JOURNAL

OF THE PROCEEDINGS OF THE

CONVENTION OF DELEGATES

ELECTED BY THE PEOPLE OF TENNESSEE, TO

AMEND, REVISE, OR FORM AND MAKE

A

NEW CONSTITUTION

FOR THE STATE.

ASSEMBLED IN THE CITY OF NASHVILLE, JANUARY 10, 1870.

NASHVILLE:

JONES, PURVIS & CO., PRINTERS TO THE STATE.

1870.

JOURNAL

OF THE

CONVENTION OF THE STATE OF TENNESSEE,

Convened in the City of Nashville on Monday, the 10th day of January, in the year of our Lord one thousand eight hundred and seventy, and in the ninety-fourth year of American Independence, in pursuance of an Act of the General Assembly of the State aforesaid, entitled "An Act to provide for the Calling of a Convention," passed the 15th day of November, 1869.

THE ASSEMBLING.

Mr. NICHOLSON called the Convention to order, and read the following proclamation from the Governor:

"EXECUTIVE OFFICE,
NASHVILLE, January 10th, 1870.

"*To the People of the State of Tennessee, and to the Delegates to the Constitutional Convention, elected at the general election held in pursuance of an Act passed by the General Assembly of the State of Tennessee, on the 18th day of December, 1869, now assembled in Nashville:*

"WHEREAS, By the 12th section of an Act 'entitled an Act to authorize the people to call a Convention and for other purposes,' passed November 15th, 1869, it is made the duty of the Governor and Secretary of State to compare the returns made by the Commissioners of Registration, of the votes cast at the general election held on the 18th day of December, 1869, for and against the Convention therein provided for, and if a majority of those voting be in favor of a Convention, it shall be the duty of the Governor immediately to issue his proclamation announcing the result.

"Now, therefore, be it known, that upon a careful comparison of the returns made, it satisfactorily appears that a large majority of the votes so cast are in favor of said Convention, the votes for Convention being 50,520, and against 10,020, showing a majority of 40,500. I do, therefore, hereby proclaim that said Convention is carried by a majority of 40,500, as far as heard from.

"In testimony whereof, I have hereunto subscribed my official signature, and caused the Great Seal of the State to be affixed, at the Department in Nashville, this 10th day of January, 1870.

"D. W. C. SENTER."

"By the Governor:

"A. J. FLETCHER,

Secretary of State."

On motion of Mr. Nicholson, Bolling Gordon, the delegate from Hickman, was appointed temporary President of the Convention.

Mr. Gordon, on taking the Chair, addressed the Convention as follows:

Gentlemen of the Convention:

For the honor conferred upon me, unsuited as I am to preside over this body during its organization, accept my thanks. I receive it at your hands the more properly, because I am a sort of connecting link between the past and present generation. I stand before you as the sole return delegate to this body, being one who met with others, almost on this identical spot, thirty-five years ago, to give to the State a Constitution. Whether that instrument has been acceptable, it is not for me to inquire; but it certainly has to the great majority of the people of the State. I was associated with a class of men who performed great services for the State. I make mention of Blount, a man venerable in years and profound in erudition; Walton, an upright, sensible man, who occupied the same position in the Convention of 96, which I occupy in the present. To this class of men I may add the names of McKinney, of East, and Weakley, of West Tennessee. We had among us various distinguished men, whose deeds it is not necessary for me to recount. I may name the venerable Francis B. Fogg, of this city, who left his impress upon the Constitution. But society, like everything else, moves on, and we are now called upon to remodel that Constitution, to adapt it to the wants of the age.

May I not invoke this Convention, in which I see so many gray heads, and so many distinguished men, to aid in making a Constitutional Government which shall answer all the ends designed; may I not invoke you to discharge all the duties of the occasion with credit to yourselves, and with benefit to the State. I thank you, gentlemen.

The following named delegates appeared, produced their credentials, and took their seats:

From the County of Bedford—T. B. IVIE.
From the County of Blount—W. H. FINLEY.
From the County of Bradley—S. P. GAUT.
From the County of Cannon—WARREN CUMMINGS.
From the County of Carroll—W. M. WRIGHT.
From the County of Claiborne—P. G. FULKERSON.
From the County of Cocke—M. MCNABB.
From the County of Davidson—NEIL S. BROWN and JOHN C. THOMPSON.
From the County of DeKalb— ———.
From the County of Dickson—THOMAS C. MORRIS.
From the County of Fayette— ———.
From the County of Franklin—JESSE ARLEDGE.
From the County of Gibson—SPARREL HILL.
From the County of Giles—THOMAS M. JONES.
From the County of Grainger—JAMES W. BRANSON.
From the County of Green—JAMES BRITTON.
From the County of Hamilton—RICHARD HENDERSON.
From the County of Hardeman—JAMES FENTRESS.
From the County of Hardin—A. G. MCDOUGAL.
From the County of Hawkins—JOHN NETHERLAND.
From the County of Haywood—GEORGE C. PORTER.
From the County of Henderson— ———.
From the County of Henry—JAS. D. PORTER, JR.
From the County of Hickman—BOLLING GORDON.
From the County of Jackson—RICHARD P. BROOKS.
From the County of Jefferson—WM. SAMPLE.
From the County of Knox—JOHN BAXTER.
From the County of Lawrence—T. D. DEAVENPORT.
From the County of Lincoln—GEO. W. JONES.
From the County of Madison—ALEXANDER W. CAMPBELL.
From the County of Marion—WM. BYRNE.

From the Counties of Davidson, Robertson, and Montgomery—JOHN F. HOUSE.

From the Counties of Rutherford and Bedford—JNO. E. DROMGOOLE.

From the Counties of Lincoln, Marshall and Giles—JNO. C. BROWN.

From the Counties of Williamson, Maury and Lewis—A. O. P. NICHOLSON.

From the Counties of Benton and Humphreys—W. F. DOHERTY.

From the Counties of Perry and Decatur—G. W. WALTERS.

From the Counties of Carroll, Gibson, Madison and Henry—JAMES S. BROWN.

From the Counties of Dyer and Lauderdale—A. T. FIELDER.

From the Counties of Tipton, Shelby, and Fayette—HUMPHREY R. BATE.

THE ORGANIZATION.

Sixty-six members appearing, it was announced by the Chair that the first business in order was the election of a President, and that nominations were in order.

Mr. NETHERLAND nominated Mr. John C. Brown, delegate from the counties of Lincoln, Marshall and Giles.

There being no other person in nomination,

On motion of Mr. KENNEDY, Mr. Brown was declared the unanimous choice of the Convention for President.

The Chair appointed Messrs. Netherland and Jones, of Lincoln, to conduct the President elect to the chair, and on taking his seat he addressed the Convention as follows:

GENTLEMEN OF THE CONVENTION:

While I am not insensible to the distinguished honor you have conferred on me, I trust you will give me credit for candor when I say that I would have preferred that the responsibilities which your generous confidence has imposed on me, should have been confided to one more experienced in parliamentary usage.

I am a stranger to deliberative bodies. I shall therefore be under the necessity of invoking your charity for my shortcomings, and your sympathy and assistance in the discharge of my official duties.

We have assembled at a most critical period in the history of our affairs. The peace, the happiness and prosperity of our beloved State may depend, in a great measure, for years to come, upon the wisdom, prudence and moderation which shall mark our deliberations. Questions of difficulty and delicacy may arise in the course of our proceedings. Let them be met and disposed of in a spirit worthy of those to whose hands the destinies of a great Commonwealth have been committed by a gallant and confiding people. Let us raise ourselves above the passions and prejudices of the hour, and dare to be just and generous regardless of the temptations prompting a contrary course. We cannot, *we must not*, be unmindful of the great changes that have impressed themselves upon our history. Let us accept the situation, and not seek to alter circumstances which have passed beyond our control. With this spirit animating every delegate, our session will speedily arrive at results which will satisfy all our people, and make Tennessee what she deserves to be, a great, happy and prosperous State.

With a sincere hope that all our deliberations may be characterized by justice and moderation, and again thanking you for the unmerited honor conferred upon me, I enter upon the discharge of the duties you have assigned me.

On motion of Mr. Brown, of Davidson, the Rev. Mr. Rains opened the proceedings by *prayer*.

On motion of Mr. Gordon, all Ministers of the Gospel present were invited to the President's stand.

Mr. Baxter offered the following resolution:

Resolved, That before proceeding further with the business of this Convention, each member be required to take an oath to support the Constitution of the United States.

On motion of Mr. House, of Davidson, Robertson and Montgomery, the resolution was laid on the table temporarily.

Mr. Burton offered the following resolution:

Resolved, That the Convention proceed to complete its organization by the election of one Secretary, one Assistant Secretary, one Door-keeper, one Assistant Door-keeper, and one Messenger.

Mr. Porter of Henry, moved to amend by inserting "three Secretaries."

Which amendment was rejected.

The resolution of Mr. Burton was then adopted.

On motion of Mr. Kennedy, it was

Resolved, That the rules of the House of Representatives be adopted by this Convention, as rules to govern its proceedings and deliberations, as far as they are applicable.

The President announced the next business in order to be the election of a Secretary, and that nominations were in order.

Mr. WILLIAMSON nominated Samuel Donelson, of the County of Sumner.

Mr. HOUSE, of Williamson, nominated Wm. G. Marshall, of Williamson.

Mr. TURNER nominated T. E. S. Russwurm, of the County of Sumner.

There being no other nominations, a ballot was had, with the following result:

For Mr. DONELSON—Messrs. Allen, Arledge, Campbell, Chowning, Gardner, Gordon, Jones of Lincoln, Kyle, Porter of Haywood, Shepard, Thompson of Davidson, Thompson of Maury, and Williamson—13.

For Mr. MARSHALL—Messrs. Baxter, Dibbrell, Deavenport, Deaderick, Finley, Fentress, Gibbs, Hill of Gibson, House of Williamson, House of Davidson, Robertson and Montgomery, Jones of Giles, Martin, Mabry, Netherland, Nicholson, Porter of Henry, Warner, and President Brown—18.

For Mr. RUSSWURM—Messrs. Brown of Davidson, Branson, Britton, Brooks, Byrne, Blizard, Burton, Brandon, Brown of Carroll, Gibson, Madison and Henry, Carter, Coffin, Doherty, Dromgoole, Fulkerson, Fielder, Gaut, Garner, Henderson, Hill of Warren, Heiskell, Ivie, Kirkpatrick, Key, Kennedy, Morris, McDougal, McNabb, Parker, Seay, Stephens, Staley, Sample, Turner, Walters and Wright—35.

Mr. RUSSWURM having received a majority of all the votes cast, was declared duly elected Secretary of the Convention, and he appeared and entered upon his duties.

The President announced that the next business in order was the election of an Assistant Secretary, and that nominations were in order.

Mr. JONES, of Lincoln, nominated T. W. Jones, of Giles.

Mr. NETHERLAND nominated W. S. Kyle, of Hawkins.

Mr. PORTER, of Haywood, nominated Henry Noland, of Haywood.

A ballot was had, with the following result:

For Mr. JONES—Messrs. Allen, Arledge, Brown of Davidson, Brooks, Burton, Deavenport, Doherty, Dromgoole, Fielder, Gibbs, Gordon, Garner, Hill of Warren, Hill of Gibson, House of Williamson, House of Davidson, Robertson and Montgomery, Ivie, Jones of Lincoln, Jones of Giles, Martin, Morris, McDougal,

Nicholson, Thompson of Davidson, Thompson of Maury, Wright, Warner, Walters, and President Brown—29.

For Mr. KYLE—Messrs. Branson, Baxter, Britton, Byrne, Blizard, Brandon, Coffin, Chowning, Carter, Dibbrell, Deaderick, Finley, Fulkerson, Gaut, Henderson, Heiskell, Kirkpatrick, Key, Kennedy, Kyle, Mabry, McNabb, Netherland, Parker, Seay, Shepard, Staley, Sample, Turner, and Williamson—30.

For Mr. NOLAND—Messrs. Brown of Carroll, Gibson, Madison and Henry, Campbell, Fentress, Gardner, Porter of Haywood, Porter of Henry, and Stephens—7.

Mr. PORTER withdrew the name of Mr. Noland.

Another ballot was had, with the following result:

For Mr. JONES—Messrs. Allen, Arledge, Brown of Davidson, Brooks, Burton, Brown of Carroll, Gibson, Madison and Henry, Campbell, Deavenport, Doherty, Dromgoole, Fentress, Fielder, Gardner, Gibbs, Gordon, Garner, Hill of Warren, Hill of Gibson, House of Williamson, House of Davidson, Robertson and Montgomery, Ivie, Jones of Lincoln, Jones of Giles, Martin, Morris, McDougal, Nicholson, Porter of Henry, Stephens, Thompson of Davidson, Thompson of Maury, Wright, Warner, Walters, and President Brown—35.

For Mr. KYLE—Messrs. Branson, Baxter, Britton, Byrne, Blizard, Brandon, Coffin, Chowing, Carter, Dibbrell, Deaderick, Finley, Fulkerson, Gaut, Henderson, Heiskell, Kirkpatrick, Key, Kennedy, Kyle, Mabry, McNabb, Netherland, Porter of Haywood, Parker, Seay, Shepard, Staley, Sample, Turner, and Williamson—31.

Mr. JONES having received a majority of all the votes cast, was declared duly elected Assistant Secretary, and he appeared and entered upon his duties.

The Convention then proceeded to the election of a Door-keeper, when the following named persons were put in nomination:

Mr. JONES, of Lincoln, nominated John H. Taylor, of Lincoln.

Mr. SEAY nominated L. G. Stuart, of Sumner.

Mr. THOMPSON, of Davidson, nominated T. W. Ballou, of Davidson.

Mr. BROWN, of Davidson, nominated W. J. Moss, of Davidson.

Mr. DIBBRELL nominated Alexander Oliver, of White.

A ballot was had with the following result:

For Mr. TAYLOR—Messrs. Arledge, Cummings, Dromgoole, Gaut,

Gordon, Henderson, Ivie, Jones of Lincoln, Jones of Giles, Key, Martin, Nicholson, Thompson of Maury, Warner and President Brown—15.

For Mr. BALLOU—Mr. Thompson of Davidson—1.

For Mr. MOSS—Messrs. Brown of Davidson, Branson, Baxter, Britton, Brandon, Chowning, Carter, Finley, Fulkerson, Fielder, Hill of Gibson, House of Williamson, Kirkpatrick, Kennedy, Parker, Stephens and Staley—18.

For Mr. STUART—Messrs. Allen, Blizard, Burton, Brown of Carroll, Gibson, Madison and Henry, Coffin, Campbell, Deavenport, Doherty, Fentress, Gardner, Garner, Heiskell, Mabry, Morris, McDougal, McNabb, Netherland, Porter of Haywood, Porter of Henry, Seay, Shepard, Thompson of Maury, Turner, Wright, Williamson and Walters—25.

For Mr. OLIVER—Messrs. Brooks, Byrne, Dibbrell, Deaderick, Gibbs, Hill of Warren, Kyle and Sample—8.

There being no election, another ballot was had as follows:

For Mr. TAYLOR—Messrs. Arledge, Cummings, Dromgoole, Gaut, Henderson, Hill of Warren, Ivie, Jones of Lincoln, Jones of Giles, Key, Kennedy, Martin, Nicholson, Thompson of Maury, Warner and President Brown—16.

For Mr. STUART—Messrs. Allen, Blizard, Burton, Brown of Henry, Carroll, Gibson and Madison, Campbell, Carter, Deavenport, Deaderick, Doherty, Fentress, Fielder, Gardner, Garner, Gibbs, Gordon, Heiskell, House of Davidson, Robertson and Montgomery, Kirkpatrick, Mabry, McDougal, Netherland, Porter of Haywood, Porter of Henry, Seay, Shepard, Stephens, Turner, Wright, Williamson and Walters—30.

For Mr. MOSS—Messrs. Brown of Davidson, Branson, Britton, Brandon, Chowning, Finley, Hill of Gibson, House of Williamson, Morris, McNabb, Parker and Staley—12.

For Mr. OLIVER—Messrs. Brooks, Byrne, Dibbrell, Fulkerson and Mr. Kyle—5.

For Mr. BALLOU—Mr. Thompson of Davidson—1.

There being no election, another ballot was had as follows:

[Mr. DIBBRELL withdrew the name of Mr. Oliver.]

For Mr. TAYLOR—Messrs. Arledge, Baxter, Cummings, Dibbrell, Finley, Fulkerson, Gaut, Henderson, Hill of Warren, Ivie, Jones of Lincoln, Jones of Giles, Key, Martin, Nicholson, Thompson of Maury, Warner and President Brown—18.

For Mr. STUART—Messrs. Allen, Branson, Britton, Byrne, Blizard, Burton, Brown of Henry, Carroll, Gibson and Madison, Coffin, Carter, Campbell, Deavenport, Deaderick, Doherty, Dromgoole, Fentress, Fielder, Gardner, Gibbs, Gordon, Garner, Hill of Gibson, Heiskell, House of Davidson, Robertson and Montgomery, Kirkpatrick, Kennedy, Kyle, Mabry, Morris, McDougal, Netherland, Porter of Haywood, Porter of Henry, Seay, Shepard, Stephens, Sample and Turner—40.

For Mr. Moss—Messrs. Brown of Davidson, Brooks, Brandon, Chowning, House of Williamsom, McNabb, Parker, Staley and Thompson of Davidson—9.

Mr. L. G. STUART having received a majority of all the votes cast, was declared duly elected Door-keeper of this Convention for the present term.

The Convention then proceeded to the election of an Assistant Door-keeper.

Mr. MARTIN nominated John E. Bennett, of Coffee.

Mr. THOMPSON, of Davidson, nominated H. A. Ausburn, of the County of Davidson.

Mr. BAXTER nominated Abraham Brown, colored, of the County of Davidson.

Mr. THOMPSON, of Davidson, nominated E. B. Drake.

Mr. BROWN, of Davidson, nominated W. H. Grant.

There being no other nominations the Convention proceeded to ballot with the following result:

For Mr. AUSBURN—Messrs. Brown of Henry, Carroll, Gibson and Madison, Campbell, Heiskell, Mabry, Netherland, Porter of Henry, Turner and Walters—8.

For Mr. BENNETT—Messrs. Allen, Arledge, Brooks, Burton, Cummings, Coffin, Chowing, Dibbrell, Deavenport, Deaderick, Dromgoole, Fulkerson, Fentress, Fielder, Gaut, Gardner, Gibbs, Garner, Gordon, Henderson, Hill of Warren, Hill of Gibson, House of Wiliamson, Ivie, Jones of Lincoln, Jones of Giles, Kennedy, Kyle, Martin, Morris, McDougal, Nicholson, Porter of Haywood, Parker, Seay, Shepard, Stephens, Thompson of Maury, Wright, Williamson, Warner and President Brown—41.

For Mr. DRAKE—Messrs. Doherty, House of Davidson, Robert-n and Montgomery, and Thompson of Davidson—3.

For Mr. GRANT—Mr. Brown of Davidson—1.

or ABRAHAM BROWN—Messrs. Branson, Baxter, Britton, Bliz-inley, Gaut, Kirkpatrick, Key, McNabb, Staley and Sample--11.

n E. BENNETT having received a majority of all the votes cast, was declared duly elected Assistant Door-keeper of this Convention for the present term.

The Convention then proceeded to the election of a Messenger.

Mr. WILLIAMSON nominated Master Paul Jones, of Davidson.

Mr. WARNER nominated H. N. C. Davis, of Marshall.

Mr. DIBBRELL nominated —— Skipworth.

Mr. BURTON nominated G. W. Blanche, of Butherford.

Mr. KYLE nominated Wm. Polk, colored, of Davidson.

Mr. BROWN, of Davidson, nominated —— Baskett.

Mr. THOMPSON, of Davidson, nominated J. N. Todd.

Mr. THOMPSON, of Davidson, nominated H. A. Ausburn.

There being no other nominations the Convention proceeded to ballot with the following result:

For Master JONES—Messrs. Arledge, Garner, House of Davidson, Robertson and Montgomery, Morris, McDougal, Shepard and Williamson—7.

For Mr. DAVIS—Messrs. Branson, Britton, Brooks, Byrne, Deavenport, Deaderick, Doherty, Fulkerson, Fielder, Gardner, Gibbs, Gordon, Hill of Gibson, Heiskell, House of Williamson, Ivie, Jones of Lincoln, Jones of Giles, Kirkpatrick, Martin, Mabry, McNabb, Nicholson, Porter of Haywood, Parker, Stephens, Thompson of Maury, Turner, Wright, Warner, Walters and President Brown—32.

For Wm. POLK—Messrs. Baxter, Blizard, Brandon, Finley, Gaut, Henderson, Key, Kyle and Sample—9.

For Mr. SKIPWORTH—Messrs. Coffin, Chowning, Dibbrell, Kennedy, Netherland and Staley—6.

For Mr. BASKETT—Messrs. Brown of Davidson, and Hill of Warren—2.

For Mr. AUSBURN—Mr. Carter—1.

There being no election—when, on motion of Mr. GARNER,

Mr. DAVIS was declared to be the Messenger of the Convention for the present term.

This completed the organization of the Convention.

On motion of Mr. KIRKPATRICK, it was

Resolved, That the resident clergy of this city be, and they are hereby respectfully solicited to act as Chaplains of this Convention during its sittings, dividing the time among themselves in such manner as they may deem most expedient.

Mr. GARNER called up the resolution of Mr. Baxter in relation to the oath to be taken by the members of the Convention, when Mr. Jones, of Lincoln, offered the following in lieu, which was accepted by Mr. Baxter, and adopted by the Convention:

Resolved, That the following oath be administered to the members of this Convention, by some Judge or Justice of the Peace:

We, and each of us, solemnly swear upon the Evangelists of Almighty God, that we will support the Constitution of the United States, and discharge the duties of delegates of this Convention faithfully and to the best of our ability.

Resolved, That a similar oath be administered to the officers of this Convention.

On motion of Mr. KENNEDY, it was

Resolved, That the reporters of the newspapers in the city of Nashville be invited to seats within the bar for the purpose of reporting the proceedings of this Convention.

On motion of Mr. CAMPBELL, it was

Resolved, That a committee of five delegates be appointed to report permanent rules for the government of this Convention.

Resolved, That a committee of five delegates be appointed to report upon credentials of members.

On motion of Mr. JONES, of Lincoln, it was

Resolved, That the President of this Convention be authorized to appoint one porter to serve this body.

Mr. BROWN, of Davidson, offered the following resolution:

Resolved, That Clay Roberts, who arranged the present hall, be appointed to remain in charge of the same, with instructions to have the hall kept in order and furnished with all necessary fuel, stationery, and other supplies, and he shall receive the same compensation as the Secretary of the Convention.

On motion of Mr. BAXTER, the resolution was laid on the table.

Mr. Nicholson offered the following resolution:

Resolved, That the following shall be the Standing Committees to be appointed by the President:

On the Legislative Department,
On the Judicial Department,
On Taxation,
On Interest and Usury,
On Revision,
On Enrollments,
On Franchise,
Each Committee to consist of nine members.

The resolution was laid over until to-morrow.

The members who answered to their names—on the first calling of the roll—were then duly sworn, in conformity with the oath prescribed, by P. W. MAXEY, an acting Justice of the Peace for the County of Davidson.

The oath was also administered to the President, the Secretary, Assistant Secretary, Door-keeper and Messenger, by Esquire MAXEY.

On motion of Mr. BURTON, the Convention adjourned until to-morrow morning, 10½ o'clock.

TUESDAY MORNING, JANUARY 11, 1870.

The Convention met pursuant to adjournment, Mr. President BROWN in the Chair.

Prayer by the Rev. Mr. SAMPLE, a member of this body.

The Journal of yesterday was read, corrected and approved.

Mr. KENNEDY called up the resolution offered on yesterday by Mr. Nicholson, in relation to the Committees, and offered the following in lieu:

1. *Resolved*, That the Bill, or Declaration of Rights, be referred to a Committee to report to this Convention whether, in their opinion any, and if any, what amendments are proper and necessary.

2. *Resolved*, That the Legislative Department, as established by the present Constitution, be referred to a Committee, to inquire and report whether, in their opinion any, and if any, what amendments are necessary.

3. *Resolved*, That the Executive Department of the Government, as established by the present Constitution, be referred to a Committee to inquire and report whether any, and if any, what amendments are necessary.

4. *Resolved,* That the Judicial Department of the Government, as established by the present Constitution, be referred to a Committee to inquire whether any, and if any, what amendments are necessary.

5. *Resolved,* That so much of the present Constitution as relates to elections and right of suffrage, be referred to a Committee to inquire and report whether any, and if any, what amendments are necessary.

6. *Resolved,* That all such parts of the Constitution as are not included in and referred by the foregoing resolutions, be referred to a Committee to inquire and report whether any, and if any, what amendments are necessary therein.

7. *Resolved,* That each Committee appointed under the foregoing resolutions, shall consist of eleven members.

8. *Resolved,* That no original resolution offered to the Convention, proposing any amendment to the Constitution, or Declaration of Rights, be discussed on its merits till it shall have been referred to the appropriate Committee.

Mr. BURTON offered the following amendment, which was accepted by Mr. Kennedy:

Resolved, That so much of the Constitution as relates to questions of finance, internal improvements and corporations, both public and private, be referred to a Committee to report whether any, and if any, what amendments are necessary.

Mr. HEISKELL offered the following in lieu of Mr. Kennedy's first seven resolutions:

Resolved, That the Standing Committees of this Convention shall be as follows:

On the Judicial Department,
On the Legislative Department,
On the Declaration of Rights,
On Elections and Right of Suffrage,
On Taxation,
On Miscellaneous Provisions.

That these Committees shall take into consideration such resolutions as shall be submitted to them by the Convention under the rules of the House.

On motion of Mr. HOUSE, of Davidson, Robertson and Montgomery, the substitute of Mr. Heiskell was laid on the table.

Mr. HOUSE, of Davidson, Robertson and Montgomery, offered the following amendment:

Provided, That the Delegate offering resolutions, may, at the time of offering the same, make a brief statement in reference thereto, the same not to exceed five minutes in length.

Which amendment was adopted, and the resolutions, as amended, were adopted by the Convention.

QUORUM.

On motion of Mr. WARNER, it was

Resolved, That two-thirds of the entire number of Delegates elected to this Convention, shall constitute a quorum for the transaction of business.

COMMITTEES TO REPORT.

Hr. HILL, of Warren, offered the following resolution:

Resolved, That each of said Committees is hereby instructed to report fully on the subjects referred to each, on or before the 20th day of this month.

On motion of Mr. KEY, the resolution was laid on the table.

TOOK THEIR SEATS.

JOHN M. TAYLOR, delegate from the County of Henderson,

H. R. BATE, delegate from the Counties of Tipton, Shelby and Fayette,

JOS. H. BLACKBURN, delegate from the County of DeKalb, and

E. H. SHELTON, delegate from the County of Tipton, appeared, took the oath required, and took their seats.

PERFECTING ORGANIZATION.

Mr. GORDON offered the following resolution, which was adopted:

Resolved, That with a view of perfecting the organization of this Convention, and of economizing its labors, that this body proceed at once to the election of a Second Assistant or Engrossing Clerk of the Convention.

The PRESIDENT announced that nominations were in order for the office of Second Assistant or Engrossing Clerk.

Mr. GORDON nominated W. S. Kyle, of Hawkins County.

Mr. PORTER nominated Y. N. Cavitt, of Henry County.

There being no other nominations, the Convention proceeded to ballot, with the following result:

For Mr. KYLE—Messrs. Allen, Brown of Davidson, Branson,

Baxter, Britton, Brooks, Byrne, Blizard, Burton, Coffin, Chowning, Carter, Dibbrell, Deaderick, Dromgoole, Finley, Fulkerson, Fentress, Gaut, Gordon, Garner, Henderson, Hill of Warren, Hill of Gibson, Heiskell, House of Williamson, Ivie, Jones of Lincoln, Jones of Giles, Kirkpatrick, Key, Kennedy, Kyle, Martin, Mabry, Morris, McNabb, Netherland, Nicholson, Porter of Haywood, Parker, Seay, Shepard, Stephens, Staley, Sample, Shelton, Thompson of Davidson, Thompson of Maury, Williamson, Warner, and President Brown—52.

For Mr. CAVITT—Messrs. Brandon, Brown of Henry, etc., Bate, Cummings, Campbell, Deavenport, Doherty, Fielder, Gardner, Gibbs, House of Davidson, Robertson and Montgomery, McDougal, Porter, of Henry, Turner, Taylor, Wright, and Walters—17.

Mr. KYLE having received a majority of all the votes cast, was declared duly elected Engrossing Clerk for the present term of this Convention, he appeared, took the required oath, and entered upon the discharge of his duties.

JOHN E. BENNETT, elected Assistant Door-keeper on yesterday, appeared, was sworn in as such, and entered upon the discharge ot his duties.

COMMITTEES.

The PRESIDENT announced as the Committee on Permanent Rules: Messrs. Campbell, Jones of Lincoln, Netherland, Baxter, and Porter of Henry.

And the Committee on Credentials to be Messrs. House of Williamson, Williamson, Britton, Coffin, and Porter of Haywood.

STATIONERY.

Mr. JONES, of Giles, offered the following resolution:

Resolved, That the Secretary contract for such stationery as may be necessary for the use of the Convention, and when procured, the same shall be under his care and responsibility.

On motion of Mr. JONES, the rules were suspended, and the resolution adopted.

COURTESIES.

Mr. FRANCIS B. Fogg, of Davidson, who was a member of the Convention of 1834, appearing in the lobby, he was, on motion of

Mr. JONES, of Lincoln, invited to a seat within the bar of the House.

On motion of Mr. NICHOLSON, the privileges of the Hall were extended to Mr. Fogg during the session of the Convention.

On motion of Mr. STEPHENS, the same courtesy was extended to Judge West H. Humphreys, of this city, who was also a member of the Convention of 1834, and to all other members of that body who may visit the city during the session of the Convention.

Mr. GARNER offered the following resolution:

Resolved, That the members of the General Assembly of Tennessee, the Governor, Judges, and other officers of the State be, and they are hereby invited to seats within the bar of this Convention.

On motion of Mr. GARNER, the rules were suspended, and the resolution adopted.

MISCELLANEOUS.

Mr. GARNER offered the following resolution:

Resolved, That the Door-keeper be and he is hereby instructed to have seats placed within and without the bar of this Convention for the use of those who may desire to be present during the sitting of this body.

On motion of Mr. GARNER, the rules were suspended, and the resolution adopted.

Mr. JONES, of Lincoln, offered the following resolution:

Resolved, That the Committee on the Executive Department be instructed to inquire into the propriety of providing for the election of a Lieutenant-Governor, who shall be President of the Senate, and who shall receive a *per diem* during the time he may be actually engaged in the discharge of his duties as such; and in case of vacancy in the office of Governor, he shall succeed to the discharge of the Executive duties.

On motion of Mr. BROWN, of Davidson, the rules were suspended, and the resolution adopted.

Mr. President BROWN—Mr. Jones, of Lincoln, in the Chair—offered the following resolution:

Resolved, That until the adoption of permanent rules of order for the Convention, that the 51st rule, adopted for our temporary government, be and the same is suspended in favor of all resolutions looking to amendments of the Constitution.

On motion of Mr. BROWN, the rules were suspended, and the resolution adopted.

AMENDMENTS PROPOSED.

Mr. BROWN, of Davidson, offered the following:

That Section 26 of the Bill of Rights be so amended as to read as follows: "That all citizens of this State have a right to keep and bear arms for their common defense."

That Section 1 of Article IV. be so amended as to read as follows, viz: Every man of the age of twenty-one years, being a citizen of the United States, and a citizen of the County wherein he may offer his vote six months next preceding the day of election, shall be entitled to vote for members of the General Assembly and other civil officers for the County or District in which he resides; and there shall be no qualification attached to the right of suffrage except that each voter shall exhibit to the Judges of Election where he offers to vote, satisfactory evidence that he has paid his poll-tax then due by him, without which his vote cannot be received. And all male citizens of the State shall be subject to the payment of poll-tax and to performance of military duty, within such ages as may be prescribed by law.

Which was ordered to be referred to the Judiciary Committee.

Mr. BROWN, of Davidson, offered the following amendment to the Constitution of the State:

To Section 29, Article II., add: "But the General Assembly shall have no power to pass laws for the issuance of bonds of the State for any purpose, or to increase the indebtedness of the State, in any form, beyond the ordinary expenditures, without the concurrence of three-fourths of the members elect of both Houses. Nor shall the General Assembly have power to pass what is commonly called omnibus bills, or bills proposing to appropriate the credit of the State in the form of bonds or otherwise, to different objects, and combined in one bill. All laws passed in that form, by whatever vote, shall be utterly void. Nor shall the General Assembly, after the present session, have power to prolong its sessions, at any time, beyond the space of sixty days from its organization."

Section 28, Article II. Strike out the word "white" in the 11th line, and add to the end of the Section: "And all revenue derived from the tax on polls, peddlers, and privileges, shall be set apart and devoted exclusively to the payment of the interest on the public debt of the State, and of the debt itself, and when this is accomplished, such revenue shall be then applied to the use of common schools for ever, and for no other purpose."

Mr. ARLEDGE offered the following resolution:

Resolved, That no bill shall pass the Legislature of this State except upon its own merits, and not connected with any other bill.

Mr. KIRKPATRICK offered the following resolutions:

1st. *Resolved,* That the credit of this State shall never be given or loaned in aid of any person, association, municipality or corporation.

2nd. That the members of the Legislature shall receive for their services a sum not exceeding four dollars a day from the commencement of the session, but such pay shall not exceed in the aggregate, two hundred and forty dollars for *per diem* allowance, except in proceedings for impeachment. The limitation as to the aggregate compensation shall not take effect until after the first Monday of October, one thousand eight hundred and seventy-one. When convened in extra session by the Governor they shall receive four dollars per day. They shall also receive one dollar for every ten miles they shall travel going and returning from their place of meeting on the most usual route.

The Speakers of the Assembly shall, in virtue of their office, receive an additional compensation equal to one-third of their *per diem* allowance as members.

Mr. KIRKPATRICK introduced the following resolutions:

1st. *Resolved,* That the General Assembly shall pass no special act conferring corporate powers.

2nd. Corporations may be formed under general laws, but all such laws may from time to time be altered or repealed.

3rd. That dues from corporations shall be secured by such individual liability of the stockholders and other means as may be prescribed by law, but in all cases each stockholder shall be liable over and above the stock owned by him or her, and any amount unpaid thereon to a further sum at least equal in amount to such stock.

Mr. HOUSE, of Davidson, Robertson and Montgomery, introduced the following resolutions:

1st. *Resolved,* That the credit of the State shall never be given or loaned in aid of any person, association, municipality or corporation.

2nd. That the Legislature may contract debts to meet casual deficits or failures in the revenues, but such debts, direct or contingent, singly or in the aggregate, shall not at any time exceed six hundred thousand dollars, and the monies arising from loans creating such debt shall be applied to the purposes for which they were obtained or to pay such debts.

3rd. No act of the Legislature shall authorize any debt to be contracted on behalf of the State except for purposes mentioned in the foregoing section unless provision be made therein to lay and collect an annual tax sufficient to pay the interest stipulated, and to discharge the debt in thirty years; nor shall such act take effect until it shall have been submitted to the people at a general election, and shall have received a majority of all the votes cast for and against it; *Provided*, that the Legislature may contract debts by borrowing money to pay any part of the debt of the State, without submitting the question to the people, and without making provision in the act authorizing the same for a tax to discharge the debt so contracted, or the interest thereon.

4th. No one who does not own at least two hundred and fifty dollars worth of taxable property shall be entitled to vote in any election in which the question is submitted to a vote of the people, of contracting debts, or raising money on behalf of the State, any association or municipality, or corporation whatsoever.

Mr. BAXTER submitted the following amendments to the Constitution:

In lieu of the 4th and 5th Sections of the Bill of Rights, insert the following:

Sec. 4. That no religious or political test, other than an oath to support the Constitution of the United States and of this State, shall ever be required as a qualification to any office or public trust under this State.

Sec. 5. That elections shall be free and equal, and the right of suffrage, as hereinafter declared, shall never be denied to any person entitled thereto, except upon conviction by a jury of some infamous crime, previously ascertained and declared by law, and the judgment thereon by a court of competent jurisdiction."

Strike out the 31st section of the Bill of Rights, and insert the following:

Sec. 31. The erection of safe and comfortable prisons, the inspection of prisons, and the humane treatment of prisoners, shall be provided for by law.

Sec. 32. That slavery and involuntary servitude, except as a punishment for crime, whereof the party shall have been duly convicted, are forever prohibited in this State.

Sec. 33. The General Assembly shall make no law recognizing the right of property in man.

"Every free man of the age of twenty-one years, being a citizen of the United States, and a citizen of the County where he may offer his vote, six months next preceding the day of election, and who shall have paid one month before the day of election all poll taxes legally due from him for the preceding year, shall be entitled to vote for members of the General Assembly and other civil officers for the County or District in which he resides."

Mr. PORTER, of Haywood, offered the following amendment to the Constitution of the State:

" *Resolved*, That Section 4, of Article II, shall be so amended as to read as follows:

The Governor shall hold his office for four years, and until a successor shall be elected and qualified. He shall not be eligible more than eight years in a term of twelve."

Resolved, That it be referred to the proper Committee to enquire into and report upon the expediency of the abolition of the office of County Trustee, as provided in Article VII, Section 1, of the Constitution.

Mr. HEISKELL offered the following amendments to the Constitution:

Resolved, Article I, Section 4, ought to be so amended that no religious test shall ever be required as a qualification for any office or public trust under this State or to the exercise of voting.

Nor shall any political test, or any oath relating to past time or conduct, except the oath to prevent dueling.

That Article VI, Section 11, of the Constitution, requires to be amended so as to provide that the Legislature may provide by law for the appointment of Judges of the Supreme Court, in the event any Judge shall be unable for any cause to attend or sit.

Resolved, That so much of Article II, Section 28, as excepts " merchants, peddlers and privileges" from the rule of equal taxation, is against the theory and principle of constitutional law, as it excepts a minority from the protection of the Constitution, and the same ought to be amended.

Mr. JONES, of Giles, offered the following resolution:

Resolved, That the Committee on the Legislative Department be instructed to inquire and report whether it is expedient and proper to limit the duration of the sessions of the Legislature to one hundred days.

Mr. KENNEDY offered the following resolution:

Resolved, That the members of the General Assembly shall not receive per diem for a longer period than ninety days for a regular session, and thirty days for a called session of the same.

Mr. TURNER offered the following amendments to the Constitution:

Resolved, That Article II, Section 8, of the present Constitution, be so amended, commencing at the last word of said Section so as to read as follows:

" And their sessions shall not continue for more than one hundred days during its term of office, unless it shall be convened in extraordinary session by the Executive, and its deliberations shall then be confined to the subjects embraced in the message of the Executive."

Resolved, That Article IV, Section 1, of the present Constitution be so amended as to strike out the last sentence of said Section.

Mr. WARNER offered the following resolution:

Resolved, That the Legislature shall not make the State debt exceed 5 per cent. on the taxable property of the State after the adoption of this Constitution; but this has no reference to the debt already created.

Mr. BROWN, of Henry, Carroll, Gibson and Madison, offered the following resolutions:

Resolved, That the General Assembly shall never authorize any county, city or town by vote of its citizens, or otherwise, to become a stockholder in any joint stock company, corporation or association whatever, or to raise money for or loan its credit to or in aid of any such company, corporation or association.

Resolved, That the bonds of the State shall never be issued for any purpose whatever except in renewal of existing liabilities.

Mr. GARDNER offered the following resolution:

Resolved, That the Committee on the Judicial Department inquire as to the expediency of providing that in case of the incompetency of any Judge to try a cause pending in his Court the practicing Attorneys present may elect a special Judge to try such cause. Also, when from sickness, or other cause, the regular Judge is unable or fails to attend to hold a term of his Court, the licensed lawyers present may elect a special Judge to hold such term, who shall be paid out of the salary of the regular Judge.

On motion of Mr. BROWN, of Davidson, it was ordered that the foregoing resolutions and proposed amendments be referred to the respective Committees hereafter to be appointed by the President.

Mr. GARNER offered the following resolutions:

Resolved, That the Committee on Elections and Right of Suffrage be instructed to inquire into and report what change, if any, should be made in the Constitution so as to require all voters to vote in all elections in the Civil District of their residence.

Resolved, That the Standing Committee on the Legislative Department be instructed to inquire into and report as to the expediency of so changing the Constitution as to limit the sessions of the Legislature and the per diem of the members and officers thereof to sixty days, at their regular biennial sessions; and also as to the propriety of limiting the number of Representatives in the General Assembly to fifty.

On motion of Mr. GARNER, the rules were suspended, and the resolutions were adopted, and ordered to be referred to the appropriate Committees.

On motion of Mr. KENNEDY, the House adjourned until to-mor row morning at 10 o'clock.

WEDNESDAY MORNING, JANUARY 12, 1870.

The Convention met pursuant to adjournment, Mr. President BROWN in the Chair.

The Journal of yesterday was read and approved.

AMENDMENTS PROPOSED.

Mr. WARNER offered the following resolution :

Resolved, That the Chancery Court Clerks and Masters be elected by the qualified voters of their respective Counties, and the time, place and manner of their election and the term of their office be the same as the Circuit and County Court Clerks.

Ordered that the resolution be referred to the Committee on the Judiciary.

Mr. STALEY offered the following resolutions :

Resolved, That the Judges of the Supreme Court, and the Judges of the Circuit Courts and Chancery Courts, and the Attorney General for the State, and the Attorneys General for the several Judicial Circuits in the State, shall be nominated, and by and with the advice and consent of the Senate, appointed by the Governor.

Resolved, That Judges of the Supreme Court shall not be less than forty years of age, and Judges of the Circuit and Chancery Courts shall not be less than thirty-five years of age.

Mr. STALEY offered the following resolution :

Resolved, That Section 1 of Article IX of the present Constitution, whereby Ministers of the Gospel are rendered ineligible to seats in the General Assembly, be abrogated.

Resolved, That Section 1, of Article IV, be so modified as to read as follows:

Every male citizen of the age of twenty-one years being a citizen of the United States, and a citizen of the County wherein he may offer his vote six months next preceding the day of election, shall be entitled to vote for Governor and members of the General Assembly, and for other civil officers for the County or District in which he may reside.

Be it further resolved, That the other two clauses of said Section 1, of Article IV, be annulled and stricken out.

TOOK THEIR SEATS.

T. M. BURKETT, Delegate from the Counties of Polk, McMinn and Meigs, and

H. R. GIBSON, Delegate from the Counties of Anderson and Campbell,

Appeared, took the oath required, and took their seats.

AMENDMENTS PROPOSED.

Mr. WARNER offered the following resolution:

Resolved, That Article II, Section 12, of the Constitution of the State of Tennessee, be so amended, as to insert the words "of the entire number," between "two-thirds" and "expel."

Mr. McDOUGAL offered the following resolution:

Resolved, That the Committee on the Legislative Department inquire into the expediency of striking out the 1st Section of Article IX, of the Constitution, which disqualifies Ministers of the Gospel of any denomination whatever, to be members of either House of the Legislature.

Mr. JONES, of Lincoln, offered the following resolution, which was adopted:

Resolved, That the Committee on the Legislative Department inquire into the propriety of providing for the pardoning of persons convicted in impeachments.

Mr. HOUSE, of Davidson, Robertson and Montgomery, offered the following as an amendment to the Constitution:

Strike out Section 4, Article III, and insert, "The Governor shall hold his office for four years, and until his successor is elected and qualified, and shall be ineligible to re-election."

Add the following as an independent section to said Article:

"Every bill which may pass both Houses of the General Assembly, shall, before it becomes a law, be presented to the Governor for his signature, if he approve he shall sign it, and the same shall become a law; but if he refuse to sign it, he shall return it with his objections thereto in writing, to the House in which it originated, and said House shall cause said objections to be entered at large upon their Journals, and proceed to reconsider the bill. If, after such reconsideration, a majority of all the members elected to that House, shall agree to pass the bill, notwithstanding the objections of the Executive, it shall be sent with said objections to the other House, by which it shall be likewise reconsidered. If approved by a majority of the whole number elected to that House, it shall become a law; the votes of both Houses shall be determined by yeas and nays, and the names of all the members voting for or against the bill, shall be entered upon the Journals of their respective Houses. If the Governor shall fail to return any bill with his objections within five days (Sundays excepted) after it shall have been presented to him, the same shall become a law without his signature; unless the General Assembly, by their adjournment, prevent its return, in which case it shall not become a law.

Every joint resolution or order (except on questions of adjournment) shall likewise be presented to the Governor for his signature, and before it shall take effect shall receive his signature, and on being disapproved by him shall in like manner be returned with his objections, and the same, before it shall take effect, shall be repassed by a majority of all the members elected to both Houses, in the manner and according to the rules prescribed in case of a bill.

Mr. HEISKELL offered the following resolution:

Resolved, That the Legislature shall have no power to restrict the rights of parties to contract for a rate of interest not exceeding ten per cent. per annum on money actually loaned.

Mr. SEAY introduced the following resolution:

Resolved, That the Constitution be amended so that new Counties may be established by the Legislature, to consist of not less than two hundred square miles, and to contain a population of three hundred and fifty voters; no line of such County shall approach the Court-house of any old County from which it may be taken nearer than eight miles, and no part of a County shall be taken to form such County or a part thereof, without a majority of the qualified voters in such part taken off shall consent. And where an old County may be reduced for the purpose of forming a new one, the area of said old County shall not be reduced to less than three hundred and fifty square miles.

Mr. SEAY introduced the following resolutions, which were adopted:

1st. *Resolved,* That a Committee of seven be appointed upon the subject of New Counties and changing County Lines, to take into consideration the sections of the present Constitution embracing said subjects, and report to this Convention, whether any, and if any, what amendments or changes are necessary therein.

2nd. That all memorials and petitions upon said subjects, and all resolutions submitted to this Convention proposing amendments or changes of said sections of the Constitution be referred to said Committee, under the rule heretofore adopted by this Convention.

Mr. THOMPSON, of Davidson, offered the following resolution:

Be it resolved, That Section 6, of Article II, be amended by words to the following effect: All debts created by operation of law, and all judgments shall bear interest at the rate of six *per centum per annum.* But the Legislature shall have no power to restrict by law the rate of interest which may be stipulated in writing to be paid for the use of money loaned in cash, at the time of the execution of the written agreement. *Provided,* That at the maturity of every debt evidenced by writing, the debtor, in person or by Attorney may confess judgment thereon in open court in favor of the named payee for the use of the party entitled.

Resolved, Every citizen having a claim against the State may pursue his claim to a judgment by the same judicial remedies, and in the same courts as those in and by which claims against citizens are reduced to judgments.

Mr. HEISKELL offered the following resolution:

Resolved, That the rights and privileges of the municipal corporations of this State shall not be infringed, or their charters changed by the Legislature without their consent.

Mr. HENDERSON introduced the following resolution:

Resolved, That the Committee on the Legislative Department be instructed to report whether the power of the Legislature to lay taxes should be limited, and to what amount.

Mr. DROMGOOLE introduced the following resolution:

1st. *Resolved,* That no power in this State shall ever solemnize or make lawful the rites of matrimony between white and colored people.

2d. *Resolved,* That the regular rate of interest in this State shall be six per cent. per annum, but on all notes or obligations, given for money actually loaned, and so stated in the face of the instrument, if not paid within twenty days after maturity, or if collected by suit, eight per cent. per annum shall be computed.

8d. *Resolved,* That there shall be five Supreme Judges in this State, and that their residence shall not be confined to any particular grand division of the State.

PRINTING FOR THE CONVENTION.

Mr. KENNEDY introduced the following resolution:

Resolved, That the Printers of the General Assembly be and they are hereby made and constituted the Printers for this Convention, upon the same terms and contract as now exists between them and the General Assembly.

AMENDMENTS PROPOSED.

Mr. CAMPBELL offered the following resolution:

Resolved, "That this Government was made for the white man and his posterity forever."

And that Section 1, Article IV, of the Constitution of Tennessee, be so amended as to read: "Every free white man of the age of twenty-one years, being a citizen of the County wherein he may offer his vote six months next preceding the day of election, shall be entitled to vote for members of the General Assembly and other civil officers for the County or District in which he resides.

On motion of Mr. CAMPBELL, the foregoing resolutions were referred to the Committee on Franchise.

Mr. MARTIN offered the following resolution, which was read and referred to the Committee on the Legislative Department:

Resolved, That no member of the Legislature shall receive compensation only for such time as he may be present in his seat attending to his duties.

THE DIVINE BLESSING.

Mr. FENTRESS offered the following resolution, which was adopted under a suspension of the rules:

Resolved, That a Committee of three be appointed, whose duty it shall be to inform the resident Clergy of this city, of all denominations, of the desire of this body that some one of them should be present and invoke the Divine blessing upon the deliberations of this House, for each day.

And thereupon the President appointed Messrs. Fentress, Thompson of Davidson, and Stephens, said Committee.

AMENDMENTS PROPOSED.

Mr. STEPHENS introduced the following resolution, which was read and referred to the Committee on the Judiciary:

Resolved, That the Clerks of the Supreme Courts shall be elected by the qualified voters of their respective divisions, for the term of six years.

Mr. PORTER, of Haywood, introduced the following resolution, which was read and referred to the Legislative Department.

Resolved, That Section 7, of Article II, of the Constitution, under the head of Legislative Department, be so amended as to lengthen the membership of the lower branch of the Legislature from two to four years, and the Senate from two to eight years. Further, that this be referred to the Committee on said Department for consideration and action.

Mr. PORTER, of Haywood, offered the following resolution, which was referred to the Committee on Finance:

Resolved, That a reference be had, to the proper Committee, to take into consideration and report upon the expediency of requiring the Sheriffs of the Counties, excepting the Counties of Knox, Davidson, and Shelby, to collect and pay over the State and County taxes.

Mr. WILLIAMSON introduced the following resolutions, which were read and referred to the Committee on Franchise:

Resolved, That no well organized Government has or can ever exist where the political power is divided between men of different races; that all social and natural society, in its inception, was predicated upon the instinct of race or kind, and that not only men, but the lower order of animals, and even the small insects, are controlled by the same great natural law.

Resolved, That any voluntary departure from this law of natural existence should only be made after the gravest deliberation.

Resolved, That the Committee on Franchise be directed to report an amendment to the Constitution of Tennessee restricting the right of suffrage to white men only.

Mr. MARTIN introduced the following resolution, which was read and referred to the Committee on Franchise:

Resolved, That no man shall be eligible to an office of honor, trust, or profit, in this State, whether such office be elective or conferred by appointment, unless he shall have been a citizen of the State of Tennessee for three years, and of the County in which he may reside one year next before election or appointment.

Mr. BRANSON offered the following resolution, which was read and referred to the Committee on the Legislative Department:

Resolved, That the Constitution be so amended as to allow each and every County in this State, having as many as one thousand qualified voters, to have a Representative in the lower branch of the State Legislature.

Mr. IVIE offered the following resolution, which was also read and referred to the Committee on Franchise:

Resolved, That Section 1, Article IV, of the present Constitution be amended so as to read as follows: "That all male citizens of the age of twenty-one years, being a citizen of the United States, and a citizen of the County wherein he may offer his vote six months next preceding the day of election, shall be entitled to vote for members of the General Assembly and other civil officers, for the County or District in which he resides, but shall in all cases be required to vote in the Civil District or Ward in which he resides, unless otherwise authorized by law.

Mr. KEY offered the following resolution, which was read and referred to the Judiciary Committee:

Resolved, That the Committee on the Judiciary be instructed to report whether any modifications and changes of the present organic law establishing the judicial system of the State are required for the public good, and if so, what changes or system will best secure the ends of justice, and a speedy and impartial trial of causes before, or which may be brought before the Court.

Mr. BLIZARD offered the following resolutions, which were read and referred to the Committee on the Judiciary:

Resolved, That the Judges of the Supreme Court, and of the Circuit and Chancery Court, and the Attorney General and Reporter for the State, and the District Attorneys and Clerks of the Circuit and Chancery Courts shall, after the adoption of this Constitution, be elected by the qualified voters of the State of Tennessee, in the following manner:

1st. The Judges of the Supreme Court and Attorney General and Reporter shall be elected by the qualified voters of the State at large.

2d. The Judges of the Circuit and Chancery Courts shall be elected by the qualified voters of their respective Circuits and Districts or Divisions.

3rd. The Clerks of the Circuit, and the Clerks and Masters of the Chancery Courts, shall be elected by the qualified voters of their respective Counties.

4th. That the Judges of the Supreme Court, and Chancellors and Circuit Judges of this State, shall hold their offices for two years from the date of their qualification, and shall be ineligible to the same office for the second term.

Mr. BROWN, of Henry, Caroll, Gibson and Madison, offered the following resolution, which was referred to the Committee on Franchise:

Resolved, That Section 1, of Article IV, of the Constitution of

Tennessee be so amended as to read: "Every free white man of the age of twenty-one years, being a citizen of the United States, and a citizen of the County wherein he may offer his vote six months next preceding the day of election, shall be entitled to vote for members of the General Assembly and other civil officers for the County or District in which he resides. *Provided,* He has paid all poll-taxes legally due from him for the year next preceding that in which he shall offer his vote."

Mr. FENTRESS offered the following resolutions, which were read and referred to the Committee on Franchise:

Resolved, That the white man is and ought to be the controller of the political affairs of the State, and that any attempt to incorporate in the body politic laws compelling or authorizing social or political equality of the negro with the white man, being contrary to truth, is dangerous to the peace and prosperity of the Government and the general good, and has a tendency to create estrangement and ill-will between the races.

Resolved, That no law shall be made authorizing or making legal marriages between the negro and the white race, or authorizing the negro to hold office or sit on juries.

Mr. BROOKS offered the following resolution, which was referred to the Committee on the Legislative Department:

Resolved, That the Constitution be so amended as that the members of the General Assembly shall be elected for a term of four years, and to be restricted to one session of not more than one hundred and twenty days in such four years, except in cases of emergency, when the Governor shall have power to convene the Legislature in special session for a term of not more than thirty days for such special session.

Mr. BROOKS offered the following resolution, which was referred to the Committee on New Counties and County Lines:

Resolved, That the Constitution be so amended as to allow new Counties to be formed; *Provided,* The same can be done without reducing the old Counties out of which the same shall be formed, below five hundred square miles; *Provided further,* That the line of a new County shall not approach the County seat of any old County nearer than ten miles; and that three hundred square miles of territory shall be required to form a new County, and shall contain four hundred qualified voters. *Provided further,* That the County seat of an old County shall not be moved without the concurrence of two-thirds of both branches of the Legislature.

Mr. DIBBRELL offered the following resolution, which, under a suspension of the rules, was adopted.

Resolved, That the Door-keeper be required to purchase a water-urn for the use of the Hall, and also a letter-box and a delivery-box.

Mr. FULKERSON offered the following resolution, which was read and referred to the Committee on the Legislative Department:

Resolved, That no Minister of the Gospel shall cease his work of love and mercy by holding any office whatever in the gift of the people.

Mr. BURTON offered the following resolution, which was read and referred to the Committee on the Legislative Department:

Resolved, That every law enacted by the Legislature shall embrace but one subject or object, and that it shall be distinctly expressed in its title. No law shall be revised or amended by reference to its title, but in such case the act revised or amended shall be re-enacted and published at length.

Mr. IVIE offered the following resolution, which was read and referred to the Committee on Franchise:

Resolved, That Section twenty-eight (28), Article second (2), be amended by striking out the word "slave" between the ages of twelve and forty years, in the second line. Also by striking out the word "white" before the word "poll."

Mr. DOHERTY offered the following resolution, which was read and referred to the Committee on Finance and Internal Improvements:

Be it resolved, That the Constitution be so amended that the State shall not be a stock-holder in any enterprise with private persons or other corporations.

Mr. BRANSON offered the following resolution, which was referred to the Committee on Franchise:

Resolved, That every free man of the age of twenty-one, being a citizen of the United States, and a citizen of the county wherein he may offer his vote, six months preceding the day of election, shall be entitled to vote for members of the General Assembly and other civil officers for the County or District in which he may reside.

Mr. THOMPSON, of Davidson, offered the following amendments to the Constitution, which were read and referred to the Committee on the Legislative Department:

Be it resolved, That Section 18, Article II, should be amended by words to the following effect: "No bill shall embrace more than one subject, which shall be clearly expressed in the title, and no law shall be revised or amended unless the new act contain the entire act revised, or the section or sections as amended, and the section or sections so amended shall be repealed.

"If any subject shall be embraced in an act but not expressed in the title thereof, such act shall be void only as to so much of the subject matter thereof as is not expressed in the title."

ORDER OF BUSINESS.

Mr. GIBSON offered the following:

As soon as the Journal is read and approved, the President shall, through the Clerk, call: 1st, For petitions, memorials and resolutions—calling the delegates in alphabetical order. 2nd, For reports from Standing Committees; and 3rd, For reports from Special Committees.

On motion of Mr. GIBSON the rules were suspended and the resolution adopted.

AMENDMENT PROPOSED.

Mr. TAYLOR offered the following resolution, which was read and referred to the Committee on the Executive Department:

Resolved, That the Committee upon the Executive Department of Government, be instructed and required to report whether or not the Constitution should be so amended as to submit the election of Secretary of State, Treasurer and Comptroller, to a direct vote of the people.

PRINTING FOR THE CONVENTION.

Mr. GARNER offered the following resolution:

Resolved, That a committee of five be appointed to inquire into and report as to the best mode of having such printing done, as either already has or may hereafter be ordered by this body.

On motion of Mr. GARNER, the rules were suspended and the resolution adopted.

The President thereupon appointed Messrs. GARNER, HEISKELL, KENNEDY, MABRY and CARTER, as said Committee.

AMENDMENTS PROPOSED.

Mr. GIBBS offered the following resolutions, which were read and referred to the Committee on New Counties and County Lines:

Resolved, That Section 4 of Article X of the present Constitution be so amended as to read as follows: "New Counties may be established by the Legislature, to consist of not less than three hundred square miles of territory, and to contain not less than five hundred qualified voters. No part of a county shall be taken off to form a new county, or a part thereof, without the consent of a majority of the qualified voters in such part taken off; nor shall such old county be so reduced therefor to less than four hundred square miles: *Provided, however,* That the present, or any succeeding Legislature, may establish a new county out of that portion of Obion County, lying west of low water mark, on the west bank of Reelfoot Lake, with a less territory than three hundred square miles, and less than five hundred qualified voters.

Mr. DIBBRELL offered the following resolution, which was read and referred to the Committee on Finance and Incorporations:

Resolved, That the Legislature shall have no power to pass laws chartering towns and cities, or private companies, unless the State of Tennessee shall be a stock-holder in said company; but may, by appropriate legislation, give the various Courts of Record of this State power to grant such charters and incorporations.

Mr. THOMPSON, of Davidson, offered the following resolution, which was read and referred to the Committee on Franchise:

Be it resolved, That Section 1 of Article IV of the Constitution be so amended as to omit the word "white;" and also be amended by adding the following words: "*Provided,* That no citizen shall be entitled to a vote at a State election who has not paid in full all of his State taxes due on the 1st of January preceding said State election; and no citizen shall be entitled to vote in a County election who has not paid in full all of his County taxes due on the 1st of January preceding said County election.

Mr. SAMPLE offered the following resolutions, which were read and referred to the Committee on Franchise:

Resolved, That every male person having arrived at the age of twenty-one years, and having not forfeited his right by crime, being a citizen of the United States, and a citizen of the County for six months previous to the day of election, shall be entitled to vote, without regard to race or color.

Resolved, That no hymenial contract or amalgamation between the white and colored race shall ever be countenanced or tolerated by law in the State of Tennessee.

Mr KENNEDY offered the following resolutions, which were read and referred to the Committee on the Legislative Department:

Resolved, That the Senate shall be elected for four years, one-half biennially.

Resolved, That the power of the Legislature to impose taxes ought to be so limited as to prohibit the imposition on property, either real or personal, of any other than an *ad valorem* tax; and that in apportioning this tax either for State, County or Municipal purposes, real estate and all the other visible property of each individual should be valued and taxed at their value: *Provided, however*, That household furniture to the value of five hundred dollars, and farming utensils to the value of five hundred dollars, shall be exempt from taxation.

Mr. FENTRESS offered the following resolution, which was read and referred to the Committee on Franchise:

Resolved, That Section 1 of Article IV of the Constitution of Tennessee be so amended as to read, "Every free white man of the age of twenty-one years, being a citizen of the United States, and a citizen of the County wherein he may offer his vote, twelve months next preceding the day of election, shall be entitled to vote for members of the General Assembly and other civil officers for the County or District in which he resides.

Mr. SAMPLE offered the following resolutions, which were read and referred to the Committee on the Legislative Department:

Resolved, That the Legislature be limited in their sessions to sixty days, and after that length of time if they continue longer, that they remain on their own expense. At a call session, thirty days, and no longer.

Resolved, That the 1st Section of the 9th Article be stricken out entirely, and the following be inserted in lieu thereof: "That Ministers of the Gospel, if elected by the qualified voters of their County or District in which they may reside, shall be admitted to take a seat in either House of the Legislature as a member of the same.

Resolved, That the following words be added in 2nd Section, 9th Article, after the words, "No person denying the existence of a God," shall be added, "or the divinity of Jesus Christ, or a future state of rewards and punishment," etc.

Mr. HOUSE, of Williamson, offered the following resolution, which was read and referred to the Committee on the Legislative Department:

Resolved, That Section 2 of Article V be so amended as to read as follows: "That the Senate shall have sole power to try impeachments. When sitting for that purpose the members shall be upon oath or affirmation, and shall be presided over by one of the Judges of the Supreme Court, selected for that purpose by *viva voce* vote of the Senate, and no person shall be convicted without the concurrence of two-thirds of the Senate, sworn to try the officer impeached.

Mr. THOMPSON, of Davidson, offered the following resolution, which was referred to the Committee on the Judicial Department:

Be it resolved, That Section 13 of Article VI of the Constitution be amended by words to the following effect: "Every Clerk of a Court of Record shall be appointed by the Judge or Judges thereof, to hold office for a term of six years. But all Clerks who are in office, or elected to office at the date of the organization of the Govment under the new Constitution, shall be entitled to hold their offices respectively until the full end and term of the period for which they are so elected.

Mr. MORRIS offered the following resolution, which was referred to the Committee on the Judiciary:

Resolved, That the Constitution be so amended as to make the Clerks and Masters of the Chancery Courts elective by the people at the same time and for the same length of time as the Chancellors; that the Clerks of the Circuit Courts be elected by the people at the same time and for the same length of time as the Judges of the Circuit Courts.

Mr. BROWN, of Davidson, offered the following resolution, which was read and referred to the Committee on the Judiciary:

Resolved, That Section 2 of Article VI shall be so amended as to read: "The Supreme Court shall be composed of six Judges, two of whom shall reside in each of the Grand Divisions of the State; they shall be nominated by the Governor to the Senate, and by that body confirmed, and such confirmation shall require two-thirds of all the Senators elect; and if, upon three successive nominations, the Senate should fail to concur, thereupon the Governor shall issue his proclamation, fixing a day for an election by the people, to be conducted as now provided by law. When said Judges are so elected, they shall be commissioned and qualified as at present. Three of said Judges shall be assigned to try cases upon the Law Docket, and three, cases upon the Chancery Docket.

The jurisdiction of this Court shall be appellate only, as at present: *Provided,* It shall have original jurisdiction to hear and determine all questions involving merely the constitutionality of any act of the General Assembly. Also, all questions touching the official duty or powers of any officer of the State Government. Such cases shall be presented by petition under such rules and regulations as may be prescribed by the Court so as to insure a speedy trial, and when exercising such original jurisdiction, all of said Judges shall preside upon the trial; and in case of a tie, notice shall be given to the Governor, who shall appoint some one learned in the law, to sit with the other Judges to hear and determine the question. The salaries of the Judges shall be as prescribed by law, and the Court shall be held at one place only in each of the Grand Divisions of the State.

Mr. IVIE offered the following resolution, which was read and referred to the Committee on the Legislative Department:

Resolved, That Section 23 of Article II of the present Constitution shall be so altered and amended as to read as follows:

"The sum of four dollars per day, and four dollars for every twenty-four miles traveling to and from the seat of Government, shall be allowed to the members of the First General Assembly as a compensation for their services. The compensation of the members of the succeeding Legislature shall be ascertained by law, but in no case shall the *per diem* compensation for any one session exceed the sum of three hundred and sixty dollars ($360 00), which shall be paid in such funds as the Collectors of Revenue are authorized by law to receive in payment of the State taxes. But no law increasing the compensation of members shall take effect until the commencement of the next regular session after such law shall have been enacted.

REPORT ON RULES.

Mr. CAMPBELL from the Committee appointed to draft rules and regulations for the Convention, reported the following, to-wit:

1st. Touching the duties of the President.

He shall take the Chair every day at the hour to which the Convention shall have adjourned on the preceding day; he shall immediately call the members to order, and, on the appearance of two-thirds of the members, shall cause the Journal of the preceding day to be read; he shall preserve decorum and order; may speak to points of order, in preference to other members, rising from his seat for that purpose; and shall decide questions of order, subject to an appeal to the Convention by any two members; he shall rise to put a question, but may state it sitting; questions shall be distinctly put in this form, to-wit: "As many as are of opinion that (as the question may be) say aye," and after the affirmative voice is expressed, "as many as are of a contrary opinion, say no." If the President doubts, or a division be called for, the Convention shall decide; those in the affirmative of the question shall first rise from their seats, and afterwards those in the negative. All Committees shall be appointed by the President, unless otherwise directed by the Convention, in which case they shall be appointed by ballot, and if upon such ballot the number required shall not be elected by a majority of votes given, the Convention shall proceed to a second ballot, in which a plurality of votes shall prevail; and in case a greater number than is required to compose or to complete the Committee, shall have an equal number of votes, the Convention shall proceed to a fourth ballot or ballots. In all cases of ballot by the Convention, the President shall vote. All acts, addresses and resolutions shall be signed by the President, and all writs, warrants or subpœnas, issued by order of the Convention, shall be under his hand and seal, attested by the Secretary. In case of any disturbance or disorderly conduct in the lobby, the President, or Chairman of the Committee of the whole Convention, shall have power to order the same to be cleared. Stenographers shall be admitted, and the President shall assign such places to them on the floor as shall not interfere with the convenience of the Convention.

2nd. Of decorum in debate.

When any member is about to speak in debate, or to deliver any matter to the Convention, he shall rise from his seat uncovered, and respectfully address himself to "Mr. President," or "Mr. Chairman," (as the case may be) and await the notice of the President or Chairman, and shall confine himself to the question under debate, and avoid disrespectful personalities. If any member, when speaking or otherwise, transgress the rules of the Convention, the President *shall*, or any member, may call to order, in which case the member so called to order shall immediately sit down, unless permitted to explain; and the Convention shall, if appealed to, decide on the case, but without debate; if there be no appeal, the decision of the Chair shall be submitted to. If the decision shall be in favor of the person called to order, he shall be at liberty to proceed; if otherwise, and the case require it, he shall be liable to the censure of the Convention. When two or more persons happen to rise at once, the President shall name the person who is to speak. No member shall speak more than twice on the same question without leave of the Convention, nor more than once until every member choosing to speak shall have spoken. Whilst the President is putting any question or addressing the Convention, no one shall walk out of or across the House; nor whilst a member is speaking, shall any one entertain private discourse; nor whilst a member is speaking, shall any one pass between him and the Chair. Every member who shall be in the Convention when a question is put, shall give his vote, unless the Convention, for special reasons, shall excuse him.

When a motion is made and seconded, it shall be stated by the President; or being in writing, it shall be handed to the Chair, and read aloud by the Secretary before it is debated.

Every motion shall be reduced to writing if the President or any member desire it.

After a motion is stated by the President, or read by the Secretary, it shall be deemed to be in possession of the Convention, but may be withdrawn at any time before a decision or amendment.

When a question is under debate no motion shall be received, unless to amend it, to commit it, or for the *previous question;* to postpone to a day certain, or to lay on the table, or to adjourn.

A motion to adjourn shall always be in order, and shall be decided without debate.

When a question made once and carried in the affirmative or negative, it shall be in order for any member of the majority to move for the reconsideration thereof.

The Convention shall have the power to compel the attendance of absent members.

No member shall absent himself from the service of the Convention, unless he has leave, or be sick and unable to attend.

The first member named on a Committee shall be Chairman of the same.

The Convention may be resolved into a Committee of the Whole for the discussion of any question that may be pending before the Convention.

The Convention, at all times, shall be considered in session when the President takes the Chair, and the roll shall not be called unless on application of a member.

The previous question shall be in this form: "Shall the main question now be put?" and may be demanded by any member if seconded; and if sustained by a majority, shall prevail; and, until it is decided, shall preclude all amendment and further debate of the main question.

The unfinished business in which the Convention was engaged at the last preceding adjournment, shall have preference in the orders of the day; and no motion on any other business shall be received, without special leave of the Convention, until the former is disposed of.

On a motion made and seconded a call of the Convention shall be had.

No member shall vote on any question touching his own conduct in, or rights and privileges, as a member of this Convention.

The Secretary shall not suffer any records or papers to be taken from the table, or out of his custody, by any member or any other person, without leave of the Convention.

It shall be a standing rule of the Convention that the President be authorised to call any member of the Convention to occupy the Chair, and exercise the functious of President until he may resume the Chair; with this proviso, that the power given by this rule shall not be construed to confer on the President a right to place any member in the Chair for a longer period than one day.

Upon the motion of any member, if seconded, the ayes and noes may be called for and spread upon the Journal. Any person voting in the negative of any proposition, shall have the right of entering his protest and reasons for such vote upon the Journal, provided he shall use no disrespectful personalities, in such protest, against any member of this Convention. After the question is put and the affirmative vote taken, there shall be no further debate.

The preceding rules shall be observed in Committee of the Whole, so far as they are applicable, except that part of the rule which restricts members from speaking more than twice upon the same question, and except the rule in regard to the previous question.

All resolutions shall lie on the table for one day for consideration, unless in special cases when the Covention shall think proper to suspend the rule.

All of which is respectfully submitted

ALEX. W. CAMPBELL,
Chairman.

On motion of Mr. CAMPBELL the rules reported by the committee were adopted, and one hundred copies ordered to be printed for the use of the Convention.

Mr. JONES, of Lincoln, moved to reconsider the vote ordering one hundred copies to be printed, which motion was rejected.

STANDING COMMITTEES.

The President announced the following as the Standing Committees of the Convention:

COMMITTEE ON THE BILL OF RIGHTS.

JOHN BAXTER.
R. P. BROOKS,
JOSEPH H. BLACKBURN,
WM. B. CARTER,
W. F. DOHERTY,
GEO. C. PORTER, of Haywood,.
MATT. MARTIN,
M. MCNABB,
T. C. MORRIS,
WM. SAMPLE,
JOHN M. TAYLOR.

COMMITTEE ON THE LEGISLATIVE DEPARTMENT.

W. H. STEPHENS,
JAMES S. BROWN, of Henry,
NATHAN BRANDON,
JAMES BRITTON,
H. R. GIBSON,
RICHARD HENDERSON,
N. S. BROWN, of Davidson,
T. B. IVIE,
GEO. W. JONES, of Lincoln,
E. H. SHELTON,
W. V. THOMPSON, of Maury.

COMMITTEE ON THE EXECUTIVE DEPARTMENT.

George W. Jones, of Lincoln.
John Allen,
Jas. W. Branson,
John E. Dromgoole,
W. H. Finley,
A. T. Feilder,
H. L. W. Hill, of Warren,
J. C. Parker,
S. G. Shepard,
Richard Warner, Jr.,
W. M. Wright.

COMMITTEE ON THE JUDICIARY DEPARTMENT

J. B. Heiskell,
John Baxter,
John W. Burton,
Alexander W. Campbell,
John F. House, of Montgomery,
Thomas M. Jones, of Giles,
A. O. P. Nicholson,
John Netherland,
James D. Porter, Jr., of Henry.
Jno. C. Thompson, of Davidson,
W. B. Staley,

COMMITTEE ON ELECTIONS AND RIGHT OF SUFFRAGE

A. O. P. Nicholson,
H. R. Bate,
Neil S. Brown, of Davidson
Warren Cummings,
W. V. Deaderick,
James Fentress,
Sparrel Hill, of Gibson,
Bolling Gordon,
A. A. Kyle,
D. M. Key,
W. H. Williamson.

COMMITTEE ON FINANCE, INTERNAL IMPOVEMENTS AND CORPORATIONS.

John A. Gardner,
Jesse Arledge,

A. BLIZARD,
JAMES A. COFFIN,
GEO. G. DIBBRELL,
SAMUEL S. HOUSE, of Williamson,
D. N. KENNEDY,
JOSEPH A. MABRY,
A. G. McDOUGAL,
GEORGE E. SEAY,
W. H. STEPHENS.

COMMITTEE ON MISCELLANEOUS SUBJECTS.

JAMES J. TURNER,
WM. BYRNE,
T. M. BURKETT,
Z. R. CHOWNING,
T. D. DEAVENPORT,
S. P. GAUT,
CHAS. N. GIBBS,
JOHN E. GARNER,
S. J. KIRKPATRICK,
P. G. FULKERSON,
G. W. WALTERS.

AMENDMENTS PROPSED.

Mr. TURNER offered the following amendments to the Constitution, which were read and referred to the Committee on the Judicial Department.

Resolved, That Art. VI, Sec. 2 of the Constitution be amended as follows, viz: by striking out the first sentence and inserting in lieu of the same:

The Supreme Court shall be composed of six judges, two of whom shall reside in each of the grand Divisions of the State.

Said Court shall meet at least once each year in each grand Division of the State. And three of them shall hear and determine all questions coming up from the Chancery Courts, and the other three shall hear and determine all causes coming up from other than the Chancery Courts.

The concurrence of two of the judges trying the cause, shall in every case be necessary to a decision.

The three judges trying the cause may, in writing, ask the other branch of the Court to sit with them on questions of great and general importance, and in such cases a majority of the Court shall determine them.

The Governor, with the concurrence of the Senate, shall designate the judges composing each Court.

The said Courts shall sit at the same time and place, and an election shall be held on the first Saturday of May, 1870, to supply the number of judges required by this section.

Mr. HOUSE, of Williamson, offered the following resolution which was referred to the Committee on the Legislative Department:

Resolved, That the General Assembly shall have no power to make or change election precincts; nor to establish bridges or ferries; nor to change names, or legitimate children; but it shall prescribe by law the manner in which said powers shall be exercised by the Courts.

Mr. MORRIS, offered the following resolution, which was referred to the Committee on the Legislative Department:

Resolved, That the Constitution of the State, be so amended that there shall be but one regular session of the General Assembly in three (3) years, with power to the Governor to convene them in extra session when necessary; that the members be allowed *per diem*, at the regular session for not exceeding one hundred (100) days; and in extra session not exceeding (30) thirty days.

Mr. WARNER offered the following resolution, which was referred to the Committee on the Legislative Department:

Resolved, That Article II, Section 19, of the Constitution of Tennessee be so amended as to allow the words "after being considered and acted upon by both Houses, or in each House," to be inserted between the words "rejected" and "no."

Mr. MARTIN offered the following, which was referred to the Committee on Miscellaneous Provisions:

Resolved, That no member of the Legislature, or Executive, or Judicial Officer of this State, shall receive while in office, either directly or indirectly, any gift, gratuity, fee or reward from any person or corporation.

LIST OF MEMBERS.

Mr. GARNER offered the following resolution:

Resolved, That the Principal Doorkeeper be directed to make out and have printed for the use of the Convention 300 copies of an accurate statement of the name, age, occupation, postoffice, place of nativity, and whether married or single, of the officers and delegates of this Convention.

On motion of Mr. GIBSON, the resolution was laid on the table.

AMENDMENTS PROPOSED.

Mr. IVIE offered the following, which was referred to the Committee on the Legislative Department:

Resolved, That Section 7 Article II of the present Constitution be amended by adding: "*Provided further,* That the Legislature shall not grant charters of incorporation to any corporation of a local or private character."

Mr. THOMPSON, of Davidson, offered the following, which was referred to the Committee on Finance:

Be it resolved, That it is expedient and for the honor of the State that due and unpaid coupons of bonds of the State of Tennessee, issued prior to May, 1861, shall be receivable in payment of all State taxes; and that due and unpaid coupons of the bonds of any County of this State, issued prior to the month of May, 1861, shall be receivable in payment of all County taxes of such County.

Mr. THOMPSON, of Davidson, offered the following, which was referred to the Committee on the Judiciary:

Be it resolved, That Section 1, of Article VII, be amended by words to the following effect: There shall be elected for each County, by the Justices thereof, one Clerk, one Sheriff, one Tax Collector, one Register, one Coroner, and one Ranger, who shall hold office respectively for two years, or until their successors are appointed. The Clerk, the Register, the Sheriff and the Tax Collector to be respectively appointed at different terms of the Quarterly Court; but every person holding or elected to one of said County offices, at the date of the organization of the government under the new Constitution, shall be entitled to hold their offices respectively until the full end and term of the period for which they are so elected.

Mr. BROWN, of Davidson, offered the following amendments, which were referred to the Committee on Finance:

To Section 6 of Article 11, add: "But the Legislature shall have power to pass laws establishing conventional interest, and within the limits therein prescribed, contracts shall be binding."

New Section 13, Article XI: The faith of the State is hereby pledged for the redemption of all of its obligations, and shall forever remain inviolate. And the General Assembly is required, without delay, to take such steps, and to adopt such measures, as may be necessary and adequate to meet the interest on the public debt, and to discharge the debt itself as fast as it matures.

Strike out Section 31 in Article II, and insert: "That the General Assembly shall have power to provide by law that all voters shall be required to vote within the Civil Districts or Wards in which they reside; and shall have power also to pass laws to protect all voters in the free exercise of their choice.

That the following sentence in Section 28, Article II, be stricken out, viz: But the Legislature shall have power to tax merchants, peddlers and privileges, in such manner as they may from time to time direct, and insert: But the Legislature shall have power to require all persons who buy and sell as a vocation to take out a license, for which they shall pay a sum not exceeding one per cent. proportion of the taxes assessed on their capital for the current year.

FINANCE, ETC.

Section 7, Article II., strike out the following, viz:

Provided, always, the Legislature shall have power to grant such charters of incorporation as they may deem expedient for the public good, and insert: and shall have no power to grant charters of incorporation, either municipal or private, but may pass laws authorizing the Chancery, Circuit, or County Courts to grant all such charters, under such rules and regulations as are, or may be prescribed by law; *Provided*, that no municipal corporations or counties shall be authorized to create any debt without an adequate levy of taxes to meet the same, except by a vote of two thirds of all the voters of such corporation or county, counting by the last preceding Gubernatorial election.

Mr. HOUSE, of Williamson, offered the following resolution, which was referred to the Committee on the Legislative Department:

Resolved, That no law or section of the Code shall be amended or repealed by mere reference to its title, or to the number of the section in the Code, but the amending or repealing act shall distinctly and fully describe the law to be amended or repealed, as well as the alteration to be made.

Mr. GAUT, offered the following resolution which was referred to the Committee on the Legislative Department:

Resolved, That the Committee on the Legislative Department enquire into and report whether the Legislature should have power to grant *any* private charters, or pass any act exclusively for private or individual benefit, or relief and also to enquire whether the Legislature should invest the Courts of Chancery of this State with the exclusive power under proper application to grant such private charters, privileges and relief.

On motion, of Mr. GORDON, the Convention adjourned until to-morrow morning at 10 o'clock.

THURSDAY MORNING JANUARY 13, 1870.

The Convention met pursuant to adjournment, Mr. President BROWN in the Chair.

Prayer by the Rev. Mr. FALL.

AMENDMENTS OF THE RULES.

Mr. GIBSON, offered the following—which was read and referred to the Committee on Rules:

Rule — No petition or memorial containing language disrespectful to this body, or to the State or General Governments, or any department thereof, shall be read if objected to.

Mr. HOUSE, of Montgomery, offered the following amendments to the Rules which were adopted, and ordered to be printed with the rules for the government of the Convention:

That the last permanent rule of this Convention be amended by adding the following:

But this rule shall not apply to resolutions proposing to amend the Constitution, but the same shall be referred at once to the appropriate Committee, and the delegate proposing such resolution shall have five minutes, within which to make explanatory remarks.

Mr. TURNER, offered the following resolution which was referred to the Committee on Rules.

Resolved, That all petitions and memorials shall be received and read, and referred without debate to the appropriate committee.

Mr. GARDNER, offered the following resolution, which was read and ordered to be referred to the Committee on Rules.

Resolved, That a committee of seven be appointed on Petitions, Memorials and Grievances, to whom all petitions and memorials, addressed to this body shall be referred without reading or debate.

AMENDMENTS PROPOSED.

Mr. ALLEN, offered the following resolution, which was read and ordered to be referred to the Committee on the Legislative Department:

Resolved, That the Committee on Corporations be instructed to report an amendment to the Constitution which will forever guarantee to the cities and other incorporated towns, in this State, the right to elect their own municipal officers, including officers of police.

Mr. Arledge offered the following, which was read and referred:

Resolved, That the Committee on Finance, Internal Improvements and Corporations, report such changes in the Constitution as will prohibit any further issuance of State bonds.

Mr. Britton submitted the following resolutions, which were read and referred to the Committee on Miscellaneous Provisions:

Resolved 1st, That we are admonished by the embarrassing condition of our own internal affairs, as well as the threatening aspect of the surroundings, that it is a matter of the highest importance to make the work of this Convention harmonious and as expeditious as possible, doing full justice to ourselves, and looking well to the interest of the people of the whole State, white and colored, present and future.

Resolved 2nd, That in the opinion of this Convention, our present Constitution is a model Constitution, well adapted to the times for which it was intended, and wisely balancing the independent powers of the co-ordinate departments of the State government, and was the work of wise, patriotic and good men.

Resolved 3rd, That this Cenvention, with a high reverence for the work of a noble and patriotic ancestry, and fully appreciating the importance and responsibility of the position in which we have been placed, will proceed to the work assigned us, aided by the reports of Standing Committees, and such Special Committees as may hereafter be appointed, by reading the present Constitution in full Convention, article by article, and section by section, and in this way making such amendments, as we proceed, as time and experience have shown to be necessary, with as little disturbance as possible of the symmetry and harmony of our present Constitution, but guided alone by the necessities arising out of the changed condition of our affairs.

Mr. Brooks offered the following resolution, which was read and referred to the Committee on the Legislative Department:

Resolved, That the Constitution be so amended as to limit the Legislature to one thousand dollars as appropriation for internal improvement by the State, and all appropriations over one thousand dollars shall be void until ratified by a majority of the qualified voters of the State of Tennessee.

Mr. Burton offered the following, which was read and referred to the Committee on the Judicial Department:

Resolved, That Article VI, Section 2, of the Constitution be amended so as to read as follows: "The Supreme Court shall be composed of five Judges, one of whom shall reside in and be elected by the qualified voters of each of the three grand divisions of the State, the remaining two to be nominated by the Governor from the State at large, and confirmed by the Senate."

Mr. BURTON offered the following, which was read and referred:

Resolved, That it be referred to the Committee on the Bill of Rights to report upon the propriety of the following amendment, to-wit:

"That no person shall be held to answer for a capital crime, or crime above the grade of petit larceny, unless on a presentment or indictment of a Grand Jury, except in cases of impeachment or military trials, otherwise provided for in the Constitution. The Legislature shall pass no laws making the stealing of more than $50 personalty petit larceny."

JOHN H. MEEKS, delegate elect from the county of McNairy, appeared, presented his credentials, was sworn and took his seat as a member of this Convention.

COMMITTEE ON NEW COUNTIES, ETC.

The President announced the following gentlemen to constitute the Committee on New Counties and County Lines: Messrs. SEAY, COFFIN, DEADERICK, WARNER, JONES, of Giles, GIBBS, and TAYLOR.

AMENDMENTS PROPOSED.

Mr. DIBBRELL, submitted the following resolution, which was referred to the Committee on New Counties and County Lines.

Resolved, That the last clause of Section 4, Article X of the Constitution, which says: "That the counties of Marion and Bledsoe shall not be reduced below one thousand qualified voters each, in forming a new county or counties," be stricken out of the Constitution.

Mr. DEAVENPORT, submitted the following resolution, which was read and referred to the Committee on Miscellaneous Subjects:

Resolved, That the appropriate Committee be instructed to inquire and report upon the propriety of ordering an election for all Judicial and County officers as soon after the ratification of the New Constitution as practicable.

4

Mr. FULKERSON, offered the following, which was read and referred to the Committee on the Legislative Department.

Resolved, That secret political organizations are dangerous to the liberties of Republican Governments, and the Legislature have power to enact laws to disperse and punish the members of the same.

Mr. FENTRESS offered the following resolution, which was read and referred to the Committee on the Bill of Rights:

Resolved, That Section 22 of the Declaration of Rights, be so amended as to read as follows:

"That no man's particular services shall be demanded, or property taken, or applied to public use without the consent of his representative, or without just compensation being made therefor. And as to any property taken for the public use, without the consent of the owner, a just compensation shall be made therefor at the time, or before the said property is so taken."

AMENDMENT OF THE RULES.

Mr. KENNEDY submitted the following resolution, which was read and referred to the Committee on Rules:

That the last of the Rules of this Convention be amended as follows:

"All resolutions on which the mover desiring action of the Convention shall lie on the table one day for consideration, unless the Convention shall suspend the rule. But resolutions may be referred to a committee at the time of presentation.

Mr. HOUSE, of Davidson, Robertson and Montgomery, submitted the following resolution:

Resolved, That the rule requiring resolutions to lay on the table one day shall not apply to resolutions proposing amendments to the Constitution, but the same shall be referred at once to the appropriate committee, and the delegate proposing such resolution shall have five minutes within which to make any explanatory remarks he may desire.

AMENDMENTS PROPOSED.

Mr. GIBSON submitted the following amendment to the Constitution, which was read and referred to the Committee on Finance:

Article —, Section —. The Legislature shall not remit or release any pecuniary or other penalty debt, or claim due or accruing to the State, or audit, allow, or direct to be paid, any private claim or account against the State, or pass any special law relative to any of the foregoing matters. But the Legislature may pass general laws whereunder such penalties, debts or claims due or accruing to the

State may be remitted or released, and may appropriate money to pay these last claims or accounts; but this section shall not be so construed as to refer to official salaries, or other compensation fixed by law, or to payment for such work or materials as may have been or may hereafter be authorized by law, or to the necessary and incidental expenses incurred by the Legislature, or a Constitutional Convention while in session.

Mr. GIBSON submitted the following amendments to the Constitution, which were read and referred to the Committee on Finance:

Article —, Section —. The officers of the State Treasury, and all other State officers, shall be liable, on their official bonds for any moneys paid by them in violation of this Constitution; but the written opinion of the majority of the Judges of the Supreme Court shall be sufficient authority in all doubtful cases.

Article —, Section —. The public debt of the State shall never exceed five per centum of the taxable wealth of the State. And no public money shall be voted for any purpose by the Legislature other than to pay or provide for existing liabilities and the ordinary expenses of the State Government, until said debt is reduced to the limit fixed in this section.

Mr. GIBSON submitted the following amendment to the Constitution, which was read and referred to the Committee on Finance:

Article —, Section —. The credit of the State shall never be given or loaned to, or in aid of, any individual, association, or corporation; nor shall the State subscribe for, or purchase shares, stock, or any other interest in any company, or corporation, or other private enterprise. And every act appropriating public money or property for or to any purpose other than to meet the ordinary expenses of government and existing liabilities, shall receive a two-thirds vote, and the yeas and nays shall be entered on the journals.

Mr. GIBSON submitted the following amendment to the Constitution, which was read and referred to the Committee on Finance:

Article —, Section —. No extra or increased pay, or compensation, shall be voted, given or allowed by the Legislature to the members or officers thereof, or to any other officer or agent of the State, on any pretence, or in any shape whatever; but the compensation of every officer shall be declared and fixed by law, and shall not in any way be increased, diminished or varied during incumbency. And all compensation shall be paid in such funds as are received at par at the State Treasury.

Mr. HOUSE, of Davidson, Robertson and Montgomery, submitted the following amendments to the Bill of Rights, which were referred to the appropriate Committee:

In the 14th section of the Bill of Rights strike out the words "shall be put to answer any criminal charge" and insert in lieu thereof the following: "shall be held to answer for a capital or otherwise infamous crime." In said section strike out also the words "free man" and insert in lieu thereof the word "person" so as to make said section read as follows:

"That no person shall be held to answer for a capital or otherwise infamous crime, but by presentment, indictment, or impeachment."

Mr. KIRKPATRICK offered the following resolution, which was refered to the Committee on the Bill of Rights:

Resolved, That the 18th section of the Declaration of Rights be stricken out and the following substituted therefor:

"No person shall be imprisoned for debt."

Mr. IVIE offered the following resolution, which lies over under the rule:

Resolved, That the President appoint a Special Committee, to consist of one delegate from each Judicial Circuit, who shall report to the Convention what changes, if any, are necessary to be made in the Chancery Divisions and Judicial Circuits of the State, and the counties that shall compose the same.

Mr. KIRKPATRICK offered the following resolution, which was referred to the Committee on the Legislative Department:

Resolved, That the General Assembly shall pass laws to protect from execution a reasonable amount of the property of a debtor, not exceeding in value the sum of five hundred dollars.

Mr. KIRKPATRICK submitted the following resolution, which was read and referred to the Committee on the Legislative Department:

Resolved, That the rate of interest in this State shall not exceed six per cent. per annum, and no higher rate shall be taken or demanded, and the Legislature shall provide by law all necessary forfeitures and penalties against usury.

Mr. KIRKPATRICK submitted the following preamble and resolutions, which were read and referred to the Committee on Miscellaneous Provisions.

WHEREAS, A general diffusion of knowledge being essential to the preservation of the rights and liberties of the people, inasmuch as an enlightened public opinion is the only conservative power in which we can confide for the protection of our Republican institutions, against fraud, intrigue, corruption and violence: And, Whereas, it is an object of cardinal solicitude with this Convention to provide for the maintenance within the reach of every child in this State, the means of such an education as will qualify him to discharge the duties of a citizen of the Republic: Therefore be it

Resolved, That the Committee on Miscellaneous Provisions be instructed to inqnire into the expediency of providing for the establishment of a uniform system of free public schools for the benefit of the children of the State between the ages of 5 and 21 years, to be maintained by taxation or otherwise.

Mr. MABRY submitted the following preamble and resolution, which were read and referred to the Committee on Finance:

WHEREAS, The people of Tennessee are in no condition to be taxed to pay illegal and unjust obligations: Therefore, be it

Resolved, That the Committee on Finance, Internal Improvements and Corporations take into consideration and report to this body whether it is properly within the province of this body to enquire and determine which are the legal and which are the illegal obligations of the State.

Mr. PORTER, of Haywood, submitted the following amendments to the Constitution of the State, which were read and referred to the Committee on Executive Department:

Addenda to the resolution of Mr. HOUSE granting veto power to the Governor.

That after the clause: "Every bill which may pass both Houses of the General Assembly, shall before it becomes a law, be presented to the Governor for his signature" shall be inserted the following clause: "If he approve he shall sign and deposit it in the office of the Secretary of State for preservation, and notify the House, where it originated, of the fact, and the same shall become a law;" and then continue as in resolution. The whole to conclude with the following clause: "The Governor may approve, sign and file in the office of Secretary of State, within five days after the adjournment of the Legislature, any act passed during the last five days of the session, and the same shall become a law."

Mr. PORTER, of Haywood, submitted the following resolution, which was read and referred to the Committee on the Legislative Department:

Resolved, That the appointment of Secretary of State be vested alone in the Governor, subject to the approval and ratification of the Senate.

Mr. PARKER submitted the following resolution, which was read and referred to the Committee on Miscellaneous Provisions:

Resolved, That the County Surveyors be elected by the qualified voters of their respective counties, and the time, place and manner of their election, and term of office be the same as Circuit and County Court Clerks.

Mr. PARKER submitted the following amendment to the Constitution, which was read and referred to the Committee on the Legislative Department:

Resolved, That Sec. 8, of Art. 1st, of the amendment to the Constitution, adopted February 22d, 1865, be so changed as to allow the counties of Scott and Morgan to send one member to the House of Representatives; and the counties of Fentress and Cumberland one Representative.

Mr. PARKER offered the following amendment, which was read and referred to the Committee on Miscellaneous Provisions:

Article —, Section —. In all elections by the people, and also by the Senate and House of Representatives, jointly or separately, the votes shall be personally and publicly given, *viva voce.*

Mr. SEAY offered the following resolution, which was read and referred to the Committee on the Legislative Department:

Resolved, That the Committee on the Legislative Department inquire into the propriety of so amending Sec. 29 of Art. II of the Constitution, as to empower the General Assembly to authorize any one, or more civil districts of a county or counties in this State, to impose taxes for corporation or other purposes, in snch manner as may be prescribed by law. All property to be taxed according to its value, upon the principles established in regard to State taxation.

Mr. SHEPARD submitted the following resolution, which was read and referred to the Committee on Franchise:

Resolved, That the right of suffrage is a fundamental right, and it is the opinion of the delegates of this Convention that they cannot delegate to the General Assembly any power to legislate upon the subject.

Mr. STEPHENS, offered the following resolution, which was read and referred to the Committee on Franchise:

Resolved, That the Committee on Elections and the Right of Suffrage be instructed to report the Article touching the question of suffrage by colored persons, in such a form that it may be conveniently submitted to the people of the State, to be voted on as an independent proposition, separate and apart from all others.

Mr. THOMPSON, of Maury, submitted the following resolution, which was read and referred to the Committee on the Judiciary:

Resolved, That the Judiciary Committee be requested to inquire into and report as to the propriety of providing, by Constitutional provision, for the prohibition of the exercise by any Judge of this State of judicial authority, both civil and criminal, and requiring the Legislature to provide for the election or appointment of a suitable number of Criminal Judges for this State.

Mr. TAYLOR offered the following resolution:

Be it resolved, That the credit of this State shall never be given or loaned in aid of any person, association, municipality or corporation. That this be referred to the Committee on the Legislative Department.

Mr. TURNER offered the following resolution, which was read and referred to the Committee on the Legislative Department:

Resolved, That Article II, Section 18 of the Constitution, be amended by adding after the word "Speakers," "Nor until the same has been signed by the Executive. If the Executive shall refuse to sign the same, he shall, in two days, return the bill to the House in which it originated, with his reasons for refusing to sign it. The bill may then become a law; *Provided,* a majority of all the members of each House shall vote for it."

Mr. TURNER offered the following resolution, which was read and referred to the Committee on the Legislative Department:

Resolved. That Senators hereafter shall be elected for the term of four years. That upon the meeting of the Legislature on the first Monday of October, 1871, the Senators elect shall draw lots for the long and short terms. The members drawing the short terms shall serve for two years, and those drawing the long term shall serve for four years. At each biennial election after the next general election for members of the Legislature, no election shall be held for Senators except in cases of vacancies."

Mr. WARNER submitted the following amendments to the Constitution, which were read and referred to the Committee on the Legislative Department:

Resolved, That Article III, Section 9, of the Constitution of the State of Tennessee, be so amended as to strike out the words "and shall state to them when assembled, the purposes for which they shall have been convened," and insert in their stead the following words: "And shall state to them specifically, in the proclamation calling them together, the purposes for which they are to convene."

Resolved, That Article III, Section 16, of the Constitution of the State of Tennessee, be so amended as to add the following words after the word "Governor," "in person."

REPORT ON PRINTING.

Mr. GARNER, from the Committee on Printing, made the following report:

The Committee on Printing have directed me to report that they find that the Public Printers for this State, Messrs. JONES, PURVIS & Co., (proprietors of the Union and American and of the Republican Banner) are prepared to do such printing as this body may order, with neatness and dispatch, and upon the terms now prescribed by law.

Your Committee request further time in which to make report as to the printing of such number of copies of the Journal of the proceedings of this Convention as may be ordered, and recommend the passage of the following resolution, viz:

Resolved, That the Secretary of this Convention procure to be printed by JONES, PURVIS & Co., on the terms prescribed by law, such job printing as has or may be ordered by this body, and that the Committee on Printing be allowed time in which to make further report as to the printing of the Journal of the proceedings of this body.

Respectfully submitted,

JOHN E. GARNER,
Chairman.

Which report was received, and the resolution adopted.

REPORT ON CREDENTIALS.

Mr. HOUSE, of Williamson, from the Committee on Credentials, made the following report, which was received, adopted, and ordered to be spread on the minutes:

The Committee on Credentials respectfully report that they have examined the credentials of the following-named persons, and find them to be entitled to seats as members of this Convention, to-wit:

From the County of Bedford—THOMPSON BAKER IVIE.

From the County of Blount—WM. HENDERSON FINLEY.

From the County of Bradley—SIMEON PERRY GAUT.

From the County of Cannon—WARREN CUMMINGS.

From the County of Carroll—WM. MOORE WRIGHT.

From the County of Claiborne—PETER GRAHAM FULKERSON.

From the County of Cocke—MALCOLM MCNABB.

From the County of Davidson—NEIL SMITH BROWN, and JOHN CLAIBORNE THOMPSON.

From the County of Dickson—THOMAS CARTER MORRIS.

From the County of DeKalb—JOSEPH HAYES BLACKBURN.

From the County of Fayette—EDWIN HENRY SHELTON.

From the County of Franklin—JESSE ARLEDGE.

From the County of Gibson—SPARREL HILL.

From the County of Giles—THOMAS MCKISSICK JONES.
From the County of Grainger—JAMES WESLEY BRANSON.
From the County of Greene—JAMES BRITTON.
From the County of Hamilton—RICHARD HENDERSON.
From the County of Hardeman—JAMES FENTRESS.
From the County of Hardin—ARCHIBALD GARRETT MCDOUGAL.
From the County of Hawkins—JOHN NETHERLAND.
From the County of Haywood—GEORGE CAMP PORTER.
From the County of Henderson—JOHN MAY TAYLOR.
From the County of Henry—JAMES DAVIS PORTER, JR.
From the County of Hickman—BOLLING GORDON.
From the County of Jackson—RICHARD PRICE BROOKS.
From the County of Jefferson—WILLIAM SAMPLE.
From the County of Knox—JOHN BAXTER.
From the County of Lawrence—THOS. DANIEL DEAVENPORT.
From the County of Lincoln—GEORGE WASHINGTON JONES.
From the County of Madison—ALEXANDER WM. CAMPBELL.
From the County of Marion—WILLIAM BYRNE.
From the County of Marshall—RICHARD WARNER, JR.
From the County of Maury—WILLIAM VANCE THOMPSON.
From the County of McNairy—JOHN HENDERSON MEEKS.
From the County of McMinn—ARCHIBALD BLIZARD.
From the County of Monroe—JAMES AYER COFFIN.
From the County of Montgomery—DAVID NEWTON KENNEDY.
From the County of Obion—CHAS. NICHOLAS GIBBS.
From the County of Overton—ZACH. ROBINSON CHOWNING.
From the County of Roane—WILLIAM BROWN STALEY.
From the County of Robertson—JOHN EWING GARNER.
From the County of Rutherford—JOHN WILLIAMS BURTON.
From the County of Stewart—NATHAN BRANDON.
From the County of Sullivan—WM. VAN ALBADE DEADERICK.
From the County of Sumner—JAMES JONES TURNER.
From the County of Shelby—WILLIAM HENRY STEPHENS and JOSEPH BROWN HEISKELL.
From the County of Smith—JOHN ALLEN.
From the County of Warren—HUGH LAWSON WHITE HILL.
From the County of Wayne—ROBERT PERRY CYPERT.
From the County of Washington—SAM'L JACOB KIRKPATRICK.
From the County of Weakley—JOHN ALMUS GARDNER.

From the County of White—GEORGE GIBBS DIBBRELL.

From the County of Wilson—SAMUEL GEORGE SHEPARD and WILLIAM HENRY WILLIAMSON.

From the County of Williamson—SAMUEL SMITH HOUSE.

From the Counties of Carter and Johnson—WILLIAM BLOUNT CARTER.

From the Counties of Greene, Hawkins, Hancock and Jefferson—ARTHUR ABSALOM KYLE.

From the Counties of Knox and Sevier—JOSEPH ALEXANDER MABRY.

From the Counties of Anderson and Campbell—HENRY RICHARD GIBSON.

From the Counties of Scott, Morgan and Fentress—JAMES CRAWFORD PARKER.

From the Counties of Polk, McMinn, and Meigs—THEOPHILUS MERIKEN BURKETT.

From the Counties of Rhea, Bledsoe, Hamilton, and Sequatchie—DAVID McKENDREE KEY.

From the Counties of Grundy, Coffee and Van Buren—MATT. MARTIN.

From the Counties of Smith, Sumner and Macon—GEORGE EDWARD SEAY.

From the Counties of Davidson, Robertson and Montgomery—JOHN FORD HOUSE.

From the Counties of Rutherford and Bedford—JOHN EASTER DROMGOOLE.

From the Counties of Lincoln, Giles and Marshall—JOHN CALVIN BROWN.

From the Counties of Williamson, Maury and Lewis—ALFRED OSBORNE POPE NICHOLSON.

From the Counties of Benton and Humphreys—WM. FRENCH DOHERTY.

From the Counties of Perry and Decatur—GEORGE WASHINGTON WALTERS.

From the Counties of Carroll, Gibson, Madison and Henry—JAMES STEPHEN BROWN.

From the Counties of Dyer and Lauderdale—ALFRED TYLER FIELDER.

From the Counties of Tipton, Shelby and Fayette—HUMPHREY RASCOE BATE.

AMENDMENTS PROPOSED.

Mr. DIBBRELL submitted the following resolution:

Resolved, That the Judiciary Committee be instructed to inquire into and report the propriety of amending the Constitution so as to adopt the two-term system of the Circuit Courts, and of reducing the number of Circuits in this State to twelve, and of reducing the number of Chancery Divisions to eight. The Chancellors and Judges, as well as Clerks of said Courts, to be elected by the qualified voters of their respective Counties, Circuits or Divisions.

Mr. STALEY offered the following resolution, which was referred to the Committee on the Judiciary:

Resolved, That the Circuit Judges of this State shall be required to reduce to writing their charges to traverse juries before delivering the same. After the charges have been delivered they shall be filed with the papers in the cause, and shall not afterwards be altered or added to.

Mr. TAYLOR submitted the following resolution, which was read and referred to the Committee on the Judiciary:

Resolved, That Section 2, of Article IV., be so amended as to read as follows: The Supreme Court shall consist of a Chief Justice and four Associate Justices. The number of Associate Justices may be increased or decreased by law, but shall never be less than two. That this be referred to the Committee on the Judiciary.

REPORT OF THE COMMITTEE ON BILL OF RIGHTS.

Mr. BAXTER, from the Committee on the Bill of Rights, made the following report, which was ordered to be laid on the table and printed:

WHEREAS, The people of the territory of the United States south of the Ohio river, having the right of admission into the General Government as a member State thereof, consistent with the Constitution of the United States, and the act of cession of the State of North Carolina, recognizing the ordinance for the government of the territory of the United States north-west of the Ohio River, by their Delegates and Representatives in Convention assembled, did, on the sixth day of February, in the year of our Lord one thousand seven hundred and ninety-six, ordain and establish a Constitution, or form of government, and mutually agreed with each other to form themselves into a free and independent State, by the name of the State of Tennessee; and

WHEREAS, The General Assembly of said State of Tennessee, (pursuant to the third Section of the tenth Article of the Constitution,) by an act passed on the twenty-seventh day of November, in the year of our Lord one thousand eight hundred and thirty-three, entitled, "An Act to provide for the calling of a Convention," did authorize and provide for the election by the people of delegates and representatives, to meet at Nashville, in Davidson County, on the third Monday in May, in the year of our Lord one thousand eight hundred and thirty-four, for the purpose of revising and amending or changing the Constitution; and

WHEREAS, *The General Assembly of the State of Tennessee, under and in virtue of the first Section of the first Article of the Declaration of Rights, contained in and forming a part of the existing Constitueion of the State, by an act passed on the fifteenth day of November, in the year of our Lord one thousand eight hundred and sixty-nine, entitled, "An Act to authorize the people to call a Convention, and for other purposes," did authorize the people of the State to call a Convention, to meet at Nashville, on the second Monday in January, in the year of our Lord one thousand eight hundred and seventy, and to elect delegates thereto, for the purpose of amending, revising, or forming and making a new Constitution;* and

WHEREAS, *The people of the State, in pursuance of, and in the mode authorized by said Act, have called said Convention, and elected delegates to represent them therein;* now, therefore,

We, the Delegates and Representatives of the people of the State of Tennessee, duly elected and in Convention assembled, in pursuance of said Act of Assembly, have ordained and established the following Constitution and form of government for this State, which we recommend to the people of Tennessee for their ratification: that is to say—

ARTICLE I.

DECLARATION OF RIGHTS.

Sec. 1. That all power is inherent in the people, and all free governments are founded on their authority, and instituted for their peace, safety, and happiness; for the advancement of those ends they have, at all times, an unalienable and indefeasible right to alter, reform, or abolish the government in such manner as they may think proper.

Sec. 2. That government being instituted for the common benefit, the doctrine of non-resistance against arbitrary power and oppression is absurd, slavish, and destructive of the good and happiness of mankind.

Sec. 3. That all men have a natural and indefeasible right to worship Almighty God according to the dictates of their own conscience; that no man can, of right, be compelled to attend, erect, or support any place of worship, or to maintain any minister against his consent; that no human authority can, in any case whatever, control or interfere with the rights of conscience; and that no preference shall ever be given, by law, to any religious establishment or mode of worship.

Sec. 4. That no religious *or political test, other than an oath to support the Constitution of the United States and of this State,* shall ever be required as a qualification to any office or public trust under this State.

Sec. 5. That elections shall be free and equal, *and the right of suffrage, as hereinafter declared, shall never be denied to any person entitled thereto, except upon a conviction by a jury of some infamous crime, previously ascertained and declared by law, and the judgment thereon by a court of compentent jurisdiction.*

Sec. 6. That the right of trial by jury shall remain inviolate.

Sec. 7. That the people shall be secure in their persons, houses, papers, and possessions from unreasonable searches and seizures; and that general warrants, whereby an officer may be commanded to search suspected places, without evidence of the fact committed, or to seize any person or persons not named, whose offences are not particularly described and supported by evidence, are dangerous to liberty, and ought not to be granted.

Sec. 8. That no man shall be taken or imprisoned, or disseized of his freehold, liberties or privileges, or outlawed or exiled, or in any manner destroyed, or deprived of his life, liberty, or property, but by the judgment of his peers, or the law of the land.

Sec. 9. That in all criminal prosecutions, the accused hath a right to be heard by himself and his counsel; to demand the nature and cause of the accusation against him, and to have a copy thereof: to meet the witnesses face to face; to have compulsory process for obtaining witnesses in his favor; and in prosecutions by indictment or presentment, a speedy public trial by an impartial jury of the County or District in which the crime shall have been committed, *unless the same shall be changed, for good cause, to another County or District in the mode to be prescribed by a general public law, passed before the alleged commission of the offense;* and shall not be compelled to give evidence against himself.

Sec. 10. That no person shall, for the same offence, be twice put in jeopardy of life or limb.

Sec. 11. That laws made for the punishment of acts committed previous to the existence of such laws, and by them only declared criminal, are contrary to the principles of a free government; wherefore no *ex post facto* law shall be made.

Sec. 12. That no conviction shall work corruption of blood or forfeiture of estate. The estate of such persons as shall destroy their own lives shall descend or vest as in case of natural death. If any person be killed by casualty, there shall be no forfeiture in consequence thereof.

Sec. 13. That no person arrested and confined in jail shall be treated with unnecessary rigor.

Sec. 14. That no citizen shall be put to answer any criminal charge but by presentment, indictment or impeachment.

Sec. 15. That all prisoners shall be bailable by sufficient sureties, unless for capital offenses, when the proof is evident or the presumption great. And the privilege of the writ of *habeas corpus* shall not be suspended, unless when in case of rebellion or invasion *the General Assembly shall declare* the public safety requires it.

Sec. 16. That excessive bail shall not be required, nor excessive fines imposed, nor cruel and unusual punishments inflicted.

Sec. 17. That all courts shall be open; and every man, for an injury done him in his lands, goods, person or reputation, shall have remedy by due course of law, and right and justice administered without sale, denial or delay. Suits may be brought against the State, in such manner and in such courts as the Legislature may, by law, direct.

Sec. 18. That the person of a debtor, where there is not strong presumption of fraud, shall not be continued in prison after delivering up his estate for the benefit of his creditor or creditors, in such manner as shall be prescribed by law.

Sec 19. That the printing presses shall be free to every person who undertakes to examine the proceedings of the Legislature, or of any branch or officer of the government; and no law shall ever be made to restrain the right thereof. The free communication of thoughts and opinions is one of the invaluable rights of man, and every citizen may freely speak, write and print on any subject, being responsible for the abuse of that liberty. But in prosecutions for the publication of papers investigating the official conduct of officers or men in public capacity, the truth thereof may be given in evidence; and in all indictments for libels, the jury shall have a right to determine the law and the facts, under the direction of the court, as in other criminal cases.

Sec. 20. That no retrospective law, or law impairing the obligations of contracts, shall be made.

Sec. 21. That no man's particular services shall be demanded, or property taken, or applied to public use, without the consent o his representatives, or without just compensation being made therefor.

Sec. 22. That perpetuities and monopolies are contrary to the genius of a free State, and shall not be allowed.

Sec. 23. That the citizens have a right in a peaceable manner to assemble together for their common good, to instruct their representatives, and to apply to those invested with the powers of government for redress of grievances, or other purposes, by address or remonstrance.

Sec. 24. That the sure and certain defense of a free people is a well regulated militia; and, as standing armies in time of peace are dangerous to freedom, they ought to be avoided as far as the circumstances and safety of the community will admit; and that in all cases the military shall be kept in strict subordination to the civil authority.

Sec. 25. That no citizen of this State, except such as are employed in the army of the United States, or militia in actual service, shall be subjected to punishment under the martial law.

Sec. 26. That the citizens of this State have a right to keep and to bear arms for their common defense.

Sec. 27. That no soldier shall, in time of peace, be quartered in any house without the consent of the owner; nor in time of war, but in a manner prescribed by law.

Sec. 28. That no citizen of this State shall be compelled to bear arms, provided he will pay an equivalent to be ascertained by law.

Sec. 29. That an equal participation of the free navigation of the Mississippi is one of the inherent rights of the citizens of this State; it cannot, therefore, be conceded to any prince, potentate, power, person or persons whatever.

Sec. 30. That no hereditary emoluments, privileges or honors, shall ever be granted or conferred in this State.

Sec. 31. That the limits and boundaries of this State be ascertained, it is declared they are as heretofore mentioned, that is to say: Beginning on the extreme height of the Stone Mountain, at the place where the line of Virginia intersects it, in latitude thirty-six degrees and thirty minutes north; running thence along the extreme height of said mountain, to the place where Watauga River breaks through it; thence in a direct course to the top of the Yellow Mountain, where Bright's road crosses the same; thence along the ridge of said mountain, between the waters of Doe River and the waters of Rock Creek, to the place where the road crosses the Iron Mountain; from thence along the extreme height of said mountain, to the place where Nolichucky River runs through the same; thence to the top of the Bald Mountain; thence along the extreme height of said mountain, to the Painted Rock, on French Broad River; thence along the highest ridge of said mountain, to the place where it is called the Great Iron or Smoky Mountain; thence along the extreme height of said mountain, to the place where it is called Unicoi or Unaka Mountain, between the Indian towns of Cowee and Old Chota; thence along the main ridge of said mountain, to the southern boundary of this State, as described in the act of cession of North Carolina to the United States; and that all the territory, lands and waters lying west of said line, as before mentioned, and contained within the chartered limits of the State of

North Carolina, are within the boundaries and limits of this State, over which the people have the right of exercising sovereignty, and the right of soil, so far as is consistent with the Constitution of the United States, recognizing the Articles of Confederation, the Bill of Rights, and Constitution of North Carolina, the cession act of the said State, and the ordinance of Congress for the government of the territory North-west of the Ohio; *Provided*, nothing herein contained shall extend to affect the claim or claims of individuals to any part of the soil which is recognized to them by the aforesaid cession act; *And provided also*, that the limits and jurisdiction of this State shall extend to any other land and territory now acquired, by compact or agreement, with other States or otherwise, although such land and territory are not included within the boundaries hereinbefore designated.

Sec. 32. *The erection of safe and comfortable prisons, the inspection of prisons, and the humane treatment of prisoners shall be provided for.*

Sec. 33. *That Slavery and involuntary servitude, except as a punishment for crime, whereof the party shall have been duly convicted, are forever prohibited in this State.*

Sec. 34. *The General Assembly shall make no law recognizing the right of property in man.*

JOHN BAXTER, Chairman.

On motion of Mr. JONES, of Lincoln, the Convention adjourned until to-morrow morning, at 10 o'clock.

FRIDAY MORNING, JANUARY 14, 1870.

The Convention met pursuant to adjournment, Mr. President Brown in the Chair.

Prayer by the Rev. Dr. Redford.

The Journal of yesterday was read, corrected and approved.

The roll was called for petitions and memorials, when—

FEDERAL REPRESENTATION.

Mr. BLACKBURN offered the following resolutions, which were read and referred to the Committee on Miscellaneous Provisions:

WHEREAS, All power being inherent in the people, as guaranteed by the Constitution of Tennessee, as well as the Constitution of the United States, set forth in the first Article of the Bill of Rights of each; therefore, be it

Resolved, That it is the duty of this Convention to see that no law shall be passed calculated to destroy, impair or diminish the representation of this State in the Congress of the United States;

Resolved, That this Convention, deriving its power from the people, will not make, pass, alter, change or amend the fundamental law of the State, so as to diminish or alter the power of this State in the Congress of the United States;

Resolved, That these resolutions be referred to the Committee on the Constitution.

AMENDMENTS PROPOSED.

Mr. BRITTON offered the following resolution which was referred to the Committee on Miscellaneous Provisions:

Resolved, That as all power is inherent in the people, and as free governments were instituted for their mutual protection and security, it is therefore eminently proper that all the offices created by the Coustitution in the various co-ordinate branches of the State government should be elected by and derive their power directly from the people.

Mr. CARTER submitted the following amendments to the Constitution, which were read and referred to the Committee on Franchise and Elections:

Article II, Section 7. The first election for Senators and Representatives shall be held on the first Tuesday in November, one thousand eight hundred and seventy; and forever thereafter, elections for members of the General Assembly shall be held once in two years, on the first Tuesday in November; said election shall terminate the same day.

Sec. 8. The first session of the General Assembly shall commence on the first Monday in January, one thousand eight hundred and seventy-one; and forever thereafter the General Assembly shall meet on the first Monday in January next ensuing the election.

Mr. DEAVENPORT introduced the following resolution, which was read and referred to the Committee on the Legislative Department:

Resolved, That the appropriate committee be instructed to inquire and report upon the expediency and practicability of establishing natural and permanent boundaries to govern and control the representation in the General Assembly of the State, instead of the two-thirds ratio, as provided for in Section 5, Article II, of the present Constitution.

Mr. DOHERTY offered the following preamble and resolution, which were read and referred to the Committee on the Legislative Department:

WHEREAS, Much of the valuable time of the Legislature is appropriated in the passage of local and private laws, to the hindrance of the public interest:

Resolved, That the Committee on the Legislative Department be requested to examine and report whether or not it would be to the interest of the State to divest the Legislature of the power of enacting private acts, and that power be vested in such court or courts as shall be designated by law.

Mr. FINLEY offered the following resolution, which was read and referred to the Committee on Franchise:

Resolved, That every male person, regardless of race or color, if qualified, having arrived at the age that may hereafter be prescribed by law, shall be eligible to any office to which he may be elected by a popular vote of the qualified voters of the County or District where he resides.

Mr. FINLEY offered the following resolution, which was read and referred to the Committee on Franchise, etc.:

Resolved, That every male person of the age of twenty-one years, regardless of race or color, not convicted of infamous crime, being a citizen of the United States and of the State of Tennessee twelve months, and of the county where he may offer his vote three months preceding the day of election, shall be entitled to vote for members of the General Assembly and all other civil officers for the County or District where he resides.

Mr. FENTRESS offered the following resolution, which was read and referred to the Committee on the Bill of Rights:

Resolved, That the Committee on the Bill of Rights be requested to report whether Section 15 of the Bill of Rights should not be so amended as to provide that the writ of *habeas corpus* shall not be suspended or denied in any case.

Mr. FIELDER submitted the following preamble and resolution, which were read and referred to the Committee on the Legislative Department:

WHEREAS, The powers of the State Government are composed of three co-ordinate branches, viz.: the Legislative, Executive, and Judicial; therefore be it

Resolved, That the Legislative Committee be requested to inquire whether or not any amendment to the present Constitution is necessary to keep them separate and distinct, so that the one may not infringe upon the rights of the other, and if so, report the same to this body.

Mr. GIBSON submitted the following amendments to the Constitution, which were read and referred to the Committee on the Judiciary Department:

Article —, Section —. The number of Law Circuits shall never exceed one for every 75,000 inhabitants; and the number of Chancery Divisions shall never exceed one for every 100,000 inhabitants. But in establishing Circuits and Divisions, territory and population shall be so equalized that the labors of the several Judges and the several Chancellors shall be equalized as nearly as possible.

Sec. —. No Judicial officer shall be a candidate before the people for any other than a Judicial office, directly or indirectly. And the election of any such officer by the people during his incumbency, or for one year thereafter, shall be absolutely void.

Sec. —. The Legislature may, by joint resolution, two-thirds in each House concurring, remove from office any Judge, Chancellor, or State's Attorney, for crime, corruption, incompetency, drunkenness, neglect, or violation of duty, or other conduct unbecoming such an officer. *Provided*, That such officer, when accused, shall be allowed to present his evidence and argument, in writing, at the bar of the two Houses in joint session. But each House shall vote separately by ayes and noes, and the same shall be entered on the Journals of each House, together with the cause or causes of removal.

Mr. GIBSON submitted the following resolution, which was read and referred to the Committee on the Judicial Department:

Resolved, That the Judiciary Committee be requested, if they decide against the Judges and District Attorneys being chosen by the people, to consider the propriety of having Circuit Judges, Chancellors, and District Attorneys nominated by the Supreme Court and confirmed by the Senate.

Mr. HILL, of Gibson, offered the following resolution, which was read and referred to the Committee on the Judicial Department:

Resolved, That Section 10, of Article VI, of the present Constitution be so amended as to read as follows:

" Judges or Justices of such Inferior Courts of Law and *Equity* as the Legislature may establish shall have power in all civil cases to issue writs of Certiorari to remove any cause or transcript thereof from inferior jurisdiction into said Courts of *Law* on sufficient cause supported by oath or affirmation. '

MEMORIAL.

Mr. HILL, of Gibson, presented a memorial, signed by 255 citizens, praying a change in the Constitution of the State in relation to the formation of new counties, which was read and referred to the Committee on New Counties and County Lines.

AMENDMENTS PROPOSED.

Mr. HOUSE, of Williamson, submitted the following amendments to the Constitution, which were read and referred to the Committee on Judiciary.

Resolved, That Article V, of the Constitution be amended as follows:

Sec. 1. The Governor, Judges of the Supreme Court, Judges of Inferior Courts, Chancellors, Attorneys for the State and Secretary of State shall be liable to impeachment, whenever they may commit any offence in their official capacity, which may require disqualification; but judgment shall only extend to removal from office and disqualification to fill any office thereafter. The party shall nevertheless, be liable to indictment, trial, judgment and punishment according to law.

Sec. 2. The House of Representatives shall have the sole power of impeaching the Governor, Judges of the Supreme Court, the Attorney General for the State and the Secretary of State.

Sec. 3. All impeachments of any of the officers mentioned in Section 2 shall be tried by the Senate; and when sitting for that purpose the Senators shall be upon oath or affirmation—and presided over by the Senior Judge of the Supreme Court of the State. If the senior Judge should be impeached then the Senate shall be presided over by the next senior Judge of the Supreme Court.

No person shall be convicted without the concurrence of two thirds of the Senators sworn to try the officer impeached.

Sec. 4. The House of Representatives shall elect from their own body three members, whose duty it shall be to prosecute impeachments. No impeachment shall be tried until the Legislature shall have adjourned *sine die*, when the Senate shall proceed to try such impeachment.

Sec 5. All Judges of Inferior Courts, Chancellors and Attorneys for the State, for the several Judicial Districts or Circuits, shall be liable to impeachment for crimes and misdemeanors in office at the instance and upon the prosecution of any citizen in the Supreme Court of the State, in such manner as the Legislature may by law direct.

Sec. 6. Justices of the Peace and other civil officers not herein before mentioned, for crimes and misdemeanors in office, shall be liable to indictment in such courts as the Legislature may direct; and upon conviction, shall be removed from office by said court as if found guilty on impeachment; and shall be subject to such other punishment as may be prescribed by law.

Mr. House, of Davidson, Robertson and Montgomery, offered the following resolution, which was read and referred to the Committee on New Counties and County Lines.

Resolved, That the county of Cheatham, as now established, be, and the same is hereby declared to be a Constitutional county.

Mr. Ivie offered the following resolution, which was read and referred to the Committee on the Legislative Department:

Resolved, That Section —, Article —, of the present Constitution be amended so as to prohibit the Legislature of this State from granting any charter of incorporation, except to Banks and Internal Iprovements. And that no charter shall be granted for any bank unless the same shall have a capital stock of five hundred thousand dollars. One half of which shall be paid in before said corporation shall be entitled to do business under the charter.

Mr. Jones, of Giles, submitted the following amendment to the Constitution, which was read and referred to the Committee on Franchise:

" *Resolved*, That the Committee on Elections and Franchise be instructed to so amend Article IV, of the Constitution of Tennessee, as that the same shall read: "Every freeman of the age of twenty-one years, being a citizen of the United States, and a resident of the State two years, and of the county, in which he may offer his vote, twelve months next preceeding the day of election, and having paid his poll tax, shall be entitled to vote for members of the General Assembly, and other civil officers for the county or district in which he resides."

Mr. McNabb offered the following resolution, which was read and referred to the Committee on Franchise:

Resolved, That no law shall ever be passed in the State of Tennessee, debarring any man from voting in any election in consequence of not having paid his tax, prior to said election.

Mr. Ivie offered the following resolution, which was read and referred to the Committee on the Legislative Department:

Resolved, That the present Constitution of the State of Tennessee be so amended as to prohibit the State Legislature from passing any bill granting State aid to Internal Improvements. And so as to prohibit the Legislature from passing any bill by the provisions of which the State shall become a joint stock-holder in any incorporation; Provided the State may build roads or improve the navigation of rivers, if authorized so to do by the Legislature.

Mr. McNabb offered the following resolution, which was read and referred to the Committee on Miscellaneous Provisions:

Resolved, That the Legislature of the State of Tennessee, shall pass a common school law, and such an one as in their judgment will be for the very best interest to the children of the State, and a reasonable school tax.

Mr. Porter, of Haywood, offered the following resolution, which was read and referred to the Committee on Miscellaneous Provisions:

Resolved, That the body having the power to fix and determine the salary of the Governor and Judges of the State, shall not reduce that of the Governor below the sum of $4,000 per annum; that of the Judges of the Supreme Court, below $4,000 per annum; that of Chancellors and Circuit Judges, below $3,000 per annum.

REPORTS CALLED FOR.

Mr. Porter, of Haywood, offered the following resolution, which lies over under the rule:

Resolved, That the Standing Committees, of this body, be and the same are hereby required to report in some way upon all propositions or resolutions, that have been or may hereafter be referred to them. That in case of rejection of any resolution, the same shall be returned to this body, labelled "*rejected,*" simply, or "rejected because the substance thereof, has, or will be acted upon and reported in another form and manner."

JURISDICTION OF MAGISTRATES

Mr. Porter, of Haywood, submitted the following resolution:

"*Resolved,* That reference be had to the Judiciary Committee, to enquire into and report to this Convention how far and to what extent, if any, the jurisdiction of Justices of the Peace in this State, now obtaining on notes of hand to the sum of $500, and on open accounts to the sum of $250, conflict with Article VII, of the amendments to the Constitution of the United States." Said Art. being in words and figures as follows: 'In suits at Common law, when the value in controversy shall exceed ($20) Twenty Dollars, the right of trial by Jury shall be preserved; and no fact tried by a Jury shall be otherwise re-examined in any Court of the United States than according to the rules of the common law.'"

REPORT OF PROCEEDINGS.

Mr. THOMPSON, of Maury, offered the following resolution, which was read and referred to the Committee on Printing:

Resolved, That William H. Drapier, be and he is hereby appointed stenographic reporter for this Convention and that he be authorized to furnish three thousand copies of his reports, in book form for which he shall receive the same compensation as is now paid, by law, for public printing, of the same grade.

AMENDMENTS PROPOSED.

Mr. WARNER offered the following resolution, which was read and referred to the Committee on the Legislative Department:

Resolved, That Article II, Section 15, of the Constitution of 1834, be so amended as to insert the words "without delay" between the word "shall" and "issue," and that the Legislative Committee enquire into the propriety of said amendment.

Mr. WARNER offered the following, which was also referred to the Committee on the Legislative Department:

Resolved, That the Committee on the Legislative Department be required to report upon the propriety of conferring on two-thirds of the Senate, and a majority of all the members of the House of the General Assembly the power to grant pardons in cases of impeachments.

Mr. WARNER offered the following, which was read and referred to the Committee on Bill of Rights:

Resolved, That the following proposition be presented to the Committee on the Bill of Rights:

1st. That Article I, Section 5, be so amended as to strike out the words "free man" between the words "no" and "shall," and insert the word "person;" and to insert the words "or her" between the words "his" and "freehold," and that the words "or her" be inserted between the words "his" and liberty," and that the words "or her" be inserted between the words "his" and "peers," which will make said section read thus: "That no person shall be taken or imprisoned, or disseized of his or her freehold, liberties or privileges, or outlawed or exiled, or in any manner distrained or deprived of his or her life, liberty or property, but by the judgment of his or her peers, or the law of the land."

Be it also resolved, That Section 9 of said Article be amended as follows: That the letters "*self*" be stricken out between the words "himself," and the words "or" "herself" be inserted," and that the words "*or her*" be inserted between the words "his" and "counsel," and that the words "or her" be inserted between the words "him" and "and," and that the words "*or her*" be inserted between the words "his" and "favor," and that the letters "*self*" in the last word in said section be stricken out, and the words "or herself" be added, which will make said section read thus: "That in all criminal prosecutions the accused hath a right to be heard by him or herself and his or her counsel, to demand the nature and cause of the accusation against him or her, and to have a copy thereof; to meet the witnesses face to face; to have compulsory process for obtaining witnesses in his or her favor; and in prosecutions by indictment or presentment, a speedy, public trial by an impartial jury of the County or District in which the crime shall have been committed; and shall not be compelled to give evidence against him or herself.

Be it further resolved, That section 13 of said Article be so amended as to strike out the word "jail ' and insert the word "prison;" and that Section 14 of said Article be so amended as to strike out the words "free man," and insert in their stead the word "*person.*"

Resolved further, That Section 17 of said Article be so amended as to insert the word "person" in the place of "man" between the words "every" and "for," and to insert the words "*or her*" after the word "him" before the word "in," and the words "*or her*" between the words "his" and "lands."

Resolved further, That Section 26 of said Article be so amended as to insert the word "person's" instead of "man's" between the the words "no" and "particular," and that the words "*or her*" be inserted between the words "his" and "representatives."

Resolved further, That Section 26 of same Article be so amended as to strike out the words "*the free white men*" and insert the words "all persons."

Resolved further, That Section 3 of said Article be so amended as to strike out the word "men" between "all" and "have," and insert the word "*persons*" and strike out the word "man" between the words "no" and "can," and insert the word "person."

Mr. Warner also offered the following, which was read and referred to the Committee on the bill of Rights:

Resolved, That the Committee on the Bill and Declaration of Rights be directed to inquire into and report on the propriety of amending Article I, Section 1, of the Declaration of Rights, so that in calling conventions of the people of this State, other than in the mode of amending the Constitution in accordance with Article II, Section 3, of the Constitution, that a majority of the qualified voters of the State, and a majority voting for Governor on the last preceding election, shall vote in favor of any Convention that may be called to amend or alter the Constitution, before said Convention or other sovereign body of the people, as it may be called, shall be authorized to act as delegates of the people in altering, reforming, or abolishing the Constitution of this State, subject to the ratification of the people.

Mr. WALTERS offered the following resolution, which was read and referred to the Committee on the Judicial Department:

Resolved, That there shall be an act enacted by the General Assembly of the State of Tennessee, authorizing the election of a County Judge for the respective Counties, and who shall have jurisdiction to try all offenses under the laws of this State, under the grade of grand larceny; that he shall try them under the *same rules* and *regulations* that they are now triable by the Circuit Courts, other than they shall not be required to refer the charges to a Grand Jury to find a bill of indictment, but may proceed to trial upon the warrant of arrest. But that the *quarterly County Courts shall* be held under such rules and regulations as may be prescribed by law.

FORM OF REPORTS OF COMMITTEES.

Mr. BROWN, of Davidson, offered the following resolution:

Resolved, That the different Committees, in making their reports, shall designate the section, or part of section and Article of the Constitution proposed to be amended; or if a new section is reported it should be numbered, and its appropriate place in the Constitution designated.

Mr. HOUSE, of Davidson, Robertson and Montgomery, offered the following in lieu of Mr. Brown's resolution:

Resolved, That the different Committees shall report as a whole all the amendments which they wish to propose to the Constitution; and they shall make no report to the Convention upon any matter referred to them until they are ready to make a general report of all the amendments they wish to recommend in the respective departments referred to them.

On motion of Mr. HOUSE, of Davidson, Robertson and Montgomery, the rules were suspended, and the resolution offered by him was adopted in lieu of Mr. Brown's:

Mr. HEISKELL offered the following amendment to Mr. House's resolution:

" But that the several Committees of this House may, in their discretion, report to this House by resolution, drawn up in such form as they may deem advisable, to test the sense of the House upon such principles as may be material so to present.

Which amendment was rejected.

On motion of Mr. Jones, of Lincoln, the vote rejecting said amendment was reconsidered, and the amendment adopted.

Mr. Kennedy offered the following amendment:

"And that the reports of said Committees shall lie upon the table, and be printed for the use of the Convention."

Which was rejected, and the resolution, as amended, was adopted by the Convention.

ADJOURNMENT OVER.

Mr. Thompson, of Maury, moved that when the Convention adjourn, it adjourn until Monday morning next, at 10 o'clock.

Mr. Baxter demanded the yeas and nays upon the motion.

A vote was taken, and the Convention refused to so adjourn.

Those voting aye are:

Messrs. Allen, Arledge, Burton, Brandon, Bate, Cummings, Jones of Lincoln, Jones of Giles, Kennedy, Porter of Haywood, Thomoson of Maury, Thompson of Davidson, Turner and Mr. President Brown—14.

Those voting no are:

Messrs. Burkett, Brown of Davidson, Branson, Baxter, Britton, Brooks, Byrne, Blizard, Brown of Carroll, Gibson, Madison and Henry, Coffin, Campbell, Chowning, Cypert, Carter, Dibbrell, Deavenport, Deaderick, Doherty, Dromgoole, Finley, Fulkerson, Fentress, Fielder, Gatt, Gibson, Gardner, Gibbs, Gordon, Garner, Henderson, Hill of Warren, Hill of Gibson, Heiskell, House of Williamson, House of Davidson, Robertson and Montgomery, Ivie, Kirkpatrick, Key, Kyle, Martin, Mabry, Morris, Meeks, McDougal, McNabb, Netherland, Nicholson, Porter of Henry, Parker, Seay, Shepard, Stephens, Staley, Sample, Shelton, Taylor, Wright, Williamson, Warner, and Walters—60.

On motion, the Convention adjourned until to-morrow morning, 10 o'clock.

SATURDAY MORNING, JANUARY 15, 1870.

The Convention met pursuant to adjournment, Mr. President BROWN in the Chair.

Prayer by the Rev. Dr. SOMERS.

The Journal of yesterday was read, corrected and approved.

AMENDMENTS PROPOSED.

The roll was called for petitions and memorials, when Mr. BRANSON offered the following resolution, which was read and referred to the Committee on the Legislative Department:

Resolved, That the Legislature of this State shall pass a Common School Law, and such an one as, in their judgment, will be for the very best interest of all the children of the State, and that they assess, or cause to be assessed, a sufficient tax to raise a fund for such educational purposes, and that the same be known as the "Common School Fund of Tennessee," and that the same shall never be otherwise applied than for that of Common School purposes.

Mr. BROOKS offered the following resolution, which was read and referred to the Committee on the Judicial Department:

Resolved, That the Constitution be so amended that the Judges of the Supreme Court shall not be allowed a salary to exceed two thousand five hundred dollars per annum, and that the salary of the Chancellors and Circuit Judges shall not exceed two thousand dollars per annum.

Mr. BLIZARD offered the following amendment to the Constitution, which was read and referred to the Committee on Franchise and Elections:

Resolved, That the Constitution of Tennessee be so amended as to provide for the election of the Secretary of State, Comptroller and Treasurers of the State, by the qualified voters of the State at large, at the same time and for the same term that the Governor and members of the General Assembly are elected.

Mr. CYPERT offered the following resolution, which was read and ordered to be referred to the Committee on the Legislative Department:

Resolved, That the best interests of the State demand that manufacturing and agricultural pursuits should be favored and encouraged, and to this end the products of these important branches of industry should forever remain exempt from taxation.

Mr. DIBBRELL offered the following resolution, which was read and referred to the Committee on the Legislative Department:

Resolved, That the Legislature shall be composed of one hundred members, as follows: Twenty-five Senators and seventy-five Representatives; *Provided*, That each county in this State with a voting population of fifteen hundred shall be entitled to one Representative in the lower branch of the Legislature.

Mr. FULKERSON offered the following resolution as an amendment to the Constitution, which was read and referred to the Committee on Franchise and Elections:

Resolved, That Section 5, of Article VII, of the Constitution be altered and amended as follows:

The Legislature shall provide that the election of the county officers, by the people, shall take place at the same time the general elections are held for members of Congress, members of the Legislature and Governor. The election shall commence and terminate the same day.

Mr. PORTER, of Haywood, offered the following resolution, which was read and referred to the Committee on the Judicial Department:

Resolved, That the Judges of the Supreme Court shall be elected by the people. That no person shall be eligible to said position unless he shall have had the experience of 25 years practice at the bar, and whose term of service shall end when he shall have attained the age of seventy years, or during good behavior.

Mr. GIBSON offered the following amendment, which was read and referred to the Committee on the Legislative Department:

Article —, Section —. The Legislature shall have no power whatever, to give, grant lease or sell any portion of the territory of the State, or the control, or dominion of any portion thereof to any individual, association, corporation or State by special law; nor shall any portion of the territory of this State, or any private property within the State, or any individual association or corporation be exempted from State or county taxes: *Provided*, always, that this nor any other section shall be so construed as to prevent the United States from acquiring dominion and control, exclusive or otherwise over such places as the Legislature may authorize, by any law, general or special; and *Provided further*, that the Legislature may pass general laws whereunder the County Court may exempt honorably discharged soldiers and indigent persons from the payment of the poll tax.

Mr. SAMPLE offered the following resolution, which was referred to the Committee on Franchise and Elections:

Resolved, That all offices to be filled, from the highest to the lowest grade, shall be filled by the popular vote of the qualified voters in the State, county or district, as the case may be, so as thereby not to conflict with the Constitution of the United States, viz: Supreme, Circuit and Chancery Judges, Clerks of the different Courts, Magistrates and Constables, Sheriffs, Surveyors, Trustees, Revenue Collectors, etc. Also all military officers shall be elected by the qualified voters of the State, county or district as the case may be.

Mr. PORTER, of Haywood, offered the following resolution, which was read and referred to the Committee on the Judicial Department:

Resolved, That the Committee on said Department take under consideration, and make report to this Convention, as to the expediency and propriety of abolishing the office of District, or Circuit Attorney General of the State, and the creation of the office of State Attorney for each county. The person filling the same to be elected by the qualified voters thereof, and whose term of service shall be the same as that of Circuit Judge. The salary of said office, in addition to the compensation now allowed by law, to be determined and fixed by the County Court, at the January Term of each year.

Mr. SEAY offered the following resolution, which was read and referred to the Committee on the Bill of Rights:

Resolved, That Section 6 of Article I be so amended as to read as follows:

"That the right of trial by Jury shall remain inviolate, and no religious or political test shall ever be required as a qualification to sit on Juries in this State."

PRINTING RULES, ETC.

Mr. KENNEDY offered the following resolution, and moved a suspension of the rules.

Resolved, That the Secretary be directed to have one hundred copies of the Constitution of Tennessee and of the United States, with the amendments adopted and proposed thereto, printed under cover with the rules of this body.

Mr. PORTER, of Henry, demanded the ayes and noes, but withdrew the call, which was afterwards renewed by Mr. PORTER, of Haywood. The resolution was then put upon its passage and resulted as follows:

Those voting in the affirmative are:

Messrs. Allen, Arledge, Brown, of Davidson, Britton, Byrne, Burton, Brandon, Cummings, Coffin, Campbell, Chowning, Cypert, Dibbrell, Deavenport, Deaderick, Dromgoole, Finley, Fulkerson, Fentress, Fielder, Gibbs, Gordon, Garner, Hill, of Warren, Heiskell, House, of Williamson, Ivie, Kirkpatrick, Kennedy, Kyle, Martin, Mabry, Morris, Meeks, McDougal, McNabb, Nicholson, Seay, Shepard, Stephens, Thompson, of Davidson, Thompson, of Maury, Turner, Taylor, Walters, Williamson and President Brown—47.

Those voting in the negative are:

Messrs. Burkett, Branson, Baxter, Brooks, Blizard, Carter, Doherty, Gaut, Gibson, Gardner, Henderson, Hill of Gibson, Jones of Lincoln, Key, Netherland, Porter of Haywood, Porter of Henry, Parker, Staley, Sample, Shelton, Warner, and Wright—24.

MEMORIALS.

Mr. HOUSE, of Williamson, presented a memorial from sundry citizens of Williamson, Maury, and other counties, which was read and referred to the Committee on New Counties and County Lines:

Mr. THOMPSON, of Maury, presented a memorial from sundry citizens of Maury and Marshall counties, which was referred to the Committee on New Counties and County Lines, without being read.

AMENDMENTS PROPOSED.

Mr. WARNER offered the following amendment to the Constitution of this State, which was read and referred to the Committee on Miscellaneous Provisions:

WHEREAS, Article V, of the Constitution of the United States, provides that "The Congress, whenever two-thirds of both Houses shall propose amendments to the Constitution, or on the application of the Legislatures of two-thirds of the several States, shall call a Convention for proposing amendments, which in either case shall be valid, to all intents and purposes, as part of the Constitution, when ratified by the Legislatures of three-fourths of the several States, or by Convention in three fourths thereof, as the one or the other mode of ratification may be proposed by Congress.

AND WHEREAS, It is manifest from said Article V that proposed amendments ought to be ratified or rejected by Legislatures or Conventions, chosen in the several States by the people thereof, after the Congress or the Convention, as the case may be, have prepared such amendment or amendments, to the several States for ratification.

AND WHEREAS, Amendments have been ratified by Legislatures elected before such amendments were proposed to the several States by Congress, thus preventing the people from having a voice in the election of their Legislatures, with a view of having their wishes and interests regarded in changing or altering the Constitution of the United States; therefore,

Be it resolved, That the following amendment be proposed to the Constitution of this State: "That when any amendment or amendments to the Constitution of the United States shall be proposed to the several States thereof, no Legislature or Convention of this State shall ever ratify such proposed amendment or amendments, unless the Legislature or Convention shall have been elected by the people of this State after the period of time when the Congress or Convention of the United States shall have proposed such amendment or amendments to the several States for ratification.

REPORT OF THE COMMITTEE ON EXECUTIVE DEPARTMENT.

Mr. JONES, of Lincoln, Chairman of the Committee on the Executive Department, offered the following report, which was read, laid upon the table, and ordered to be printed:

The Committoe on the Executive Department have had under consideration the several propositions referred to them, and have instructed me to report and recommend the adoption of the following amendment, two-wit:

In Article III, Section 9, of the Constitution of the State of Tennessee, strike out the words, "And shall state to them when assembled the purposes for which they shall have been convened," and insert in lieu thereof the words, "*In which he shall state* to them, specifically, the purposes for which they are to convene," so that it will read: Article III, Section 9. He may, on extraordinary occasions, convene the General Assembly by proclamation, in which he shall state specifically the purposes for which they are to convene; but they shall enter on no legislative business except that for which they were specifically called together.

I am also instructed to report adversely upon all other propositions referred to the Committee.

Respectfully submitted.

GEORGE W. JONES.

REPORT OF COMMITTEE ON BILL OF RIGHTS.

Mr. BAXTER, from the Committee on the Bill of Rights, made a verbal report, asking to be discharged from the further consideration of sundry petitions referred to them, which was accordingly ordered by the Convention.

LEAVES OF ABSENCE.

On application of Mr. BURTON, leave of absence was granted him until Tuesday next.

Mr. ARLEDGE was also granted leave of absence until Tuesday next.

On motion of Mr. PORTER, of Haywood, the Convention adjourned until Monday morning, at 10½ o'clock.

MONDAY MORNING, JANUARY 17, 1870.

The Convention met pursuant to adjournment, Mr. President BROWN in the Chair.

Prayer by the Rev. Mr. Sample, a member of this body.

The Journal of Saturday was read and approved.

AMENDMENTS PROPOSED.

The roll was called for petitions and memorials, when

Mr. BURKETT offered the following resolutions, which were read and referred to the Committee on the Judicial Department:

Resolved, 1st. That the attention of the proper Committee be called to the propriety of presenting such alterations or amendments to our present State Constitution as will provide for the election of only one Justice of the Peace for each Civil District of every County in the State, except in such districts as include a County seat, or shall have over a given number of qualified voters, and that in such Districts, so excepted, an additional Justice of the Peace shall be elected.

2d. That the attention of the proper Committee be called to the propriety of presenting such amendments to the Constitution as will provide that County Courts hold their sessions quarterly, or once only in every three months, looking to legislation that will confer power on the Chairman of the several County Courts to grant letters of administration or testamentary out of term time upon proper qualification of applicants for such letters.

Mr. BURKETT introduced the following resolution, which was read and referred to the Committee on Franchise and Elections:

Resolved, That the attention of the proper committee be called to the propriety of combining two or more civil districts, so that the voting population of such combined districts shall not exceed some given number to be presented by such committee, and that such, two or more, combined civil districts shall form a district, which shall elect only one Constable, who shall discharge all the duties now by law made incumbent on the Constables of the said combined districts and in addition thereto, such Constables shall be required to collect the State and county revenue, due from citizens of such combined districts.

Mr. BRITTON submitted the following resolution, which was referred to the Committee on the Legislative Department:

Resolved, That the Committee on the Legislative Department be requested to enquire into and report how far the Constitution should be amended allowing the General Assembly to pass laws authorizing the people of any County, District, incorporated Town, one half or two thirds of the qualified voters in such County, District, or incorporated Town voting therefor, to prohibit the exercise of privileges within their respective limits.

RETRENCHMENT AND REFORM.

Mr. BROOKS offered the following resolution, which lies over under the rule:

Resolved, That the President of this Convention appoint a Special Committee of seven on Retrenchment and Reform.

REPORT REQUESTED.

Mr. BROOKS offered the following resolution, which lies over one day under the rule:

Resolved, That the Committee on the Franchise be requested to eport their action at as early a day as practicable and consistent with their labors.

AMENDMENTS PROPOSED.

Mr. BLIZARD offered the following resolution, which was read and referred to the Committee on the Legislative Department:

Resolved, That the Constitution of the State of Tennessee be so amended as to provide that the Legislature shall be elected for two years, and that each member shall receive for his services a stated salary of one thousand dollars in lieu of all other pay or allowance to be made to him; *Provided,* that four dollars per day of the salary of any member absenting himself from the Legislature during its sessions, without leave of the House of which he is a member, shall be withheld upon the final settlement of his account.

IMPEACHMENT OF JUDGE FRAZIER.

Mr. BAXTER offered the following preamble and resolutions, which, the House refusing to supend the rules, lies over for one day:

WHEREAS, the House of Representatives of this State on — day of ——, 1867, exhibited articles of impeachment against the Honorable Thomas N. Frazier, Judge of the Criminal Court of Davidson County, for alleged high crimes and misdemeanors, upon which he was subsequently arraigned before and tried by the Senate, sitting as a High Court of Impeachment, found guilty, removed from his office and disqualified from ever thereafter holding any office in this State; and

WHEREAS, In the opinion of this Convention, the said Thomas N. Frazier, was an honest, upright, just and able Judge; that his judgment complained of in said articles of Impeachment, was not only dictated by honest convictions of duty, but was a just and correct exposition of the law involved in the case; and that said Impeachment, trial, conviction and judgment of disqualification, originated in a corrupt conspiracy, and was conducted to a final conclusion for the accomplishment of partizan purposes; *It is, therefore*

Resolved, That a Select Committee of five be appointed to prepare and report, to this Convention, an article to be incorporated into the Constitution, relieving the said Thomas N. Frazier from the disabilities imposed upon him by the conviction and judgment aforesaid.

THE ORGANIZATION OF THE LEGISLATURE.

Mr. CAMPBELL submitted the following amendments to the Constitution of the State, which were read and referred to the Committee on the Legislative Department:

Resolved, That the Legislature of the State of Tennessee shall consist of ninety members; thirty of whom are to be Senators.

Resolved, That the State be laid off into fifteen (15) Senatorial Districts, from each of which, two (2) Senators shall be elected.

Resolved, That the Senators shall be elected by freeholders (of value $——) in their respective Districts; that the Senators first elected, shall be elected for nine (9) years; that on the first convening of the Senate the Senators shall be classed into three (3) classes; the term of service of the first class, shall expire at the expiration of three (3) years, from date of election; the second class at the end of six (6) years, and the third class at the expiration of nine (9) years, so that one-third be elected every third year, and in case of vacancy in either class, the vacancy to be filled by special election.

Resolved, That an election for Senators and Representatives be held on the first Thursday in August, 1871, and ever thereafter triennially on the first Thursday in August.

Resolved, That the House of Representatives be elected by the qualified voters of the respective Counties and Districts, based upon the voting population.

Resolved, That after the first session of the General Assembly, the sessions of the General Assembly shall be limited to ninety (90) days; the Governor to convene the Legislature for special purpose and legislation to be confined to that purpose.

Resolved, That no person be eligible for Senator until he is thirty-five (35) years of age, and for member of the House until twenty-eight (28) years of age.

Resolved, That no person who has heretofore been convicted of any crime, punishable by confinement in the Penitentiary, or who shall hereafter be convicted of any crime punishable by confinement in the Penitentiary, shall ever be entitled to vote.

Resolved, That the House of Representatives have the sole right of originating bills for laying and collecting taxes; subject to be amended or rejected by the Senate.

EXECUTIVE DEPARTMENT.

Mr. CAMPBELL submitted the following propositions to amend the Constitution of the State, which were read and ordered to lie on the table:

Resolved, That on the first Thursday in August, 1871, the Governor be elected, and ever thereafter on the first Thursday in August every fourth year; and shall hold office until his successor is elected and qualified, (the oath of office of Governor to be administered by any Judge of the Courts.)

Resolved, That no one shall be eligible to the office of Governor until he has arrived at the age of 35 and shall have been a citizen of the State of Tennessee three years next preceding the day of his election.

Resolved, That there be an election for Lt. Governor on the same day (Governor's election,) who shall possess the same qualifications as Governor: The Lt. Governor shall be ex-officio President of the Senate, but shall have no vote except in a tie vote of Senators. In event of death, resignation, removal from office, or absence from the State, the Lt. Governor shall discharge the duties of Governor.

Resolved, That the Governor, by and with the advice and consent of the Senate, appoint the Judges, Chancellors, Justices of the Peace, Secretary of State, Comptroller of the State, Secretary, Treasurer, Attorney General for State and District Attorneys General, two-thirds of the Senators elected concurring therein.

JUDICIAL DEPARTMENT.

Mr. CAMPBELL submitted the following propositions to amend the Constitution of the State, which were read and referred to the Committee on the Judicial Department:

Resolved, That there be instituted a Court of Appeals in Law, consisting of three (3) Judges, one of whom shall be Chief Justice of that Court.

Resolved, That there be established a Court of Appeals in Equity, consisting of four Judges, one of whom shall be Chief Justice of that Court.

Resolved, That the Judges of Courts of Appeals, in Law and Equity, shall constitute a Supreme Court of the State of Tennessee for the correction of errors in Law and Equity: That the Chief Justice of the Court of Appeals in Equity shall be Chief Justice of the Supreme Court and that said Supreme Court hold its sessions once a year in the city of Nashville.

Resolved, That the Court of Appeals in Law shall be held in each of the Grand Divisions of the State, at such times and place as the Legislature shall prescribe.

Resolved, That the Court of Appeals in Equity shall be held in each of the three Grand Divisions of the State, at such times and places as the Legislature shall prescribe.

Resolved, That Appeals in the nature of writs of Error, Appeals and Writs of Error, shall lie from the Court of Appeals in Equity and the Court of Appeals in Law to the Supreme Court for correction of Errors in Equity and Law, and causes may be transferred from either of the Courts of Appeals into the Supreme Court for final determination under such rules and regulations as the Legislature may prescribe.

Resolved, That there be established in each county in the State, except Davidson and Shelby Counties, one Court of Law, to be styled the Circuit Court, to hold its sessions twice a year; that causes in said Circuit Court shall be tried under such rules and regulations as the Legislature may prescribe—at the first term after commencing suit—that the forms of action and pleading in said Circuit Courts shall be such as were used and practiced in said Courts prior to the 1st day of October, 1851, except in the action of ejectment.

Resolved, That the Legislature, by law, require the Judges to interchange, so that no one of the Judges will hold more than one Court in the County in one year. The Counties of Davidson and Shelby may be divided into as many Circuits and Chancery Districts as may be deemed necessary.

Resolved, That there be established and held one Chancery Court in each Law Circuit; that the Legislature shall provide, by law, for the appointment of Clerks and Masters in Chancery, to reside at the respective county seats, with the authority of the Clerk and Master at the place where the Court is held, for the convenience of the people for that particular County.

Resolved, That there be established in each County a Court styled the Court of Common Pleas of that County; that the Court of Common Pleas possess such jurisdiction as is now exercised by the Quorum Courts; that the said Court be held by one Judge, who shall preside over the meetings of the Quarterly Courts, have power to assess taxes, etc., and be financial agent of the County under such rules and regulations as are now prescribed for the action of the Judges and Chairmen of the present County Courts as now prescribed by law, and as may be prescribed by law, and his salary to be $——, and paid by the County. That said Court of Common Pleas shall have exclusive jurisdiction of all causes of action arising *ex contractu,* to the amounts of from $100 to $500, and exclusive and original jurisdiction of all causes of action arising *ex delicto,* from $50 to $200. That the mode of proceeding may be prescribed by the Legislature.

Resolved, That the Judges, Chancellors and Justices, be appointed during good behavior; that the Clerks of the several Courts be appointed by the Courts to hold during good behavior, and that the salary of Judges and Chancellors shall not be diminished while in office.

Resolved, That the Court of Appeals in Law, and the Court of Appeals in Equity, and the Supreme Court, shall have original jurisdiction to issue writs of mandamus.

Mr. Gibson submitted the following propositions to amend the Constitution of the State, which were read and referred to the Committee on Miscellaneous Provisions :

Section —. A tax of twenty-five cents on every taxable poll, and twenty-five cents on every one hundred dollars' worth of taxable property in this State is hereby levied for each and every year forever, and shall be collected each year in the same manner, at the same time, and by the same officer as and by whom the State taxes are collected, and shall be by such officers deposited with the State Treasurer, who shall pay over the same to the several Counties of the State, in proportion to their respective populations, between eight and eighteen years of age. The money thus collected and deposited shall never be applied or used for any purpose other than the maintenance and support of free schools; and the Legislature is hereby commanded to pass all necessary laws to effectuate the objects of this Section. But should the Legislature fail or refuse to act as commanded, then the said Revenue Officers shall collect and deposit the said tax as aforesaid, and the State Treasurer shall apportion said money thus collected and deposited among the several Counties as aforesaid, and shall, without unnecessary delay, pay over said apportionment to such person or persons as have general charge of the financial interests of such Counties, to be by them disbursed in the maintenance of free schools in their respective Counties: *Provided*, That in making his apportionment, the State Treasurer shall be governed by the last reliable enumeration of the scholastic population in each County: *And provided further*, That each of said officers, whose duty it is under this Section, to collect, deposit, pay over or disburse said money, or any part thereof, shall be and are hereby made liable on their respective official bonds, for any failure, default, delay or malfeasance, in discharging the duties herein and hereby imposed, and may be proceeded against summarily by motion by any citizen in any Court of original jurisdiction in the County where such default, failure, delay or malfeasance, may have occurred; and such summary proceeding shall be heard and decided by the Court upon its merits without a jury, and no other form shall be necessary than five days' notice in writing: *And provided still further*, That nothing in this or any other Section of this Constitution shall be so construed as to prohibit or prevent the Legislature or any County from levying an additional tax or taxes for the support and maintenance of free schools and academies.

Mr. KIRKPATRICK submitted the following resolution, which was read and referred to the Committee on the Legislative Department:

Resolved, That the General Assembly shall have no power, at any time, to call into question the validity of the public debt of this State.

Mr. MARTIN submitted the following amendments to the Constitution, which were read and referred to the Committee on Franchise and Elections:

Resolved, That Article IV, Section 4, be amended to read as follows:

"Section 4. Electors shall, in all elections, vote *viva voce,* and the General Assembly shall enact all necessary laws for carrying this provision into effect."

In all elections to be made by the General Assembly, or either House thereof, the votes of the several members voting shall be entered on the Journal.

Mr. McNabb offered the following resolution, which was read and referred to the Committee on New Counties and County Lines:

Resolved, That in the formation of new Counties in the State of Tennessee, no part of any old County shall be stricken off only by the consent of the qualified voters of said old County or Counties, and that a majority of the votes polled in such elections shall carry.

Mr. McNabb offered the following resolution, which was read and referred to the Committee on Miscellaneous Provisions:

Resolved, That no County seat in any County in the State of Tennessee, shall be moved only by a vote of the people qualified to vote, and that a majority of the votes polled shall carry.

Mr. Sample offered the following resolution, which was read and referred to the Committee on the Judicial Department:

Resolved, That the Legislature may, by law, empower the County Courts to have Grand and traverse Juries, and to have power to try all cases of petit larceny and assault and battery; petit larceny to extend to $25, but no higher; and the Legislature shall, by law, prescribe the penalties of those crimes, and the Court have power to inflict it; said Court to consist of at least three Magistrates.

Mr. Thompson, of Davidson, submitted the following resolution:

Be it resolved, That the following provision be inserted in the Bill of Rights:

"Any proscribed class of citizens in the community is contrary to the genius of a free government. No citizen of this State shall ever be disfranchised of any civil or political rights, except by impeachment or conviction of infamous crime in a Court of Record."

Which was referred as directed.

Mr. Warner submitted the following resolution, which was read and referred to the Committee on Finance, Internal Improvements and Incorporations:

Resolved, That the Committee on Internal Improvements inquire as to what railroads are in default, and what disposition this Convention shall make of the defaulting railroads.

Mr. WARNER submitted the following resolution, which was read and referred to the Committee on Finance:

Resolved, That the Committee on Finance inquire into and report what bonds of the State are *bona fide,* and what ones are not, and that the State be required to pay only such bonds as are just and *bona fide.*

Mr. DROMGOOLE submitted the following, to be added to the Bill of Rights:

No power can legitimately deprive the people of this State from defining the qualifications of their own electors.

BILL OF RIGHTS CONSIDERED.

On motion of Mr. Brown, of Davidson, the report of the Committee on Bill of Rights was taken up and considered;

Whereupon, Mr. Jones, of Lincoln, offered the following amendment:

Insert after the word Convention, in line 12, "passed in obedience to the declared will of the voters of the State as expressed at the general election of August, in the year of our Lord one thousand eight hundred and thirty-three."

Mr. GIBSON submitted the following in lieu of the preamble:

We the people of the State of Tennessee, in order to organize liberty, secure justice, and protect property, do ordain and establish this Constitution for our government."

After discussion, Mr. Gibson withdrew his substitute.

Mr. STEPHENS submitted the following amendment:

After the word "and" in the 15th line, add the words "Said Convention did accordingly meet and form a Constitution, which was submitted to the people and ratified by them the first Friday in March, 1835."

And the amendment was adopted.

Mr. CAMPBELL submitted the following amendments:

Resolved, That the 3d section of the Preamble be so amended as to read as follows:

WHEREAS, The General Assembly of said State of Tennessee, under and in virtue of the first Section of the first Article of the Declaration of Rights, contained in and forming a part of the existing Constitution of the State, by an act passed on the 15th day of November, in the year of our Lord one thousand eight hundred and sixty-nine, the people of the State did, by a vote at an election, held on the 18th day of December, 1869, determine to call a Convention to meet at Nashville, on the 2d Monday in January, in the year of our Lord one thousand eight hundred and seventy, and elected delegates thereto for the purpose of amending, revising, or forming and making a new Constitution.

Mr. PORTER, of Haywood, submitted the following resolution:

Resolved, That the 4th section of the Preamble be so amended as to dispense with the word "authorize" altogether.

Mr. PORTER subsequently withdrew his resolution.

Mr. GARDNER offered the following, in lieu of Mr. Campbell's:

In the 19th and 20th lines strike out the following:

"Entitled an act to authorize the people to call a Convention and for other purposes, did authorize the people of the State to call a Convention," and insert in lieu thereof the following: "Provide for the calling of a Convention by the people of the State."

Mr. THOMPSON, of Davidson, offered the following, in lieu of Mr. Campbell's and Mr. Gardner's:

Resolved, That after the word "did," at the end of the nineteenth line, the word "authorize" be stricken out, and the following inserted in lieu thereof: "In obedience to the expressed will of the people provide a mode for."

Which was rejected by the Convention.

Mr. BROWN, of Davidson, submitted the following amendment to the proposition of Mr. Gardner, which was accepted:

"Provide for the calling of a Convention by the people."

And the amendment as amended was adopted by the Convention.

Mr. GARDNER proposed to amend as follows:

In the 21st line strike out the words, "and to elect delegates," and insert the words "for the election of delegates."

Which was adopted.

Mr. GARNER submitted the following amendments:

After the word "mode," in line 23, *strike out,* "Authorized by said act have called said Convention and elected delegates," and insert, "Provided for by said act, did on the eighteenth day of December, in the year of our Lord one thousand eight hundred and sixty-nine, at a general election, call said Convention and elected delegates"

Mr. PORTER, of Henry, offered the following in lieu of Mr. Garner's which was accepted and adopted by the Convention:

WHEREAS, The people of the State, in the mode prescribed by

said act, have called said Convention and elected delegates to represent them therein.

Mr. NICHOLSON offered the following amendments, which were adopted:

In line 22, after "amending," insert *or*, and after "revising," insert *the present Constitution;* after "or" insert *of*, so that it will read:

"Amending or revising the present Constitution, or of forming and making a new Constitution.

On motion of Mr. THOMPSON, of Davidson, the Convention adjourned until to-morrow morning, at 10 o'clock.

TUESDAY MORNING JANUARY 18, 1870.

The Convention met pursuant to adjournment, Mr. President BROWN in the Chair.

Prayer by the Rev. Mr. KELLY.

The Journal of yesterday was read and approved.

The President announced that the unfinished business of yesterday was the order of the day.

On motion of Mr. Baxter, the order of the day was set aside to permit the introduction of memorials and petitions.

AMENDMENTS PROPOSED.

Mr. GARDNER submitted the following amendments to the Constitution of the State, which were read and referred to the Committee on Miscellaneous Provisions:

Resolved, That the Committee on Miscellaneous Provisions be instructed to prepare and report an amendment to section 3, of Article XI, as an addition to said section, in substance as follows:

The Legislature shall have the right, at any time, by law, to submit to the people the question of calling a Convention to alter, reform, or abolish this Constitution; and when, upon such submission, a majority of the votes cast shall be in favor of said proposition, the delegates shall be chosen, and the Convention shall assemble in such mode and manner as shall be prescribed by law.

MISCELLANEOUS.

Mr. HOUSE, of Williamson, offered the following resolution:

Resolved, That the Door-keeper be instructed to purchase two filters for the use of the Convention.

On motion of Mr. House, the rules were suspended, and the resolution was adopted.

MEMORIALS.

Mr. KIRKPATRICK presented a communication in relation to the establishment of the County of Powell, which, without being read, was referred to the Committee on New Counties and County Lines.

Mr. SAMPLE presented a memorial from a large number of the citizens of Grainger, Hawkins, Jefferson, Greene, and Cocke Counties for the establishment of a new County, which was read and referred to the Committee on New Counties and County Lines.

AMENDMENTS PROPOSED.

Mr. SAMPLE submitted the following resolution, which was read and referred to the Committee on New Counties and County Lines:

Resolved, That a new County may be formed out of territory to be taken from the Counties of Jefferson, Grainger, Hawkins, Greene and Cocke, to contain not less than 250 square miles, and have in its bounds 1000 qualified voters; and lines of said new County not to approach nearer to the old County seats or Courthouses than ten miles. *Provided,* The residents of said new County assume their proportionable part of the debts of the Counties from which they are taken.

MEMORIAL.

Mr. WARNER presented a memorial from sundry citizens of Marshall, Williamson and Rutherford Counties, praying for the establishment of a new county and county lines.

REPORT ON THE FRANCHISE.

Mr. NICHOLSON, from the Committee on Elections and the Right of Suffrage, submitted the following:

The Committee on Elections and Right of Suffrage have considered the several propositions referred to them on the subject of the Elective Franchise, and have instructed me to make the following report:

REPORT.

1. A majority of the Committee recommend that the Elective Franchise shall not be withdrawn from the colored men, but that they shall be secured in the continued exercise thereof.
2. A majority of the Committee have rejected the proposition to submit the question of suffrage by colored persons, as an independent proposition, separate and apart from all others.
3. A majority of the Committee recommend that the payment of such poll taxes as may be assessed by law, shall be made a condition precedent to the exercise of the elective franchise.
4. A majority of the Committee recommend that the General Assembly be empowered to pass laws for requiring voters to vote in the election precincts in which they may reside, and to secure the freedom of elections and the purity of the ballot box.

For the purpose of carrying out the conclusions of the Committee, a majority of them recommend that the following be adopted by the Convention, in lieu of Section 1, Article IV, of the present Constitution, viz:

ARTICLE IV.

Sec. 1. Every man of the age of twenty-one years, being a citizen of the United States, and a citizen of the county wherein he may offer his vote six months preceding the day of election, shall be entitled to vote for members of the General Assembly, and other civil officers for the county or district in which he resides; and there shall be no qualification attached to the right of suffrage, except that each voter shall give to the Judges of the election, where he offers to vote, satisfactory evidence that he has paid the poll taxes then due by him, without which his vote cannot be received: And all male citizens of the State shall be subject to the payment of poll taxes and to the performance of military duty, within such ages as may be prescribed by law; *Provided*, That the General Assembly shall have power to enact laws requiring voters to vote in the election precincts in which they may reside, and laws to secure the freedom of elections and the purity of the ballot box.

On motion of Mr. NICHOLSON, the report of the Committee was laid on the table.

BILL OF RIGHTS FURTHER CONSIDERED.

The Convention proceeded to the consideration of the report of the Committee on Bill of Rights.

Sections 1, 2 and 3 were adopted.

Mr. KIRKPATRICK proposed the following amendment to Section 4:

" Except as now provided by Section 3, of the Fourteenth Amendment to the Constitution of the United States."

On motion of Mr. WRIGHT, the amendment of Mr. Kirkpatrick was laid on the table.

Mr. HEISKELL submitted the following amendment to Section 4:

" That no religious test, or any oath relating to conduct prior to the administration thereof, shall ever be required as a condition to the exercise of the right of suffrage, or holding any office or public trust in this State;"

Which was rejected by the Convention.

Section 4 was then adopted.

Section 5 was passed over informally.

Mr. HOUSE, of Davidson, Robertson and Montgomery, offered the following amendment to Section 6:

" And no political test shall ever be prescribed by the Legislature as a qualification for jurors," so that said section shall read as follows:

The right of trial by jury shall remain inviolate, and no political test shall ever be prescribed by the Legislature as a qualification for jurors.

Mr. TURNER offered the following in lieu of the amendment of Mr. House:

Sec. 6. That the right of trial by jury shall remain inviolate, " and no religious or political test shall ever be required as a qualification for jurors."

Which was accepted by Mr. House.

Mr. GIBSON moved to amend the amendment of Mr. Turner, as follows:

Insert " other than the ordinary juror's oath at Common Law," between words " test " and " shall."

On motion of Mr. FULKERSON, the amendment of Mr. Gibson was laid on the table.

Mr. SEAY offered the following amendment in lieu of Mr. Turner's:

Resolved, That Section 6, Article I, be amended so as to read as follows:

That the right of trial by jury shall remain inviolate, and no religious or political test shall ever be required, either directly or indirectly, as a qualification to sit on juries in this State.

On motion of Mr. FULKERSON, the amendment of Mr. Seay was laid on the table.

The amendment of Mr. TURNER was adopted, and the section as amended was adopted by the Convention.

Sections 7 and 8 were adopted without amendment.

Mr. BURTON proposed the following amendment to Section 9:

Resolved, That Section 9, of the amended Bill of Rights reported by the Committee, be amended by striking out all the words therein printed in italics.

Mr. BROWN, of Davidson, submitted the following additional amendment:

Provided, That the venue shall not be changed in behalf of the State in any instance, until the whole panel of the County shall be exhausted.

Mr. TURNER offered the following in lieu of the pending amendments:

Inserting after the word offense, "*Provided*, That the State shall not change the venue unless a panel of two-thirds of the qualified jurors of the county has been exhausted, nor shall the venue be changed to any other than an adjoining county."

On motion of Mr. BAXTER, all of the pending amendments, except the motion to strike out, were laid on the table.

Mr. GARDNER offered the following amendment:

Strike out in the 5th and 6th lines the words, "for a good cause to another;" and insert "because an impartial jury cannot be empanneled in the county where the offender is arraigned, to an adjoining;" and strike out the words "or district," in the 6th line. The section will then read "Unless the venue shall be changed, because after an actual and honest effort to make one, an impartial jury can not be empanneled in the county where the offender is arraigned, to an adjoining county, in the mode to be prescribed by a general public law, passed before the alleged commission of the offense.

Mr. Kirkpatrick submitted the following amendment to Mr. Gardner's amendment:

"To the nearest county free from like objection."

On motion of Mr. Blizard, the amendments were laid on the table.

Mr. Kennedy demanded the previous question, which was sustained.

Mr. Thompson, of Davidson, submitted the following, which was read for information:

Be it resolved, That Section 9, of the Bill of Rights, be amended by adding the following:

But where the offense shall have been committed within one-fourth of a mile of a county line, the trial may be had either in the county where it was committed, or in the county nearest to the place where the offense was committed.

The question recurring on Mr. Burton's proposition to strike out,

Mr. Burton demanded the yeas and nays, which were ordered, and the resolution to strike out sustained.

Those voting in the affirmative were:

Messrs. Allen, Brown of Davidson, Branson, Burton, Cummings, Campbell, Carter, Dibbrell, Deavenport, Deaderick, Dromgoole, Finley, Fentress, Fielder, Gibson, Gibbs, Gordon, Garner, Hill of Warren, Hill of Gibson, Heiskell, House of Davidson, Robertson and Montgomery, Jones of Lincoln, Kennedy, Kyle, Mabry, Meeks, Netherland, Porter of Henry, Parker, Seay, Shepard, Stephens, Shelton, Thompson of Davidson, Thompson of Maury, Taylor, Wright, Williamson and Warner—39.

Those voting in the negative were:

Messrs. Arledge, Burkett, Baxter, Britton, Brooks, Byrne, Blizard, Brandon, Bate, Coffin, Chowning, Cypert, Doherty, Fulkerson, Gaut, Gardner, Henderson, House of Williamson, Ivie, Jones of Giles, Kirkpatrick, Key, Martin, Morris, McDougal, McNabb, Nicholson, Porter of Haywood, Sample and Turner—30.

On motion of Mr. Heiskell the words "or Districts" were stricken out, and the 9th Section, as thus amended, was adopted by the Convention.

On motion of Mr. Fentress, the Convention adjourned until to-morrow morning at 10 o'clock.

WEDNESDAY MORNING, JANUARY 19, 1870.

The Convention met pursuant to adjournment, Mr. President BROWN in the Chair.

Prayer by the Rev. Dr. MOORE.

The Journal of yesterday was read and approved.

AMENDMENTS PROPOSED.

The roll was called for memorials and petitions, when Mr. KYLE submitted the following resolutions, which were read and referred to the Committee on the Judiciary:

Resolved, That the Judiciary Committee inquire into and make such alterations or amendments to our existing State Constitution so as to provide for the election of only one Justice of the Peace in each Civil District in the various Counties of the State, except the Town Districts, where there shall be two.

2. That the said Committee be directed to inquire into the propriety of so reorganizing our present County Court system, as to increase their jurisdiction over all misdemeanors, and of making petit larceny a misdemeanor; and in default of the payment of fines and costs, the said Court shall have power to force payment either in a County work-house or public roads of the County.

3. That each County Court in the State shall have the power to elect a Prosecuting Attorney, whose duty it shall be to prosecute all misdemeanors, receiving the fees now fixed, or that may hereafter be fixed by law.

That the fees of Magistrates be increased.

Mr. WARNER submitted the following resolutions, which were read and referred to the Committee on New Counties and County Lines:

Resolved, That the Committee on New Counties and County Lines inquire into the propriety of establishing a new County out of the North part of Marshall, North-west part of Bedford, South-west part of Rutherford, South part of Williamson, and East part of Maury, to consist of an area of not less than two or three hundred square miles, and containing a voting population of not less than eight hundred or one thousand.

Resolved further, That in forming said new County, the line or lines shall not run nearer the County sites of the old Counties than ten miles, and that neither one of the old Counties mentioned shall be reduced in *area* less than three hundred square miles.

Resolved further, That this shall be left to the qualified voters living within the fractions out of which the new County is to be formed, whether or not they want or will have said new County, and if a majority of the voters contained therein vote for the same, then the same may be established.

Resolved, That the said Committee also inquire into the propriety of taking off from the County of Giles, on the North part adjoining Marshall County, fifty square miles, and adding the same to said Marshall: *Provided, however*, That a majority of the qualified voters in said fraction shall vote in favor of the same.

Resolved further, That in taking off said fraction the line shall not run nearer the County site of Giles County than ten miles, and the area of said County of Giles shall not be reduced to less than five hundred square miles.

Resolved further, That as soon as this Constitution is adopted, the Legislature shall fix the time and place, and prescribe the manner of voting, consistent with the above, for the new County or against it, and for the fraction of Giles to come to Marshall or against it.

Resolved further, That as soon as the vote has been taken, as above specified, if a majority of the various fractions shall vote for a new County, if a new County can be had according to the aforesaid specifications, then the lines may be run and the County laid off and established; and if the majority of the fraction from Giles shall vote to come into Marshall, then the line shall be run in accordance with the rules or lines above specified, and if in accordance therewith the same can be done, then the same shall be a part of Marshall.

MINORITY REPORT ON THE ELECTIVE FRANCHISE.

Mr. FENTRESS, from the Minority of the Committee on Elections and Franchise, made the following report, which was read, and 150 copies of it and the Report of the Majority ordered to be printed:

We, the undersigned, members of the Committee on Elective Franchise, beg leave to submit the following report, to-wit:

We cannot concur with the Majority of the Committee in drawing a black line across the word "white" in the Constitution of Tennessee, and in their action, refusing to submit the question of negro suffrage to be voted upon as a separate proposition by the people.

We hold that the negro race is the lowest order of human beings, incapable in themselves of a virtuous, intelligent or free government; and for the truth of this, we appeal to history, and challenge the world to show a single exception.

We hold that the inferiority of the negro to the white man, in race, color and capacity for permanent, well-ordered government, has been fixed by Him, who "doeth all things well," and whose natural or revealed law has never been violated by any human government without disaster and confusion. The proud Castilian violated this natural law, when, instead of recognizing in the body politic, the distinction which God had made between him and the Aztec, the Indian and the negro, he made them politically equal, and swift destruction came upon him, insomuch that his *pure* blood cannot now be traced in the mongrel, miscegenating horde, who, by never-ceasing revolution and civil strife, desolate the rich and beautiful lands of Mexico.

We hold that the elective franchise is the highest crowning right which can be held by a freeman; the which, when a man shall be legally entitled to enjoy, there doth necessarily follow those incidentals—the right to sit on juries, to hold office, and (what is more terrible to contemplate) the right to social equality and intermarriage.

We hold that this Convention should not be moved by fear of arbitrary power, to shut their eyes to the light of experience, and falling in with the fanaticism of the hour, deny the *truth*, and blindly rush, in defiance of the natural law of God, to the *confusion* of our *race*, and *destruction* of the government our fathers left us.

We hold that the people of Tennessee have the *right* to consider this tremendous question for themselves, as a separate, distinct proposition, as the people of New York, Ohio, Michigan, Minnesota, Colorado, Kansas, Missouri and Connecticut, have lately done; and, having considered it in all its bearings, to decide it for themselves, free from the incumbrance of any other questions; and that any attempt by this Convention to prevent a fair expression of their will, by refusing to allow the people to vote upon it as a separate question, will be a gross violation of the *rights* of the *people*, and of the principles of republican and democratic government; especially so in this case, because no expression of the will of the people, or general discussion upon it was had, pending the election, in a large majority of the Districts, represented by Delegates in this Convention; and, in a great many, the question was not even mentioned; and deliberate discussion was impossible in the brief time between the call of the Convention and election of Delegates; therefore,

In behalf of the people of Tennessee, and in view of the fact that no Convention of any State in the United States has refused to submit this question as a separate proposition back to the people, and following the precedent of the States above mentioned, and in order that due discussion and deliberation, and the light of events which may transpire between the adjournment of this Convention and the time fixed for the vote of the people, may be had; having also the utmost confidence that when said subject has been discussed, deliberated upon and weighed, the people will do right. It is recommended that this Convention adopt the following, to-wit:

That on the —— day of ——, A. D. 18—, the polls shall be opened at the respective voting places in each County in this State, by the proper officers; and those who are in favor of extending the right of suffrage to the negro equally with the white man, shall have printed or written on their ballots, "negro suffrage," and those who are opposed to the negro being allowed equally with the white man the right of the elective franchise, shall have written or printed on their ballots, "white suffrage," and in case a majority of the qualified electors vote in said election "negro suffrage," then the word "white" in the first line of Article IV, Section 1, of the Constitution of Tennessee, shall be stricken out; but if a majority of said electors shall vote "white suffrage," then said section shall read as follows, to-wit: "Every *free white* man, of the age of twenty-one years, being a citizen of the United States, and a citizen of the county wherein he may offer his vote, six months next preceding the day of election, shall be entitled to vote for members of the General Assembly and other civil officers for the County or District in which he resides."

Respectfully submitted,

JAMES FENTRESS,
WM. H. WILLIAMSON,
H. R. BATE,
W. CUMMINGS.

REPORT OF COMMITTEE ON PRINTING.

Mr. GARNER, from the Committee on Printing, made the following report:

The Committee on Printing have had under consideration the resolution offered by Mr. Thompson, of Maury, relative to the printing of stenographic reports of the proceedings of this Convention, and have instructed me to report the following resolution, and recommend its adoption, viz.:

Resolved, That the Committee on Printing be authorized to contract with the Public Printers of this State, Jones, Purvis & Co., (Proprietors of the Union and American and Republican Banner) for stenographic reports of the proceedings and debates of this Body, and for the printing and binding of 2000 copies of said reports, in one volume, to be as well done as Caldwell's Reports of the Decisions of the Supreme Court of Tennessee. All to be done under the supervision of said Committee, and the prices for the printing to be those fixed by law. Respectfully submitted,

JOHN E. GARNER, Chairman.

On motion of Mr. Key, the resolution and report was laid on the ab le.

BILL, OF RIGHTS FURTHER CONSIDERED.

The Convention proceeded to the consideration of the report of the Committee on the Bill of Rights, the unfinished business of yesterday.

On motion of Mr. NICHOLSON, the 5th section, which was passed over informally yesterday, was taken up.

Mr. CARTER submitted the following amendment:

"Strike out all of said section after the word equal."

Mr. CARTER demanded the yeas and nays, which were ordered, and the resolution was rejected.

Those voting in the affirmative are:

Messrs. Allen, Arledge, Brown of Carroll, Gibson, Madison, and Henry, Bate, Cummings, Campbell, Carter, Deavenport, Deaderick, Dromgoole, Fentress, Fielder, Gordon, Hill of Gibson, Jones of Lincoln, Porter of Henry, Turner, Taylor, Wright, and Williamson—20.

Those voting in the negative are:

Messrs. Burkett, Brown of Davidson, Branson, Baxter, Britton, Brooks, Byrne, Blizard, Burton, Brandon, Coffin, Chowning, Cypert, Dibbrell, Doherty, Finley, Fulkerson, Gaut, Gibson, Gardner, Gibbs, Garner, Henderson, Hill of Warren, Heiskell, House of Williamson, House of Davidson, Robertson, and Montgomery, Ivie, Kirkpatrick, Key, Kennedy, Kyle, Martin, Mabry, Morris, Meeks, McDougal, McNabb, Netherland, Nicholson, Porter of Haywood, Parker, Seay, Stephens, Staley, Sample, Shelton, Thompson of Davidson, Thompson of Maury, and Warner—50.

The fifth section, as reported by the Committee, was then adopted by the Convention.

Sections 10, 11, 12 and 13 were adopted as reported by the Committee.

Section 14 was taken up, when Mr. HOUSE of Davidson, Robertson and Montgomery, offered the following in lieu of said section:

Strike out the 14th Section of Bill of Rights, and insert in place thereof the following:

No person shall be held to answer for a capital or otherwise infamous crime except by presentment, indictment or impeachment; but the Legislature, in case of petit larceny, and in cases of assault, assault and battery, affray, riot, unlawful assembly, vagrancy, and other misdemeanors of a like character, may dispense with inquest of a grand jury, on indictment or presentment, and may authorize prosecutions for such offences, before such inferior court or courts as may be established by the Legislature; and the proceedings in such cases shall be regulated by law. *Provided*, That all defendants, so arraigned, shall have the right of trial by jury, unless the same shall be expressly waived in such mode as may be established by law.

Mr. WARNER offered the following in lieu of Mr. House's amendment:

"Except in cases of misdemeanors." So said section would read thus: That no citizen shall be put to answer any criminal charge but by presentment, indictment, or impeachment, except in cases of misdemeanors, when the crime does not merit imprisonment as a penalty.

Mr. BAXTER moved to lay the amendment and the amendment in lieu on the table.

Mr. HOUSE, of Montgomery, demanded the yeas and nays, which were ordered, and the motion to lay on the table sustained.

Those voting in the affirmative are:

Messrs. Allen, Arledge, Bate, Baxter, Blizard, Branson, Brandon, Britton, Brown of Davidson, Burkett, Byrne, Carter, Coffin, Cummings, Cypert, Deaderick, Fentress, Fielder, Finley, Garner, Gaut, Gibbs, Gibson, Heiskell, Henderson, Hill of Warren, Hill of Gibson, Ivie, Jones of Lincoln, Kirkpatrick, Mabry, McDougal, McNabb, Martin, Meeks, Morris, Netherland, Parker, Sample, Shepard, Shelton, Stephens, Thompson of Maury and Williamson—44.

Those voting in the negative are:

Messrs. Brooks, Brown of Henry, etc., Burton, Campbell, Chowning, Deavenport, Dibbrell, Doherty, Dromgoole, Fulkerson, Gardner, Gordon, House of Williamson, House of Davidson, Robertson, and Montgomery, Kennedy, Key, Kyle, Nicholson, Porter of Haywood, Porter of Henry, Seay, Staley, Taylor, Thompson of Davidson, Turner, Warner, and Wright—27.

On motion of Mr. BAXTER, the section was amended by striking out the word *citizen* and inserting *person.*

Mr. HEISKELL moved to amend by inserting "*free man*" in lieu of person.

Mr. HEISKELL demanded the yeas and nays on his amendment, which were ordered, and the amendment rejected.

Those voting in the affirmative are:

Messrs. Burkett, Campbell, Carter, Deaderick, Deavenport, Dromgoole, Fentress, Fielder, Fulkerson, Garner, Gibbs, Gordon, Heiskell, Henderson, Hill of Gibson, Jones of Lincoln, Kirkpatrick, Kyle, Morris, Netherland, Porter of Henry, Shepard, Taylor, Thompson of Davidson, Thompson of Maury, Turner and Williamson—27.

Those voting in the negative are:

Messrs. Allen, Arledge, Bate, Baxter, Blizard, Brandon, Branson, Britton, Brooks, Brown of Davidson, Brown of Henry, etc., Burton, Byrne, Coffin, Cummings, Cypert, Dibbrell, Doherty Finley, Gardner, Gaut, Gibson, Hill of Warren, House of Williamson, House of Davidson, Robertson, and Montgomery, Ivie, Kennedy, Key, Mabry, McDougal, McNabb, Martin, Meeks, Nicholson, Parker, Porter of Haywood, Sample, Shelton, Staley, Stephens, Warner and Wright—43.

The section, as amended, was then adopted by the Convention.

Mr. FENTRESS offered the following amendment to Section 15:

Resolved, That the following words be added as an amendment at the end of the 4th line of the 15th Section of the Bill of Rights: "And then only to soldiers in actual service." So that the same shall read as follows:

Sec. 15. That all prisoners shall be bailable by sufficient sureties, unless for capital offences, when the proof is evident, or presumption great. And the privilege of the writ of *habeas corpus* shall not be suspended, unless when in case of rebellion or invasion the General Assembly shall declare the public safety requires it, and then only as to soldiers in actual service.

On motion of Mr. BAXTER, the amendment was laid on the table.

The section, as reported by the Committee, was then adopted by the Convention.

Section 16 was adopted as reported by the Committee.

Mr. NETHERLAND proposed the following amendment to Section 17:

Be it resolved, That Section 17 be amended by adding the words: "In the same tribunals and in the same remedies as suits against individuals."

Mr. GIBSON submitted the following additional amendment:

"The Legislature shall pass laws whereunder suits may be brought against the State."

Mr. WILLIAMSON submitted the following, in lieu of the last clause of the section:

"*Provided,* No suit shall be brought against the State."

On motion of Mr. HEISKELL, the pending amendments were laid on the table, and the section, as reported by the Committee, was adopted.

Mr. McDOUGAL submitted the following amendment:

Strike out the 18th section and insert in lieu thereof: The Legislature shall pass no law authorizing imprisonment for debt in civil cases.

Mr. BAXTER moved to lay the amendment on the table, and demanded the yeas and nays, which were ordered, and the motion to lay on the table failed.

Those voting in the affirmative are:

Messrs. Allen, Baxter, Brooks, Byrne, Blizard, Burton, Carter, Dromgoole, Finley, Gardner, Henderson, Heiskell, House of Davidson, Robertson, and Montgomery, Ivie, Key, Kennedy, Martin, McNabb, Porter of Haywood, and Sample—20.

Those voting in the negative are:

Messrs. Arledge, Burkett, Brown, of Davidson, Britton, Brandon, Brown, of Henry, etc., Bate, Cummings, Coffin, Campbell, Chowning, Cypert, Dibbrell, Deavenport, Deaderick, Doherty, Fulkerson, Fentress, Fielder, Gaut, Gibson, Gibbs, Gordon, Garner, Hill, of Warren, Hill, of Gibson, House, of Williamson, Jones, of Lincoln, Jones, of Giles, Kirkpatrick, Kyle, Mabry, Morris, Meeks, McDougal, Netherland, Nicholson, Porter, of Henry, Parker, Seay, Stephens, Staley, Shelton, Thompson, of Davidson, Thompson, of Maury, Turner, Taylor, Wright, Williamson and Warner—52.

Mr. HOUSE, of Williamson, offered the following amendment, in lieu of Mr. McDougal's:

Strike out 18th Section and insert:

That imprisonment for debt cannot exist in this State except for fines and penalties imposed for violation of law.

Mr. WRIGHT demanded the previous question, which was sustained, and a vote had on Mr. McDOUGAL's amendment, which was adopted, and Section 18 as amended was adopted by the Convention.

On motion of Mr. WRIGHT, the Convention adjourned until tomorrow morning, 10 o'clock.

THURSDAY MORNING, JANUARY 20, 1870.

The Convention met pursuant to adjournment, Mr. President BROWN in the Chair.

Prayer by the Rev. Mr. INMAN.

The Journal of yesterday was read and approved.

The roll was called for Memorials and Petitions.

AMENDMENT PROPOSED.

Mr. BROOKS submitted the following amendment to the Constitution, which were read and referred to the Committee on the Judiciary.

Section 1. *Resolved,* That the Constitution be so amended that Justices of the Peace shall have full jurisdiction on promissory notes to the amount of five hundred dollars.

Sec. 2. *Be it resolved,* That said Justices of the Peace shall have full jurisdiction of two hundred and fifty dollars on Accounts and Attachments or Replevin.

Sec. 3. *Be it resolved,* That at trials under the above section the Justice on application of either party cause to be summoned a Jury of three or five men to try the cause and hear the testimony, and render a verdict on the same, and be governed by the rules governing Juries in Courts of Record subject to appeal by either party.

MEMORIAL.

Mr. COFFIN presented a memorial from 933 citizens of East Tennessee, praying a change of the Constitution in regard to the sale of intoxicating liquors, so that the same may be submitted to a vote of the towns and Districts, which was read and referred to the Committee on the Legislative Department.

HOUR OF MEETING.

Mr. GIBSON offered the following resolution, which lies over under the rules:

Resolved, That hereafter, and until further ordered, the Convention shall meet at 9½ A. M.

AMENDMENTS PROPOSED.

Mr. HILL, of Warren, submitted the following resolution, which was read and referred to the Committee on New Counties and County Lines:

Resolved, That the Committee on New Counties and County Lines be instructed to report an amendment to Article X, Section 4, of the Constitution, so as to declare Sequatchie County constitutionally established as its boundaries are now defined by Legislative enactments.

Mr. KYLE submitted the following preamble and resolution, which were read and referred to the Committee on Internal Improvements, Finance, etc.:

WHEREAS, It is notorious that the Legislative Department of the Government have granted privileges to Express and Telegraphic Companies that are in conflict with the interest of the great mass of our people; *Therefore*,

Resolved, That the proper Committee be directed to enquire into the propriety of so amending our Constitution, as to restrain and prohibit the said companies from making exorbitant and unreasonable charges for their services.

Mr. KYLE submitted the following preamble and resolution, which were read and referred to the Committee on Miscellaneous Provisions:

WHEREAS, The office of County Trustee costs the various counties of the State, annually, from $80,000 to $100,000, the incumbents thereof, rendering inadequate and but little service therefor, and,

WHEREAS, It behooves every lover of the State in our straightened financial condition to look well to an economical administration of our State Government; *Therefore*,

Resolved, That the proper Committee be directed to enquire into the propriety of abolishing the office of County Trustee and substituting the County Court Clerk, or some other County official to the duties thereof.

Mr. KEY presented a Memorial from sundry citizens of the counties of Roane, Monroe and Blount, praying the establishment of a new County out of portions of those counties, which, without being read, was referred to the Committee on New Counties.

Mr. KEY submitted the following resolution, which was referred to the Committee on New Counties and County Lines:

Resolved, That a new County may be formed by the Legislature out of the territory around the town of Loudon and Philadelphia, in Monroe County, to be composed of fractions of the Counties of Roane, Monroe and Blount; *Provided*, that said new County shall not approach within less than ten miles of the County sites of either of said Counties, and shall not reduce the territorial limits of either of said old Counties to less than five hundred square miles, and said new County shall contain an area of at least three hundred square miles and a voting population of not less than six hundred.

Mr. MEEKS offered the following resolution, which was read and referred to the Committee on Elections and Right of Suffrage:

Resolved, That the Committee on Elections be requested to inquire into the propriety of this Convention not interfering with the elections, which are to take place on the —— day of March next, for County officers of this State.

MEMORIALS.

Mr. THOMPSON, of Maury, presented a petition from numerous citizens of Maury, asking that Clerks and Masters of the Chancery Court be elected by the people of their respective Counties or Districts, which, without being read, was referred to the Committee on the Judiciary.

Mr. SEAY presented a memorial from a large number of citizens, of Wilson, Smith, Macon and Sumner, praying the establishment of a new County out of portions of said Counties, which, without being read, was referred to the Committee on New Counties and County Lines.

Mr. SEAY also presented a memorial from citizens of Sumner County, praying a change in the Constitution, in relation to the establishment of new counties, so that a county can be formed with a less area than now required, which was referred to the Committee on New Counties.

AMENDMENTS PROPOSED.

Mr. WILLIAMSON submitted the following amendment, which was read and on his motion ordered to be laid on the table:

Resolved. That Section 11, Article III, of the Constitution be amended by adding the following:

"And every bill which shall have passed the Senate and House of Representatives, shall before it becomes a law, be presented to the

Governor; if he approve, he shall sign it; but if not, he shall return it, with his objections, to that House in which it shall have originated, who shall enter the objections at large on their Journal and proceed to reconsider it. If, after such reconsideration, two thirds of the members present shall agree to pass the bill, it shall be sent, with the objections, to the other House, by which it shall be likewise reconsidered, and if approved by two thirds of all the members present, it shall become a law, notwithstanding the objection of the Governor: But in all such cases, the votes of both Houses shall be determined by yeas and nays, and the names of the members voting for and against the bill shall be entered on the Journal of each House respectively. If any bill shall not be returned by the Governor within ten days (Sundays excepted) after it shall have been presented to him, the same shall be a law in like manner as if he had signed it, unless the Legislature shall, by their adjournment, prevent its return; in which case it shall not become a law.

BILL OF RIGHTS FURTHER CONSIDERED.

The Convention proceeded to the consideration of the report of the Committee on Bill of Rights—the unfinished business of yesterday:

Mr. CYPERT offered the following amendment to Section 19:

That the nineteenth Section of the Bill of Rights as reported by the Committee be so amended as to read as follows:

That the printing presses shall be free to every person who undertakes to examine the proceedings of the Legislature or of any branch thereof, or officer of the Government, and no law shall ever be made to restrain the right thereof. The free communication of thoughts and opinions is one of the invaluable rights of man, and every citizen may freely speak, write and print on any subject, being responsible for the abuse of that liberty. And in prosecutions for the publication of papers, investigating the *official or private conduct of any officer or person,* the truth thereof may be given in evidence, and in all indictments for libels the jury shall have a right to determine the law and the facts, under the direction of the Court as in other criminal cases.

Sec. 19, line —, strike out the word "but" and insert "and." Line 6, after the word "*official,*" strike out the words "conduct of officers or men in public capacity," and insert the words "or private conduct of any officer or person."

On motion of Mr. FULKERSON, the amendments were laid on the table.

Section 19, as reported by the Committee, was adopted.

Section 20 was taken up, when Mr. DEAVENPORT submitted the following amendment:

That Section 20 be so amended that "other" may be inserted between *or* and *law*, so that said section will read—

Sec. 20. That no retrospective law, or other law impairing the obligations of contracts, shall be made.

Which amendment was rejected, and Section 20, as reported by the Committee, was adopted.

Mr. GIBSON submitted the following amendment to Section 21:

Strike out "or" in second line, and insert "and," and add the words "*in money*," after the word "compensation."

Sec. 21. That no man's particular services shall be demanded or property taken or applied to public use, without consent of his representatives, *and* without just compensation in money being made therefor.

Which amendment was rejected by the Convention, and Section 21, as reported by the Committee, was adopted.

Sections 22, 23 and 24, as reported by the Committee, were adopted.

Mr. HEISKELL proposed to amend Section 25, by striking out the word "martial," and substituting the word "military."

Mr. CAMPBELL proposed as an amendment in lieu, that the words "either under martial or under military law," be inserted.

Which was adopted in lieu of Mr. Heiskell's.

Mr. FIELDER demanded the previous question, which was sustained, and the amendment of Mr. CAMPBELL was adopted, and Section 25, as amended, was adopted.

Mr. HEISKELL offered the following clause to Section 25:

"That martial law, in the sense of the unrestricted power of military officers or others to dispose of the persons, liberties or property of the citizen, is inconsistent with the principles of free government, and is not confided to any department of the government of this State."

Which was adopted.

Mr. GARDNER offered the following amendment to Section 26, by adding to the end of the Section:

"But the Legislature shall have power, by law, to regulate the wearing of arms with a view to prevent crime."

Which was adopted, and Section 26, as thus amended, was adopted by the Convention.

Section 27 was adopted as reported by the Committee, without amendment.

Mr. CYPERT proposed to amend Section 28, as follows:

That Section 28 be stricken out, and in lieu thereof the following words be inserted:

"All citizens of this State, between such ages as now prescribed, or as may hereafter be prescribed by law, may be compelled to bear arms, and no equivalent in money shall ever be received by the State in lieu of such services."

Which amendment was rejected, and the section, as reported by the Committee, adopted.

Sections 29, 30, 31, 32, 33 and 34 were adopted by the Convention, as reported by the Committee, without amendment.

Mr. HEISKELL moved to reconsider the vote adopting the fourteenth Section.

Mr. BAXTER moved to lay the motion to reconsider on the table, and demanded the yeas and nays, which were ordered, and the motion to lay on the table lost.

Those voting in the affirmative are:

Messrs. Allen, Arledge, Bate, Baxter, Blackburn, Blizard, Branson, Britton, Brooks, Carter, Chowning, Cummings, Deaderick, Fielder, Finley, Gibbs, Henderson, Hill of Warren, Hill of Gibson, Ivie, Jones of Lincoln, Kirkpatrick, Mabry, McDougal, McNabb, Morris, Netherland, Sample, Stephens and Thompson of Maury—30.

Those voting in the negative are:

Messrs. Brandon, Brown of Davidson, Brown of Henry, etc., Burkett, Burton, Byrne, Campbell, Coffin, Cypert, Deavenport, Dibbrell, Doherty, Dromgoole, Fentress, Fulkerson, Gardner, Garner, Gaut, Gibson, Gordon, Heiskell, House of Williamson, House of Davidson, Robertson and Montgomery, Jones of Giles, Kennedy, Key, Kyle, Martin, Meeks, Nicholson, Parker, Porter of Haywood, Porter of Henry, Seay, Shepard, Taylor, Thompson of Davidson, Turner, Warner, Williamson and Wright—41.

The motion to reconsider was then adopted.

On motion of Mr. HEISKELL, the consideration of the fourteenth Section of the Bill of Rights was postponed until to-morrow, and made the special order, to be taken up immediately after the call of the roll for memorials and petitions.

Mr. JONES, of Giles, moved to reconsider the vote adopting the ninth Section of the Bill of Rights.

On motion of Mr. STEPHENS, the motion to reconsider was laid on the table.

Mr. PORTER, of Henry, moved to adjourn until to-morrow morning at 10 o'clock.

Mr. BAXTER demanded the yeas and nays, which were ordered, and the motion to adjourn failed.

Those voting in the affirmative are:

Messrs. Allen, Arledge, Bate, Brooks, Brown of Henry, etc., Burton, Campbell, Deavenport, Doherty, Droomgoole, Fentress, Gardner, Gordon, House of Davidson, Robertson and Montgomery, Jones of Giles, Morris, Porter of Haywood, Porter of Henry, Seay, Shepard, Shelton, Stephens, Taylor, Thompson of Davidson, Williamson and Wright--26.

Those voting in the negative are:

Messrs. Baxter, Blackburn, Blizard, Branson, Brandon, Britton, Brown of Davidson, Burkett, Byrne, Carter, Chowning, Coffin, Cummings, Cypert, Deaderick, Dibbrell, Fielder, Finley, Fulkerson, Garner, Gaut, Gibbs, Gibson, Heiskell, Henderson, Hill of Warren, Hill of Gibson, House of Williamson, Ivie, Jones of Lincoln, Kennedy, Key, Kirkpatrick, Kyle, Mabry, McDougal, McNabb, Martin, Meeks, Netherland, Nicholson, Parker, Sample, Thompson of Maury, Turner and Warner—46.

REPORT ON EXECUTIVE DEPARTMENT CONSIDERED.

On motion of Mr. BROWN, of Davidson, the Convention proceeded to the consideration of the report of the Committee on the Executive Department.

The report of the Committee was read, when, on motion of Mr. HOUSE, of Davidson, Robertson and Montgomery, the Convention proceeded to the consideration of the third Article of the Constitution of the State, section by section.

Sections 1, 2 and 3 were adopted without amendment.

Mr. HOUSE, of Davidson, Robertson and Montgomery, offered the following in lieu of the fourth Section:

The Governor shall hold his office for the term of four years, and until his successor shall be elected and qualified, and shall not be eligible for more than four years in a period of eight years.

Mr. JONES, of Giles, demanded the yeas and nays, which were ordered, and the amendment was adopted.

Yeas.. 40
Nays.. 30

Those voting in the affirmative are:

Messrs. Allen, Bate, Baxter, Branson, Brandon, Britton, Brooks, Brown of Davidson, Brown of Henry, etc., Burton, Byrne, Campbell, Carter, Cummings, Deaderick, Doherty, Dromgoole, Fentress, Fulkerson, Gibson, Heiskell, House of Williamson, House of Davidson, Robertson and Montgomery, Jones of Giles, Kennedy, Key, Kirkpatrick, Kyle, Mabry, McNabb, Morris, Nicholson, Parker, Porter of Haywood, Porter of Henry, Shelton, Thompson of Davidson, Turner, Williamson and Wright—40.

Those voting in the negative are:

Messrs. Arledge, Blackburn, Blizard, Burkett, Chowning, Cypert, Deavenport, Dibbrell, Fielder, Finley, Gardner, Garner, Gaut, Gibbs, Gordon, Henderson, Hill of Warren, Hill of Gibson, Ivie, Jones of Lincoln, McDougal, Martin, Meeks, Netherland, Sample, Shepard, Stephens, Taylor, Thompson of Maury and Warner—30.

Mr. HOUSE submitted the following, as an independent section to said Article:

Every bill which may pass both Houses of the General Assembly shall, before it becomes a law, be presented to the Governor for his signature. If he approve, he shall sign it, and the same shall become a law; but if he refuse to sign it, he shall return it, with his objections thereto in writing, to the House in which it originated; and said House shall cause said objections to be entered at large upon their Journal, and proceed to reconsider the bill. If, after such reconsideration, a majority of all the members elected to that House shall agree to pass the bill, notwithstanding the objections of the Executive, it shall be sent, with said objections, to the other House, by which it shall likewise be reconsidered. If approved by a majority of the whole number elected to that House, it shall become a law: the votes of both Houses shall be determined by yeas and nays, and the names of all the members voting for or against the bill, shall be entered upon the Journals of their respective Houses.

If the Governor shall fail to return any bill, with his objections, within five days (Sundays excepted) after it shall have been presented to him, the same shall become a law without his signature, unless the General Assembly, by their adjournment, prevent its return, in which case it shall not become a law.

Every joint resolution, or order, (except on questions of adjournment) shall likewise be presented to the Governor for his signature, and before it shall take effect, shall receive his signature; and on being disapproved by him, shall, in like manner, be returned with his objections; and the same, before it shall take effect, shall be repassed by a majority of all the members elected to both Houses in the manner and according to the rules prescribed in case of a bill.

It was ordered by the Convention that said amendment be laid on the table and one hundred copies printed, and that the consideration of said section be postponed temporarily.

Sections 5 and 6 were adopted without amendment and without a division.

To Section 7 Mr. WILLIAMSON offered the following amendment:

"He shall receive, as compensation for his services, at least five thousand dollars per annum, but his salary shall not be increased during the period for which he shall have been elected."

During the pendency of said amendment, on motion, the Convention adjourned until to-morrow morning at 10 o'clock.

FRIDAY MORNING, JANUARY 21, 1870.

The Convention met pursuant to adjournment, Mr. President BROWN in the Chair.

Prayer by the Rev. Mr. SAMPLE, a member of this body.

The Journal of yesterday was read, corrected and approved.

The roll was called for memorials and petitions.

TO AMEND THE RULES.

Mr JONES, of Lincoln, proposed to amend the rules of the Convention as follows:

Insert after the word "order," in the second line of the last rule on page 5, the words "within two days thereafter."

On motion of Mr. JONES, the rules were suspended and the amendment adopted.

Mr. JONES, of Lincoln, moved to reconsider the vote adopting the amendment, and further moved that the motion to reconsider be laid on the table, which latter motion prevailed.

PAY OF MEMBERS.

Mr. JONES, of Lincoln, submitted the following resolution, which was adopted by the Convention:

Resolved, That the Treasurer of the State of Tennessee is hereby authorized and required to pay the members of this Convention their *per diem* and mileage, and the officers of this Convention their *per diem* the same as members and officers of the Legislature, due up to the time of calling for the same.

AMENDMENTS PROPOSED.

Mr. WRIGHT submitted the following resolution, which was read and referred to the Committee on Miscellaneous Provisions:

Resolved, That it be engrafted in the Constitution of Tennessee that any officer or officers having in charge public moneys for the benefit of the Common Schools, shall, for any violation of public trust be dismissed from office, and become ineligible to any office of trust or honor in the State, and shall be subject to severe penalties, pecuniary and corporeal.

BILL OF RIGHTS FURTHER CONSIDERED.

On motion of Mr. KEY, the vote by which Mr. Campbell's amendment to Section 25 of the Bill of Rights was adopted, was reconsidered.

On motion of Mr. BAXTER, the amendment was altered so as to read, "under the martial or military law;" and thus amended, was adopted by the Convention.

The Convention proceeded to the consideration of special order—the 14th Section of the Bill of Rights.

Mr. HOUSE, of Davidson, Robertson and Montgomery, offered the following in lieu of the 14th Section of the Bill of Rights, as reported by the Committee:

Strike out Section 14 of the Bill of Rights, and insert, "No person shall be held to answer any criminal charge, except by presentment, indictment or impeachment; but the Legislature, in cases of petit larceny, assault, assault and battery, affray and vagrancy, may dispense with an inquest of a Grand Jury, an indictment or presentment, and may authorize prosecutions for said offenses, before such inferior Court or Courts as may be established by law; and the proceedings in such cases shall be regulated by law; and all defendants so arraigned, shall have the right of trial by jury, unless the same shall be expressly waived in such manner as may be prescribed by the Legislature."

Mr. WARNER offered the following in lieu of Mr. House's:

Amend the 14th Section by adding after *impeachment*, "Except in cases of misdemeanors meriting impeachment, which may be fixed by the Legislature."

Mr. BROWN, of Davidson, offered the following amendment to Mr. House's amendment:

"*Provided*, That in all cases of trial of the offenses above specified, the prosecution shall be required to prefer an information on oath, describing the matter of the offense, with reasonable certainty, and the place and time of its commission."

Which was accepted by Mr. HOUSE.

Mr. JONES, of Lincoln, moved to lay the pending amendments on the table.

Mr. BAXTER demanded the yeas and nays, which were ordered, and the motion to lay on the table sustained.

Yeas.. 37.
Nays.. 35.

Those voting in the affirmative are:

Messrs. Arledge, Bate, Baxter, Blackburn, Blizard, Branson, Brandon, Britton, Burkett, Carter, Deaderick, Fentress, Fielder, Finley, Garner, Gaut, Gibbs, Gibson, Henderson, Hill of Warren, Hill of Gibson, Ivie, Jones of Lincoln, Kirkpatrick, Mabry, McDougal, McNabb, Martin, Morris, Meeks, Netherland, Parker, Sample, Shepard, Shelton, Stephens, and Thompson of Maury—37.

Those voting in the negative are:

Messrs. Brooks, Brown of Davidson, Brown of Henry, Carroll, Gibson and Madison, Burton, Byrne, Campbell, Chowning, Coffin, Cummings, Cypert, Deavenport, Dibbrell, Doherty, Dromgoole, Fulkerson, Gardner, Gordon, Heiskell, House of Williamson, House of Davidson, Robertson and Montgomery, Jones of Giles, Kennedy, Key, Kyle, Nicholson, Porter of Haywood, Porter of Henry, Seay, Staley, Taylor, Thompson of Davidson, Turner, Warner, Williamson, and Wright—35.

Section 14 of the Bill of Rights was then adopted as reported by the Committee.

REPORT ON ELECTIONS.

Mr. NICHOLSON, from the Committee on Elections and the Rights of Suffrage, submitted the following

REPORT:

The Committee on Elections and Rights of Suffrage, have had under consideration various propositions, suggesting amendments to the Constitution in regard to the times of holding certain elections and the mode of voting, and have rejected all of them, except one which proposes to change the time of holding the elections for members of the General Assembly, and the time for the regular sessions of that body. This is a proposition to amend Sections 7 and 8 of Article II, by striking out of Section 7 the words "on the first Thursday in August, 1835," and inserting in lieu thereof the words "*on the first Tuesday in November, one thousand eight hundred and seventy,*" and in the same section, in lines four and five, to strike out the words "on the first Thursday in August," and to insert in lieu thereof the words "*on the first Tuesday in November,*" so that the section, as amended, will read as follows:

Article II, Section 7. The first election for Senators and Representatives shall be held on the first Tuesday in November, one thousand eight hundred and seventy, and forever thereafter elections for members of the General Assembly shall be held once in two years on the first Tuesday in November; said elections shall terminate the same day.

In Section 8, Article II, it is proposed to strike out the words, in lines two and three, ("one thousand eight hundred and thirty-five") and to insert in lieu thereof the words: *One thousand eight hundred and seventy-one*; and in line 4 of said Section, to strike out the words ("first Monday in October") and insert in lieu thereof the words, *first Monday in January*, so that the 8th Section, Article II, as amended will read as follows:

Article II, Section 8. The first session of the General Assembly shall commence on the first Monday in January, one thousand eight hundred and seventy-one; and forever thereafter, the General Assembly shall meet on the first Monday in January next ensuing the election.

The Committee recommend the amendment of Sections 7 and 8 as proposed, and their adoption as Sections 7 and 8 in Article II, of the Constitution.

All of which is respectfully submitted,

A. O. P. NICHOLSON.

On motion of Mr. NICHOLSON, it was ordered that the report be laid on the table, and one hundred copies ordered to be printed.

MARRIAGES BETWEEN WHITES AND BLACKS.

Mr. NICHOLSON, from the same Committee, reported back the resolution of Mr. Sample in relation to marriages between whites and colored persons, and asked that the Committee be discharged from its further consideration, which was so ordered, and the resolution referred to the Committee on Miscellaneous Provisions.

REPORT ON EXECUTIVE DEPARTMENT FURTHER CONSIDERED.

Mr TURNER moved to reconsider the vote adopting Mr. HOUSE's amendment in lieu of Section 4, of Article III, on yesterday.

Mr. HEISKELL moved to lay the motion to reconsider on the table.

Mr. KENNEDY demanded the yeas and nays, which were ordered and the motion to lay on the table failed:

Yeas..29.
Nays..44.

Those voting in the affirmative are:

Messrs. Bate, Baxter, Blackburn, Branson, Brandon, Brooks, Brown of Henry. Carroll, Gibson and Madison, Campbell, Carter, Deaderick, Doherty, Dromgoole, Fentress, Fulkerson, Gibson, Heiskell, House of Williamson, House of Davidson, Robertson and Montgomery, Jones of Giles, Kennedy, Key, Kyle, Mabry, Porter, of Haywood, Porter of Henry, Shelton, Staley, Williamson and Wright—29.

Those voting in the negative are:

Messrs. Allen, Arledge, Blizard, Britton, Brown, of Davidson, Burkett, Burton, Byrne, Chowning, Coffin, Cummings, Cypert, Deavenport, Dibbrell, Fielder, Finley, Gardner, Garner, Gaut, Gibbs, Gordon, Henderson, Hill of Warren, Hill, of Gibson, Ivie, Jones of Lincoln, Kirkpatrick, McDougal, McNabb, Martin, Morris, Meeks, Netherland, Nicholson, Sample, Seay, Shepard, Stephens, Taylor, Thompson of Davidson, Thompson of Maury, Turner and Warner—44.

The motion to reconsider was then adopted.

The question recurring upon the adoption of Mr. HOUSE's amendment:

Mr. BURTON demanded the yeas and nays, which were ordered and the amendment was rejected

Yeas..29
Nays..43

Those voting in the affirmative are:

Messrs. Bate, Baxter, Brandon, Brown of Davidson, Burton, Byrne, Campbell, Deaderick, Doherty, Dromgoole, Fentress, Fulkerson, Gibson, Heiskell, House of Williamson, House of Davidson, Robertson and Montgomery, Jones of Giles, Kennedy, Key, Kyle, Mabry, McNabb, Porter of Haywood, Porter of Henry, Shelton, Staley, Thompson of Davidson, Williamson and Wright —29.

Those voting in the negative are:

Messrs. Allen, Arledge, Blackburn, Blizard, Branson, Britton, Brooks, Burkett, Carter, Chowning, Coffin, Cummings, Cypert, Deavenport, Dibbrell, Fielder, Finley, Gardner, Garner, Gaut, Gibbs, Gordon, Henderson, Hill of Warren, Hill of Gibson, Ivie, Jones of Lincoln, Kirkpatrick, McDougal, Martin, Morris, Meeks, Netherland, Nicholson, Parker, Sample, Seay, Shepard, Stephens, Taylor, Thompson of Maury, Turner and Warner—43.

The 4th Section, of Article III, of the present Constitution was then adopted without amendment.

Mr. MARTIN moved to reconsider the vote by which the 5th Section, of Article III, was adopted, on yesterday, and submitted the following amendment, which was read for information:

AMENDMENT TO SECTION FIFTH, ARTICLE III.

After the words United States insert as follows:

"And he shall not in any event call into service the militia for any party or political purpose; and shall not call them into service in any case, except that of rebellion or invasion, and in such case the General Assembly shall declare the public safety requires it."

On motion of Mr. TURNER, the motion to reconsider was laid on the table.

The amendment of Mr. WILLIAMSON to Section 7, in relation to the salary to be paid to the Governor, was rejected and the Section as it is in the present Constitution, was adopted by the Convention.

Section 8 was adopted without amendment.

The amendment of the Committee on the Executive Department to Section 9, was adopted.

Mr. CYPERT demanded the yeas and nays, which were ordered, and resulted as follows:

Yeas..57
Nays..13

Those voting in the affirmative are:

Messrs Allen, Arledge, Bate, Blackburn, Blizard, Branson, Brandon, Britton, Brooks, Brown of Davidson, Burkett, Byrne, Campbell, Carter, Chowning, Cummings, Cypert, Deaderick, Deavenport, Dibbrell, Doherty, Dromgoole, Fentress, Fielder, Finley, Fulkerson, Gardner, Garner, Gaut, Gibson, Gordon, Henderson, Hill of Warren, Ivie, Jones of Lincoln, Kennedy, Key, Kirkpatrick, Kyle, McDougal, McNabb, Martin, Morris, Meeks, Netherland, Nicholson, Parker, Sample, Seay, Shepard, Shelton, Staley, Taylor, Thompson of Davidson, Thompson of Maury, Turner, Warner and Wright—57.

Those voting in the negative are:

Messrs. Baxter, Burton, Gibbs, Heiskell, Hill of Gibson, House of Williamson, House of Davidson, Robertson and Montgomery, Jones of Giles, Mabry, Porter of Haywood, Porter of Henry, Stephens and Williamson—13.

LEAVES OF ABSENCE

On motion of Mr. PORTER, of Henry, Mr. BROWN, of Henry, Carroll, Gibson and Madison, was granted leave of absence on account of sickness.

On motion of Mr. GIBBS, leave of absence was grented Mr. CUMMINGS, until Tuesday next.

On motion of Mr. GORDON, leave of absence was granted Mr. ALLEN, until Tuesday next.

CONSIDERATION OF EXECUTIVE DEPARTMENT RESUMED.

Sections 10, 11, 12, 13, 14, 15, and 16, as they exist in the present Constitution, were adopted without amendment.

Mr. DIBBRELL offered the following amendment to Section 17.

Section 17. After the words "shall be" strike out the words "appointed by joint vote of the General Assembly" and insert "*shall be elected by the qualified voters of the State, at the same time and in the same manner that the Governor is elected.*" So that the section will read as follows:

Secion 17. A Secretary of State shall be elected by the qualified voters of the State, at such time and in the same manner that the Governor is elected, once in two years, and commissioned during the term of two years. He shall keep a fair register of all the officials acts and proceedings of the Governor, and shall, when required, lay the same, and all minntes and vouchers relative thereto, before the General Assembly, and shall peform such other duties as shall be enjoined by law.

Mr. KYLE moved to lay the amendment on the table.

Mr. DIBRELL demanded the yeas and nays, which were ordered, and the motion to lay on the table prevailed.

Yeas..41
Nays..29

Those voting in the affirmative are:

Messrs. Allen, Bate, Baxter, Blackburn, Brown of Davidson, Burkett, Campbell, Carter, Cummings, Deaderick, Dromgoole, Fielder, Fulkerson, Garner, Gibbs, Gibson, Gordon, Heiskell, Henderson, Hill of Gibson, House of Williamson, House of Davidson, Robertson and Montgomery, Ivie, Jones of Giles, Kennedy, Key, Kyle, Mabry, Netherland, Nicholson, Parker, Porter of Haywood, Shepard, Shelton, Staley, Stephens, Thompson of Davidson, Thompson of Maury, Turner and Williamson—41.

Those voting in the negative are:

Messrs. Blizard, Branson, Brandon, Britton, Brooks, Burton, Byrne, Chowning, Cypert, Deavenport, Dibbrell, Doherty, Fentress, Finley, Gaut, Hill of Warren, Jones of Lincoln, Kirkpatrick, McDougal, McNabb, Martin, Morris, Meeks, Porter of Henry, Sample, Seay, Taylor, Warner and Wright—29.

Mr. PORTER, of Haywood, offered the following amendment:

That said section be so amended as to read as follows:

"The Secretary of State shall be appointed by the Governor and confirmed by the Senate, and shall be commissioned during the term of two years."

Mr. CYPERT moved to lay the amendment on the table, and demanded the yeas and nays, which were ordered, and the motion to lay on the table prevailed.

Yeas..43
Nays..28

Those voting in the affirmative are:

Messrs. Allen, Baxter, Blackburn, Blizard, Britton, Brooks, Brown of Davidson, Burkett, Burton, Campbell, Chowning, Cummings, Cypert, Deavenport, Doherty, Dromgoole, Fentress, Fielder, Finley, Fulkerson, Gaut, Gibbs, Gordon, Henderson, Hill of Warren, Hill of Gibson, Ivie, Jones of Giles, Mabry, McDougal,

Martin, Morris, Meeks, Netherland, Porter of Henry, Sample, Seay, Shepard, Stephens, Taylor, Thompson of Davidson, Warner and Wright—43.

Those voting in the negative are:

Messrs. Bate, Branson, Brandon, Byrne, Carter, Coffin, Deaderick, Dibbrell, Gardner, Garner, Gibson, Heiskell, House of Williamson, House of Davidson, Robertson and Montgomery, Jones of Lincoln, Kennedy, Key, Kirkpatrick, Kyle, McNabb, Nicholson, Parker, Porter of Haywood, Shelton, Staley, Thompson of Maury, Turner, and Williamson—28.

Mr. PORTER, of Henry, offered the following amendment:

Strike out the words "joint vote of the General Assembly," and insert the words "by the Governor of the State."

On motion of Mr. BAXTER, the amendment was laid on the table.

The section was then passed without amendment.

The amendment of Mr. HOUSE of Montgomery, etc., conferring on the Governor a qualified veto power, was postponed until to-morrow.

IMPEACHMENT PENALTIES.

Mr. HEISKELL submitted the following resolution:

Resolved, That a Committee of five be appointed, to whom it shall be referred to report whether it is proper that this Convention take any action in regard to relieving persons impeached from the penalties imposed.

With instructions further to report whether any action is proper and necessary in reference to the case of Judge Thomas N. Frazier.

On motion of Mr. HEISKELL, the rules were suspended and the resolution adopted.

On motion of Mr. House of Davidson, Robertson and Montgomery, the Convention adjourned until to-morrow morning at 10 o'clock.

SATURDAY MORNING, JANUARY 22, 1870.

The Convention met pursuant to adjournment, Mr. President BROWN in the Chair.

Prayer by the Rev. Mr. Sample, a member of this body.

The Journal of yesterday was read and approved.

COMMITTEE ON IMPEACHMENT.

The PRESIDENT announced the following gentlemen as constituting the Select Committee, under Mr. Heiskell's resolution in relation to impeachment, and the case of Judge Thos. N. Frazier, viz: Messrs. Baxter, Heiskell, Key, House of Montgomery, and Porter of Henry.

The roll was called for memorials and petitions.

AMENDMENTS PROPOSED.

Mr. BROOKS submitted the following resolution, which was read and referred to the Committee on New Counties and County Lines:

Resolved, That the Constitution be so amended that there may be a new county formed out of the Counties of Jackson and Overton. *Provided*, That in the formation it shall contain at least 400 qualified voters; and further, said new county shall contain at least 300 square miles of territory, and shall not reduce either of the old counties, from which it is taken, below 500 square miles. *Provided further*, That the line of said new county shall not approach either of the old county seats nearer than ten miles. *Provided further*, That a majority of the qualified voters contained in said new county vote in favor of said new county. The county seat of the old counties, from which said new county is formed, shall not be removed without a concurrence of two-thirds vote of both Branches of the Legislature.

MEMORIALS.

Mr. MEEKS presented a memorial from sundry citizens of McNairy County, praying a change of the Constitution in relation to the formation of new counties, which, without being read, was referred to the Committee on New Counties and County Lines.

Mr. NETHERLAND presented a memorial from sundry citizens of Hawkins County, against the creation of a new county out of said county and others, and against any change in the Constitution in regard to the creation of new counties, which was read and referred to the Committee on New Counties and County Lines.

Mr. WARNER presented a memorial from a large number of citizens of Bedford and Marshall Counties for the formation of a new county, which was, without being read, referred to the Committee on New Counties and County Lines.

AMENDMENTS PROPOSED.

Mr. DEAVENPORT submitted the following amendment to the Constitution:

Resolved, That Article VII, Section 2, be so amended as to read:

Sec. 2. Should a vacancy occur, subsequent to an election, in the office of Sheriff, Trustee, or Register, it shall be filled by the County Judge, or Justices of the Quarterly or Quorum Courts; if in that of the clerks to be elected by the people, it shall be filled by the Courts. And the person so appointed shall continue in office until his successor shall be elected and qualified; and such office shall be filled by the qualified voters at the first election for any of the county officers.

Mr. HEISKELL, on behalf of the majority of the Committee on the Judicial Department, made a report, which was ordered to be laid on the table and printed.

Mr. STALEY, from the minority of said Committee, made a report, which was read and ordered to be printed with the report of the majority.

Mr. GARNER moved to print 300 copies, which was rejected.

On motion of Mr. KENNEDY, it was ordered that 100 copies be printed.

Said reports are as follows:

MAJORITY REPORT OF THE COMMITTEE ON THE JUDICIARY.

A majority of the Judiciary Committee, to whom were referred divers propositions for the amendment of the existing Constitution, have had the same under consideration, and have instructed me to report, in lieu of all the proposed amendments, the following, as a substitute for the fifth and sixth articles of the existing Constitution, and for such portion of the schedule to be attached to the Constitution as relates to the subjects referred to them.

J. B. HEISKELL, Chairman.

ARTICLE V.

Sec. 1. The House of Representatives shall have the sole power of impeachment.

Sec. 2. All impeachments shall be tried by the Senate; when sitting for that purpose the Senators shall be upon oath or affirmation, *and the Chief Justice of the Supreme Court, or if he be on trial the Senior Associate Judge, shall preside over them.* No person shall be convicted without the concurrence of two-thirds of the Senators sworn to try the officer impeached.

Sec. 3. The House of Representatives shall elect, from their own body, three members, whose duty it shall be to prosecute impeachments. No impeachment shall be tried unless the Legislature shall have adjourned *sine die*, when the Senate shall proceed to try such impeachment.

Sec. 4. The Governor, Judges of the Supreme Court, Judges of Inferior Courts, Chancellors, Attorneys for the State, and Secretary of State, shall be liable to impeachment, whenever they may, in the opinion of the House of Representatives, commit any crime in their official capacity which may require disqualification; but judgment shall only extend to removal from office, and disqualification to fill any office thereafter. The party shall, nevertheless, be liable to indictment, trial, judgment and punishment according to law.

Sec. 5. Justices of the Peace, and other civil officers not hereinbefore mentioned, for crimes or misdemeanors in office, shall be liable to indictment in such courts as the Legislature may direct; and, upon conviction, shall be removed from office by said court, as if found guilty on impeachment; and shall be subject to such other punishment as may be prescribed by law.

ARTICLE VI.

Sec. 1. The Judicial power of this State shall be vested in one Supreme Court, and in such *Circuit, Chancery and other* inferior courts as the Legislature shall, from time to time, ordain and establish; in the Judges thereof, and in Justices of the Peace.

The Legislature may also vest such jurisdiction in Corporation Courts as may be deemed necessary.

Courts to be holden by Justices of the Peace may also be established.

Sec. 2. The Supreme Court shall consist of *five Judges, of whom not more than two shall reside in any one of the grand divisions of the State.*

The Judges shall designate one of their own number who shall preside as Chief Justice.

The concurrence of three of the Judges shall in every case be necessary to a decision.

The jurisdiction of this court shall be appellate only, under such restrictions and regulations as may, from time to time, be prescribed by law; but it may possess such other jurisdiction as is now conferred by law on the present Supreme Court. Said courts shall be held at one place, and at one place only, in each of the three grand divisions of the State.

Sec. 3. *The Governor of the State shall nominate, and by and with the advice and consent of the Senate, shall appoint the Judges of the Supreme Court.*

The consent of the Senate to such nominations shall require the concurrence of two-thirds of the whole number required by law to compose that body.

Every Judge of the Supreme Court shall be thirty-five years of age, *and shall, before his appointment, have been a resident of the State for five years. His term of service shall be twelve years.*

Sec. 4. The Judges of the Circuit and Chancery Courts, and of other inferior courts, shall be elected by the qualified voters of the *district or circuit to which they are to be assigned.*

Every Judge of such court shall be thirty years of age, and shall, before his appointment, have been a resident of the State for *five* years. *His term of service shall be ten years.*

Sec. 5. *An Attorney General and Reporter for the State shall be appointed by the Judges of the Supreme Court, and shall hold his office for a term of twelve years.*

An Attorney for the State for any circuit or district, for which a judge *having criminal jurisdiction shall be provided by law,* shall be elected by the qualified voters of such circuit or district, and shall hold his office for a term of six years.

In all cases where the Attorney for any district fails or refuses to attend and prosecute according to law, the court shall have power to appoint an Attorney *pro tempore.*

Sec. 6. Judges and Attorneys for the State may be removed from office, by a concurrent vote of both Houses of the General Assembly, each House voting separately; but two-thirds of all the members elected to each House must concur in such vote; the vote shall be determined by ayes and noes, and the names of the members voting for or against the Judge or Attorney for the State, together with the cause or causes of removal, shall be entered on the Journals of each House respectively. The Judge or Attorney for the State, against whom the Legislature may be about to proceed, shall receive notice thereof, accompanied with a copy of the causes alleged for his removal, at least ten days before the day on which either House of the General Assembly shall act thereupon.

Sec. 7. The Judges of the Supreme or Inferior Courts shall, at stated times, receive a compensation for their services, to be ascertained by law, which shall not be increased or diminished during the time for which they are elected. They shall not be allowed any fees or perquisites of office, nor hold any other office of trust or profit under the State, or the United States.

Sec. 8. *The jurisdiction of the Circuit, Chancery, and other inferior courts shall be as now established by law, until changed by the Legislature.*

Sec. 9. Judges shall not charge juries with respect to matters of fact, but may state the testimony and declare the law.

Sec. 10. The Judges or Justices of the Inferior Courts of Law shall have power, in all civil cases, to issue writs of *certiorari* to remove any cause, or the transcript *of the record* thereof, from any inferior jurisdiction into such court, on sufficient cause, supported by oath or affirmation.

Sec. 11. No Judge of the Supreme or Inferior Courts shall preside on the trial of any cause in the event of which he may be interested, or where either of the parties shall be connected with him by affinity or consanguinity, within such degrees as may be prescribed by law, or in which he may have been of counsel, or in which he may have presided in any inferior court, except by consent of all the parties. In case all or any of the Judges of the Supreme Court shall thus be disqualified from presiding on the trial of any cause or causes, the Court, or the Judge thereof, shall certify the same to the Governor of the State, and he shall forthwith specially commission the requisite number of men, of law knowledge, for the trial and determination thereof.

The Legislature may, by general laws, make provision that Special Judges may be appointed to hold any courts the Judge of which shall be unable or fail to attend or sit; or to hear any cause in which the Judge may be incompetent.

Sec. 12. All writs and other process shall run in the name of the State of Tennessee; and bear test and be signed by the respective clerks. Indictments shall conclude, "*against the peace and dignity of the State.*"

Sec. 13. Judges of the Supreme Court shall appoint their clerks, who shall hold office for six years. Chancellors (if Courts of Chancery shall be established,) shall appoint their Clerks and Masters, who shall hold their offices for a period of six years. Clerks of such inferior courts as may be hereafter established, which shall be required to be holden in the respective counties of this State, shall be elected by the qualified voters thereof for the term of four years; they shall be removed from office for malfeasance, incompetency, or neglect of duty, in such manner as may be prescribed by law.

Sec. 14. No fine shall be laid on any citizen of this State that shall exceed fifty dollars, unless it shall be assessed by a jury of his peers, who shall assess the fine at the time they find the fact, if they think the fine should be more than fifty dollars.

Sec. 15. The different counties of this State shall be laid off, as the General Assembly may direct, into districts of convenient size, so that the whole number in each county shall not be more than twenty-five, or four for every one hundred square miles. There shall be two Justices of the Peace and one Constable elected in each District, by the qualified voters therein, except districts including county towns, which shall elect three Justices and two Constables. The jurisdiction of said officers shall be co-extensive with the county. Justices of the Peace shall be elected for the term of six, and Constables for the term of two years. Upon the removal of either of said officers from the district in which he was elected, his office shall become vacant from the time of such removal. Justices of the Peace shall be commissioned by the Governor. The Legislature shall have power to provide for the appointment of an additional number of Justices of the Peace in incorporated towns.

SCHEDULE.

Section 1. That no inconvenience may arise from a change of the Constitution, it is declared that all civil officers, except Attorneys-General of the State and the Judges for the several Courts, shall hold their offices until the expiration of their present term of service.

So much of this Constitution as provides for the appointment of the permanent Judges of the Supreme Court, shall not go into cperation until the first day of November, 1871.

Immediately after the ratification of this Constitution, the Governor shall nominate, and by and with the advice and consent of the Senate, shall appoint four additional Judges, who, together with the Judges of the present Supreme Court, shall constitute the Supreme Court until the first of November, 1871, and until the appointment and qualification of the Supreme Court provided for in this Constitution.

The compensation of each of said four additional Judges shall be five thousand dollars annually.

Said Judges may sit in two sections, and hear and determine causes at the same time; but they shall not sit in different grand divisions at the same time.

An Attorney-General for the State shall be appointed after the appointment and qualification of the four Judges of the Supreme Court, herein provided for.

The present Judges of the Circuit, Chancery and other inferior Courts, shall hold their offices until their successors are elected, under this schedule.

The election for Judges of said inferior Courts shall be held on the —— day of ———, 1870, by the Sheriffs of the several counties, in the manner prescribed by the Code.

MINORITY REPORT OF THE COMMITTEE ON THE JUDICIARY.

The undersigned, a minority of the Committee on the Judiciary, not being able to concur in the conclusion arrived at by a majority, begs leave to submit the following:

Being the youngest member of the Committee, of experience less enlarged, and of knowledge less accurate and extensive than those with whom he has had the honor to be associated, he presents this report with great deference, and urges, as his excuse for so doing, his utter inability to reconcile with his sense of duty the action of the majority. He would have great distrust of his own judgment if he stood alone in his views, but as he knows himself to be supported by the ablest writers, and by the most eminent Judges who have adorned the jurisprudence both of our own and other countries, and as he feels assured that the majority of the Committee entertain views not dissimilar to his own on the main question which has received their consideration, he has entire confidence in the opinions which have actuated him to submit this report.

Ever since the undersigned was led to reflect upon the subject at all, he has never had a doubt as to the proper method of choosing Judges. It seems to him to be so plain that the method of their appointment and the tenure of their office should be such as to secure their independence and impartiality, and that these cannot be secured by popular election, that he is at a loss to understand how any diversity of opinion could have arisen upon the subject. Every good citizen recognizes the importance, nay, the necessity, of an upright, an impartial, an independent Judiciary. This can never be secured, as the undersigned firmly believes and confidently asserts, by popular elections. If our Judges are to be constantly looking forward to re-election, as they will be, and shaping their conduct accordingly—if they are to engage in strife and demoralizing contests for office—if they are to witness the zealous efforts of friends to retain them in place, and the determined endeavors of those who are not friends, to pull them down—they cannot, they will not, as long as human nature is what it now is—be independent and impartial.

It is in vain to say that if the election of Judges be taken from the people, an unwillingness to trust them will be shown. The undersigned has quite as much confidence in the people as those who urge this objection. He believes in the honesty of the people, and that their disposition is to do right. He cannot disguise from himself, however, the fact that they are frequently misled; but is happy to know that the "sober second thought" always brings them back to the true path. Whilst the undersigned entertains no distrust of the people, he has a very great distrust of those who habitually seek office before them. The people themselves have no great confidence in this class; and if we establish a system by which our Judges will be compelled to enter the arena and become office-seekers, this lack of confidence will soon attach to them, who, above all other men, should be without reproach. If they are to engage in indecent scuffles for place, they cannot escape infection, and will not be long in learning the arts of the political trickster, and in resorting to his practices. It may be safely assumed that their conduct will be shaped with a view to their continuance in office.

The undersigned does not forget that for some years past the Judges in our State have been elected by the people; but this will hardly be appealed to by the advocates of an elective Judiciary. The recollection is not encouraging. The system has not given satisfaction, and its operation should be a sufficient warning without reference to the experience of other States in which the same system has been adopted, and to which the attention of the advocates of this doctrine might be directed with profit.

There is nothing in the objection that the non-election of Judges by the people is inconsistent with the principles of a free government. The undersigned believes it not only to be in accordance with such principles, but necessary to their maintenance. History, were it necessary to appeal to it, would abundantly fortify this conclusion. In England, the freest and the most enlightened country on the globe except our own, the Judges have always been appointed by the Crown. She can point to a long list of names of illustrious men in the history of her Judiciary who were an honor to their country and to humanity. Her people are, to-day, indebted, in a great measure, to the unswerving impartiality and sturdy independence of her Judges for the fixed and stable character of her institutions. Under this system she has grown solid as a mountain rock; her power and her wealth have become almost boundless; her limits have been extended, until she boasts that the sun never sets on her territory, and that her morning reveille is heard all round the globe.

In our own country, the wisest body of men that ever assembled, provided, in Convention, in 1787, that Judges should not be elected by the people. That act of theirs was ratified by the States of the Confederation, and has been in operation, under our federal system, for more than three-quarters of a century. It has, during all that time, worked well. Independent, enlightened and upright Judges, have presided in our Federal Courts. Every American refers with pride to such men as Marshall and Story, whose names shine among the brightest stars in the galaxy of jurisprudence. Has any one ever seriously entertained a thought of changing this system to an elective Judiciary? The undersigned has never so much as heard of a proposition of the kind on the part of any party or person, and he believes that any attempt of the kind would be regarded by the people as an insane project.

The majority of the Committee have reported that Judges of the Supreme Court should be nominated, and by and with the advice and consent of the Senate, appointed by the Governor. If it be right and proper so to appoint Supreme Judges, *a fortiori*, the

Judges of the inferior Courts should be likewise appointed. Supreme Judges are, in a great degree, removed from the influences of the prejudices and passions of the day, whilst the Judges of inferior Courts are daily brought in contact with them and with the multitude swayed by them. How important, then, to remove as far as possible from these officials all temptation to yield. It is idle to dream of human perfection. Judges have the same imperfections, are liable to the same errors, and are moved by the same excitements with ourselves. When we invest a man with the robes of judicial office, we do not, at the same time, invest him with any additional virtue—he is not so panoplied as to ward off all extraneous influences—nor doth his dignity so hedge him in as to repel all improper approach. We must frame our plans for man as he is, and not for man as he would be, were he free from vice.

There is one other proposition reported by the majority to which the undersigned cannot assent. It is this: the majority propose to vacate the offices of all the Circuit Judges and Chancellors in the State immediately upon the ratification of the amended Constitution. With all due deference for the opinion of the Committee, the undersigned cannot see the justice of the measure proposed. In no view that he has been able to take of it can he perceive its propriety or its necessity. It is believed that the impolicy of such a step will present itself to the mind of every member of the Convention upon the slightest reflection. We cannot be oblivious, if we would, of the circumstances which surround us. It is the part of wisdom, nay, common prudence dictates, that in all our acts we should have reference to the exigencies upon us, whenever we can do so, as we can in this case, without a sacrifice of principle or violation of right.

Dismissing this consideration, there are other reasons, satisfactory to the mind of the undersigned, why these offices should not be vacated as proposed. The Convention may have the power to vacate them, and if the exercise of the power be approved by the people, it will be rendered effectual; but something more will be required to demonstrate its justice and expediency. During the early part of the last year, and previously thereto, a clamorous demand was raised for the election of Judges and Chancellors. It was urged, on all sides that the Constitution had been, and was continually being violated by the Executive in appointing men to fill these offices. The powerful influence of the press was brought to bear in this direction. The pressure of *public* opinion (not the opinion of any one class or party) become so great that the General Assembly yielded and passed a law to bring about the election of Judges, Chancellors and Attorneys-General. The present incumbents yielded to the solicitations of friends and members of the Bar to become candidates—they left their practice, in many instances lucrative; they were elected for the term of eight years, with the understanding and the undoubted expectation that they should discharge the duties, and enjoy the emoluments and privileges of their offices for the full period. Yet the proposition is to turn them out before the lapse of one-fourth of their terms, and that without the preferment of any charge. It occurs to the undersigned that we ought not to disappoint the reasonable expectations of these officers, under the circumstances, unless an imperious necessity demanded it. The objection that the present incumbents were elected at a time when no fair expression of the popular will could be had by vote, is more specious than solid. There was a fair, a decided, an overwhelming expression of public opinion in favor of the law to bring about the election at the time therein specified, and the present officials were favored and encouraged to become candidates, by men of all parties. Were we about to inaugurate a new system, it might be proper to put it into operation as soon as practicable; but to retain the present plan, and to arbitrarily eject these men from office, and fill their places in the same manner by which they were chosen, would seem to many to be the dictate of party spirit, and to savor of injustice. Besides, it would bring to bear against our labors an opposition too formidable to be despised or disregarded; and, in all probability, under the plan proposed by the majority, and as it now exists, we would get no better men than we now have. The undersigned has not been able to see how the difficulties of the situation can be better met than to change the method of choosing Judges, but to permit those now in office to continue until the expiration of the time for which they were elected. Whilst the new system would be delayed, we would at once reap some of its advantages, and rid ourselves of a great evil incident to the existing system, for the present Judges, knowing that they could not again be elected by the people, would be uninfluenced by any such consideration. No necessity for precipitate action can be perceived. We are not sitting here as a legislative assembly, whose acts may, in a few months, be repealed and set aside. We hope and expect our work to last for generations; and if, by a little delay, we can get a good system, we can well afford to wait.

The same reasons which have led to these conclusions apply with equal force to Attorneys-General.

Other amendments have been reported by a majority of the Committee about which there is no material disagreement. Although not in all respects such as could be desired, they are matters about which an opinion may be yielded in deference to the opinions of others or in a spirit of compromise. The undersigned offers, therefore, the following amendments, viz.:

ARTICLE VI.

Section 1. The judicial power of this State shall be vested in one Supreme Court; in the Circuit and Chancery Courts, and in such inferior Courts as the Legislature shall, from time to time, ordain and establish; and in the Judges thereof and in Justices of the Peace. The Legislature may also vest such jurisdiction as may be deemed necessary in corporation Courts.

Sec. 2. The Supreme Court shall be composed of three Judges, one of whom shall reside in each of the grand divisions of the State; the concurrence of two of said Judges shall, in every case, be necessary to a decision. The jurisdiction of this Court shall be appellate only, under such restrictions and regulations as may, from time to time, be prescribed by law; but it may possess such other jurisdiction as is now conferred by law on the present Supreme Court. Said Courts shall be held at one place, and at one place only, in each of the three grand divisions of the State.

Sec. 3. The Judges of the Supreme Court, and the Judges of the Circuit and Chancery Courts, and of such inferior Courts as the Legislature may establish, shall be nominated, and by and with the advice and consent of the Senate (a majority of the Senators concurring) be appointed by the Governor. Courts may be established to be holden by Justices of the Peace. Judges of the Supreme Court shall not be less than forty years of age.

Sec. 4. The Judges of the Circuit and Chancery Courts, and of the inferior courts, shall not be less than thirty-five years of age.

Sec. 5. Judges of the Supreme Court shall hold their office for twelve years, and Judges of the Circuit and Chancery and inferior courts for eight years.

Sec. 6. An Attorney-General for the State at large, and an Attorney-General for the State in each judicial circuit, shall be nominated, and by and with the advice and consent of the Senate, (a majority of the Senators concurring) appointed by the Governor.

Sec. 7. The Attorney-General for the State shall hold his office for twelve years, and each of the Attorneys-General in the judicial circuits of the State shall hold his office for eight years.

SCHEDULE.

Section 1. That no inconvenience may arise from a change of the Constitution, it is declared that all laws shall remain in full force until changed by the General Assembly, which shall sit under this amended Constitution, and all civil officers shall continue to hold their offices and discharge all the duties appertaining to the same until the expiration of the time for which they were elected.

Sec. 2. To remedy the inconvenience that has arisen from an accumulation of business in the Supreme Court, it is declared, that immediately upon the ratification of this amended Constitution, the Governor shall nominate, and by and with the advice and consent of the Senate, appoint three Judges, one from each of the grand divisions of the State, who, with the present Supreme Judges, shall for the time being, constitute the Supreme Court of Tennessee. They shall sit in the same division of the State, but in different chambers, or at different hours, so as in effect to constitute two courts. One of these courts shall hear and determine all the equity causes; the other all the law causes in said Court, under the laws, rules and regulations as now prescribed in said court. The Judges herein appointed shall receive the same compensation as the present Judges, and shall continue in office until the expiration of the term for which the present Judges were elected; forever afterwards the Supreme Court shall consist of three Judges, to be appointed as prescribed in Section 3, of Article VI, of this Constitution.

In all else the undersigned would leave the Judiciary system unchanged. He does not so far mistake the temper of this Convention as to flatter himself that these amendmends will be made. He expects to see them rejected or disregarded; but whatever may be their fate, he has discharged his duty, and his conscience is at rest.

Respectfully submitted,

W. B. STALEY.

REPORT ON FINANCE, INTERNAL IMPROVEMENTS AND CORPORATIONS.

Mr. GARDNER, from the Committee on Finance, Internal Improvements and Corporations, made the following report, which was read, and

On motion of Mr. HOUSE, of Williamson, 100 copies were ordered to be printed:

MR. PRESIDENT:

The Committee on "Finance, Internal Improvements and Corporations," having had under consideration the subjects referred to them, instruct me to report the following amendments, and recommend their adoption by the Convention:

CORPORATIONS.

Strike out the proviso at the end of Article XI, Section 7, and insert the following:

"No corporation shall be created by special laws, but the General Assembly shall provide by general laws for the organization of all corporations, hereafter created, which laws may, at any time, be altered, or repealed."

TAXATION.

Strike out the 28th Section of the 2nd Article, and insert the following:

"All property, real, personal or mixed, shall be taxed, except such as may be held by the State, by counties, cities or towns, and used for public or corporation purposes, and such as may be held for purposes purely religious, charitable, scientific, literary or educational; and except one thousand dollars' worth of personal property in the hands of each tax-payer, and the direct products of the soil in the hands of the producer.

"All property shall be taxed according to its value—that value to be ascertained in such manner as the Legislature shall direct, so that the same shall be equal and uniform throughout the State. No one species of property, from which a tax may be collected, shall be taxed higher than any other species of property of the same value.

"Capital invested in the buying and selling of merchandise shall be estimated for taxation at the highest value of the stock of merchandise on hand at any one period in the year preceding its assessment, and merchants shall pay in addition to an *ad valorem* tax thereupon, a specific tax which shall not exceed five hundred dollars per annum, to be graduated as the Legislature shall direct; but peddlers and privileges, may be taxed in such manner as may, from time to time, be prescribed by law.

"The Legislature shall have power to levy a special tax upon incomes derived from stocks and bonds exempted by the laws of the United States from taxation.

"All male citizens of this State, over the age of twenty-one years, shall be liable to a poll tax of not less than one nor more than five dollars *per annum*, until such age as may be fixed by law."

INTEREST.

Strike out Article XI, Section 6, and insert the following:

"The legal rate of interest in this State shall be six per centum per annum; but the Legislature shall have power to provide by law for a conventional rate of interest."

All of which is respectfully submitted,

JNO. A. GARDNER,
Chairman.

EXECUTIVE DEPARTMENT FURTHER CONSIDERED.

The Convention proceeded to the consideration of the special order of the day.

Mr. House's amendment giving the Governor a qualified veto, was taken up, when Mr. Porter, of Haywood, offered the following amendment in lieu of Mr. House's:

Section —. Every bill which shall have passed both Houses of the General Assembly, shall, before it becomes a law, be presented to the Governor. If he approve the bill he shall sign it and deposit it in the office of Secretary of State for preservation, and notify the House where it originated of the fact, and the same shall become a law. But if he disapprove of it, or any part or parts of it, containing separate and distinct provisions, he shall return it to that House in which it shall have originated, with his objections to the whole or to such part or parts of it as he shall disapprove, which shall enter the objections at large on their Journal and proceed to reconsider it. If after such reconsideration either of an entire bill or of a part or parts of said bill objected to, as the case may be, two-thirds of all the members elected to that House, shall agree to pass the whole bill, it shall be sent together with the objections to the other House, by which it shall be reconsidered, and if approved by two-thirds of all the members elected to that House, it shall become a law, notwithstanding the objections of the Governor.

If either of the two Houses shall not thus approve of the part or parts objected to, the bill containing such part or parts shall be approved by the Governor, shall, without unnecessary delay after the the vote is taken on such reconsideration, be engrossed as a separate bill, and returned to the Governor for his signature. But in all such cases the votes of both Houses shall be determined by the yeas and nays, and the names of the members voting for and against the bill shall be entered on the Journals of each House respectively. In case any bill shall not be returned by the Governor within five days (Sundays excepted) after it shall have been presented to him, the same shall be a law in like manner as though he had signed it, and he may approve, sign, and file in the office of the Secretary of State, within five days after the adjournment of the Legislature, any act passed within the last five days of the session, and the same shall become a law; but unless signed within that time the same shall not become a law.

Mr. Porter subsequently withdrew his amendment.

Mr. Thompson, of Maury, demanded the previous question, which demand was sustained.

Mr. Wright demanded the yeas and nays on the passage of the amendment, which were ordered, and the amendment of Mr. House was adopted.

Yeas.. 43
Nays.. 25

Those voting in the affirmative are:

Messrs. Bate, Baxter, Brandon, Burkett, Burton, Byrne, Campbell, Carter, Chowning, Coffin, Cypert, Deavenport, Doherty, Dromgoole, Fentress, Gardner, Garner, Gibson, Gordon, Heiskell,

House of Williamson, House of Davidson, Robertson, and Montgomery, Jones of Giles, Kennedy, Key, Mabry, McDougal, Morris, Meeks, Netherland, Nicholson, Porter of Haywood, Porter of Henry, Seay, Shelton, Staley, Stephens, Taylor, Thompson of Davidson, Thompson of Maury, Turner, Williamson and Wright—43.

Those voting in the negative are:

Messrs. Arledge, Blizard, Branson, Britton, Brooks, Brown of Davidson, Deaderick, Dibbrell, Fielder, Finley, Gaut, Gibbs, Henderson, Hill of Warren, Hill of Gibson, Ivie, Jones of Lincoln, Kirkpatrick, Kyle, McNabb, Martin, Parker, Sample and Warner—25.

Mr. House of Davidson, Robertson and Montgomery, moved to reconsider the vote adopting the amendment, and further moved to lay the motion to reconsider on the table, which latter motion prevailed.

PRINTING THE JOURNAL AND DEBATES.

Mr. GARNER called up the resolution heretofore offered by him, from the Committee on Printing, in relation to printing the Journal and Debates.

Mr. BAXTER moved to amend the resolution by striking out the words "*and debates,*" and demanded the yeas and nays, which were ordered, and the amendment adopted.

Yeas..48
Nays..17

Those voting in the affirmative are:

Messrs. Arledge, Bate, Baxter, Blizard, Branson, Brandon, Britton, Brooks, Brown of Davidson, Burkett, Burton, Byrne, Campbell, Carter, Chowning, Cypert, Deaderick, Deavenport, Dibbrell, Doherty, Dromgoole, Fielder, Finley, Gardner, Gaut, Gibbs, Gibson, Gordon, Henderson, Hill of Warren, Hill of Gibson, Jones of Lincoln, Kirkpatrick, Kyle, Mabry, McDougal, McNabb, Martin, Morris, Meeks, Netherland, Nicholson, Parker, Sample, Staley, Stephens, Taylor, and Warner—48.

Those voting in the negative are:

Messrs. Fentress, Garner, Heiskell, House of Williamson, House of Davidson, Robertson and Montgomery, Ivie, Jones of Giles, Key, Porter of Haywood, Porter of Henry, Seay, Shelton, Thompson of Maury, Turner, Williamson and Wright—17.

On motion of Mr. JONES of Lincoln, the resolution of the Committee on Printing was laid on the table.

MEMORIAL.

Mr. KIRKPATRICK presented a memorial from a number of citizens of Hawkins, Grainger and other counties, praying the establishment of a new county, which, without being read, was referred to the Committee on New Counties and County Lines.

REVISION AND ENROLLMENT.

Mr. STEPHENS offered the following resolution:

Resolved, That a Committee on Revision and Enrollment, to consist of five members, shall be appointed, whose duty it shall be to have correctly enrolled upon parchment, in a fair round hand, the Constitution as proposed to be amended by this Convention, in correct language, and have the amendments properly inserted in the places and as adopted by the Convention.

On motion of Mr. STEPHENS, the rules were suspended and the resolution adopted.

EXECUTIVE DEPARTMENT FURTHER CONSIDERED.

Mr. MARTIN offered the following resolution, as an independent section to Article III of the Constitution:

The Governor shall not, in any event, call into service the militia for any party or political purpose, and shall not call them into service in any case except that of rebellion and invasion, and in such case the General Assembly shall declare the public safety requires it.

On motion of Mr. FENTRESS, it was ordered that 100 copies be printed for the use of the Convention.

On motion of Mr. NICHOLSON, the Convention adjourned until Monday morning, at 10½ o'clock.

MONDAY MORNING, JANUARY 24, 1870.

The Convention met pursuant to adjournment, Mr. President BROWN in the Chair.

Prayer by the Rev. Mr. WESCHLER.

The Journal of Saturday was read and approved.

COMMITTEE ON REVISION, ETC.

The PRESIDENT announced the following gentlemen as constituting the Committee on Revision and Enrollment: W. H. Stephens, H. R. Bate, A. Blizard, A. O. P. Nicholson, John F. House.

LEAVE OF ABSENCE.

On motion of Mr. DOHERTY, leave of absence was granted Mr. Meeks on account of sickness.

Leave of absence was also granted Mr. THOMPSON, of Davidson, on account of sickness.

MEMORIAL.

Mr. KIRKPATRICK presented a memorial from citizens of Washington, Green, Hawkins and Sullivan Counties, praying for a new county to be formed out of fractions of said counties, which, without being read, was referred to the Committee on New Counties and County Lines.

REPORT OF COMMITTEE ON LEGISLATIVE DEPARTMENT.

Mr. STEPHENS, from the Committee on the Legislative Department, made the following report, 100 copies of which were, on motion of Mr. Gardner, ordered printed for the use of the Convention.

MR. PRESIDENT:

I am instructed by the Committee on the Legislative Department to report that they have had under consideration the various matters referred to them; and not supposing it necessary to repeat here each proposition, or to discuss its merits, they have deemed it sufficient to announce the following as their unanimous conclusion upon the whole matter.

The change of dates in some of the sections of Article II, which they recommend, are such as are necessary to adapt the Constitution to the new starting point from which we are setting out. The more important amendments which they propose to engraft on Article II, such as those regulating the compensation of members of the General Assembly, and the mode of enacting laws, and the power of the Legislature to embark the State in debt, and the power of counties and incorporated cities and towns to loan their credit, and to become joint stockholders with others, are, all of them, the result of an earnest conviction on the part of the committee that some such changes in the organic law are essential to the prosperity of the State.

It appearing that the subjects embraced within Section 28 of Article II, were properly within the jurisdiction of the Committee on Finance, Internal Improvements, and Corporations, the consideration of that section, by mutual agreement, was referred to that committee. The section recommended by them, in lieu of Section 28, is inserted in its proper order in this report.

Taking up Article II, I am instructed to recommend that said Article be amended as follows:

Sectiou 3—To the end of this section add the words, "who shall hold their offices for two years from the day of the general election."

Section 4—Strike out the word "forty-one" in the third line, and insert the word "seventy-one."

Section 7—Strike out the word "thirty-five" in the third line, and insert "seventy-one."

Sec. 8—Strike out the word "thirty-five" in the third line, and insert "seventy-one."

Sec. 11—Strike out in the fourth line the words "Two-thirds of each House," and insert "Not less than two-thirds of all the members to which each House shall be entitled."

Sec. 17—Add to the end of this section the words, "No bill shall pass which embraces more than one subject; that subject to be expressed in the title. All acts which repeal, revive or amend former laws, shall recite in their caption or otherwise the title or substance of the law repealed, revived or amended."

Sec. 18—Strike out all after the word "shall," near the end of the third line, and insert "have been read and pased on three different days in each house, the assent of a majority of all the members to which that house shall be entitled under this Constitution; and shall have been signed by the respective Speakers, in open session, the fact of such signing to be noted on the Journal; and shall have received the approval of the Governor, or shall have been otherwise passed under the provisions of this Constitution."

Sec. 21—Strike out "*two,*" in the sixth line, and insert "five."

Sec. 23—Strike out the word "first" in the third line.

After the word "Assembly," at the end of the third line, insert "elected after the ratification of the Constitution."

After the word "services," in the fourth line, strike out all of said section, and insert, "But no member shall be paid for more than seventy-five days of a regular session, or for more than twenty days of an extra or called or adjourned session, or for any day when absent from his seat in the Legislature, unless physically unable to attend. The Senators, when sitting as a Court of Impeachment, shall each receive four dollars per day of actual attendance.

Sec. 28—Amended as reported by the Chairman of the Committee on Finance, etc.

Sec. 29—Add to the end as follows: "But the credit of no

county, city, or town shall be given or loaned to or in aid of any person, company, association or corporation, except upon an election to be first held by the qualified voters of such county, city, or town, and the assent of three-fourths of the votes cast at said election. Nor shall any county, city or town become a stockholder with others in any company, association, or corporation, except upon a like election, and the assent of a like majority."

Section 31—Strike out this section and insert: "The credit of this State shall not be hereafter loaned or given to or in aid of any person, association, company, corporation or municipality; nor shall the State become a stockholder with others in any association, company, corporation or municipality."

With these amendments, Article II, in its complete form, will read as hereinafter written.

Respectfully submitted,

WM. H. STEPHENS, Chairman.

January 24th, 1870.

ARTICLE II.

DISTRIBUTION OF POWERS.

Sec. 1. The powers of the Government shall be divided into three distinct departments: the Legislative, Executive and Judicial.

Sec. 2. No person or persons belonging to one of these departments shall exercise any of the powers properly belonging to either of the others, except in the cases herein directed or permitted.

LEGISLATIVE DEPARTMENT.

Sec. 3. The legislative authority of this State shall be vested in a General Assembly, which shall consist of a Senate and House of Representatives, both dependent on the people, who shall hold their office for two years from the day of the general election.

Sec. 4. An enumeration o the qualified voters and an apportionment of the Representatives in the General Assembly, shall be made in the year one thousand eight hundred and seventy-one, and within every subsequent term of ten years.

Sec. 5. The number of Representatives shall, at the several periods of making the enumeration, be apportioned among the several counties or districts according to the number of qualified voters in each; and shall not exceed seventy-five until the population of the State shall be one million and a half, and shall never thereafter exceed ninety-nine. *Provided*, That any county having two-thirds of the ratio shall be entitled to one member.

Sec. 6. The number of Senators shall, at the several periods of making the enumeration, be apportioned among the several counties or districts, according to the number of qualified voters in each, and shall not exceed one-third the number of Representatives. In apportioning the Senators among the different counties, the fraction that may be lost by any county or counties, in the apportionment of members to the House of Representatives, shall be made up to such county or counties in the Senate as near as may be practicable. When a district is composed of two or more counties, they shall be adjoining; and no county shall be divided in forming a district.

Sec. 7. The first election for Senators and Representatives shall be held on the first Thursday in August, one thousand eight hundred and seventy-one; and forever thereafter, elections for members of the General Assembly shall be held once in two years, on the first Thursday in August; and elections shall terminate the same day.

Sec. 8. The first session of the General Assembly shall commence on the first Monday in October, one thousand eight hundred and seventy-one; and forever thereafter the General Assembly shall meet on the first Monday in October next ensuing the election.

Sec. 9. No person shall be a Representative unless he shall be a citizen of the United States of the age of twenty-one years, and shall have been a citizen of this State for three years, and a resident in the county he represents one year immediately preceding the election.

Sec. 10. No person shall be a Senator unless he shall be a citizen of the United States, of the age of thirty years, and shall have resided three years in this State, and one year in the county or district immediately preceding the election. No Senator or Representative shall, during the time for which he was elected, be eligible to any office or place of trust, the appointment to which is vested in the Executive or the General Assembly, except to the office of trustee of a literary institution.

Sec. 11. The Senate and House of Representatives, when assembled shall each choose a Speaker and its other officers, be judge of the qualifications of its members, and sit upon its own adjournments from day to day. Not less than two-thirds of all the members to which each House shall be entitled, shall constitute a quorum to do business; but a smaller number may adjourn from day to day, and may be authorized by law to compel the attendance of absent members.

Sec. 12. Each House may determine the rules of its proceedings, punish its members for disorderly behavior, and, with the concurrence of two-thirds, expel a member, but not a second time for the same offence; and shall have all other powers necessary for a branch of the Legislature of a free State.

Sec. 13. Senators and Representatives shall in all cases, except treason, felony, or breach of the peace, be privileged from arrest during the session of the General Assembly, and in going to and returning from the same; and for any speech or debate in either House, they shall not be questioned in any other place.

Sec. 14. Each House may punish by imprisonment, during its session, any person, not a member, who shall be guilty of disrespect to the House, by any disorderly or any contemptuous behavior in its presence.

Sec. 15. When vacancies happen in either House, the Governor for the time being, shall issue writs of election to fill such vacancies.

Sec. 16. Neither House shall, during its session, adjourn without the consent of the other for more than three days, nor to any other place than that in which the two Houses shall be sitting.

Sec. 17. Bills may originate in either House; but may be amended, altered, or rejected by the other. No bill shall pass which embraces more than one subject; that subject to be expressed in the title. All acts which repeal, revive or amend former laws shall recite in their caption or otherwise the title or substance of the law repealed, revived or amended.

Sec. 18. Every bill shall be read once on three different days, and be passed each time in the House where it originated, before transmission to the other. No bill shall become a law until it shall have been read and passed, on three different days in each House, and shall have received, on its final passage in each House, the assent of a majority of all the members to which that House shall be entitled under this Constitution; and shall have been signed by the respective Speakers in open session—the fact of such signing to be noted on the Journal; and shall have received the approval of the Governor, or shall have been otherwise passed under the provisions of this Constitution.

Sec. 19. After a bill has been rejected, no bill containing the same substance shall be passed into a law during the same session.

Sec. 20. The style of the laws of this State shall be, "*Be it enacted by the General Assembly of the State of Tennessee.*"

Sec. 21. Each House shall keep a Journal of its proceedings, and publish it, except such parts as the welfare of the State may require to be kept secret; the ayes and noes shall be taken in each House upon the final passage of every bill of a general character, and bills making appropriations of public moneys; and the ayes and noes of the members on any question, shall, at the request of any five of them, be entered on the Journal.

Sec. 22. The doors of each House, and of Committees of the Whole, shall be kept open, unless when the business shall be such as ought to be kept secret.

Sec. 23. The sum of four dollars per day, and four dollars for every twenty-five miles traveling to and from the seat of government, shall be allowed to the members of the General Assembly elected after the ratification of this Constitution, as a compensation for their services. But no member shall be paid for more than seventy-five days of a regular session, or for more than twenty days of any extra or called or adjourned session; or for any day when absent from his seat in the Legislature unless physically unable to attend. The members, when sitting as a court of impeachment, shall each receive four dollars per day of actual attendance.

Sec. 24. No money shall be drawn from the treasury, but in consequence of appropriations made by law; and an accurate statement of the receipts and expenditures of the public money shall be attached to and published with the laws at the rise of each stated session of the General Assembly.

Sec. 25. No person who heretofore hath been, or may hereafter be, a collector or holder of public moneys, shall have a seat in either House of the General Assembly, until such person shall have accounted for, and paid into the Treasury, all sums for which he may be accountable or liable.

Sec. 26. No Judge of any Court of Law or Equity, Secretary of State, Attorney General, Register, Clerk of any Court of Record, or person holding any office under the authority of the United States, shall have a seat in the General Assembly: nor shall any person in this State hold more than one lucrative office at the same time; *Provided*, that no appointment in the militia, or to the office of Justice of the Peace, shall be considered a lucrative office, or operative as a disqualification to a seat in either House of the General Assembly.

Sec. 27. Any member of either House of the General Assembly shall have liberty to dissent from and protest against, any act or resolve which he may think injurious to the public or to any individual, and to have the reasons for his dissent entered on the journals.

Sec. 28. "All property, real, personal or mixed, shall be taxed, except such as may be held by the State, by counties, cities or towns, and used for public or corporation purposes, and such as may be held for purposes purely religious, charitable, scientific, literary or educational, and except one thousand dollars's worth of personal property in the hands of each tax-payer, and the direct product of the soil in the hands of the producer.

All property shall be taxed according to its value, that value to be ascertained in such manner as the Legislature shall direct, so that the same shall be equal and uniform throughout the State. No one species of property from which a tax may be collected shall be taxed higher than any other species of property of the same value.

Capital invested in the buying and selling of merchandise shall be estimated at the highest value of the stock of merchandise on hand at any one period of the year preceeding its assessment; and merchants shall pay, in addition to an *ad volarem* tax thereupon, a specific tax, which shall not exceed five hundred dollars per annum, to be graduated as the Legislature shall direct; but peddlers and privileges may be taxed in such manner as may from time to time be prescribed by law.

The Legislature shall have power to levy a special tax upon incomes derived from stocks and bonds, exempted by the laws of the United States from taxation.

All male citizens of this State, over the age of twenty-one years, shall be liable to a poll tax of not less than one nor more than five dollars per annum, until such age as may be fixed by law.

Sec. 29. The General Assemly shall have power to authorize the several counties and incorporated towns in this State, to impose taxes for county and corporation purposes respectively, in such manner as shall be prescribed by law, and all property shall be taxed according to its value, upon the principles established in regard to State taxation.

But the credit of no county, city or town shall be given or loaned to or in aid of any person, company, association or corporation except upon an election to be first held by the qualified voters of such county, city or town, and the assent of three-fourths of the votes cast at said election. Nor shall any county, city or town become a stockholder with others in any company, association, or corporation, except upon a like election and the assent of a like majority.

Sec. 30. No article manufactured of the produce of this State, shall be taxed otherwise than to pay inspection fees.

Sec. 31. The credit of this State shall not be hereafter loaned or given to or in aid of any person, association, company, corporation or municipality: nor shall the State become a stockholder with others in any association, company, corporation or municipality.

THE RIGHT OF SUFFRAGE CONSIDERED.

On motion of Mr. Nicholson the Convention proceeded to the consideration of the report of the Committee on Franchise and Right of Suffrage.

Mr. Warner moved to pospone the consideration of the report until to-morrow, which motion was rejected.

Mr. Jones, of Lincoln, moved the adoption of the report of the minority of the Committee in lieu of the recommendation of the majority—pending the consideration of said motion, the Convention,

On motion of Mr. Bate, adjourned until to-morrow morning, at 10 o'clock.

TUESDAY MORNING JANUARY 25, 1870.

The Convention met pursuant to adjournment, Mr. President BROWN in the Chair.

Prayer by the Rev. Mr. McNEELEY.

The Journal of yesterday was read and approved.

The Roll was called for Memorials and Petitions.

TO AMEND THE RULES.

Mr. BRITTON submitted the following amendment to the Rules:

Resolved, That the rules governing the proceedings of this House be so amended, that no member shall be permitted to speak more than fifteen minutes upon any single proposition proposing an amendment to the Constitution, unless he shall first obtain leave of the Convention to do so.

Resolved, further, That this rule shall not apply to the proposition now under consideration, but to all propositions that may hereafter come up for consideration in this House.

MEMORIAL.

Mr. IVIE presented a memorial from a large number of citizens of Bedford, Marshall and Rutherford counties, in favor of establishing a new county, which, without being read, was referred to the Committee on New Counties and County Lines.

EXECUTIVE DEPARTMENT FURTHER CONSIDERED.

On motion of Mr. JONES, of Lincoln, the unfinished business of yesterday was postponed and the resolution of Mr. MARTIN, defining the terms on which the militia shall be called into service, was taken up.

On motion of Mr. JONES, of Lincoln, the resolution of Mr. MARTIN was amended by striking out the words "for any party or political purpose, and shall not call them into service in any case." The resolution as amended will read:

The Governor shall not, in any event, call into service the militia except that of rebellion or invasion; and in such case the General Assembly shall declare the public safety requires it.

Mr. DROMGOOLE offered the following in lieu:

"The Governor shall not call into service the militia of this State in any case, unless the General Assembly shall declare the public safety requires it."

Mr. HOUSE, of Davidson, Robertson and Montgomery, submitted the following, in lieu of the original resolution and the amendment in lieu:

The Governor shall have no power to call the militia into service except in case of armed rebellion or invasion; and in such case the General Assembly, by a majority of two-thirds of all the members elected to each House, shall first declare, by joint resolution that, the public safety requires it.

Mr. HEISKELL submitted the following in lieu of the original resolutions and all pending amendments:

The General Assembly shall have no power to authorize the militia to be called into actual service, except when in case of rebellion or invasion the public safety may require it.

In case the law shall be resisted by combinations too powerful to be controlled by the civil authorities of the State, such call may be authorized for not more than ten days at a time, and then only by a law declaring the necessity to exist and defining the powers to be conferred.

Mr. JONES, of Lincoln, moved to lay the original resolution and the amendments on the table.

Mr. MARTIN demanded the yeas and nays, which were ordered and the motion to lay on the table lost.

Yeas..14
Nays..54

Those voting in the affirmative are:

Messrs. Bate, Branson, Britton, Carter, Finley, Garner, Gibson, Hill of Warren, Jones of Lincoln, Kirpatrick, Mabry, Parker, Staley and Thompson of Maury—14.

Those voting in the negative are:

Messrs. Allen, Arledge, Baxter, Blackburn, Blizard, Brandon, Brooks, Brown of Davidson, Brown of Henry, etc., Burkett, Burton, Byrne, Campbell, Chowning, Coffin, Cypert, Deaderick, Deavenport, Dibbrell, Doherty, Dromgoole, Fentress, Fielder, Fulkerson, Gardner, Gaut, Gibbs, Gordon, Heiskell, Henderson, Hill of Gibson, House of Davidson etc., Ivie, Jones of Giles, Kennedy, Key, Kyle, McDougal, McNabb, Martin, Morris, Meeks, Netherland, Nicholson, Porter of Henry, Sample, Seay, Shepard, Shelton, Stephens, Taylor, Warner, Williamson and Wright—54.

Mr. HOUSE, of Davidson, Robertson and Montgomery, moved to refer the resolution and amendment to the Committee on the Executive Department.

Mr. MARTIN moved to amend the motion by referring the whole subject to a special Committee of five, which motion was concurred in by the Convention.

LEAVE OF ABSENCE.

On motion of Mr. Hill, of Warren, leave of absence was granted Mr. Cummings, on account of sickness.

AMENDMENTS PROPOSED.

Mr. GARNER submitted the following resolution, which was read and referred to the Committee on Miscellaneous Provisions:

Resolved, That the Committee on Miscellaneous Subjects be instructed to enquire into and report as to the expediency of adopting the following as Section 14, of Article XI, of the Constitution, viz:

Section 14. A homestead in the hands of each head of a family in this State, occupied as a residence, together with all the improvements on the same, to the value of not exceeding two thousand dollars shall be exempt from forced sale under any process of law during the life time of such head of a family and the minority of his or her children, and shall not be alienated without the joint consent of husband and wife when that relation exists; but no property shall be exempt from sale for taxes, or for the payment of obligations contracted for the purchase of said premises, or for the erection of improvements thereon.

THE ELECTIVE FRANCHISE FURTHER CONSIDERED.

The Convention proceeded to the consideration of the report of the Committee on Franchise and the Right of Suffrage, and the substitute offered by Mr. JONES, of Lincoln.

Before coming to a conclusion, the Convention, at 2 o'clock, P. M.,

On motion of Mr. HEISKELL, took a recess until 3 o'clock, P. M.

AFTERNOON SESSION.

The Convention assembled at 3 o'clock P. M., Mr. President BROWN in the Chair.

Mr. JONES, of Lincoln, moved that the Convention adjourn until to-morrow morning at 10 o'clock.

Mr. HILL, of Warren, demanded the yeas and nays, which were ordered, and the motion to adjourn failed.

Yeas.. 7
Nays.. 39

Those voting in the affirmative are:

Messrs. Allen, Arledge, Burton, Dromgoole, Jones of Lincoln, Porter of Henry, and Williamson—7.

Those voting in the negative are:

Messrs. Baxter, Blizard, Brandon, Branson, Britton, Brooks, Brown of Davidson, Burkett, Byrne, Campbell, Carter, Chowning, Deaderick, Finley, Fulkerson, Gardner, Garner, Gibbs, Gibson, Gordon, Hill of Warren, Hill of Gibson, House of Davidson, Robertson and Montgomery, Ivie, Jones of Giles, Mabry, McDougal, McNabb, Morris, Nicholson, Parker, Seay, Shepard, Staley, Stephens, Thompson of Davidson, Thompson of Maury, Turner and Warner—39.

Mr. STALEY submitted the following amendment to the report of the majority:

Strike out in seventh, eighth and ninth lines the following:

"Except that each voter shall give to the Judges of Election, where he offers to vote, satisfactory evidence that he has paid the poll taxes then due from him, without which his vote cannot be received."

The section will then read: "Every man of the age of twenty-one years, being a citizen of the United States, and a citizen of the county wherein he may offer his vote, six months next preceding the day of election, shall be entitled to vote for members of the General Assembly and other civil officers, for the county or district in which he resides, and there shall be no qualification attached to the right of suffrage. All male citizens of the State shall be subject to the payment of poll taxes and to the performance of military duty within such ages as may be prescribed by law; *Provided*, that the General Assembly shall have power to enact laws requiring voters to vote in the election precincts in which they may reside, and laws to secure the freedom of elections and the purity of the ballot box."

Without coming to a conclusion, the Convention, on motion of Mr. HOUSE, of Montgomery, adjourned until to-morrow morning, at 10 o'clock.

WEDNESDAY MORNING, JANUARY 26, 1870.

The Convention met pursuant to adjournment, Mr. President BROWN in the Chair.

Prayer by the Rev. Mr. SAMPLE, a member of the Convention.

The Journal of yesterday was read and approved.

The roll was called for memorials and petitions.

AMENDMENT PROPOSED.

Mr. GARDNER submitted the following resolution, which was read and referred to the Committee on Elections:

Resolved, That in filling vacancies in all offices under this Constitution, occasioned by death, resignation or removal, the appointment or election shall be made for the unexpired term.

HOUR OF MEETING.

Mr. JONES, of Lincoln, submitted the following resolution:

Resolved, That hereafter the hour of meeting of the Convention shall be 9 o'clock, A. M.; it shall sit until 1 o'clock, P. M., and take a recess until 2½ o'clock, P. M., unless otherwise ordered by the Convention.

On motion of Mr. GARNER the rules were suspended, and the resolution was taken up, when,

On motion of Mr. BAXTER the resolution was amended by striking out 9 and substituting 9½ o'clock, and the resolution as amended was adopted by the Convention.

PROPOSITION IN LIEU OF THE MAJORITY REPORT OF THE JUDICIARY COMMITTEE.

Mr. HILL, of Gibson, submitted the following in lieu of the report of the majority of the Committee on the Judicial Department, which, on motion of Mr. HOUSE, of Montgomery, was ordered to be laid on the table, and 100 copies ordered to be printed:

ARTICLE V.

Section 1. The House of Representatives shall have the sole power of impeachment.

Sec. 2. All impeachments shall be tried by the Senate. When sitting for that purpose the Senators shall be upon oath or affirmation, *and the Chief Justice of the Court of Errors and Appeals, or, if he be on trial, the Senior Associate Judge shall preside over them.* No person shall be convicted without the concurrence of two-thirds of the Senators sworn to try the officer impeached.

Sec. 3. The House of Representatives shall elect, from their own body, three members, whose duty it shall be to prosecute impeachments. No impeachment shall be tried until the Legislature shall have adjourned *sine die*, when the Senate shall proceed to try such impeachment.

Sec. 4. The Governor, Judges of the Court of Errors and Appeals, Judges of the Supreme Courts, Judges of the Inferior Courts, Chancellors, Attorneys for the State, and Secretary of State, shall be liable to impeachment, whenever they may, in the opinion of the House of Representatives, commit any crime in their official capacity which may require disqalification; but judgment shall only extend to removal from office, and disqualification to fill any office thereafter. The party shall, nevertheless, be liable to indictment, trial, judgment and punishment, according to law.

Sec. 5. Justices of the Peace, and other civil officers, not hereinbefore mentioned, for crimes or misdemeanors in office, shall be liable to indictment in such courts as the Legislature may direct; and upon conviction, shall be removed from office by said court, as if found guilty on impeachment; and shall be subject to such other punishment as may be prescribed by law.

ARTICLE VI.

Section 1. The Judicial power of this State shall be vested in one Court of Errors and Appeals, and in three Supreme Courts, and in such Circuit, Chancery and other inferior Courts as the Legislature shall from time to time ordain and establish, and the Judges thereof, and in Justices of the Peace. The Legislature may also vest such jurisdiction in corporation courts as may be deemed necessary. Courts to be holden by Justices of the Peace may also be established.

Sec. 2. The Court of Errors and Appeals shall consist of three Judges, of whom not more than one shall reside in any one of the grand divisions of the State. They shall be elected by the qualified voters of the State at large. They shall hold one term of the Court of Errors and Appeals annually, in the city of Nashville, at such times as the Legislature shall fix. They shall designate one of their number who shall preside as Chief Justice. The concurrence of two of said Judges shall, in every case, be necessary to a decision. Every Judge of the Court of Errors and Appeals shall be not less than thirty-five years of age, and shall, before his election, have been a resident of the State five years. The jusisdiction of this Court shall be appellate only under such restrictions and regulations as may be prescribed, from time to time, by law; *Provided*, that this Court shall have jurisdiction of no cause except such as may be prosecuted to this Court from the Supreme Courts, under such restrictions and regulations as may now exist or may be fixed, from time to time, by law, for the removing of causes from Inferior Courts to Superior Courts for the correction of errors; *Provided*, that the Court of Errors and Appeals shall have jurisdiction of no civil cause, except in cases involving questions of the constitutionality of an Act of the General Assembly, or the rights and duties of public officers, when the amount involved is less than $500 00; *Provided*, the Legislature shall have power to fix, from time to time—with the exception before named—the amount over which this Court shall have jurisdiction; *Provided*, the amount shall not be less than $500 00; *Provided*, that causes involving the constitutionality of an Act of the General Assembly, or the rights and duties of public officers, shall be prosecuted direct to the Court of Errors and Appeals from such Inferior Courts as may now exist or be established, from time to time, by law, in the same manner as causes are now removed from said Inferior Courts to the present Supreme Court, and under such other restrictions and regulations as may be fixed from time to time, by law.

Sec. —. There shall be three Supreme Courts. One of said Courts shall be held at Knoxville, for the Grand Division of East Tennessee; one shall be held at Nashville, for the Grand Division of Middle Tennessee; one shall be held at Jackson, for the Grand Division of West Tennessee. The Legislature shall fix the time for the holding of these Courts. Each Court shall be composed of three Judges, one of whom shall be one of the Judges of the Court of Errors and Appeals, who shall preside as Chief Justice of the

Supreme Court. The other two Judges shall reside in the respective Grand Divisions of the State where the Court is to be held, and shall be elected by the qualified voters of said Grand Division. The concurrence of two of said Judges shall, in every case, be necessary to a decision. No Judge of the Supreme Courts shall be less than thirty years of age, and he shall, before his election, have been a resident of the State five years. His term of office shall be eight years. The jurisdiction of the Supreme Courts shall be the same as is now by law conferred upon the present Supreme Court under such other restrictions and regulations as may be fixed, from time to time, by law; *Provided*, that the Supreme Courts shall have no jurisdiction over any cause wherein is involved any question of the constitutionality of any Act of the General Assembly, or the rights and duties of public officers.

Sec. —. An Attorney General and Reporter for the State shall be appointed by the Judges of the Court of Errors and Appeals, and he shall hold his office for the term of eight years. An Attorney General for each Grand Division of the State shall be elected by the qualified voters thereof, and he shall hold his office for eight years. Attorneys for the State for any Circuit or District, as may now exist, or hereafter be established by law, shall be elected by the qualified voters of said Circuit or District, and shall hold their offices for the term of six years, or as may be fixed from time to time by law. In all cases where the Attorney for any Division or District fails or refuses to attend and prosecute, according to law, the Courts shall have power to appoint an Attorney *pro tem.*

Sec. —. Judges and Attorneys for the State may be removed from office by a concurrent vote of both Houses of the General Assembly, each House voting separately; but two-thirds of all the members elected to each House must concur in such vote; the vote shall be determined by ayes and noes, and the names of the members voting for or against the Judge or Attorney for the State, together with the cause or causes of removal, shall be entered on the Journals of each House, respectively. The Judge or Attorney for the State, against whom the Legislature may be about to proceed, shall receive notice thereof, accompanied with a copy of the causes alleged for his removal, at least ten days before the day on which either House of the General Assembly shall act thereupon.

Sec. —. The Judges of the Courts of Errors and Appeals, and the Supreme Courts and Inferior Courts, shall, at stated times, receive a compensation for their services, to be ascertained by law, which shall not be increased or diminished during the time for which they are elected. They shall not be allowed any fees or perquisites of office; nor hold any other office of trust or profit under this State, or the United States.

Sec. —. The jurisdiction of the Circuit, Chancery and other Inferior Courts, shall be as now established by law, until changed by the Legislature.

Sec. —. Judges shall not charge juries with respect to matters of fact, but may state the testimony and declare the law.

Sec. —. The Judges, Chancellors, or Justices of the Inferior Courts of Law and Equity, shall have power, in all civil cases, to issue writs of *certiorari* to remove any cause, or the transcript of the record thereof, from any inferior jurisdiction into such courts of law, on sufficient cause, supported by oath or affirmation.

Sec. —. No Judge of the Court of Errors and Appeals, or of the Supreme Courts or Inferior Courts, shall preside on the trial of any cause in the event of which he may be interested, or where either of the parties shall be connected with him by affinity or consanguinity, within such degress as may be prescribed by law, or in which he may have been of counsel, or in which he may have presided in any Inferior Court, except by the consent of all the parties. In case any or all of the Judges of the Supreme Court shall be thus disqualified from presiding on the trial of any cause or causes, the Court, or the Judges thereof, shall certify the same to the Governor of the State, and he shall forthwith specially commission the requisite number of men, of law knowledge, for the trial and determination thereof. In case of sickness of any of the Judges of the Supreme or Inferior Courts, so that they or any of them are unable to attend, the Legislature shall be authorized to make provision, by general laws, that special Judges may be appointed to attend said courts. The Legislature may, by general laws, make provision that special Judges may be appointed to hold any courts, the Judges of which shall be unable, or fail to attend or sit, or to hear any cause in which the Judge may be incompetent.

Sec. —. All writs and other process shall run in the name of the State of Tennessee; and bear test and be signed by the respective clerks. Indictments shall conclude, "*against the peace and dignity of the State.*"

Sec. —. Judges of the Court of Errors and Appeals, and of the Supreme Courts, shall appoint their clerks, who shall hold their terms of office for six years. Chancellors shall appoint their Clerks and Masters, who shall hold their offices for a period of eight years. Clerks of such Inferior Courts, as may be hereafter established, which shall be required to be holden in the respective counties of this State, shall be elected by the qualified voters thereof, for the term of four years; they shall be removed from office for malfeasance, incompetency, or neglect of duty, in such manner as may be prescribed by law.

Sec. —. No fine shall be laid on any citizen of this State that shall exceed fifty dollars, unless it shall be assessed by a jury of his peers, who shall assess the fine at the time they find the fact, if they think the fine should be more than fifty dollars.

Sec. —. The different counties of this State shall be laid off as the General Assembly may direct, into districts of convenient size, so that the whole number in each county shall not be more than twenty-five, or four for every one hundred square miles. There shall be two Justices of the Peace and one Constable elected in each district by the qualified voters therein, except districts including county towns, which shall elect three Justices and two Constables. The jurisdiction of said officers shall be co-extensive with the county. Justices of the Peace shall be elected for the term of six, and Constables for the term of two years. Upon the removal of either of said officers from the district in which he was elected, his office shall become vacant from the time of such removal. Justices of the Peace shall be commissioned by the Governor. The Legislature shall have power to provide for the appointment of an additional number of Justices of the Peace in incorporated towns.

SCHEDULE.

Sec. 1. That no inconvenience may arise from a change of the Constitution, it is declared that all civil officers of the State, except Attorney General and Reporter for the State, and the Attorneys General for the Criminal Districts or Courts of the State, and the Judges of the several courts, shall hold their offices until the expiration of their terms of service.

Sec. 2. The present Judges of the Supreme Court, and of the Circuit, Chancery, and other Inferior Courts, shall hold their offices until their successors are elected under this schedule.

Sec. 3. The election of Judges and Attorneys General, under this Constitution, shall be held on the —— day of ———, 1870, by the Sheriffs in the several counties in the manner prescribed by the Code.

AMENDMENTS PROPOSED.

Mr. McDougal submitted the following resolution, which was read and referred to the Committee on the Judicial Department:

Resolved, That the Committee on the Judicial Department be directed to inquire into and report as to the propriety of striking out the amendment adopted to the Constitution of Tennessee in 1853, which requires that the elections for Judges and Attorneys General shall not be held on the same day with elections for the State and county officers.

Mr. Stephens submitted the following amendments to Section 1, Article IV, as reported by the Committee on Elections:

1st. Strike out from the first line the word "man" and insert the word "male person."

2d. Strike out the word "six" in the third line, and insert the word "twelve."

3d. After the word "district," in the fifth line, insert the words "*or municipal corporation.*"

4th. Strike out all after the fifth line, and insert: "Each voter shall give to the judges of election where he offers to vote, satisfactory evidence that he has, at a time to be prescribed by law, paid the full taxes due by him, without which his vote cannot be received. All male citizens of the State shall be subject to the payment of poll-taxes, and to the performance of military duty within such ages as may be prescribed by law. The General Assembly shall have power to require voters to vote in the election precincts in which they may reside, and to pass laws to secure the freedom of elections and the purity of the ballot-box.

Mr. WRIGHT submitted the following resolution in lieu of Section 1 of the Schedule as reported by the majority of the Judiciary Committee:

Resolved, That in order that the interest of the people may be subserved, and that justice may be established, it be declared by this Convention that all civil officers of the State, except those in whose elections the people generally were allowed to participate, (to-wit: the Governor and Legislature,) are vacant, and that elections *by the people*, to fill all such vacancies, shall take place immediately upon the ratification of the Constitution proposed by this Convention and submitted to the people.

On motion of Mr. WRIGHT, the resolutions were referred to the Committee on Elections.

COMMITTEE ON MILITIA.

The PRESIDENT announced the following gentlemen as constituting the Special Committee on Mr. Martin's resolution, defining the terms on which the militia shall be called into service: Messrs. Martin, Stephens, Brown of Davidson, Netherland and Deaderick.

THE ELECTIVE FRANCHISE FURTHER CONSIDERED.

The Convention resumed the consideration of the unfinished business of yesterday—the report of the Committee on Franchise and Right of Suffrage, and the amendments proposed thereto; and before coming to a conclusion thereon, at 10 o'clock the Convention took a recess until 2½ o'clock P. M.

AFTERNOON SESSION.

The PRESIDENT, at 2:30 o'clock, called the Convention to order, and the Convention proceeded again to the consideration of the report of the Committee on Franchise, etc.

At 5 o'clock P. M., on motion of Mr. NICHOLSON, the Convention adjourned until to-morrow morning, at 9:30 o'clock.

THURSDAY MORNING, JANUARY 27, 1870.

The Convention met pursuant to adjournment, Mr. President BROWN in the Chair.

The Journal of yesterday was read and approved.

The roll was called for memorials and petitions.

LENGTH OF SPEECHES.

Mr. BRITTON called up his resolution, offered on Tuesday, fixing the length of time a delegate shall be allowed to speak.

Mr. BROOKS moved to amend the resolution by striking out "fifteen" and inserting "thirty."

Mr. JONES, of Giles, moved to lay the resolution and amendment on the table.

Mr. GARNER demanded the yeas and nays, which were ordered, and the motion to lay on the table failed.

Yeas...30
Nays...38

Those voting in the affirmative are:

Messrs. Allen, Bate, Baxter, Cummings, Deavenport, Dromgoole,

Fentress, Fulkerson, Gibbs, Heiskell, Henderson, Hill of Gibson, House of Williamson, House of Davidson, Robertson and Montgomery, Ivie, Jones of Giles, Key, Mabry, McDougal, Meeks, Netherland, Porter of Haywood, Porter of Henry, Shepard, Shelton, Stephens, Taylor, Thompson of Davidson, Thompson of Maury, and Williamson—30.

Those voting in the negative are:

Messrs. Arledge, Branson, Brandon, Britton, Brooks, Brown of Davidson, Brown of Henry, etc., Burkett, Byrne, Campbell, Carter, Chowning, Coffin, Deaderick, Dibbrell, Doherty, Fielder, Finley, Gardner, Garner, Gaut, Gibson, Hill of Warren, Jones of Lincoln, Kennedy, Kirkpatrick, Kyle, McNabb, Martin, Morris, Nicholson, Parker, Sample, Seay, Staley, Turner, Warner and Wright—38.

Mr. BROOKS' amendment was rejected.

Mr. JONES, of Lincoln, moved to amend the resolution by striking out "*fifteen*" and inserting "*twenty-five,*" which was accepted by Mr. Britton.

Mr. HILL, of Warren, moved to amend by inserting *fifteen* in lieu of twenty-five.

Mr. GIBBS moved the indefinite postponement of the resolution and amendment.

Mr. HEISKELL demanded the previous question, which was sustained.

Mr. GIBBS' motion to postpone indefinitely was sustained.

Yeas	44
Nays	28

Those voting in the affirmative are:

Messrs. Allen, Bate, Baxter, Blizard, Brooks, Brown of Davidson, Brown of Henry, Burton, Byrne, Campbell, Chowning, Coffin, Cummings, Cypert, Deavenport, Doherty, Dromgoole, Fentress, Fulkerson, Gibbs, Gordon, Heiskell, Henderson, Hill of Gibson, House of Williamson, House of Davidson, Robertson and Montgomery, Ivie, Jones of Giles, Key, McDougal, Martin, Meeks, Netherland, Porter of Haywood, Porter of Henry, Shepard, Shelton, Stephens, Taylor, Thompson of Davidson, Thompson of Maury, Turner, Williamson, and Wright—44.

Those voting in the negative are:

Messrs. Arledge, Branson, Brandon, Burkett, Carter, Deaderick, Dibbrell, Fielder, Finley, Gardner, Garner, Gaut, Gibson, Hill of Warren, Jones of Lincoln, Kennedy, Kirkpatrick, Kyle,

Mabry, McNabb, Morris, Nicholson, Parker, Sample, Seay, Staley, and Warner—28.

NIGHT SESSIONS.

Mr. GARNER offered the following resolutions, which lie over under the rules:

Resolved, That this Convention will meet each night of its daily sessions at 7 o'clock P. M., unless otherwise ordered.

Resolved, That this Convention will adjourn *sine die* on Monday, the 7th day of February, 1870.

ELIGIBILITY OF DELEGATES TO OFFICE.

Mr. GIBSON submitted the following preamble and resolution, which were read and referred to the Committee on Miscellaneous Provisions:

WHEREAS, It is gravely proposed to vacate and create a large number of offices upon the ratification of this Constitution; and

WHEREAS, The people may well have serious doubts as to whether these offices and vacancies are created by an uninterested disposition to benefit them, and not the members of this Convention; and

WHEREAS, It is highly proper that this Convention should show the people that delegates have not voted to create these offices and vacancies in order to fill them themselves, but that they are prompted by the purest and most disinterested patriotism; therefore,

Be it resolved and incorporated in the schedule, That no delegate in this Convention shall be eligible to fill any vacancy, or the first term of any office, created by this Constitution.

MEMORIAL.

Mr. WRIGHT presented a memorial from sundry citizens of Carroll County, against taking any portion of said county to form a new county or counties, which, without being read, was referred to the Committee on New Counties and County Lines.

AMENDMENTS WITHDRAWN.

Mr. STALEY asked and obtained leave to withdraw the amendment offered by him to the report of the majority of the Committee on Elections and the Elective Franchise, in order that the Convention may vote *singly* on the proposition of the minority, with notice that he would again offer it before final action on the report of the majority.

REPORT ON THE MILITIA.

Mr. MARTIN, from the Special Committee appointed to consider and report what limitations should be made in the manner of calling out the militia, made the following report:

The Special Committee, appointed to report upon the proposition to amend Article III in such a manner as to limit the power to call out the militia, have had the matter under consideration, and have instructed me to report the following in addition to said Article, to be styled Section 18:

"The militia shall only be called into service in case of rebellion or invasion, and then only when the General Assembly shall declare by law that the public safety requires it."

MATT. MARTIN.

On motion of Mr. JONES, of Lincoln, the Convention proceeded to the consideration of the report.

Mr. MARTIN demanded the yeas and nays upon the adoption of the amendment proposed by the Committee, which were ordered, and the amendment adopted.

Yeas.. 50
Nays.. 20

Those voting in the affirmative are:

Messrs. Blizard, Brandon, Brooks, Brown of Davidson, Brown of Henry, etc., Burkett, Burton, Byrne, Campbell, Chowning, Coffin, Cummings, Cypert, Deaderick, Deavenport, Dibbrell, Doherty, Dromgoole, Fentress, Fielder, Finley, Fulkerson, Gardner, Gaut, Gibbs, Gordon, Heiskell, Henderson, Hill of Gibson, House of Williamson, Ivie, Key, Kyle, McDougal, McNabb, Martin, Meeks, Netherland, Nicholson, Porter of Haywood, Porter of Henry, Sample, Seay, Shelton, Stephens, Taylor, Thompson of Davidson, Turner, Warner, and Wright—50.

Those voting in the negative are:

Messrs. Arledge, Bate, Baxter, Branson, Britton, Carter, Garner, Gibson, Hill of Warren, Jones of Lincoln, Jones of Giles, Kennedy, Kirkpatrick, Mabry, Morris, Parker, Shepard, Staley, Thompson of Maury, and Williamson—20.

FOR ENROLLMENT.

On motion of Mr. JONES, of Lincoln, it was ordered that Articles I and III of the Constitution as adopted by the Convention be referred to the Committee on Revision and Enrollment.

LEAVE OF ABSENCE.

On motion of Mr. STEPHENS, leave of absence was given Mr. Blackburn until Tuesday next.

THE ELECTIVE FRANCHISE FURTHER CONSIDERED.

The Convention resumed the consideration of the unfinished business of yesterday—the report of the Committee on Franchise and the proposition in lieu, and without coming to a conclusion at 1 o'clock P. M., took recess to 2½ o'clock P. M.

AFTERNOON SESSION.

Mr. HOUSE, of Davidson, Robertson and Montgomery, at 2½ o'clock called the Convention to order, and stated that the President was prevented from presiding over this body this afternoon by indisposition, and on his motion Mr. Gordon, of Hickman was called to the Chair.

THE ELECTIVE FRANCHISE FURTHER CONSIDERED.

The Convention resumed the consideration of the report of the Committee on Franchise and Right of Suffrage, and the amendment of Mr. Jones, of Lincoln, in lieu.

Mr. JONES, of Lincoln, demanded the yeas and nays upon the adoption of the amendment in lieu, which were ordered, and the amendment rejected:

Yeas.. 20
Nays.. 54

Those voting in the affirmative are:

Messrs. Arledge, Bate, Brown of Henry, etc., Campbell, Carter,

Cummings, Deavenport, Fentress, Fielder, Heiskell, Jones of Lincoln, Porter of Haywood, Porter of Henry, Shepard, Shelton, Stephens, Taylor, Warner, Williamson, and Wright—20.

Those voting in the negative are:

Messrs. Allen, Baxter, Blizard, Branson, Brandon, Britton, Brooks, Brown of Davidson, Burkett, Burton, Byrne, Chowning, Coffin, Cypert, Deaderick, Dibbrell, Doherty, Dromgoole, Finley, Fulkerson, Gardner, Garner, Gaut, Gibbs, Gibson, Gordon, Henderson, Hill of Warren, Hill of Gibson, House of Williamson, House of Davidson, Robertson and Montgomery, Ivie, Jones of Giles, Kennedy, Key, Kirkpatrick, Kyle, Mabry, McDougal, McNabb, Martin, Morris, Meeks, Netherland, Nicholson, Parker, Sample, Seay, Staley, Thompson of Davidson, Thompson of Maury, Turner, Walters, and President Brown—54.

Mr. Fentress offered the following in lieu of the majority report of the Committee on Franchise and Right of Suffrage:

ARTICLE IV.

Section 1. Every free white man of twenty-one years, being a citizen of the United States, and a citizen of the county wherein he may offer his vote six months next preceding the day of election, shall be entitled to vote for members of the General Assembly and other civil officers for the county or district in which he resides, and all persons in the State who are or may hereafter be entitled to vote in this State, shall be subject to the payment of poll-taxes and to the performance of military duty, within such ages as may be prescribed by law, but no one who is not legally entitled to vote, shall ever be required to pay a poll-tax. It is further ordered by this Convention that the question whether the negro and mulatto shall be allowed to vote equally with the white man, shall be submitted to the people of Tennessee on such day as this Convention may hereafter direct, as a separate question, so that the will of the people may be clearly gotten upon it, in such manner as this Convention may direct, and if a majority of the electors who are legally entitled to vote at said election and who do vote at said election, declare by their votes in favor of the negro or mulatto voting equally with the white man, then there shall be added as a part of Article IV the following as

Sec. 2. Every negro or mulatto of twenty-one years, being a citizen of the United States and a citizen of the county where he may offer his vote, six months next preceeding the day of election shall be entitled to vote for members of the General Assembly and other civil officers for the county or district in which he resides:

But in case a majority of the electors voting at said election shall be against allowing the negro or mulatto, equally with the white man, the elective Franchise, then Section 4, as hereinbefore first set out in Section 1.

Mr. NICHOLSON moved to lay the amendment in lieu on the table.

Mr. WILLIAMSON demanded the yeas and nays, which were ordered, and the motion to lay on the table sustained.

Yeas...52
Nays...20

Those voting in the affirmative are:

Messrs. Allen, Baxter, Blizard, Branson, Brandon, Britton, Brooks, Brown of Davidson, Burkett, Burton, Byrne, Chowning, Coffin, Cypert, Deaderick, Dibbrell, Doherty, Finley, Fulkerson, Gardner, Garner, Gaut, Gibbs, Gibson, Gordon, Henderson, Hill of Warren, Hill of Gibson, House of Williamson, House of Davidson, Robertson and Montgomery, Ivie, Jones of Giles, Kennedy, Key, Kirkpatrick, Kyle, Mabry, McDougal, McNabb, Martin, Morris, Meeks, Netherland, Nicholson, Porter of Haywood, Sample, Seay, Staley, Thompson of Davidson, Thompson of Maury and Turner—52.

Those voting in the negative are:

Messrs. Arledge, Bate, Brown of Henry, Carroll, Gibson and Madison, Campbell, Carter, Cummings, Deavenport, Dromgoole, Fentress, Fielder, Heiskell, Jones of Lincoln, Porter of Henry, Shepard, Shelton, Stephens, Taylor, Warner, Williamson and Wright—20.

On motion of Mr. TAYLOR the Convention adjourned until tomorrow morning at 9½ o'clock.

FRIDAY MORNING, JANUARY 28, 1870.

The Convention met pursuant to adjournment, Mr. President BROWN in the Chair.

The Journal of yesterday was read, and approved.

The roll was called for memorials and petitions.

11

MEMORIALS.

Mr. DIBBRELL presented memorials from a member of citizens of the County of Sequatchie praying that said County be declared a Constitutional County, which without being read were referred to the Committee on New Counties and County Lines.

Mr. FIELDER, presented a memorial from a large number of citizens, of Madison, Gibson, Haywood and Dyer Counties, praying the establishment of the County of Crockett out of portions of said Counties, which, without being read, was referred to the Committee on New Counties and County Lines.

PROPOSITION IN LIEU OF THE REPORTS OF THE MAJORITY AND MINORITY OF THE JUDICIARY COMMITTEE.

Mr. GAUT presented the following in lieu of the report of the majority and minority of the Committee on the Judiciary, which, on motion of Mr. BAXTER, was ordered to be laid on the table, and 100 copies printed for the use of the Convention :

Resolved, That that the following be received and adopted in lieu of the Majority and Minority Reports of the Committee on the Judiciary :

ARTICLE V.

IMPEACHMENT.

First Section to remain as in the present Constitution, to-wit :

Section 1. The House of Representatives shall have the sole power of impeachment.

Sec. 2. All impeachments shall be tried by the Senate; when sitting for that purpose, the Senators shall be upon oath or affirmation, and the senior Judge of the Supreme Court, or if he be on trial, the senior of the two remaining Judges, shall preside over them. No person shall be convicted without the concurrence of two-thirds of the Senators sworn to try the officer impeached.

Here follow Sections 3, 4 and 5, as in the present Constitution, to-wit :

Sec. 3. The House of Representatives shall elect, from their own body, three members, whose duty it shall be to prosecute impeachments. No impeachment shall be tried until the Legislature shall have adjourned, *sine die*, when the Senate shall proceed to try such impeachment.

Sec. 4. The Governor, Judges of the Supreme Court, Judges of the Inferior Courts, Chancellors, Attorneys for the State, and Secretary of State, shall be liable to impeachment, whenever they may, in the opinion of the House of Representatives, commit any crime in their official capacity which may require disqualification; but judgment shall only extend to removal from office, and disqualification to fill any office thereafter. The party shall, nevertheless, be liable to indictment, trial, judgment and punishment according to law.

Sec. 5. Justices of the Peace, and other civil officers, not hereinbefore mentioned, for crimes or misdemeanors in office, shall be liable to indictment in such courts as the Legislature may direct; and, upon conviction, shall be removed from office by said Court, as if found guilty on impeachment; and shall be subject to such other punishment as may be prescribed by law.

ARTICLE VI.

JUDICIAL DEPARTMENT.

Sec. 1. The Judicial power of this State shall be vested in one Supreme Court, and in such Circuit, Chancery, Criminal and other Inferior Courts, as the Legislature shall, from, time to time, ordain and establish, in the Judges thereof and in Justices of the Peace.

The 2d and 3d Sections as our present Constitution except strike out the word "*eight*" in the last clause of Section 3, and insert *twelve*, to-wit:

Sec. 2. The Supreme Court shall be composed of three Judges, one of whom shall reside in each of the grand divisions of the State; the concurrence of two of said Judges shall, in every case, be necessary to a decision. The jurisdiction of this Court shall be appellate only, under such restrictions and regulations as may, from time to time, be prescribed by law; but it may possess such other jurisdiction as is now conferred by law on the present Supreme Court. Said courts shall be held at one place, and at one place only, in each of the three grand divisions of the State.

Sec. 3. The Judges of the Supreme Court shall be elected by the qualified voters of the State at large, and the Judges of such inferior courts as the Legislature may establish shall be elected by the qualified voters residing within the bounds of any district or circuit to which such inferior Judge or Judges, either of law or equity may be assigned, by ballot, in the same manner that members of the General Assembly are elected. Courts may be established to be holden by Justices of the Peace. Judges of the Supreme Court shall be thirty-five years of age, and shall be elected for the term of *twelve* years.

Section 4, to remain as in the present Constitution, except strike out "*eight*" and insert *ten*, to-wit:

Sec. 4. The Judges of such inferior courts as the Legislature may establish, shall be thirty years of age, and shall be elected for the term of *ten* years.

Sections 5 and 6 as in our Constitution, to-wit:

Sec. 5. An Attorney General for the State shall be elected by the qualified voters of the State at large, and the Attorney for the State for any circuit or district to which a Judge of an inferior court may be assigned, shall be elected by the qualified voters within the bounds of such district or circuit, in the same manner that members to the General Assembly are elected; all said Attorneys, both for the State and circuit or district, shall hold their offices for the term of six years. In all cases where the Attorney for any district fails or refuses to attend and prosecute according to law, the court shall have power to appoint an Attorney *pro tempore.*

Sec. 6. Judges and Attorneys for the State may be removed from office by a concurrent vote of both Houses of the General Assembly, each House voting separately; but two-thirds of all the members elected to each House must concur in such vote; the vote shall be determined by ayes and noes, and the names of the members voting for or against the Judge or Attorney for the State, together with the cause or causes of removal, shall be entered on the Journals of each House respectively. The Judge or Attorney for the State, against whom the Legislature may be about to proceed, shall receive notice thereof, accompanied with a copy of the causes alleged for his removal, at least ten days before the day on which either House of the General Assembly shall act thereupon.

Sec. 7. The Judges of the Supreme Court shall, at stated times, receive a compensation for their services to be ascertained by law, which shall not be less than four thousand dollars per annum. The salaries of Circuit Judges and Chancellors, and Judges of Criminal Courts, shall be fixed by law, but shall not in any case be less than three thousand dollars per annum. No fees or perquisites of office shall attach to the office of Supreme, Circuit or Chancery Judge, or Judge of a Criminal Court, nor shall either of them hold any other office of trust or profit, under this State or the United States.

Sec. 8. The jurisdiction of the Circuit, Chancery and other Inferior Courts shall be as now established by law until changed by the Legislature.

Section 9 as in the present Constitution, to-wit:

Sec. 9. Judges shall not charge juries with respect to matters of fact, but may state the testimony and declare the law.

Sec. 10. The Judges of Inferior Courts of Law and Equity, shall have power in civil cases to issue writs of *certiorari*, to remove any cause or the transcript of the record thereof from any inferior jurisdiction into such court, on sufficient cause supported by oath or affirmation.

Sec. 11. No Judge of the Supreme or Inferior Courts shall preside on the trial of any cause in the event of which he may be interested, or where either of the parties shall be connected with him by affinity or consanguinity within such degrees as may be prescribed by law, or in which he may have been of counsel, or in which he may have presided in an inferior court, except by the consent of all the parties. In case all or any of the Judges of the Supreme Court shall be thus disqualified from presiding on the trial of any cause or causes, the Court or the Judges thereof shall certify the same to the Governor of the State, and he shall forthwith specially commission the requisite number of men of law knowledge for the trial and determination thereof.

The Legislature may by general laws make provision that Special Judges may be appointed to hold any courts, the Judges of which shall be unable, or fail to attend or sit; or to hear any cause in which the Judge may be incompetent.

Sections 12, 13, 14 and 15, as in the present Constitution, to-wit:

Sec. 12. All writs and other process shall run in the name of the State of Tennessee, and bear test and be signed by the respective Clerks. Indictments shall conclude, "against the peace and dignity of the State."

Sec. 13. Judges of the Supreme Court shall appoint their Clerks, who shall hold their offices for six years. Chancellors (if Courts of Chancery shall be established) shall appoint their Clerks and Masters, who shall hold their offices for a period of six years. Clerks of such inferior courts, as may be hereafter established, which shall be required to be holden in the respective counties of this State, shall be elected by the qualified voters thereof, for the term of four years; they shall be removed from office for malfeasance, incompetency, or neglect of duty, in such manner as may be prescribed by law.

Sec. 14. No fine shall be laid on any citizen of this State that shall exceed fifty dollars, unless it shall be assessed by a jury of his peers, who shall assess the fine at the time they find the fact, if they think the fine should be more than fifty dollars.

Sec. 15. The different counties of this State shall be laid off, as the General Assembly may direct, into districts of convenient size, so that the whole number in each county shall not be more than twenty-five, or four for every one hundred square miles. There shall be two Justices of the Peace and one Constable elected in each district, by the qualified voters therein, except districts including county towns, which shall elect three Justices and two Constables. The jurisdiction of said officers shall be co-extensive with the county. Justices of the Peace shall be elected for the term of six, and Constables for the term of two years. Upon the removal of either of said officers from the district in which he was elected, his office shall become vacant from the time of such removal. Justices of the Peace shall be commissioned by the Governor. The Legislature shall have power to provide for the appointment of an additional number of Justices of the Peace in incorporated towns.

SCHEDULE.

To meet present emergencies, and relieve the dockets of the Supreme Court of the great accumulation of causes *now* upon them, it shall be the duty of the Governor of the State, immediately after the ratification of the amended Constitution, to appoint two additional Supreme Judges, who, together with the present Supreme Judges or their successors, shall compose the Supreme Court of the State, for the time being—who shall sit together and try causes—the concurrence of three being necessary to a decision. Said two additional Supreme Judges shall receive, each, the same compensation as each one of the other three Judges. And said five Supreme Judges shall hold their office until the first election for Supreme Judges under this schedule. At the first election of Supreme Judges under this schedule, and forever thereafter, only three Supreme Judges shall be elected, as provided for in Section 3, Article VI, of this Constitution.

That no inconveniencies may arise from a change of the Constitution, it is declared that all civil officers of this State, except the Attorney-General and Reporter for the State, the several District Attorneys-General, and the Judges of the several courts, shall hold their respective offices until the expiration of the present term of service.

The present Supreme Judges and those to be appointed by the Governor, also the Circuit Judges and Chancellors, and Judges of Criminal Courts and other inferior courts, shall hold their office until their successors are elected under this schedule. The present Attorney-General and Reporter, and the several District Attorneys-General, shall hold their office until their successors are elected under this schedule.

The first election for Circuit Judges and Chancellors and Judges of Criminal Courts, and District Attorneys-General, shall be held on the —— day of ———, 1870, by the Sheriffs of the several counties, in the manner prescribed by the Code of Tennessee.

The first election for Judges of the Supreme Court and for an Attorney-General and Reporter for the State, shall be held on the first Tuesday of May, 1872.

MEMORIAL.

Mr. JONES, of Lincoln, presented a memorial from sundry citizens, praying the creation of a new county out of portions of Lincoln, Franklin and Bedford Counties; which, without being read, was referred to the Committee on New Counties and County Lines.

Mr. TURNER, from the Committee on Miscellaneous Provisions,

made the following report, which, on motion of Mr. TAYLOR, was ordered to be laid on the table, and 100 copies printed for the use of the Convention:

REPORT ON MISCELLANEOUS MATTERS.

MR. PRESIDENT: The Committee on Miscellaneous Provisions, having under consideration the various subjects referred to them, instruct me to report the following amendments, and recommend their adoption. The Committee ask to be discharged from the consideration of those questions not reported upon:

Taking up Article XI, I am instructed to recommend that said Article be amended as follows:

At the end of Section 3, add as follows:

"The Legislature shall have the right, at any time, by law, to submit to the people the question of calling a Convention to alter, reform or abolish this Constitution, and when, upon such submission, a majority of all the votes cast shall be in favor of said proposition, then delegates shall be chosen, and the Convention shall assemble in such mode and manner as shall be prescribed."

After Section 5, add a section as follows:

Sec. —. "The Legislature shall have no power to change the names of persons, or to pass Acts adopting or legitimating persons, but shall, by general laws, confer this power on the courts."

After Section 11, insert a section as follows:

Sec. —. "No member of the Legislature nor Convention, or judicial officer of this State shall receive, while in office, either directly or indirectly, any gift, gratuity, fee or reward from any person or corporation, otherwise than by the general law of the land."

After the last Section, insert the following Section:

Sec. —. "A homestead, in the hands of each head of a family, in this State, occupied as a residence, together with all the improvements on the same, to the value of not less than one thousand dollars, shall be exempt from forced sale under any process of law during the lifetime of such head of a family, and the minority of his or her children, and shall not be alienated without the joint consent of husband and wife, when that relation exists; but no property shall be exempt from sale for taxes or for the payment of obligations contracted for the purchase of said premises, or for the erection of improvements thereon.

"The Legislature may increase the amount of this exemption."

After the last Section insert the following Section:

Sec. —. "The intermarriage of white persons with negroes, mulattoes, or persons of mixed blood, descended from a negro to the third generation, inclusive, is prohibited."

"The Legislature shall enforce this section by appropriate legislation."

I am instructed to report an amendment to Article II, Section 25, so as to make it read as follows:

"No person who heretofore hath been, or may hereafter be a collector or holder of public moneys, shall hold any civil office under this State, until such person shall have accounted for and paid into the Treasury all sums for which he may be accountable or liable."

I am instructed to report the following section, in lieu of Article VII, Section 1, so as to make the office of Trustee a Legislative office, if the same shall be retained by them, instead of having it a Constitutional office.

Section 1. "There shall be elected in each county, by the qualified voters therein, one Sheriff and one Register—the Sheriff for two years, and the Register for four years; *Provided*, that no person shall be eligible to the office of Sheriff more than six years in any term of eight years."

"There shall be elected for each county, by the Justices of the Peace, one Coroner and one Ranger, who shall hold their offices for two years. Said officers shall be removed for malfeasance, or neglect of duty, in such manner as may be prescribed by law."

A portion of the Committee differ with a majority as to a portion of the propositions before them, but agree to the greater part of the report.

Respectfully submitted,
JAMES J. TURNER,
Chairman.

LEAVES OF ABSENCE.

On motion of Mr. STEPHENS, leave of absence was granted Mr. Hill, of Gibson, for to-morrow.

On motion of Mr. TURNER, leave of absence was granted Mr. Seay for to-morrow.

On motion of Mr. BURTON, leave of absence for to-morrow was granted to Mr. Arledge.

SPECIAL ORDER.

On motion of Mr. HEISKELL, the report of the Judiciary Committee was made the special order for Tuesday next.

THE ELECTIVE FRANCHISE FURTHER CONSIDERED.

The Convention proceeded to the consideration of the unfinished business of yesterday—the report of the Committee on Franchise.

Mr. STALEY offered the following amendment:

That all parts of the report of the majority of the Committee on Elections and Elective Franchise contained in Article IV, Section 1, as recommended by said Committee, beginning with the word "and" in the 6th line, and ending with the word "received" in the 9th line be stricken out.

The foregoing amendment having been acted on in a different form, was not urged by Mr. Staley.

Mr. STEPHENS offered the following in lieu of Section 1, Article IV, as reported by the Committee on Elections:

ARTICLE IV.

Section 1. Every male person of the age of twenty-one years, being a citizen of the United States, and of the county wherein he may offer his vote for one year next preceeding the day of election, and a resident in the civil district wherein he may offer his vote for six months next preceding the day of election, shall be entitled to vote for members of the General Assembly and other civil officers of the county or district in which he may reside. Each voter shall give to the Judges of election satisfactory evidence that he has paid all poll taxes due by him up to some preceding period to be fixed by the Legislature: without which his vote cannot be received.

All male citizens of the State shall be subject to the payment of poll taxes and to the performance of military duty, within such ages as may be prescribed by law. The Legislature shall pass laws securing the freedom of elections and the purity of the ballot box.

Mr. STEPHENS subsequently withdrew his amendment.

Mr. JONES, of Lincoln, submitted the following amendment:

Strike out all after the word "except" in the seventh line, to and including the word "received" in the ninth line, and insert as herein prescribed, and the right to vote shall be determined by the Judges of the election without a tax receipt or certificate of registration.

Mr. HEISKELL moved to lay the amendment of Mr. Jones on the table.

Mr. JONES, of Lincoln, demanded the yeas and nays, which were ordered, and the motion to lay on the table sustained.

Yeas...45
Nays...28

Those voting in the affirmative are:

Messrs. Allen, Baxter, Brandon, Brown of Davidson, Brown of

Henry, etc., Burkett, Burton, Byrne, Campbell, Coffin, Cypert, Deaderick, Deavenport, Dibbrell, Doherty, Dromgoole, Fielder, Gardner, Garner, Gibbs, Gordon, Heiskell, Henderson, Hill of Gibson, House of Williamson, House of Davidson, Robertson and Montgomery, Ivie, Jones of Giles, Kennedy, Key, Kirkpatrick, Mabry, McDougal, Meeks, Nicholson, Porter of Haywood, Porter of Henry, Seay, Shepard, Shelton, Stephens, Thompson of Davidson, Thompson of Maury, Turner and Wright—45.

Those voting in the negative are:

Messrs. Arledge, Bate, Blizard, Branson, Britton, Brooks, Carter, Chowning, Cummings, Finley, Fentress, Fulkerson, Gaut, Gibson, Hill of Warren, Jones of Lincoln, Kyle, McNabb, Martin, Morris, Netherland, Parker, Sample, Staley, Taylor, Walters, Warner and Williamson—28.

LEAVE TO VOTE.

Mr. President BROWN, in accordance with leave granted on yesterday, recorded his vote against the amendment in lieu of the majority report of the Committee on Franchise, offered by Mr. Jones, of Lincoln.

Mr. WALTERS was granted leave to record his vote on the same proposition.

ELECTIVE FRANCHISE RESUMED.

Mr. HEISKELL offered the following amendment:

Article IV. In third line strike out the word "six" and insert "twelve."

On motion of Mr. SEAY the amendment was laid on the table.

Mr. PORTER, of Henry, submitted the following amendment:

Every male person of the age of twenty-one years, being a citizen of the United States, and a citizen of the county wherein he may offer his vote six months next preceding the day of election shall be a voter; but such voter shall have been for thirty days next preceding the election, a resident of the precinct or ward in which he offers to vote, and he shall vote in said precinct or ward, and not elsewhere. And there shall be no further qualification attached to the right of suffrage. All male citizens of the State shall be subject to the payment of poll taxes and to the performance of military duty, and the General Assembly shall prescribe by law the ages within which military service shall be rendered.

Mr. SEAY offered the following in lieu of Mr. Porter's amendment:

Resolved, That Article IV, Section 1, as reported by the majority of the Committee on Elections and Elective Franchise, be amended by striking out all after the words "shall be" in the fourth line, to the word "resides" in the fifth line, inclusive, and insert the words "*a voter*" so that the first five lines of said Article and Section shall read as follows: "Every man of the age of twenty-one years, being a citizen of the United States, and a citizen of the county wherein he may offer his vote, six months next preceding the day of election, shall be a voter."

Mr. FULKERSON moved to lay the amendment on the table.

Mr. SEAY demanded the yeas and nays, which were ordered, and the motion to lay on the table sustained.

Yeas..62
Nays..11

Those voting in the affirmative are:

Messrs. Allen, Baxter, Blizard, Branson, Brandon, Britton, Brooks, Brown of Davidson, Brown of Henry, etc., Burkett, Byrne, Campbell, Carter, Chowning, Coffin, Cummings, Cypert, Deaderick, Deavenport, Doherty, Dromgoole, Fielder, Finley, Fulkerson, Garner, Gaut, Gibbs, Gibson, Gordon, Heiskell, Henderson, Hill of Gibson, House of Williamson, House of Davidson, Robertson and Montgomery, Ivie, Jones of Lincoln, Jones of Giles, Kennedy, Key, Kirkpatrick, Kyle, Mabry, McDougal, McNabb, Morris, Meeks, Netherland, Nicholson, Parker, Porter of Henry, Sample, Shepard, Shelton, Staley, Stephens, Taylor, Thompson of Davidson, Turner, Walters, Warner, Williamson and Wright—62.

Those voting in the negative are:

Messrs. Arledge, Bate, Burton, Dibbrell, Fentress, Gardner, Hill of Warren, Martin, Porter of Haywood, Seay, and Thompson of Maury—11.

Mr. BAXTER moved to lay the amendment of Mr. Porter, of Henry, on the table.

Mr. TAYLOR demanded the yeas and nays, which were ordered, and the motion to lay on the table sustained.

Yeas..47
Nays..26

Those voting in the affirmative are:

Messrs. Allen, Bate, Baxter, Blizard, Brandon, Brown of Davidson, Burkett, Burton, Byrne, Campbell, Chowning, Coffin, Cypert, Deaderick, Deavenport, Doherty, Dromgoole, Fielder, Gardner,

Garner, Gaut, Gibson, Gordon, Heiskell, Henderson, House of Williamson, House of Davidson, Robertson and Montgomery, Jones of Giles, Kennedy, Key, Kirkpatrick, Mabry, McDougal, Meeks, Netherland, Nicholson, Parker, Sample, Seay, Shepard, Shelton, Stephens, Thompson of Davidson, Thompson of Maury, Turner, Walters and Warner—47.

Those voting in the negative are:

Messrs. Arledge, Branson, Britton, Brooks, Brown of Henry, etc., Carter, Cummings, Dibbrell, Fentress, Finley, Fulkerson, Gibbs, Hill of Warren, Hill of Gibson, Ivie, Jones of Lincoln, Kyle, McNabb, Martin, Morris, Porter of Haywood, Porter of Henry, Staley, Taylor, Williamson and Wright—26.

The Convention took a recess until 2½ o'clock P. M.

AFTERNOON SESSION.

Mr. President BROWN called the Convention to order at 2½ o'clock P. M.

Mr. HEISKELL submitted the following amendment to the report of the majority of the Committee on Franchise, which was adopted by the Convention:

AMENDMENT IN SECOND LINE.

After the words "citizen of the United States and a" strike out "citizen," and insert "*resident of this State for twelve months, and,*" so as to read, "Being a citizen of the United States and resident of this State for twelve months, and of the county," etc.

Mr. KENNEDY offered the following amendment:

After the word "months," in third line, insert "and of the election district or ward sixty days."

Mr. NICHOLSON moved to amend the amendment by striking out "sixty" and inserting "thirty," which was accepted by Mr. Kennedy.

Mr. BURTON moved to lay the amendment on the table.

Mr. Cypert demanded the yeas and nays, which were ordered, and the motion to lay on the table was sustained.

Yeas...45
Nays...24

Those voting in the affirmative are:

Messrs. Baxter, Blizard, Branson, Britton, Burkett, Burton, Carter, Coffin, Cummings, Cypert, Deaderick, Deavenport, Dibbrell, Doherty, Finley, Fulkerson, Gaut, Gibbs, Gibson, Gordon, Henderson, Hill of Warren, House of Williamson, Ivie, Jones of Lincoln, Key, Kirkpatrick, Kyle, Mabry, McNabb, Martin, Morris, Meeks, Netherland, Nicholson, Parker, Sample, Seay, Shepard, Staley, Taylor, Walters, Warner, Williamson and Wright —45.

Those voting in the negative are:

Messrs. Bate, Brandon, Brooks, Brown of Davidson, Brown of Henry, etc., Byrne, Campbell, Chowning, Dromgoole, Fentress, Fielder, Gardner, Garner, Heiskell, House of Davidson, Robertson and Montgomery, Jones of Giles, Kennedy, McDougal, Porter of Haywood, Porter of Henry, Shelton, Stephens, Thompson of Davidson and Turner—24.

Mr. Gibson offered the following amendment:

Strike out all between the words "suffrage," in the 6th line, and the word "provided," in the 12th line, and insert the word "other" after the word "no" in the 6th line, so that the section shall read thus:

Sec. 1st. Every man of the age of twenty-one years, being a citizen of the United States and a citizen of the county wherein he may offer his vote six months next preceding the day of election, shall be entitled to vote for members of the General Assembly and other civil officers for the county or district in which he resides, and there shall be no other qualification attached to the right of suffrage: *Provided,* That the General Assembly shall have power to enact laws requiring voters to vote in the election precincts in which they may reside, and laws to secure the freedom of elections and the purity of the ballot-box.

The amendment was ruled out of order, as another proposition, embracing the same in substance, had been voted on and rejected.

Mr. Gibson moved to reconsider the vote laying the amendment of Mr. Jones of Lincoln, on the table.

Mr. Kennedy moved to lay the motion to reconsider on the table.

Mr. Gibson demanded the yeas and nays, which were ordered, and the motion to lay on the table was sustained.

Yeas..40
Nays...... 27

Those voting in the affirmative are:

Messss. Bate, Baxter, Blizard, Brandon, Brown of Davidson, Burkett, Burton, Byrne, Campbell, Coffin, Cummings, Deaderick, Deavenport, Dibbrell, Doherty, Dromgoole, Fielder, Gardner, Garner, Gordon, Heiskell, Henderson, House of Williamson, House of Davidson, Robertson and Montgomery, Jones of Giles, Kennedy, Key, Kirkpatrick, McDougal, Meeks, Nicholson, Porter of Haywood, Seay, Shepard, Shelton, Stephens, Taylor, Thompson of Davidson, Turner and Walters--40.

Those voting in the negative are:

Messrs. Branson, Britton, Brooks, Brown of Henry, Carroll, Gibson and Madison, Carter, Chowning, Cypert, Finley, Fulkerson, Gaut, Gibbs, Gibson, Hill of Warren, Ivie, Jones of Lincoln, Kyle, Mabry, McNabb. Martin, Netherland, Parker, Porter of Henry, Sample, Staley, Warner, Williamson and Wright—27.

Mr. HEISKELL offered the following amendment:

In the 9th line strike out the words " then due by him," and insert, " For such preceding period as the Legislature shall prescribe." Which was adopted.

Mr. HEISKELL submitted the following amendment:

In the 9th line, after the words of last amendment, insert, "And at such time as may be prescribed by law." Which was adopted by the Convention.

Mr. WARNER moved to amend by striking out the word " poll " wherever it occurs in the report of the majority, etc.

Mr. HOUSE of Davidson, Robertson and Montgomery, moved to lay the motion on the table.

Mr. WARNER demanded the yeas and nays, which were ordered, and the motion to lay on the table sustained.

Yeas..54
Nays..14

Those voting in the affirmative are:

Messrs. Bate, Baxter, Blizard, Brandon, Britton, Brown of Davidson, Brown of Henry, etc., Burkett, Burton, Byrne, Campbell, Carter, Chowning, Coffin, Cummings, Cypert, Deaderick, Deavenport, Dibbrell, Doherty, Dromgoole, Fentress, Fielder, Fulkerson, Gardner, Garner, Gaut, Gibbs, Gordon, Heiskell, Henderson, House of Williamson, House of Davidson, Robertson and Montgomery, Ivie, Jones of Giles, Kennedy, Key, Kirkpatrick, Kyle, Mabry, McDougal, McNabb, Meeks, Nicholson, Porter of

Haywood, Seay, Shepard, Shelton, Staley, Stephens, Taylor, Turner, Walters and Wright—54.

Those voting in the negative are:

Messrs. Branson, Brooks, Finley, Gibson, Hill of Warren, Jones of Lincoln, Martin, Netherland, Parker, Porter of Henry, Sample, Thompson of Davidson Warner, and Williamson—14.

Mr. KENNEDY submitted the following amendment:

Strike out the words "laws requiring voters to vote in the election precincts in which they may reside," and insert at end of the 5th line, "*who shall vote in the district or ward in which they may reside.*"

Mr. CYPERT moved to lay the amendment on the table, and demanded the yeas and nays on his motion, which were ordered, and the motion to lay on the table sustained.

Yeas..45
Nays..23

Those voting in the affirmative are:

Messrs. Bate, Baxter, Blizard, Branson, Britton, Burkett, Burton, Byrne, Carter, Coffin, Cummings, Cypert, Deaderick, Deavenport, Dibbrell, Dromgoole, Fentress, Finley, Fulkerson, Gibbs, Gibson, Gordon, Henderson, House of Williamson, Ivie, Jones of Lincoln, Key, Kirkpatrick, Kyle, Mabry, McDougal, McNabb, Martin, Meeks, Netherland, Nicholson, Parker, Sample, Seay, Shepard, Staley, Taylor, Walters, Warner and Williamson—45.

Those voting in the negative are:

Messrs. Brandon, Brooks, Brown of Davidson, Brown of Henry, Carroll, Gibson and Madison, Campbell, Chowning, Doherty, Fielder, Gardner, Garner, Gaut, Heiskell, Hill of Warren, House of Davidson, Robertson and Montgomery, Jones of Giles, Kennedy, Porter of Haywood, Porter of Henry, Shelton, Stephens, Thompson of Davidson, Turner and Wright—23.

Mr. COFFIN submitted the following amendment:

ARTICLE IV.

Section 1. Every man of the age of twenty-one years, being a citizen of the United States, and a citizen of the State twelve months, and of the county wherein he may offer his vote six months next preceding the day of election, shall be a voter, and may be required by law to give to the Judges of election, where he offers to vote, satisfactory evidence that he has paid the poll-tax then due by him, without which his vote cannot be received, and all male citizens, etc., as in report of Committee.

Mr. FULKERSON moved to amend the amendment by striking out the word "may" and inserting "shall."

Mr. PORTER, of Haywood, moved to lay the amendment on the table.

Mr. COFFIN demanded the yeas and nays, which were ordered, and the motion to lay on the table sustained.

Yeas.. 41
Nays.. 25

Those voting in the affirmative are:

Messrs. Bate, Baxter, Brandon, Brooks, Brown of Davidson, Burkett, Burton, Campbell, Carter, Chowning, Cummings, Deaderick, Dibbrell, Doherty, Dromgoole, Fielder, Gardner, Garner, Gaut, Gordon, Heiskell, Henderson, House of Williamson, House of Davidson, Robertson and Montgomery, Jones of Giles, Kennedy, Key, Kirkpatrick, McDougal, McNabb, Meeks, Nicholson, Porter of Haywood, Porter of Henry, Seay, Shepard, Shelton, Stephens, Thompson of Davidson, Turner and Wright—41.

Those voting in the negative are:

Messrs. Blizard, Branson, Britton, Brown of Henry, etc., Byrne, Coffin, Cypert, Deavenport, Fentress, Finley, Fulkerson, Gibbs, Gibson, Hill of Warren, Ivie, Kyle, Mabry, Martin, Netherland, Parker, Sample, Staley, Taylor, Walters and Warner—25.

Messrs. JONES, of Lincoln, and WILLIAMSON, were excused by the Convention from voting on the foregoing proposition.

Mr. BURTON moved to amend by striking out the word "*man*" in the first line and inserting the words "male person."

Mr. NICHOLSON demanded the *previous question*, which demand was sustained.

The vote was taken, and Mr. BURTON'S amendment adopted.

Article IV, as amended, reads as follows:

Every male person of the age of twenty-one years, being a citizen of the United States, and a resident of this State for twelve months, and of the county wherein he may offer his vote six months next preceding the day of election, shall be entitled to vote for members of the General Assembly and other civil officers for the county or district in which he resides, and there shall be no qualification attached to the right of suffrage, except that each voter shall give to the Judges of election, where he offers to vote, satisfactory evidence that he has paid the poll-taxes for such preceding period as the Legislature shall prescribe, and at such time as may be prescribed by law, without which his vote cannot be received, and all male citizens of the State shall be subject to the payment of poll-taxes and to the performance of military duty, within such ages as may be prescribed by law; *Provided,* That the General Assembly shall have power to enact laws requiring voters to vote in the election precincts in which they may reside, and laws to secure the freedom of elections and the purity of the ballot-box.

Mr. JONES, of Lincoln, demanded the yeas and nays on the adoption of the Article as amended, which were ordered, and the Article adopted:

Yeas.. 56
Nays.. 18

Those voting in the affirmative are:

Messrs. Allen, Bate, Baxter, Blizard, Brandon, Britton, Brown of Davidson, Burkett, Burton, Byrne, Coffin, Chowning, Cummings, Cypert, Deaderick, Deavenport, Dibbrell, Doherty, Dromgoole, Fielder, Fulkerson, Gardner, Garner, Gaut, Gibbs, Gordon, Heiskell, Henderson, Hill of Warren, Hill of Gibson, House of Williamson, House of Davidson, Robertson and Montgomery, Ivie, Jones of Giles, Kennedy, Key, Kirkpatrick, Kyle, McDougal, McNabb, Martin, Morris, Meeks, Netherland, Nicholson, Porter of Haywood, Seay, Shelton, Stephens, Thompson of Davidson, Thompson of Maury, Turner, Warner, Walters, Wright and President Brown—56.

Those voting in the negative are:

Messrs. Arledge, Branson, Brooks, Brown of Henry, etc., Campbell, Carter, Fentress, Finley, Gibson, Jones of Lincoln, Mabry, Parker, Porter of Henry, Sample, Shepard, Staley, Taylor and Williamson—18.

Mr. NICHOLSON moved to reconsider the vote adopting said Article IV, and moved to lay the motion to reconsider on the table, which latter motion was sustained.

The Convention, on motion, adjourned until to-morrow morning at 9½ o'clock.

SATURDAY MORNING, JANUARY 29, 1870.

The Convention met pursuant to adjournment, Mr. President Brown in the Chair.

Prayer by the Rev. Mr. Sample, a member of this body.

The Journal of yesterday was read and approved.

LEAVE TO VOTE.

Mr. Allen asked and obtained leave to record his vote in favor of Article IV, adopted on yesterday.

Mr. Thompson, of Maury, was, on his motion, allowed to record his vote in favor of Article IV.

CHANGE OF VOTES.

Mr. McNabb asked and obtained leave to change his vote on Article IV, he having voted in the negative on yesterday.

Mr. Walters asked and obtained leave to change his vote on Article IV, he having voted in the negative under a misapprehension.

PROTEST.

Mr. Staley presented the following protest against the action of the majority in adopting Article IV on yesterday:

"The undersigned having voted against the amendment proposed by a majority of the Committee on Elections and Elective Franchise, avails himself of his right to enter upon the Journal the reasons for his dissent. The majority of said Committee have reported, 'That each voter shall give to the judges of election where he offers to vote, satisfactory evidence that he has paid his poll-taxes then due by him, without which his vote cannot be received.' The undersigned is unwilling to aid in placing any restriction of the kind on the exercise of this great and important right for the reasons following:

1. It is a property qualification.
2. Many good men, whose only fault is their poverty, will be deprived of the elective franchise.

3. The poll-tax may be increased to such an extent as to amount to a prohibition of the exercise of this right by many.

4. It will still further corrupt the ballot-box.

5. The tendency of power in this country is to steal continually from the hands of the many into the hands of the few. This clause in the amendment, proposed by the majority, will encourage this tendency, and give to the opulent candidate an advantage over his less fortunate opponent, which he should not have.

It is regretted that the majority of the Committee felt it their duty to insert this clause, for in all other respects the report is unobjectionable, and but for this clause would be cheerfully supported.

W. B. STALEY.

PROTEST.

Mr. GIBSON presented the following protest, which, at his request, was ordered to be spread on the Journal:

The undersigned cannot satisfy their sense of duty to themselves and to their constituents without stating in full the reasons that prompted their vote against the 1st Section of the 4th Article of the Amended Constitution, known as the Franchise Section. That section requires that every voter *before he can vote* shall produce "satisfactory evidence" to the judges of election *that he has paid his poll-tax.* Had it not been for this required prepayment of the poll-tax the undersigned would gladly have voted for said section. Their constituents now vote without any tax restriction, and they cannot consent to impose such restriction upon them; they favor the removal of *all* restrictions, and not the creation of new ones.

But the undersigned are firm believers in the doctrine that suffrage is a *right* and not a *privilege*—as much a right as life, liberty or property—a right not to be limited and not to be restricted except as to age, time and place; and above all, a right not to be bestowed on the rich *in preference* to the poor. Suffrage is the political means of self-defense, and the disfranchised man is, or soon will be, a slave. Such being their cardinal doctrine, the undersigned would enumerate the following minor reasons for their vote:

1st. *The right to restrict the elective franchise implies the right to destroy it.*

If *one* obstacle can be placed between the voter and the ballot-box, the entire road can be closed. If one qualification can be required, so can *another*, so can *many.* Is the payment of money a better pre-requisite for *voting* than is proof of loyalty, or of intelligence or morality?

2d. *The required pre-payment of the poll-tax is an unjust discrimination against the poor man.* What is taxation? Taxation is the price of protection. But the poor man, having but little property, needs but little protection. And yet, by said section, the poor man has *just the same tax* to pay before he can vote as the rich man.

3d. *The required pre-payment of the poll-tax as a qualification for voting is more oppressive to the rich than a property qualification.*

Where there is a property qualification the voter can vote and pay his poll-tax afterwards. But here he must pay his poll-tax before he can vote at all. In truth, this whole thing is nothing but a property qualification in *disguise.*

4th. *The required pre-payment of the poll-tax will give the rich candidate an unjust but great advantage over a poor candidate.*

The rich candidate, in person or through friends, can pay the poll-tax of every poor man favorable to his election, while the poor men, favorable to the poor candidate, will in many cases be unable to vote. And here the door is opened to infinite bribery and infinite corruption in Tennessee politics.

5th. *The required pre-payment of the poll-tax will enable a partisan tax collector to disfranchise many voters.* Suppose the tax-collector should refuse to receive the poll-tax from certain voters, or should absent himself, for political purposes, or should resign or die shortly before an election, how easily could he thus change the result of an election, and defeat the true will of the people. We see here commissioners of registration with a *new* name!

6th. *The required pre-payment of the poll-tax only substitutes a tax receipt for the present voting certificate.* The voter has to produce "satisfactory evidence" to the judges of election that he has paid his poll-tax. What is "satisfactory evidence?" It is legal evidence sufficient to satisfy the *judicial* mind; and that legal evidence the courts will quickly declare must be a tax receipt, the most odious of voting certificates.

7th. *The required prepayment of the poll-tax will enable partisan judges of election to disfranchise legal voters.* Democratic judges will be "satisfied" with little or no "evidence" when a Democrat offers his vote; but will require the most "satisfactory evidence," to-wit: a tax receipt, when a Republican offers his vote, and *vice versa.* How monstrous the inducement to corruption!

8th. *The required pre-payment of the poll-tax will be the mother of infinite contests and strife in elections.*

In consequence of the possible frauds above mentioned being actually perpetrated, many lawful voters will be practically disfranchised, and many unlawful voters allowed to vote. Fraudulent tax receipts will be forged. Perjury will usher in many a vote. Bribery will luxuriate around the ballot-box. Poor men will stand back with a sigh, while the rich put in their votes. Challenges will be endless; and the resulting strife and bad feeling infinite. Nobody will be satisfied. The ballot will lose its dignity. Elections will become a farce; and—but we prefer to drop the curtain upon the last scene in this horrid drama.

And therefore it is, that the undersigned predict that this required pre-payment of the poll-tax will be odious to the people. It will array the poor men of Tennessee, the men who fight your battles, and who constitute your wealth and your strength, in solid phalanx against that Constitution which strikes at the most precious of all their rights. It will awaken a breeze of opposition in every settlement from the Blue Ridge to the Mississippi; and if that breeze is swelled into a storm by the advocates of white suffrage, and that storm is swelled into a tempest by the removal of the existing judiciary; and that tempest swelled into a tornado by the friends of free schools, then will this fabric of government, we are here erecting, be swept away, and "like the baseless fabric of a vision, leave not a wreck behind."

For the foregoing considerations, the undersigned protest against so much of said franchise section as requires the pre-payment of poll-tax as the condition of voting; and ask that this their protest be spread upon the Journal.

HENRY R. GIBSON.
JAMES W. BRANSON.
JAMES C. PARKER,
W. H. FINLEY,
R. P. BROOKS.

The roll was called for Memorials and Petitions.

AMENDMENT PROPOSED.

Mr. GORDON offered the following resolution:

Resolved, That the Committee on Miscellaneous Subjects be instructed to inquire and report whether a provision shall not be inserted in the Constitution appropriating for ever all revenue derived from poll-taxes for the use of the State to the purposes of education in common schools throughout the State.

On motion of Mr. GORDON, it was ordered that the foregoing resolutions, and kindred propositions, be referred to a Special Committee of seven, to be appointed by the President.

JUDICIARY.

Mr. NICHOLSON submitted the following resolution, which was read, and on motion of Mr. Jones, of Lincoln, was ordered to be laid on the table, and 100 copies printed for the use of the Convention:

Resolved, That before taking up the reports of the majority or minority of the Judiciary Committee, or of any of the substitutes therefor offered to the Convention, it is expedient that the judgment of the Convention be taken on the following propositions, viz:

1st. It is the judgment of the Convention that the offices now held by the Supreme Judges, Chancellors, Circuit Judges, Criminal Judges, Attorney General and Reporter for the State, and District Attorneys, shall be vacated after the ratification by the people of the amended Constitution, at such time as may be therein prescribed.

2d. It is the judgment of the Convention that the Supreme Judges, Chancellors, Circuit Judges, Criminal Judges, Attorney and Reporter for the State, and the States Attorneys for the Districts be appcinted by the Governor, by and with the advice and consent of the Senate.

3d. It is the judgment of the Convention that a Special Commission be appointed by the Governor, by and with the advice of the Senate, to consist of three lawyers in each division of the State, to sit as judges, with full jurisdiction to hear and determine all the causes pending in the Supreme Court at Knoxville, Nashville, and Jackson, their commissions to expire on the 1st of October, 1871.

Resolved, That upon the determination by the Convention of these propositions, the majority and minority reports, together with the several substitutes, be recommitted to the Judiciary Committee, with instructions to prepare and report a plan of judicial reform in pursuance of the judgment of the Convention on said propositions.

AMENDMENTS PROPOSED.

Mr. HEISKELL submitted the following amendment to Article XI, Section 7:

The Legislature shall have power to pass a statute of limitations applicable to the lands which have been granted by this State, on payment of entry taker's fees only, different from the general statute of limitation in regard to lands. Which was read and referred to the Committee on the Legislative Department.

Mr. FENTRESS submitted the following resolution, which was read and referred to the Special Committee to be raised on the subject of Common Schools:

Resolved, That the Committee on Miscellaneous Provisions be instructed to inquire whether the Legislature shall not be prevented by constitutional provision from making a common school law which forces the poor white man to send his children to school with negro children, or lose entirely the benefits of the free common schools.

RATIFICATION BY THE PEOPLE.

Mr. THOMPSON, of Davidson, submitted the following resolution:

Be it resolved, That it is expedient that the new Constitution shall be submitted to the people at the next ensuing election of county officers; and, therefore, in the event that the adjournment of this Convention shall not leave a sufficient interval to elapse before the day for the county elections, as now fixed by law, to be held on the — day of March, 1870, the day of election should be postponed, not less than thirty days after the adjournment of the Convention.

Mr. HOUSE, of Davidson, Robertson and Montgomery, moved to suspend the rules and take up the resolution, and submitted the following resolution in lieu:

WHEREAS, It being expedient that the new Constitution should be submitted to a vote of the people at the ensuing election for county officers on 5th March, next; therefore,

Be it resolved, That this Convention will meet each night of its daily sessions, at 7 o'clock, P. M., commencing on Monday next.

Mr. KENNEDY moved to amend the amendment in lieu, by adding "that no vote shall be taken at any night session."

Mr. PORTER, of Haywood, moved to lay the resolution of Mr. Thompson, the resolution in lieu, and the amendment, on the table.

Mr. CYPERT demanded the yeas and nays, which were ordered, and the motion to lay on the table sustained.

Yeas..37
Nays..32

Those voting in the affirmative are:

Messrs. Bate, Baxter, Blizard, Branson, Brooks, Brown of Davidson, Burkett, Campbell, Carter, Chowning, Cypert, Doherty, Dromgoole, Fentress, Finley, Fulkerson, Gibbs, Gibson, Gordon, Heiskell, Henderson, Jones of Lincoln, Jones of Giles, Kennedy, Key, Mabry, McDougal, Meeks, Parker, Porter of Haywood, Porter of Henry, Shelton, Staley, Stephens, Taylor, Walters and Williamson—37.

Those voting in the negative are:

Messrs. Allen, Brandon, Britton, Brown of Henry, etc., Burton, Byrne, Coffin, Cummings, Deaderick, Deavenport, Dibbrell, Fielder, Gardner, Garner, Gaut, Hill of Warren, House of Williamson, House of Davidson, Robertson and Montgomery, Ivie, Kirkpatrick, Kyle, McNabb, Martin, Netherland, Nicholson, Sample, Shepard, Thompson of Davidson, Thompson of Maury, Turner, Warner and Wright—32.

AMENDMENTS PROPOSED.

Mr. BROWN, of Davidson, offered the following resolution, which was read and referred to the Special Committee on Common Schools:

Resolved, That the Constitution be so amended that all revenue derived from poll tax be applied exclusively to the payment of the public debt, and when it is accomplised it shall be applied to common schools and for no other purpose.

TO SAVE TIME.

Mr. Fentress submitted the following preamble and resolution, which were read and referred to the Committee on Miscellaneous Provisions:

Whereas, These daily discussions of how to save time consume more time than is saved by them:

Resolved, That hereafter discussions as to how to save time shall be out of order, and that this Convention proceed to the business before it, and when finished that they adjourn.

SUFFRAGE AND ELECTIONS.

On motion of Mr. Jones, of Lincoln, the Convention resumed the consideration of the unfinished business of yesterday—the report of the Committee on Franchise, Right of Suffrage and Elections.

Article II, Section 7, as reported by the Committee, was adopted.

Mr. Parker submitted the following amendment, which was rejected by the Convention:

In all elections by the people, and also by the Senate and House of Representatives, jointly or separately, the votes shall be personally and publicly given *viva voce.*

Mr. Nicholson submitted the following in lieu of Section 8, as reported by the Committee:

Article II, Section 8. The first session of the General Assembly shall commence on the first Monday in October, 1871, at which time the term of service of the members shall commence, and expire on the first Tuesday in November, 1872, and at which session the Governor elected on the first Tuesday in November, 1870, shall be inaugurated; and forever thereafter the General Assembly shall meet on the first Monday in January, next ensuing the election, at which session thereof the Governor shall be inaugurated.

Which was adopted in lieu, and the section, as thus amended, was adopted by the Convention.

LEGISLATIVE DEPARTMENT.

The Convention, on motion of Mr. JONES, of Lincoln, proceeded to the consideration of the report of the Committee on the Legislative Department.

ARTICLE II.

Sections 1 and 2, as they exist in the present Constitution, were adopted by the Convention.

Section 3, as recommended by the Committee, was adopted.

Section 4 was amended by striking out "forty-one" and inserting "seventy-one; as thus amended, was adopted by the Convention.

At 1 o'clock P. M., Mr. KENNEDY moved to adjourn until Monday morning at 9½ o'clock.

Mr. BAXTER demanded the yeas and nays, which were ordered, and the motion to adjourn until Monday lost.

Yeas..33
Nays..36

Those voting in the affirmative are:

Messrs. Allen, Bate, Brown of Davidson, Brown of Henry, etc., Burton, Byrne, Campbell, Chowning, Deavenport, Doherty, Dromgoole, Fentress, Gardner, Gibbs, Gordon, House of Williamson, House of Davidson, Robertson and Montgomery, Ivie, Jones of Lincoln, Jones of Giles, Kennedy, Kirkpatrick, Martin, Meeks, Netherland, Porter of Haywood, Porter of Henry, Shelton, Thompson of Davidson, Thompson of Maury, Turner, Williamson and Wright—33.

Those voting in the negative are:

Messrs. Baxter, Blizard, Branson, Britton, Brooks, Burkett, Carter, Coffin, Cummings, Cypert, Deaderick, Dibbrell, Fielder, Finley, Garner, Gaut, Gibson, Heiskell, Henderson, Hill of Warren, Key, Kyle, Mabry, McDougal, McNabb, Nicholson, Sample, Shepard, Staley, Stephens, Taylor, Walters, Warner and President Brown—36.

The Convention took a recess to 2½ o'clock P. M.

AFTERNOON SESSION.

Mr. GARNER offered the following amendment:

Strike out all after the word "seventy-five" in the third line of Section 5, of Article II, unto the word "*Provided*" in the 4th line, and insert "fifty," so as to limit the number of Representatives to 50 at all times.

Mr. BROWN, of Henry, etc., moved to lay the amendment on the table.

Mr. GARNER demanded the yeas and nays, which were ordered, and the motion to lay on the table sustained.

Yeas..47
Nays.. 5

Those voting in the affirmative are:

Messrs. Allen, Baxter, Blizard, Branson, Brandon, Britton, Brown of Davidson, Brown of Henry, Carroll, Gibson and Madison, Byrne, Campbell, Chowning, Coffin, Cummings, Cypert, Deaderick, Deavenport, Dibbrell, Doherty, Fielder, Finley, Fulkerson, Gaut, Gibbs, Gibson, Heiskell, Henderson, Ivie, Jones of Giles, Key, Kyle, Mabry, McDougal, McNabb, Martin, Netherland, Nicholson, Parker, Porter of Henry, Shepard, Stephens, Thompson of Davidson, Thompson of Maury, Walters, Warner, Williamson and Wright—47.

Those voting in the negative are:

Messrs. Brooks, Carter, Garner, Hill of Warren, and Kennedy —5.

Mr. DIBBRELL offered the following amendment:

In the last line of Section 5, strike out "two-thirds" and insert "1500 voters."

Mr. ALLEN moved to lay the amendment on the table.

Mr. CYPERT demanded the yeas and nays, which were ordered, and the motion to lay on the table sustained.

Yeas..31
Nays..24

Those voting in the affirmative are:

Messrs. Allen, Bate, Baxter, Blizard, Britton, Brown of Henry, etc., Campbell, Carter, Chowning, Deaderick, Fentress, Fielder, Fulkerson, Garner, Gaut, Gibbs, Heiskell, Henderson, Ivie, Key, Kirkpatrick, Kyle, Nicholson, Porter of Henry, Sample, Shepard, Shelton, Staley, Stephens, Thompson of Davidson, and Thompson of Maury—31.

Those voting in the negative are:

Messrs. Branson, Brooks, Brown of Davidson, Byrne, Coffin, Cummings, Cypert, Deavenport, Dibbrell, Doherty, Finley, Gibson, Hill of Warren, Jones of Giles, Kennedy, Mabry, McDougal, McNabb, Martin, Parker, Walters, Warner, Williams and Wright—24.

Mr. ALLEN moved that the Convention adjourn to Monday morning at 9½ o'clock, A. M.

Mr. GARNER demanded the yeas and nays, and the motion to adjourn was lost.

Yeas..18
Nays..35

Those voting in the affirmative are:

Messrs. Allen, Bate, Brown of Henry, etc., Campbell, Fentress, Gibbs, Jones of Giles, Martin, Netherland, Porter of Haywood, Porter of Henry, Shepard, Shelton, Thompson of Davidson, Thompson of Maury, Walters, Williamson and Wright—18.

Those voting in the negative are:

Messrs. Baxter, Blizard, Branson, Brandon, Britton, Brooks, Brown of Davidson, Burkett, Byrne, Carter, Chowning, Coffin, Cummings, Cypert, Deaderick, Deavenport, Dibbrell, Doherty, Fielder, Finley, Fulkerson, Garner, Gaut, Gibson, Henderson, Hill of Warren, Kennedy, Key, Kirkpatrick, Kyle, Mabry, McDougal, McNabb, Nicholson, Parker, Sample, Staley, Stephens and Warner—39.

Mr. DEAVENPORT offered the following amendment to Section 5, Article II:

"*Provided further*, That those counties entitled to one representative by the apportionment of 1851 and 1852, shall never be deprived of that representation."

On motion of Mr. CAMPBELL, the amendment was laid on the table.

Section 5, as reported by the Committee, was adopted without amendment.

Section 6, as recommended by the committee, was adopted without amendment.

Sections 7 and 8 were passed over, they having been adopted in the report of the Committee on Elections.

Mr. GARNER offered the following amendment to Section 9:

Strike out "twenty-one years" in the second line, and insert twenty-five years."

Which was rejected, and the section, as recommended by the committee, adopted.

Mr. THOMPSON, of Maury, moved to amend Section 10 by striking out "thirty" and inserting "twenty-one." Which was rejected.

Mr. DIBBRELL moved to amend Section 10 by striking out "thirty" and inserting "twenty-five." Which was rejected, and the sections, as amended by the committee, was adopted by the Convention.

Section 11 was amended by inserting "and election" after the word "qualification," in second line, and thus amended, was adopted by the Convention.

Mr. WARNER offered the following amendment to Section 12:

After the words "two-thirds," and before the word "expel," insert the words "of the entire number," so that said section will read thus:

Each House may determine the rules of its proceedings, punish its members for disorderly behavior, and, with the concurrence of two-thirds of the entire number, expel a member, but not a second time for the same offence, and shall have all other powers necessary for a branch of the Legislature of a free State.

Which was rejected, and the section, as recommended by the committee, was adopted by the Convention.

Sections 13, 14, 15 and 16, were adopted, as reported by the committee, without amendment.

On motion of Mr. GIBSON, Section 17 was amended by striking out the word "pass," and inserting the words "become a law." And the section, as thus amended, was adopted by the Convention.

Section 18, as reported by the committee, was adopted without amendment.

Mr. WARNER submitted the following, in lieu of Section 19, as reported by the committee:

"After a bill has been considered by both Houses of the General Assembly, and rejected, no bill containing the same substance shall be passed into a law during the same session."

The amendment in lieu was rejected, and the section, as recommended by the committee, was adopted.

Sections 20, 21, and 22, were adopted as recommended by the committee.

On motion of Mr. STEPHENS, Section 23 was amended by inserting the word "each" in lieu of "the," and before the words General Assembly in the second line, and as thus amended, was adopted.

Mr. GARNER moved to amend by striking out "seventy-five days" in the fourth line, and inserting in lieu thereof "sixty days."

Mr. FULKERSON moved to lay the amendment on the table, and demanded the yeas and nays, which were ordered, and the motion to lay on the table sustained.

Yeas...33
Nays...26

Those voting in the affirmative are:

Messrs. Allen, Bate, Baxter, Blizard, Branson, Brown of Henry, etc., Burkett, Byrne, Campbell, Carter, Coffin, Cummings, Cypert, Deaderick, Fentress, Fielder, Gaut, Gibbs, Gibson, Henderson, Jones of Giles, Kennedy, Key, Mabry, Nicholson, Parker, Porter of Haywood, Porter of Henry, Shepard, Shelton, Stephens, Thompson of Maury and Williamson—33.

Those voting in the negative are:

Messrs. Brandon, Britton, Brooks, Brown of Davidson, Chowning, Deavenport, Dibbrell, Doherty, Finley, Fulkerson, Garner, Hill of Warren, Kirkpatrick, Kyle, McDougal, McNabb, Martin, Netherland, Sample, Staley, Thompson of Davidson, Walters, Warner and President Brown—26.

Mr. GARNER proposed to amend said section by striking out the words "unless physically unable to attend," in the 5th line. Which was rejected, and the section, as amended, was adopted by the Convention.

Section 24 was adopted without amendment and without a division.

Mr. KIRKPATRICK offered the following amendment to Section 25:

"No person, who may at any time have been a collector of taxes, whether State or municipal, or who may have been otherwise entrusted with the public money, shall be eligible to the General Assembly, or to any office of trust or profit in the civil department of this State, until he shall have first obtained a discharge for the amount of such collection, and for all public money with which he may have been entrusted.

Mr. GIBBS offered the following in lieu of Mr. Kirkpatrick's amendment:

After the word "assembly," in second line, insert the following: "Or hold any other civil office under the State Government."

Which was adopted in lieu, and then adopted as an amendment to Section 25; and the section, as thus amended, was adopted by the Convention.

Sections 26 and 27 were adopted by the Convention without amendment.

Section 28 was paseed over informally.

Mr. KENNEDY entered a motion to reconsider the vote adopting Section 23, and gave notice that he should, if reconsidered, move to amend the same by striking out the words "or adjourned," in the fourth line.

All further consideration of the report was postponed until Monday next.

COMMITTEE ON COMMON SCHOOLS.

The PRESIDENT announced, as the Special Committee on Common Schools, etc., Messrs. Gordon, Brown of Davidson, Kirkpatrick, Gibson, Baxter, Meeks, and Taylor.

On motion, the Convention adjourned until Monday morning, at 9½ o'clock.

MONDAY MORNING, JANUARY 31, 1870.

The Convention met pursuant to adjournment, Mr. President BROWN in the Chair.

Prayer by the Rev. Mr. McNEELEY.

The Journal of Saturday was read, corrected and approved.

HOURS OF MEETING AND ADJOURNMENT.

Mr. Britton submitted the following resolution :

Resolved, That it shall be the established rule of this House, until otherwise ordered, to meet at 9½ o'clock A. M., and adjourn at 4 o'clock, which lies over under the rules.

RESOLUTION WITHDRAWN.

Mr. Brooks asked and obtained leave to withdraw the resolution introduced by him on a former day, to create a new county out of portions of Jackson and Overton Counties, for purposes of amendment.

MEMORIAL

Mr. Gaut presented a memorial from sundry citizens of Bradley County, praying that the Constitution be so amended that the Legislature shall have entire control of the subject of tippling and tippling houses, which was, without being read, referred to the Committee on Miscellaneous Provisions.

RIGHTS OF MARRIED WOMEN.

Mr. Kirkpatrick submitted the following resolution, which was read and referred to the Committee on Miscellaneous Provisions :

Resolved, That the Constitution be amended by incorporating therein the following provision, to-wit :

Sec. —. The property and pecuniary rights of every married woman, at the time of marriage, or afterward acquired by gift, devise, or inheritance, shall not be subject to the debts or contracts of the husband, and laws shall be passed providing for the registration of the wife's separate property.

MEMORIAL.

Mr. Seay presented a memorial from sundry citizens of Smith, Sumner, and Macon Counties, praying the creation of a new county out of portions of said counties, which, without being read, was referred to the Committee on New Counties and County Lines :

COMMON SCHOOLS.

Mr. Gardner submitted the following resolution, which was read and referred to the Committee on Common Schools :

Resolved, That the Committee on Common Schools inquire and report the propriety of dedicating to educational purposes, such portion of the proceeds of the poll-tax hereafter, as shall be in excess of the amount received from that source in the year 1869. Such excess to be invested by the Legislature in such manner as may be prescribed by law, for the benefit of common schools in this State, the principal not to be used until the fund amounts to half a million of dollars.

MEMORIALS.

Mr. FENTRESS presented a memorial from sundry citizens of Hardeman and Fayette Counties, praying the creation of a new county out of portions of said counties, which, without being read, was referred to the Committee on New Counties and County Lines.

Mr. SAMPLE presented a memorial from a large number of citizens against the creation of a new county out of portions of Hawkins, Jefferson and Greene, which, without being read, was referred to the Committee on New Counties and County Lines.

BANK OF TENNESSEE.

Mr. THOMPSON, of Davidson, submitted the following resolution:

Be it resolved, That in view of the undoubted intention of the State of Tennessee to pay all of her indebtedness, and in view of the embarrassed condition of the State, the Committee on Finance be instructed to enquire and report upon the expendiency of rechartering the Bank of Tennessee: And at the same time to enquire and report upon the advisability of memorializing Congress to remit in favor of the Bank of Tennessee the restrictions and penalties imposed on State Banks by the National Banking system.

Which was referred to the Committee on Finance.

LEGISLATIVE DEPARTMENT FURTHER CONSIDERED.

The Convention proceeded to the consideration of the unfinished business of Saturday—the report of the Committee on the Legislative Department.

Mr. KENNEDY called up his motion to reconsider the vote adopting Section 23, and the same was reconsidered by the Convention.

Mr. KENNEDY submitted the following amendment, which was adopted by the Convention:

Strike out "*or adjourned*," in the fourth line.

Mr. BAXTER proposed to amend the Section further by striking out the following words: "But no member shall be paid for more than seventy-five days of a regular session, or for more than twenty days of an extra or called session: or for any day when absent from his seat in the Legislature unless physically unable to attend."

Mr. GARNER moved to lay the amendment on the table.

Mr. GIBSON demanded the yeas and nays, which were ordered and the motion to lay on the table sustained.

Yeas..64
Nays.. 8

Those voting in the affirmative are:

Messrs. Branson, Brandon, Brooks, Brown of Davidson, Brown of Henry, etc., Burkett, Burton, Byrne, Campbell, Carter, Chowning, Coffin, Cummings, Cypert, Deaderick, Deavenport, Dibbrell, Doherty, Dromgoole, Fentress, Fielder, Finley, Fulkerson, Gardner, Garner, Gant, Gibbs, Gibson, Henderson, Hill of Warren, Hill of Gibson, House of Williamson, House of Davidson, etc., Ivie, Jones of Lincoln, Jones of Giles, Kennedy, Key, Kirkpatrick, Kyle, McDougal, McNabb, Martin, Meeks, Morris, Netherland, Nicholson, Parker, Porter of Haywood, Porter of Henry, Sample, Seay, Shepard, Shelton, Staley, Stephens, Taylor, Thompson of Davidson, Turner, Warner, Walters, Wright and President Brown—64.

Those voting in the negative are:

Messrs. Allen, Bate, Baxter, Blizard, Heiskell, Mabry, Thompson of Maury, and Williamson—8.

Section 23, as thus amended was adopted by the Convention.

Mr. JONES, of Lincoln, submitted the following amendment to Section 29:

Add after the word taxation in the 4th line of Section 29, the words: The ordinary County or Corporation tax shall not be greater than the State tax unless specially authorized by the General Assembly for specific objects.

Mr. GIBBS moved to lay the amendment on the table, which was rejected.

Mr. GARNER offered the following amendment in lieu of Mr. JONES'S:

After the word taxation in the 4th line of the 29th Section add these words: "The annual County or Corporation tax shall not be greater than the State tax unless first authorized by the vote of the majority of the qualified voters of said County or Corporation."

On motion of Mr. DIBBRELL the amendment and the amendment in lieu were laid on the table.

Mr. SEAY offered the following amendment:

Resolved, That Section 29, (report of Committee on Legislative Department) be amended by inserting after the words "*Counties*" in the 1st line, the words "Civil Districts," and after the words "County" in the 2nd line the words "Civil Districts." After the word "County" in the 5th line insert the words "Civil District," and in the 6th and 7th lines after the word "County" insert the word "Civil District" and that the word "*three-fourths*" in the 7th line of said section be stricken out, and the words "two-thirds" inserted in lieu thereof.

On motion of Mr. DEAVENPORT the amendment was laid on the table.

Mr. HOUSE, of Davidson, Robertson and Montgomery, submitted the following amendment:

In line 7, of Section 29, strike out the words "three-fourths," and insert in lieu thereof the word "majority," and after the word "election" in said line insert 'and no person who does not own at least $250 worth of taxable property, within said county, city or town, as the case may be, shall be entitled to vote in such election;" so that it will read:

But the credit of no county, city or town shall be given or loaned to or in aid of any person, company, association or corporation, except upon an election to be first held by the qualified voters of such county, city or town, and the assent of a majority of the votes cast at said election, and no person who does not own at least $250 worth of taxable property within said county, city or town, as the case may be, shall be entitled to vote in such election.

On motion of Mr. DEAVENPORT the amendment was laid on the table.

Mr. TURNER offered the following amendment: "After the words "the assent of" in the 7th line, insert in lieu of the words "*three fourths,*" the words "*three-fifths,*" which was rejected by the Convention.

Mr. ALLEN moved to amend by striking out all of the Section reported by the Committee in lines 5, 6, 7, 8 and 9.

Mr. BROWN, of Henry, Carroll, Gibson and Madison, submitted the following amendment:

Insert the word "whatever" after the word Corporation in the 6th line, and strike out the remainder of 6th line. Strike out all after words "*Corporation*" in the 8th line and insert the word "*whatever;*" so that the Section will read: "But the credit of no county, city or town shall be given or loaned to or in aid of any person, company, association or corporation whatever. Nor shall any county, city or town become a stockholder with others in any company, association or corporation whatever.

Mr. MABRY moved to lay the amendment on the table—pending which the Convention took a recess to 2½ P. M.

AFTERNOON SESSION.

Mr. PORTER, of Haywood, demanded the yeas and nays on Mr. Mabry's motion to lay Mr. Brown's amendment on the table, which were ordered and the motion to lay on the table sustained.

Yeas.. 44.
Nays.. 22.

Those voting in the affirmative are:

Messrs. Bate, Baxter, Blackburn, Branson, Brandon, Britton, Brooks, Brown of Davidson, Burkett, Byrne, Campbell, Carter, Chowning, Coffin, Cypert, Deaderick, Dibbrell, Finley, Fulkerson, Gardner, Garner, Gaut, Gibbs, Gibson, Heiskell, Hill of Gibson, Ivie, Jones of Giles, Kirkpatrick, Kyle, Mabry, McNabb, Martin, Meeks, Netherland, Nicholson, Parker, Sample, Seay, Shepard, Stephens, Turner and President Brown—44.

Those voting in the negative are:

Messrs. Blizard, Burton, Brown of Henry, etc., Deavenport, Doherty, Dromgoole, Fentress, Fielder, Henderson, Hill of Warren, House of Williamson, House of Davidson, etc., Jones of Lincoln, Kennedy, McDougal, Morris, Porter of Haywood, Taylor, Thompson of Maury, Warner, Williamson and Wright—22.

Mr. ALLEN's amendment was rejected and Section 29 as reported by the Committee was adopted by the Convention.

Mr. BURTON offered the following amendment to Section 30: After the word "*State*" in the first line, insert "either in the hands of the manufacturer or other person," which was rejected and the section as reported by the Committee was adopted.

Mr. KENNEDY offerred the following amendment to Section 31 by adding:

"Nor shall the bonds of the State be issued for any purpose whatever, except to provide for the payment of existing debts or liabilities and the interest thereon, and in this case only by authority of the Legislature reciting for what liability they are issued."

Mr. BROWN, of Davidson, submitted the following amendment: "Except by a vote of three-fourths of all the members of both Houses to which they are entitled under this Constitution; *Provided*, that nothing herein shall be construed to impair vested rights."

Mr. BROWN, withdrew his amendment.

Mr. HOUSE, of Williamson, proposed to amend Mr. Kennedy's amendment by adding the words "and except to suppress rebellion, invasion or insurrection," which was accepted by Mr. Kennedy.

Mr. PORTER, of Henry, moved to strike out the words "and except to suppress rebellion, invasion or insurrection."

Mr. DIBBRELL moved to lay the amendments of Mr. Kennedy and Mr. Porter on the table.

Mr. HOUSE, of Williamson, demanded the yeas and nays, which were ordered, and the motion to lay on the table sustained:

Yeas..46
Nays..23

Those voting in the affirmative are:

Messrs. Baxter, Branson, Britton, Brooks, Burkett, Campbell, Carter, Chowning, Coffin, Cummings, Cypert, Deavenport, Deaderick, Dibbrell, Fentress, Finley, Fulkerson, Gardner, Gaut, Gibbs, Gibson, Heiskell, Henderson, Hill of Gibson, Ivie, Jones of Giles, Key, Kirkpatrick, Kyle, Mabry, McNabb, Martin, Netherland, Nicholson, Parker, Porter of Haywood, Sample, Seay, Shepard Shelton, Stephens, Taylor, Thompson, of Maury, Turner, Warner and Williamson—46.

Those voting in the negative are:

Messrs. Arledge, Blizard, Brandon, Brown of Davidson, Brown of Henry, etc., Burton, Doherty, Dromgoole, Fielder, Garner, Hill of Warren, House of Williamson, House of Davidson, Robertson and Montgomery, Jones of Lincoln, Kennedy, McDougal, Morris, Meeks, Porter of Henry, Thompson of Davidson, Walters, Wright and President Brown—23.

Mr. MABRY demanded the previous question, which demand was sustained, and Section 31 was recommended by the Committee was adopted.

Mr. GIBBS moved to reconsider the vote by which Section 5, Article II, was adopted.

Mr. DEAVENPORT moved that the Convention adjourn until to-morrow morning.

Mr. GARNER demanded the yeas and nays, which were ordered, and the motion to adjourn lost.

Yeas.. 20
Nays.. 45

Those voting in the affirmative are:

Messrs. Arledge, Brown of Davidson, Brown of Henry, etc., Campbell, Cypert, Deavenport, Dibbrell, Doherty, Gibbs, House of Williamson, Jones of Giles, McDougal, Meeks, Netherland, Parker, Seay, Taylor, Thompson of Maury, Walters and Wright —20.

Those voting in the negative are:

Messrs. Baxter, Blizard, Branson, Britton, Brooks, Burkett, Burton, Byrne, Carter, Chowning, Coffin, Cummings, Deaderick, Dromgoole, Fentress, Fielder, Finley, Fulkerson, Gardner, Garner, Gaut, Gibson, Heiskell, Henderson, Hill of Warren, Hill of Gibson, House of Davidson, Robertson and Montgomery, Ivie, Jones of Lincoln, Kennedy, Key, Kirkpatrick, Mabry, McNabb, Martin, Nicholson, Porter of Haywood, Porter of Henry, Sample, Shepard, Shelton, Stephens, Thompson of Davidson, Turner and Warner —45.

Mr. HEISKELL moved to lay the motion to reconsider on the table.

Mr. DEAVENPORT demanded the yeas and nays, which were ordered, and the motion to lay on the table sustained.

Yeas.. 37
Nays.. 30

Those voting in the affirmative are:

Messrs. Arledge, Baxter, Blizard, Brandon, Britton, Burkett, Byrne, Campbell, Carter, Chowning, Coffin, Deaderick, Doherty, Dromgoole, Fentress, Fielder, Gardner, Garner, Gaut, Heiskell, Henderson, Hill of Gibson, House of Davidson, Robertson and Montgomery, Ivie, Jones of Lincoln, Kennedy, Key, McDougal,

Morris, Meeks, Porter of Haywood, Porter of Henry, Sample, Shepard, Shelton, Stephens and Thompson of Davidson—37.

Those voting in the negative are:

Messrs. Branson, Brooks, Brown of Davidson, Brown of Henry, etc., Burton, Cummings, Cypert, Deavenport, Finley, Fulkerson, Gibbs, Gibson, Hill of Warren, House of Williamson, Jones of Giles, Kirkpatrick, Kyle, Mabry, McNabb, Martin, Nicholson, Parker, Seay, Taylor, Thompson of Maury, Turner, Walters, Warner, Wright and President Brown—30.

On motion, the Convention adjourned until to-morrow morning at 9½ o'clock.

TUESDAY MORNING, FEBRUARY 1, 1870.

The Convention met pursuant to rdjournment, Mr. President BROWN in the Chair.

Prayer by the Rev. Dr. YOUNG.

The Journal of yesterday was read and approved.

MEMORIALS AND PETITIONS.

Mr. DOHERTY submitted a memorial from sundry citizens of Benton, Decatur, Henderson and Carroll Counties, praying the creation of a new county out of portions of said counties, which, without being read, was referred to the Committee on New Counties and County Lines.

Mr. DOHERTY presented a memorial from a large number of citizens, praying that the Constitution be amended so as to give towns and civil districts the right to prevent the sale or manufacture of spirits within their limits, which was referred to the Committee on Miscellaneous Provisions.

Mr. GIBBS presented a memorial from a large number of citizens of the counties of Gibson, Obion, Dyer and Weakley, praying the creation of a new county out of portions of said counties, which, without being read, was referred to the Committee on New Counties and County Lines.

Mr. JONES, of Lincoln, submitted a memorial from citizens of Lincoln, Franklin and Bedford Counties, praying the creation of a new county out of portions of said counties, which, without being read, was referred to the Committee on New Counties and County Lines.

ORDINANCES PROPOSED.

Mr. TURNER submitted the following ordinance:

Resolved, That it shall be the duty of the several officers of this State, authorized by law to hold elections for members of the General Assembly and other officers, to open and hold an election at the places of holding elections for members of the General Assembly and other officers, in their respective counties, on the first Saturday in March, 1870, for the purpose of receiving the votes of such qualified voters as may desire to vote for the adoption or rejection of this amended Constitution; *Provided*, That the qualifications of voters in this election shall be the same as that required in the election of delegates to this Convention.

2. That it shall be the duty of said returning officers in each county in this State, to prepare poll-books, which shall be opened on said day of election, and in which shall be enrolled the name of each voter by the assistance of the clerks, who shall be appointed and sworn as clerks in other elections. Said officers shall prepare a ballot-box, in which shall be placed the ticket of each voter. Each ticket shall have written or printed thereon the words "I ratify the new Constitution," or if the voter is opposed to it, "I reject the new Constitution," or the words "ratification" or "rejection," or some such words as will distinctly convey the intention of the voter.

The election shall be held, and the Judges and Clerks shall be appointed as in the case of election of members of the General Assembly, and it shall be conducted in all respects as in cases of said election of members of the General Assembly. It shall be the duty of the returning officer, in presence of the inspectors, to count the votes given for the ratification or rejection of the Constitution, of which they shall keep a true and correct estimate in said poll-book.

The returning officers shall deposit the original poll-books of said election with the Clerks of the County Court in their respective counties, and shall, within five days after said election, make out duplicate statements of the number of votes in their respective counties for ratifying and rejecting the Constitution, and shall forward by mail one of said certificates to the Governor, and one to the Secretary of State.

It shall be the duty of said several County Court Clerks carefully to examine the said poll-books, and forthwith to certify to the Secretary of State, a full, true and perfect statement of the number of votes taken for and against the Constitution, as appears from the poll-books in their offices.

Should said returning officers, or any of them, fail to make returns in due time, as above directed, the Secretary of State shall then be authorized to dispatch a special messenger for the purpose of obtaining a certified copy of the result of said election.

3. That upon the receipt of said returns, it shall be the duty of the Governor, Secretary of State, and the President of this Convention, or any two of said officers, to compare the votes given in said election for the ratification or rejection of the amended Constitution; and if it shall appear from said returns, that a majority of all the votes given in said election is for ratifying the amended Constitution, then it shall be the duty of the Governor forthwith to make proclamation of that fact, and thenceforth the amended Constitution shall be ordained and established as the Constitution of Tennessee.

That the Governor of the State is requested to issue his proclamation as to this election on the first Saturday of March, 1870, for the ratification or rejection of this amended Constitution.

Which was read and referred to the Committee on Elections.

SUBMISSION OF THE CONSTITUTION TO THE PEOPLE.

Mr. HEISKELL offered the following resolution:

Resolved, That it is the sense of this Convention that the Constitution be submitted to the people at the March elections.

On motion of Mr. HEISKELL, the rules were suspended, and the resolution taken up; whereupon,

Mr. DAVENPORT submitted the following in lieu of Mr. Heiskell's:

Resolved, That an election shall be held throughout the State, on the first Saturday in April, 1870, to elect Circuit and County Court Clerks and Justices of the Peace, and at the same time an election shall be held for the ratification or rejection of this Constitution.

Mr. DEAVENPORT subsequently withdrew his amendment.

Mr. BAXTER moved to lay the resolution of Mr. Heiskell on the table.

Mr. GARNER demanded the yeas and nays, which were ordered, and the motion to lay on the table sustained.

Yeas.. 37
Nays.. 36

Those voting in the affirmative are:

Messrs. Arledge, Baxter, Blizard, Branson, Britton, Brooks, Brown of Davidson, Brown of Henry, etc., Carter, Cummings, Cypert, Deaderick, Doherty, Dromgoole, Fentress, Finley, Fulkerson, Gardner, Gibbs, Gibson, Henderson, Hill of Gibson, Jones of Lincoln, Jones of Giles, Key, Kirkpatrick, McNabb, Martin, Parker, Porter of Henry, Sample, Shepard, Staley, Taylor, Walters, Warner and Williamson—37.

Those voting in the negative are:

Messrs. Allen, Bate, Blackburn, Brandon, Burkett, Burton, Byrne, Campbell, Chowning, Coffin, Deavenport, Dibbrell, Fielder, Garner, Gaut, Heiskell, Hill of Warren, House of Williamson, House of Davidson, Robertson, and Montgomery, Ivie, Kennedy, Kyle, Mabry, McDougal, Morris, Meeks, Netherland, Nicholson, Porter of Haywood, Seay, Shelton, Stephens, Thompson of Maury, Turner, Wright and President Brown—36.

Mr. CYPERT moved to reconsider the vote laying the resolution on the table.

Mr. GARNER demanded the yeas and nays, which were ordered, and the motion to reconsider sustained.

Yeas..38
Nays..35

Those voting in the affirmative are:

Messrs. Allen, Bate, Brandon, Brooks, Burkett, Burton, Byrne, Campbell, Chowning, Coffin, Cypert, Deavenport, Dibbrell, Fielder, Garner, Gaut, Heiskell, Hill of Warren, House of Williamson, House of Davidson, Robertson and Montgomery, Ivie, Kennedy, Key, Kyle, Mabry, McDougal, Meeks, Morris, Netherland, Nicholson, Porter of Henry, Seay, Shelton, Stephens, Thompson of Maury, Turner, Wright and President Brown—38.

Those voting in the negative are:

Messrs. Arledge, Baxter, Blackburn, Blizard, Branson, Britton, Brown of Davidson, Brown of Henry, etc., Carter, Cummings, Deaderick, Doherty, Dromgoole, Fentress, Finley, Fulkerson, Gardner, Gibbs, Gibson, Henderson, Hill of Gibson, Jones of Lincoln, Jones of Giles, Kirkpatrick, McNabb, Martin, Parker, Porter of Haywood, Sample, Shepard, Staley, Taylor, Walters, Warner and Williamson—35.

The question recurring on the adoption of Mr. Heiskell's resolution, Mr. GARDNER offered the following in lieu:

Resolved, That the Legislature now in session is hereby requested, with as little delay as possible, to pass a law changing the time of holding the election for county officers, from the first to the fourth Saturday in March next, to afford time to this Convention to finish its labors, and submit the result to the people for ratification or rejection, at said election of county officers.

On motion of Mr. HOUSE, of Williamson, the resolution and the resolution in lieu, were referred to the Committee on Elections.

IMPEACHMENT OF JUDGE FRAZIER.

Mr. BAXTER, from the Select Committee on Impeachment and the case of Judge Thos. N. Frazier, made the following report:

MR. PRESIDENT: The Select Committee charged with the duty of inquiring what action, if any, is proper to be taken by this Convention to relieve persons impeached from the penalties imposed, with instructions to report whether any action is necessary in reference to the case of the Hon. Thomas N. Frazier, have instructed me to make the following report:

REPORT.

"That the General Assembly having adjourned from May to November, 1866, the Governor, by proclamation, summoned the members thereof to meet in extraordinary session on the intervening 4th of July. Under this call, a part of the members of that body, less than a quorum, assembled on the day appointed, in the Capitol, for the purpose of organizing as an Assembly, and proceeding in the discharge of their legislative duties. The members thus assembled in the House, finding themselves without a quorum, undertook to force the attendance of absent members, and by resolution authorized and directed their Speaker to issue his warrant, commanding the Sergeant-at-Arms to arrest and bring them before the House, 'to answer for their conduct and contempt of the House.' In obedience to and under the authority of this resolution, a warrant was issued for the arrest of Pleasant Williams, a member of the House. Armed with this assumed authority, the Sergeant-at-Arms proceeded to arrest Mr. Williams, at his residence in Carter County, forced him to Nashville, and held him for several days a prisoner in one of the rooms of the Capitol. While thus held as a prisoner, Mr. Williams, through counsel, applied to Judge Frazier for a writ of *habeas corpus.* The writ, as a matter of course, was granted, duly served and returned for hearing, the questions of law and fact involved in the case were argued by able counsel, for and against the application, and after due consideration his Honor was of opinion that the petitioner, Williams, was illegally restrained of his liberty and ordered his release.

It was for this act Judge Frazier was impeached: the articles charging his judgment was erroneous, and pronounced with the corrupt intent of hindering the organization and invading the privileges of the House; and upon these charges he was arraigned, tried and convicted, removed from his office and disqualified from ever afterwards holding any office under the authority of this State.

The arrest and imprisonment of Mr. Williams proceeded from a misapprehension of the constitutional power of the House in the premises. The only clause in the Constitution of Tennessee (Article II, Section 11,) relating to this question, is in the following words: 'Two-thirds of each House shall constitute a quorum to do business, but a smaller number may adjourn from day to day, and *may be authorized by law* to compel the attendance of absent members.' But this provision does not authorize a minority or less than a quorum of either House of the General Assembly, in the absence of legislation upon the subject, to enforce the attendance of absent members. Such was not the intention of the framers of our Constitution, but their purpose was, as the language used by them clearly imports, to authorize the Legislature *to provide by law* for such a contingency. Upon this point there was no diversity of opinion until the impeachment of Judge Frazier. Mr. Cushing, a writer of acknowledged ability upon 'The Elements of the Law and Practice of Legislative Assemblies,' Section 257, commenting on this clause of our Constitution, says:

'Clauses of this description authorize the Legislatures of the States in which they prevail, to provide *by law*, that such Legislative Assembly, though containing less than a quorum, may compel the attendance of its members; and this authority may as well be exercised so as to relate to the first assembling, as after the constitution of the first Assembly. When this is the case, if the requisite number do not appear, those who do, may of course, resort to the *measures provided by law*, to compel the attendance of absent members.'"

In the absence, therefore, of the legislation contemplated by the clause of our Constitution recited above, and there was none, authorizing the arrest and imprisonment of members for non-attendance, the action against Mr. Williams was unathorized and illegal. Having no authority themselves, the members assembled could communicate none to their Sergeant-at-arms; and being illegally restrained of his liberty, it was a plain and impeartive duty imposed by law upon Judge Frazier, upon Williams' application made in pursuance of law, to issue the writ of *habeas corpus* prayed for.

A refusal to have done so under the circumstances of the case, would have been a gross direliction of duty, and subjected Judge Frazier to heavy pecuniary damages. So the Convention will perceive that in the judgment of your Committee Judge Frazier was impeached at a period of high party excitement, convicted and punished, not for any abuse of his judicial powers, but for a manly, honest, correct and enlightened administration of the law, and in consequence, there is a strong obligation resting upon this Convention, to relieve Judge Frazier of the disabilities imposed by said conviction and judgment, if he has not been already relieved by the action recently taken by the General Assembly in his behalf.

A majority of your Committee, however, believe that the Legislature possesses the constitutional power to remove disabilities imposed by the judgment of a court of impeachment, and that its action recently taken in regard to Judge Frazier's case is effective to restore him to all the rights and immunities which he possessed prior to his conviction.

But as this power is not expressly given by the existing Constitution, and as there is some conflict of opinion on this point, the committee have directed me to present the following amendment, and recommend its adoption as a part of the Constitution to be framed by this Convention, and submitted to the people for their ratification:

Insert as an additional section of the 5th Article the following:

"Sec. 5. The Legislature now has, and shall continue to have power to relieve from the penalties imposed, any person disqualified from holding office by the judgment of a Court of Impeachment."

Respectfully submitted,

JOHN BAXTER, Chairman.

On motion of Mr. House, of Williamson, the proposed amendment of the Committee was adopted as Section 5, of Article V, of the Constitution.

On motion of Mr. House, of Williamson, it was ordered that 100 copies of the report be printed for the use of the Convention.

THE JUDICIARY.

The Convention proceeded to the consideration of the special order of the day, the resolutions of Mr. Nicholson, relative to the Judiciary.

Resolution No. 1. "It is the judgment of the Convention that the offices now held by the Supreme Judges, Chancellors, Circuit Judge, Criminal Judges, Attorney-General, and Reporter for the State and District Attorneys, shall be vacated after the ratification by the people of the amended Constitution, at such time as may be therein prescribed,"

Was, under the operation of the previous question, adopted.

Mr. CYPERT demanded the yeas and nays, which were ordered, resulting as follows:

Yeas..55
Nays..16

Those voting in the affirmative are:

Messrs. Allen, Arledge, Baxter, Blizard, Brandon, Britton, Brooks, Brown of Henry, etc., Burkett, Burton, Byrne, Campbell, Carter, Chowning, Cummings, Deaderick, Deavenport, Doherty, Dromgoole, Fentress, Fielder, Fulkerson, Gardner, Garner, Gaut, Gibbs, Heiskell, Henderson, Hill of Warren, Hill of Gibson, Ivie, Jones of Lincoln, Jones of Giles, Kennedy, Kirkpatrick, Kyle, McDougal, McNabb, Martin, Morris, Meeks, Netherland, Nicholson, Porter of Henry, Seay, Shepard, Shelton, Stephens, Taylor, Thompson of Maury, Turner, Walters, Warner, Williamson and Wright—55,

Those voting in the negative are:

Messrs. Blackburn, Branson, Brown of Davidson, Coffin, Cypert, Dibbrell, Finley, Gibson, House of Williamson, House of Davidson, Roberston, and Montgomery, Key, Mabry, Parker, Porter of Haywood, Sample, and Staley—16.

Resolution No. 2. "It is the judgment of this Convention that the Supreme Judges, Chancellors, Circuit Judges, Criminal Judges, Attorney and Reporter for the State, and the States Attorneys for the District, be appointed by the Governor, by and with the advice and consent of the Senate."

Mr. KIRKPATRICK offered the following in lieu of resolution No. 2:

It is the judgment of this Convention that the Supreme Judges with the Attorney General and Reporter for the State, be elected by the qualified voters of the State at large; and that the Chancellors, Criminal and Circuit Judges, and District Attorneys-General, be elected by the qualified voters of their respective districts or circuits.

Mr. GIBSON offered the following amendment to Mr. Kirkpatrick's resolution in lieu:

Add: "And that no Delegate in this Convention shall be eligible to fill any of the vacancies created by the new Constitution."

Mr. STEPHENS moved to lay the amendment of Mr. Gibson on the table.

Mr. Gibson demanded the yeas and nays, which were ordered, and the motion to lay on the table sustained.

Yeas...61
Nays...11

Those voting in the affiative are:

Messrs. Allen, Arledge, Baxter, Blizard, Britton, Brooks, Brown of Henry, etc., Burkett, Burton, Byrne, Campbell, Carter, Chowning, Coffin, Cummings, Deaderick, Deavenport, Dibbrell, Dromgoole, Fentress, Fielder, Gardner, Garner, Gaut, Gibbs, Heiskell, Henderson, Hill of Warren, Hill of Gibson, House of Williamson, House of Davidson, Robertson and Montgomery, Ivie, Jones of Lincoln, Jones of Giles, Kennedy, Key, Kirkpatrick, Kyle, Mabry, McDougal, McNabb, Martin, Morris, Meeks, Netherland, Nicholson, Porter of Haywood, Porter of Henry, Seay, Shepard, Shelton, Stephens, Taylor, Thompson of Maury, Turner, Walters, Warner, Williamson, Wright and President Brown—61.

Those voting in the negative are:

Messrs. Blackburn, Brandon, Branson, Brown of Davidson, Cypert, Doherty, Finley, Gibson, Parker, Sample and Staley—11.

Mr. Allen moved to lay the resolution of Mr. Kirkpatrick on the table, and demanded the yeas and nays, which were ordered, and the motion to lay on the table rejected.

Yeas...19
Nays...50

Those voting in the affirmative are:

Messrs. Allen, Baxter, Brown of Davidson, Campbell, Carter, Heiskell, House of Williamson, House of Davidson, Robertson and Montgomery, Ivie, Jones of Giles, Kennedy, Kyle, Netherland, Nicholson, Porter of Haywood, Shelton, Staley, Stephens, Thompson of Maury, and Turner—19.

Those voting in the negative are:

Messrs. Arledge, Blackburn, Blizard, Branson, Brandon, Britton, Brooks, Brown of Henry, etc., Burkett, Benton, Byrne, Chowning, Coffin, Cummings, Cypert, Deaderick, Deavenport, Dibbrell, Doherty, Dromgoole, Fielder, Finley, Fulkerson, Gardner, Garner, Gaut, Gibbs, Gibson, Henderson, Hill of Warren, Hill of Gibson, Jones of Lincoln, Key, Kirkpatrick, Mabry, McDougal, McNabb, Martin, Morris, Meeks, Parker, Porter of Henry, Sample, Seay, Shepard, Taylor, Walters, Warner, Williamson and Wright—50.

The Convention took a recess until 2½ o'clock.

AFTERNOON SESSION.

Mr. JONES of Giles, offered the following in lieu of Mr. Kirkpatrick's resolution:

It is the judgment of the Convention that the Judges of the Supreme Court, Chancellors, Circuit Judges, Criminal Judges, Attorney and Reporter for the State, and the State's Attorneys for the district, be appointed by the Legislature, in joint convention assembled.

On motion of Mr. GARNER, the amendment was laid on the table.

Mr. BROWN, of Davidson, offered the following amendment in lieu of Mr. Kirkpatrick's:

Resolved, That the Supreme Judges shall be appointed by the Governor, by and with the advice and consent of the Senate, but the Chancellors, Circuit Judges, Criminal Judges, Attorney and Reporter of the State, and State's Attorneys of the district, shall be elected by the qualified voters as now provided.

Which was rejected by the Convention.

Mr. THOMPSON, of Davidson, submitted the following in lieu of Mr. Kirkpatrick's resolution:

It is the judgment of the Convention that the Supreme Judges should be appointed by the Governor and confirmed by two-thirds of the entire Senate; that the Attorney General and Reporter should be selected from the bar and appointed by the Judges of the Supreme Court; and that the Chancellors, Circuit Judges, Judges of Criminal Courts, and District Attorneys General, be elected by the qualified voters of their respective districts or circuits.

Mr. DEAVENPORT moved to lay the amendment of Mr. Thompson on the table.

Mr. KENNEDY demanded the yeas and nays, which were ordered and the motion to lay on the table sustained:

Yeas..46
Nays..21

Those voting in the affirmative are:

Messrs. Allen, Baxter, Blizard, Branson, Brandon, Britton, Brooks, Brown of Henry, etc., Burton, Chowning, Coffin, Cummings, Cypert, Deaderick, Deavenport, Dibbrell, Doherty, Dromgoole, Fentress, Fielder, Gardner, Garner, Gaut, Gibbs, Gibson, Hill of Warren, Hill of Gibson, Jones of Lincoln, Kirkpatrick, Kyle, McDougal, McNabb, Martin, Morris, Meeks, Parker, Porter of Henry, Sample, Seay, Shepard, Taylor, Turner, Walters, Warner, Williamson and Wright—46.

Those voting in the negative are:

Messrs. Blackburn, Brown of Davidson, Byrne, Carter, Gordon, Heiskell, Henderson, House of Williamson, House of Davidson, etc., Jones of Giles, Kennedy, Key, Netherland, Nicholson, Porter of Haywood, Shelton, Staley, Stephens, Thompson of Davidson and Thompson of Maury—21.

Mr. KIRKPATRICK's resolution was then adopted in lieu of resolution No. 2, of Mr. Nicholson, by the following vote:

Yeas..49
Nays..23

Those voting in the affirmative are:

Messrs. Arledge, Blizard, Brandon, Branson, Britton, Brooks, Brown of Henry, etc., Burkett, Burton, Byrne, Chowning, Coffin, Cummings, Cypert, Deavenport, Dibbrell, Doherty, Dromgoole, Fentress, Fielder, Finley, Fulkerson, Gardner, Garner, Gaut, Gibbs, Gibson, Henderson, Hill of Warren, Hill of Gibson, Jones of Lincoln. Key, Kirpatrick, Mabry, McDougal, McNabb, Martin, Meeks, Morris, Parker, Porter of Henry, Sample, Seay, Shepard, Taylor, Walters, Warner, Williamson and Wright—49.

Those voting in the negative are:

Messrs. Allen, Bate, Baxter, Brown of Davidson, Campbell, Carter, Gordon, Heiskell, House of Williamson, House of Davidson, etc., Ivie, Jones of Giles, Kennedy, Kyle, Netherland, Nicholson, Porter of Haywood, Shelton, Staley, Stephens, Thompson of Davidson, of Maury and Turner—23.

Mr. BURTON submitted the following resolution:

Resolved, That the Legislature shall so provide that but two terms of the Circuit Court shall be held in any county in each year, and shall further provide that every cause shall stand for trial at the first term.

Mr. BLIZARD moved to lay the resolution on the table. The yeas and nays were ordered and the motion to lay on the table sustained:

Yeas..59
Nays..11

Those voting in the affirmative are:

Messrs. Baxter, Blizard, Brandon, Branson, Britton, Brown of Davidson, Burkett, Carter, Chowning, Coffin, Cummings, Cypert,

Deaderick, Doherty, Dromgoole, Fentress, Fielder, Finley, Fulkerson, Garner, Gaut, Gibbs, Gibson, Gordon, Heiskell, Henderson, Hill of Warren, Hill of Gibson, House of Williamson, House of Davidson, etc., Ivie, Jones of Lincoln, Jones of Giles, Kennedy, Key, Kirkpatrick, Kyle, Mabry, McDougal, McNabb, Martin, Meeks, Morris, Netherland, Nicholson, Parker, Porter of Haywood, Sample, Seay, Shepard, Shelton, Staley, Stephens, Taylor, Thompson of Maury, Turner, Walters, Warner and Williamson—59.

Those voting in the negative are:

Messrs. Brooks, Brown of Henry, etc., Burton, Byrne, Campbell, Dibbrell, Gardner, Porter of Henry, Thompson of Davidson, Wright and President Brown—11.

On motion of Mr. NICHOLSON the further consideration of the resolutions submitted by him, was postponed, and the Convention proceeded to the consideration of the

REPORT OF COMMITTEE ON THE JUDICIARY.

Mr. HILL, of Gibson, offered the substitute presented by him on a former day in lieu of the report of the majority of the Committee:

Mr. BURTON offered the following amendment:

The Supreme Court shall be composed of five Judges to be chosen as follows:

One shall be elected by the qualified voters of each of the three Grand Divisions of the State, and the remaining two shall be nominated by the Governor from the State at large and confirmed by the Senate.

On motion of Mr. DEAVENPORT the amendment was laid on the table.

Mr. STEPHENS submitted the following amendment:

Strike out from Section 13, of Article VI, all of the first four lines except the word "clerks" at the end of fourth line and insert in lieu thereof: Clerks of the Supreme Court shall be elected for the term of six years, by the qualified voters of the Division; and Clerks and Masters of the Chancery Court shall be elected for the term of six years by the qualified voters of the County or District.

Which was adopted by the Convention.

On motion of Mr. THOMPSON, of Davidson, the Convention adjourned until to-morrow morning at 9½ o'clock.

WEDNESDAY MORNING FEBRUARY 2, 1870.

The Convention met pursuant to adjournment, Mr. President BROWN in the Chair.

Prayer by the Rev. Dr. BAIRD.

The Journal of yesterday was read and approved.

AMENDMENTS PROPOSED.

Mr. BLACKBURN presented the following amendment to the Constitution:

WHEREAS, There cannot be made any law as a part of the fundamental law of this State outside of the Constitution of the United States; *Therefore, be it resolved,* That this Convention will studiously observe the same and avoid the making, or passage, of any law infringing on said Constitution of the United States, and that the following be made a part of the Constitution of Tennessee:

Section 1. That this State shall not make, nor enforce, any law, which shall abridge the privileges, or immunities, of any of its citizens, nor shall any law be made which shall deprive any person of life, liberty or property without due process of law. Nor deny to any person within its jurisdiction, the equal protection of the laws.

Sec. 2. That when the right to vote at any election for the choice of electors for President and Vice President of the United States, Representatives in Congress, the Executive and Judicial officers of the State, or the members of the Legislature thereof, is denied to any of the male inhabitants of this State, being twenty-one years of age and citizens of the United States, or in any way abridged, the basis of representation shall be reduced in the proportion which the number of such male citizens shall bear to the whole number of male citizens, twenty-one years of age in this State.

Sec. 3. No person shall be eligible as a Senator or Representative in Congress or elector of President and Vice President, or hold any office, civil or military under this State, who, having previously taken an oath as a member of Congress or as an officer of the United States, or as a member of the State Legislature, or as an Executive or Judicial officer of the State, shall have engaged in insurrection or rebellion against the same, or given aid or comfort to the enemies thereof. Unless such person shall first have his disabilities removed as required in the 3d Section, of the 14th Amendment to the Constitution of the United States.

Sec. 4. The validity of the National debt, authorised by law, including debts incurred for the payment of pensions and bounties in suppressing insurrection or rebellion shall not be questioned. But, this State shall not assume, or pay, any debt, or obligation incurred in aid of insurrection or rebellion against the Government of the United States, or any claim for the emancipation of any slave, but all such debts, obligations and claims shall be held illegal and void.

Sec. 5. That the right to vote and hold office by any citizen of this State shall not be denied or abridged by any law of this State on account of race or color, or previous condition of servitude.

Sec. 6. That the Legislature shall have power to enforce all the above laws and parts thereof, by appropriate legislation.

Which were read and referred to the Committee on Miscellaneous Provisions.

MEMORIALS.

Mr. BROWN, of Henry, etc., presented a memorial from citizens of Henry, Carroll and Weakley counties, praying the creation of a new County out of portions of said counties, which, without being read was referred to the Committee on New Counties and County Lines.

Mr. STEPHENS presented a memorial from citizens of Marion County, praying to be attached to the County of Grundy, which, without being read, was referred to the Committee on New Counties and County Lines.

Mr. KEY presented a memorial from citizens of Roane, Monroe and Blount counties, praying for the establishment of a new county out of portions of said counties, which, without being read, was referred to the Committee on New Counties and County Lines.

REPORT OF COMMITTEE ON ELECTIONS.

Mr. NICHOLSON from the Committee on Elections made the following report:

The Committee on Elections and Right of Suffrage have had under consideration the resolutions of Mr. Heiskell and Mr. Gardner, as to the time when the amended Constitution shall be submitted to the people for their ratification or rejection, and have directed me to recommend the adoption of Mr. Gardner's resolution as follows:

"*Resolved*, That the Legislature now in session is hereby requested, with as little delay as possible, to pass a law changing the time of holding the election for county officers, from the first to the fourth Saturday in March next, to afford time to this Convention to finish its labors, and submit the result to the people for ratification or rejection, at said election of County officers.

The Committee have also considered the resolution of Mr. Wright, as to the expediency of declaring all civil officers (except those held by the Governor and Legislature) vacant upon the ratification of the amended Constitution, and have instructed me to recommend that the offices held by Justices of the Peace be declared vacant upon the ratification of the amended Constitution.

The Committee instruct me to ask to be discharged from the other portions of the resolution.

All of which is respectfully submitted,

A. O. P. NICHOLSON,
Chairman.

REPORT CONSIDERED.

On motion of Mr. GARNER the rules were suspended and the report of the Committee taken up, when Mr. Garner offered the resolution of Mr. Turner, to submit the Constitution to a vote of the people on the first Saturday in March next, in lieu of the resolution recommended by the Committee.

Mr. DEAVENPORT demanded the yeas and nays, which were ordered and the substitute offered by Mr. Garner was rejected:

Yeas.. 14
Nays.. 56

Those voting in the affirmative are:

Messrs. Allen, Blizard, Burkett, Byrne, Dibbrell, Doherty, Garner, Hill of Warren, House of Montgomery, etc., Kirkpatrick, Porter of Henry, Shelton, Thompson of Maury, and Turner—14.

Those voting in the negative are:

Messrs. Arledge, Bate, Baxter, Blackburn, Branson, Brandon, Britton, Brooks, Brown of Davidson, Brown of Henry, etc., Burton, Campbell, Carter, Coffin, Cummings, Cypert, Deaderick, Deavenport, Dromgoole, Fentress, Fielder, Finley, Fulkerson, Gardner, Gaut, Gibbs, Gibson, Gordon, Henderson, Hill of Gibson, House of Williamson, Ivie, Jones of Lincoln, Jones of Giles, Kennedy, Key, Kyle, Mabry, McDougal, McNabb, Martin, Morris, Meeks, Netherland, Nicholson, Parker, Porter of Haywood, Sample, Seay, Shepard, Staley, Stephens, Taylor, Thompson of Davidson, Walters, Warner, Williamson and Wright—56.

The resolution recommended by the Committee was then adopted.

Mr. GIBSON demanded the yeas and nays, which were ordered, and resulted as follows:

Yeas.. 48
Nays.. 24

Those voting in the affirmative are:

Messrs. Arledge, Bate, Baxter, Brandon, Brooks, Brown of Davidson, Brown of Henry, etc., Burkett, Burton, Campbell, Chowning, Coffin, Cummings, Cypert, Deavenport, Dibbrell, Doherty, Dromgoole, Fielder, Gardner, Garner, Gaut, Gordon, Henderson, Hill of Gibson, House of Williamson, Ivie, Jones of Lincoln, Jones of Giles, Kennedy, Key, Kyle, Mabry, McDougal, McNabb, Martin, Meeks, Morris, Netherland, Nicholson, Sample, Seay, Taylor, Thompson of Davidson, Thompson of Maury, Turner, Walters, Williamson, and Wright—48.

Those voting in the negative are:

Messrs. Allen, Blizard, Branson, Britton, Byrne, Carter, Deaderick, Fentress, Finley, Fulkerson, Gibbs, Gibson, Heiskell, Hill of Warren, House of Montgomery, etc., Kirkpatrick, Parker, Porter of Haywood, Porter of Henry, Shepard, Shelton, Staley, Stephens, and Warner—24.

On motion of Mr. NICHOLSON, the remainder of the report of the Committee was laid on the table.

REPORT ON JUDICIARY FURTHER CONSIDERED.

The Convention proceeded to the consideration of the unfinished business of yesterday—the Report of the Committee on the Judiciary.

Mr. BRITTON submitted the following preamble and resolution:

WHEREAS, It is the expressed judgment of this Convention to remove the present incumbents in the judiciary department at some time to be agreed upon in this Constitution; and

WHEREAS, It is also the judgment of the Convention to retain in the Constitution the right of the people to elect the Judiciary; and

WHEREAS, Such expressed judgment is more in accordance with the present Constitution than either the majority or minority reports, or any substitute; therefore,

Resolved, That the Convention will pass over informally the majority and minority reports, and take up Articles V and VI as they stand in our present Constitution, and read them section by section and amend them so as to conform to the heretofore expressed judgment of the Convention.

Which lies over under the rule.

THE MAJORITY REPORT.

Mr. BROWN, of Davidson, submitted the following resolution:

Resolved, That the Convention proceed to consider the majority report of the Judiciary Committee section by section, and when the same is perfected it shall be in order to offer any amendment in lieu of the whole.

Which was adopted by the Convention.

Section 1 of Article II, as reported by the majority of the Committee, was adopted by the Convention.

Mr. GAUT proposed to amend Section 2 by striking out the words in italics and inserting "*the senior Judge* of the Supreme Court, or *if he be on trial, the senior of the two remaining Judges* shall preside over them."

Mr. GAUT subsequently withdrew his amendment.

Section 2, as recommended by the majority of the Committee, was then adopted by the Convention.

Section 3 was adopted without amendment.

Section 4 was amended by inserting after the word State in second line, the words "*Comptroller, Treasurer,*" and as thus amended, was adopted by the Convention.

Section 5 was adopted without amendment.

Section 1, Article VI, was taken up, when Mr. HILL, of Gibson, offered the following in lieu of the report of the majority.

ARTICLE VI.

Section 1. The Judicial power of this State shall be vested in one Court of *Errors and Appeals*, and in *three* Supreme Courts, and in such *Circuit, Chancery,* and other inferior Courts as the Legislature shall, from time to time, ordain and establish, and the Judges thereof, and in Justices of the Peace. The Legislature may also vest such jurisdiction in Corporation Courts as may be deemed necessary. Courts to be holden by Justices of the Peace may also be established.

Mr. McDougal offered the following amendment, to be inserted after the 8th line, Section 2:

Immediately after the ratification of this Constitution, the Legislature, by joint ballot of both Houses, shall elect a Special Commission, to consist of two additional Judges for each Grand Division of the State, who shall, with the Supreme Judge of their respective Grand Divisions, constitute three separate Supreme Courts, with full power and jurisdiction to hear and determine all causes, now pending or which may be pending in the Supreme Court at Knoxville, Nashville and Jackson; said Commission to expire on the—— day of ——, 1871.

Mr. Porter moved to lay the amendment on the table, which motion failed.

Mr. Burton demanded the yeas and nays on the adoption of the amendment, which were ordered, and the amendment rejected.

Yeas.. 10
Nays.. 57

Those voting in the affirmative are:

Messrs. Brown of Davidson, Cypert, Deavenport, Key, McDougal, Meeks, Nicholson, Thompson of Davidson, Thompson of Maury, and Walters—10.

Those voting in the negative are:

Messrs. Blizard, Branson, Brandon, Britton, Brooks, Brown of Henry, etc., Burkett, Burton, Byrne, Campbell, Carter, Chowning, Coffin, Cummings, Deaderick, Dibbrell, Doherty, Dromgoole, Fentress, Fielder, Finley, Fulkerson, Garner, Gaut, Gibbs, Gibson, Gordon, Heiskell, Henderson, Hill of Warren, Hill of Gibson, House of Williamson, House of Davidson, etc., Ivie, Jones of Giles, Kennedy, Kirkpatrick, Kyle, Mabry, McNabb, Martin, Morris, Netherland, Parker, Porter of Haywood, Porter of Henry, Sample, Seay, Shepard, Shelton, Staley, Stephens, Taylor, Turner, Warner, Williamson and Wright—57.

The Convention took a recess until 2½ o'clock P. M.

AFTERNOON SESSION.

Mr. JONES, of Lincoln, moved to amend by striking out the words "Circuit, Chancery and other," in the first and second lines.

Mr. KEY moved to lay the amendment on the table.

Mr. McDOUGAL demanded the yeas and nays, which were ordered, and the motion to lay on the table sustained.

Yeas.. 39
Nays.. 19

Those voting in the affirmative are:

Messrs. Baxter, Branson, Brooks, Brown of Henry, etc., Burton, Chowning, Deaderick, Doherty, Fentress, Gardner, Garner, Gaut, Gibbs, Gibson, Heiskell, Henderson, Hill of Gibson, House of Williamson, House of Montgomery, etc., Ivie, Jones of Giles, Key, Kirkpatrick, Kyle, McDougal, McNabb, Martin, Netherland, Nicholson, Porter of Haywood, Porter of Henry, Seay, Shepard, Shelton, Staley, Stephens, Taylor, Thompson of Davidson, and Wright—39.

Those voting in the negative are:

Messrs. Arledge, Blizard, Brandon, Britton, Byrne, Coffin, Cummings, Dibbrell, Dromgoole, Fielder, Fulkerson, Hill of Warren, Jones of Lincoln, Kennedy, Morris, Meeks, Turner, Walters and Warner—19.

On motion of Mr. HEISKELL, the amendment of Mr. Hill of Gibson, was laid on the table.

Mr. PORTER, of Haywood, demanded the previous question, which was sustained, and Section 1, Article VI, as reported by the majority of the Committee, was adopted.

Mr. BAXTER moved to reconsider the vote adopting said section, and further moved that the motion to reconsider be laid on the table, which motion was sustained.

Mr. WARNER offered the following in lieu of Section 2, as reported by the Committee:

The Supreme Court shall be composed of three Judges, one of whom shall reside in each of the Grand Divisions of the State; the concurrence of two of said Judges shall, in every case, be necessary to a decision. The jurisdiction of this Court shall be appellate only, under such restrictions and regulations as may, from time to time, be prescribed by law; but it may possess such other jurisdiction as is now conferred by law on the present Supreme Court. Said Court shall be held at one place only in each of the three Grand Divisions of the State.

Mr. SAMPLE offered the following amendment:

Amendment to Section 2, of Article VI:

The Supreme Court shall consist of three Judges, one of whom shall reside in each grand division of the State. But for the purpose of disposing of the accumulated business now pending in the Supreme Court, there shall be elected by the qualified voters of the State, upon the —— day of ——, 1870, three additional Judges of the Supreme Court, one of whom shall reside in each grand division of the State, who shall have the same jurisdiction, powers and salary as the Supreme Judges. These three additional Judges of the Supreme Court shall only have authority to try and dispose of the cases pending in the Supreme Courts at Knoxville, Nashville and Jackson, at the time of their election, and when these cases are determined and decided by them their commission shall expire. These three additional Judges shall hold their Courts at the same time and places as the Supreme Court, but in a different hall, and they shall constitute a separate and distinct Court, whose decisions shall be reported by the Attorney-General and Reporter for the State, but in a separate volume or volumes.

On motion of Mr. PORTER, of Haywood, the amendments of Mr. Warner and Mr. Sample were laid on the table.

Mr. JONES, of Lincoln, moved to amend Section 2, by striking out all after the word "held," in the seventh line, and inserting "at Knoxville, Nashville and Jackson."

Which was adopted by the Convention.

Mr. McDOUGAL moved to amend by striking out the word "five," in the first line, and inserting "three," and by striking out the word "two," in first line, and inserting "one."

Mr. McDOUGAL demanded the previous question, which was sustained.

Mr. FIELDER demanded the yeas and nays on the adoption of the amendment of Mr. McDougal, which were ordered, and the amendment was rejected.

Yeas..........31
Nays..........38

Those voting in the affirmative are:

Messrs. Blackburn, Branson, Brandon, Britton, Brooks, Brown

of Henry, etc., Carter, Chowning, Cypert, Deaderick, Deavenport, Dibbrell, Doherty, Fielder, Finley, Fulkerson, Gardner, Gaut, Gibbs, Gibson, Hill of Warren, Hill of Gibson, Kirpatrick, Kyle, McDougal, McNabb, Meeks, Sample, Staley, Walters and Warner —31.

Those voting in the negative are:

Messrs. Arledge, Baxter, Blizard, Brown of Davidson, Burkett, Burton, Campbell, Coffin, Cummings, Dromgoole, Fentress, Garner, Gordon, Heiskell, Henderson, House of Williamson, House of Montgomery, etc., Ivie, Jones of Lincoln, Jones of Giles, Kennedy, Key, Mabry, Martin, Morris, Netherland, Nicholson, Porter of Haywood, Porter of Henry, Seay, Shepard, Shelton, Stephens, Taylor, Thompson of Davidson, Turner, Williamson and Wright—38.

Section 2, as amended, was then adopted by the Convention.

Mr. PORTER, of Henry, moved to reconsider the vote adopting said section, and further moved to lay the motion to reconsider on the table, which latter motion was adopted.

Mr. HEISKELL submitted the following in lieu of the first four lines of Section 3, as reported by the majority of the Committee:

The Judges of the Supreme Court shall be elected by the qualified voters of the State.

The Legislature shall have power to prescribe such rules as may be necessary to carry out the provisions of Section 2, of this Article.

Mr. CAMPBELL offered the following amendment to the amendment in lieu of Mr. Heiskell:

Provided, That no Indian, Asiatic, African, mulatto or mustee shall be allowed to vote in any election for judicial officers in this State.

Mr. BAXTER moved to lay the amendment of Mr. Campbell on the table.

Mr. GIBSON demanded the yeas and nays, which were ordered, and the motion to lay on the table sustained.

Yeas..58
Nays...8

Those voting in the affirmative are:

Messrs. Baxter, Blizard, Branson, Brandon, Britton, Brooks, Brown of Davidson, Burkett, Burton, Byrne, Carter, Chowning, Coffin, Cummings, Cypert, Deaderick, Dibbrell, Doherty, Dromgoole, Fielder, Finley, Fulkerson, Gardner, Garner, Gaut, Gibbs, Gibson, Gordon, Heiskell, Henderson, Hill of Warren, Hill of Gibson, House of Williamson, House of Montgomery, etc., Ivie, Jones of Lincoln, Kennedy, Key, Kirkpatrick, Kyle, Mabry, McDougal, McNabb, Martin, Morris, Meeks, Netherland, Nicholson, Porter of Haywood, Sample, Seay, Staley, Stephens, Thompson of Davidson, Turner, Walters, Warner and Wright—58.

Those voting in the negative are:

Messrs. Brown of Henry, etc., Campbell, Fentress, Jones of Giles, Porter of Henry, Shepard, Taylor and Williamson—8.

Mr. JONES, of Giles, demanded the yeas and nays on the adoption of Mr. Heiskell's amendment, which were ordered, and the amendment adopted.

Yeas.. 46
Nays.. 25

Those voting in the affirmative are:

Messrs. Arledge, Blackburn, Blizard, Branson, Brandon, Britton, Brooks, Brown of Henry, etc., Burkett, Burton, Byrne, Chowning, Cummings, Cypert, Deavenport, Dibbrell, Doherty, Dromgoole, Fentress, Fielder, Finley, Fulkerson, Garner, Gaut, Gibbs, Gibson, Hill of Warren, Hill of Gibson, Jones of Lincoln, Kirkpatrick, Mabry, McDougal, McNabb, Martin, Morris, Meeks, Netherland, Porter of Henry, Sample, Seay, Shepard, Taylor, Walters, Warner, Williamson and Wright—46.

Those voting in the negative are:

Messrs. Bate, Baxter, Brown of Davidson, Campbell, Carter, Coffin, Deaderick, Gardner, Gordon, Heiskell, Henderson, House of Williamson, House of Davidson, Robertson and Montgomery, Ivie, Jones of Giles, Kennedy, Key, Kyle, Nicholson, Porter of Haywood, Shelton, Staley, Stephens, Thompson of Davidson, and Turner—25.

Mr. JONES, of Lincoln, moved to amend by striking out the word "*twelve*," in the sixth line, and inserting "*eight*," and demanded the yeas and nays, which were ordered, and the amendment was adopted.

Yeas..37
Nays..34

Those voting in the affirmative are:

Messrs. Arledge, Blackburn, Blizard, Branson, Britton, Brooks, Brown of Henry, etc., Burkett, Burton, Chowning, Coffin, Cummings, Cypert, Deaderick, Dibbrell, Doherty, Fielder, Finley, Fulkerson, Garner, Gibbs, Gibson, Hill of Warren, Hill of Gibson, Jones of Lincoln, Mabry, McDougal, McNabb, Morris, Meeks,

Sample, Stephens, Taylor, Walters, Warner, Williamson and Wright—37.

Those voting in the negative are:

Messrs. Bate, Baxter, Brandon, Brown of Davidson, Byrne, Campbell, Carter, Deaderick, Dromgoole, Fentress, Gardner, Gaut, Gordon, Heiskell, Henderson, House of Williamson, House of Montgomery, etc., Ivie, Jones of Giles, Kennedy, Key, Kirkpatrick, Kyle, Martin, Netherland, Nicholson, Porter of Haywood, Porter of Henry, Seay, Shepard, Shelton, Staley, Thompson of Davidson, and Turner—34.

Mr. BAXTER moved to amend by striking out the word "five" and inserting the word "three," in the sixth line.

Mr. CAMPBELL moved to amend by striking out the word "five" and inserting "nine," in the sixth line, Section 3.

Mr. JONES, of Lincoln, demanded a division of the question, which was ordered, and a vote taken on the motion to strike out.

Mr. BAXTER demanded the yeas and nays, which were ordered, and the motion to strike out failed.

Yeas..17
Nays..54

Those voting in the affirmative are:

Messrs. Baxter, Blackburn, Branson, Brandon, Britton, Campbell, Carter, Deaderick, Finley, Fulkerson, Gibson, Hill of Warren, Mabry, Nicholson, Porter of Henry, Thompson of Davidson, and Wright—17.

Those voting in the negative are:

Messrs. Arledge, Bate, Blizard, Brooks, Brown of Davidson, Brown of Henry, etc., Burkett, Burton, Byrne, Chowning, Coffin, Cummings, Cypert, Deavenport, Dibbrell, Doherty, Dromgoole, Fentress, Fielder, Gardner, Garner, Gaut, Gibbs, Gordon, Heiskell, Henderson, Hill of Gibson, House of Williamson, House of Montgomery, etc., Ivie, Jones of Lincoln, Jones of Giles, Kennedy, Key, Kirkpatrick, Kyle, McDougal, McNabb, Martin, Morris, Meeks, Netherland, Porter of Haywood, Sample, Seay, Shepard, Shelton, Staley, Stephens, Taylor, Turner, Warner and Williamson—54.

Section 3, as thus amended, was adopted by the Convention.

Mr. JONES, of Lincoln, moved to reconsider the vote adopting Section 3, and further moved to lay the motion to reconsider on the table, which latter motion was adopted.

Mr. MABRY moved to amend Section 4, by inserting after the word "years" in the fourth line, "*or a native born citizen of the State.*"

Mr. TAYLOR moved to amend by striking out the word "ten" in the fourth line, and inserting "eight." It will then read, "His term of service shall be eight years."

Mr. BATE proposed to amend by striking out all after the word "age" in the third line.

On motion of Mr. BLACKBURN, the Convention adjourned until 9½ o'clock to-morrow morning.

THURSDAY MORNING, FEBRUARY 3, 1870.

The Convention met pursuant to adjournment, Mr. President BROWN in the Chair.

Prayer by the Rev. Mr. MOONEY.

The Journal of yesterday was read and approved.

The roll was called for Memorials and Petitions.

SPECIAL REPORT ON COMMON SCHOOLS.

Mr. GORDON, from the Special Committee on Common Schools, made the following report:

The Committee on Common Schools have had under consideration sundry resolutions in reference to the application of the proceeds of the poll-tax, from year to year, for the use of free schools in this State, and have unanimously agreed to submit to the consideration of the Convention the following report:

Resolved, That Section 10, Article XI, of the present Constitution be amended by striking out all after the word "end" in the fifth line, and inserting: *It shall be the duty of the General Assembly to provide for the establishment and maintenance of free schools for the gratuitous instruction of all the children of the State between the ages of —— and —— years. And the ordinary tax assessed on polls, under the provisions of this Constitution, with such other of the revenue of the State as the General Assembly may from time to to time set apart therefor, shall never be applied to other than educational purposes.*

B. GORDON, Chairman.

On motion of Mr. PORTER, of Haywood, it was ordered that the report be laid on the table, and 100 copies printed for the use of the Convention.

REPORT ON THE JUDICIARY FURTHER CONSIDERED.

The Convention proceeded to the consideration of the unfinished business of yesterday, the report of the majority of the Judiciary Committee.

The amendment of Mr. TAYLOR to Section 4, to strike out "ten" and insert "eight" years, was adopted.

Mr. MABRY withdrew his amendment.

Mr. BROOKS moved to reconsider the vote by which Mr. Taylor's amendment was adopted.

Mr. GIBSON gave notice that if the motion to reconsider was sustained, that he should move to amend by striking out "eight years" in the 4th line, and insert "six years."

Mr. TAYLOR moved to lay the motion to reconsider on the table.

Mr. GIBSON demanded the yeas and nays, which were ordered, and the motion to lay on the table sustained.

Yeas.. 61
Nays.. 9

Those voting in the affirmative are:

Messrs. Bate, Baxter, Blizard, Britton, Brown of Davidson, Brown of Henry, etc., Burkett, Burton, Byrne, Campbell, Carter, Coffin, Cummings, Deaderick, Deavenport, Dibbrell, Doherty, Dromgoole, Fentress, Fielder, Finley, Gardner, Garner, Gaut, Gibbs, Gordon, Heiskell, Henderson, Hill of Warren, Hill of Gibson, House of Williamson, House of Montgomery, etc., Ivie, Jones of Lincoln, Jones of Giles, Kennedy, Key, Kirkpatrick, Kyle, Mabry, McDougal, McNabb, Martin, Morris, Meeks, Netherland, Nicholson, Porter of Haywood, Porter of Henry, Seay, Shepard,

Shelton, Staley, Stephens, Taylor, Thompson of Davidson, Thompson of Maury, Turner, Walters, Warner, Williamson and Wright—61.

Those voting in the negative are:

Messrs. Branson, Brandon, Brooks, Chowning, Cypert, Fulkerson, Gibson, Parker and Sample—9.

Mr. BAXTER moved to amend by striking out the word "five" in the fourth line, and inserting "three."

Mr. ——— moved to lay the motion of Mr. Baxter on the table.

Mr. GIBSON demanded the yeas and nays, which were ordered, and the motion to lay on the table sustained.

Yeas..53
Nays..19

Those voting in the affirmative are:

Messrs. Arledge, Bate, Blizard, Brandon, Brooks, Brown of Davidson, Brown of Henry, etc., Burkett, Burton, Byrne, Campbell, Chowning, Cummings, Cypert, Deavenport, Dibbrell, Doherty, Dromgoole, Fentress, Fielder, Fulkerson, Gardner, Garner, Gaut, Gibbs, Henderson, Hill of Gibson, House of Williamson, Ivie, Jones of Lincoln, Jones of Giles, Kennedy, Kyle, McDougal, McNabb, Morris, Meeks, Martin, Netherland, Porter of Henry, Seay, Shepard, Shelton, Staley, Stephens, Taylor, Thompson of Davidson, Thompson of Maury, Turner, Walters, Warner, Williamson and Wright—53.

Those voting in the negative are:

Messrs. Blackburn, Baxter, Branson, Britton, Carter, Coffin, Finley, Gibson, Gordon, Heiskell, Hill of Warren, House of Montgomery, etc., Key, Kirkpatrick, Mabry, Nicholson, Parker, Porter of Haywood and Sample—19.

Mr. BURKETT offered the following:

Resolved, That in lieu of Article VI, Section 4, as reported by the majority of the Committee on the Judiciary, the following be adopted, viz:

ARTICLE VI.

Sec. 4. The Judges of the Circuit and Chancery Courts, and of other inferior courts of the State, shall be elected by the qualified voters of the district or circuit to which they are to be assigned. Every Judge of said court shall be thirty-five years of age, and shall, before his election, have practiced as an Attorney-at Law or Solicitor in Chancery ten years, in the courts of this State, before he shall be eligible to such office, and shall have resided in such district or circuit one year immediately preceding such election. His term of office shall be eight years.

On motion of Mr. BAXTER, the amendment was laid on the table.

Mr. MARTIN offered the following amendment:

Insert after the word "years" in the fourth line, "and shall have been a resident of the State five years, and of the circuit or district one year before his election."

Which was adopted by the Convention.

Section 4, as amended, was adopted by the Convention.

Mr. GARNER moved to reconsider the vote adopting Section 4, and further moved to lay the motion to reconsider on the table, which latter motion was adopted.

Mr. TURNER proposed the following in lieu of the two first lines of Section 5:

An Attorney General and Reporter for the State shall be elected by the qualified voters of the State, and shall hold his office for eight years.

Mr. HEISKELL moved to lay the amendment on the table.

Mr. TURNER demanded the yeas and nays, which were ordered, and the motion to lay on the table sustained.

Yeas...59
Nays...14

Those voting in the affirmative are:

Messrs. Arledge, Burkett, Blackburn, Brown of Davidson, Baxter, Britton, Brooks, Byrne, Blizard, Burton, Brown of Henry, etc., Bate, Cummings, Coffin, Campbell, Chowning, Cypert, Carter, Deaderick, Doherty, Dromgoole, Finley, Fulkerson, Fentress, Gaut, Gardner, Gordon, Henderson, Hill of Gibson, Heiskell, House of Williamson, House of Montgomery, etc., Ivie, Jones of Lincoln, Jones of Giles, Kirkpatrick, Key, Kennedy, Kyle, Martin, Mabry, Morris, Meeks, McDougal, McNabb, Netherland, Nicholson, Porter of Haywood, Porter of Henry, Shepard, Stephens, Staley, Shelton, Thompson of Davidson, Thompson of Maury, Taylor, Wright, Williamson and Walters—59.

Those voting in the negative are:

Messrs. Branson, Brandon, Dibbrell, Deavenport, Fielder, Gibson, Gibbs, Garner, Hill of Warren, Parker, Seay, Sample, Turner and Warner—14.

On motion of Mr. JONES, of Lincoln, the section was amended by striking out the word "twelve" and inserting "eight" in the second line.

Mr. MARTIN moved to amend by adding to the fifth line: "And shall have been a resident of the State five years, and of the circuit or district one year before his election;" which was adopted, and the section, as amended, was adopted by the Convention.

Mr. GIBSON offered the following amendment to Section 6:

Insert between the words "office" and "by," in first line, the words, "for crime, corruption, habitual drunkenness, incompetency, or neglect of duty."

Mr. FENTRESS offered the following in lieu of Mr. Gibson's amendment:

Insert after the word "State," first line, the words, "for official corruption, or for continued neglect of duty, or continued incapacity of any kind to perform the duties of his office."

Mr. HEISKELL moved to lay the amendment of Mr. Gibson, and the amendment in lieu by Mr. Fentress on the table, and demanded the yeas and nays, which were ordered, and the motion to lay on the table rejected.

Yeas.. 31
Nays.. 41

Those voting in the affirmative are:

Messrs. Arledge, Baxter, Blizard, Brown of Henry, etc., Burton, Byrne, Coffin, Cummings, Gardner, Gibbs, Heiskell, Henderson, Hill of Warren, House of Davidson, etc., Ivie, Jones of Lincoln, Kennedy, Key, Mabry, McDougal, Morris, Meeks, Porter of Haywood, Porter of Henry, Shelton, Taylor, Thompson of Davidson, Thompson of Maury, Turner, Warner and Williamson—31.

Those voting in the negative are:

Messrs. Bate, Blackburn, Branson, Brandon, Britton, Brooks, Brown of Davidson, Campbell, Carter, Chowning, Cypert, Deaderick, Deavenport, Dibbrell, Doherty, Dromgoole, Fentress, Fielder, Finley, Fulkerson, Garner, Gaut, Gibson, Gordon, Hill of Gibson, House of Williamson, Jones of Giles, Kirkpatrick, Kyle, McNabb, Martin, Netherland, Nicholson, Parker, Sample, Seay, Shepard, Staley, Stephens, Walters and Wright—41.

Mr. TURNER gave notice that he should offer the following amendment:

Add at the end of line 8th; *Provided,* The causes of his removal are such as are prescribed by a general law of the land, passed by a Legislature prior to the one taking action thereon.

Mr. CAMPBELL demanded the previous question, which demand

was sustained, and the question recurring on the adoption of Mr. Fentress' amendment in lieu of Mr. Gibson's.

Mr. CAMPBELL demanded the yeas and nays, which were ordered, and Mr. Fentress' amendment in lieu was adopted.

Yeas.. 39
Nays.. 33

Those voting in the affirmative are:

Messrs. Bate, Blizard, Brandon, Britton, Brown of Davidson, Burkett, Campbell, Carter, Coffin, Cypert, Deaderick, Deavenport, Dromgoole, Fentress, Fielder, Fulkerson, Gardner, Gaut, Gibbs, Gordon, Hill of Warren, Hill of Gibson, Jones of Giles, Kirkpatrick, Kyle, McDougal, Martin, Morris, Meeks, Netherland, Porter of Haywood, Porter of Henry, Shepard, Stephens, Thompson of Davidson, Turner, Warner, Williamson and Wright—39.

Those voting in the negative are:

Messrs. Baxter, Blackburn, Branson, Brooks, Brown of Henry, etc., Burton, Byrne, Chowning, Cummings, Dibbrell, Doherty, Finley, Garner, Gibson, Heiskell, Henderson, House of Williamson, House of Davidson, etc., Ivie, Jones of Lincoln, Kennedy, Key, Mabry, McNabb, Nicholson, Parker, Sample, Seay, Shelton, Staley, Taylor, Thompson of Maury, and Walters—33.

Mr. HEISKELL demanded the ayes and nays upon the adoption of Mr. Fentress' amendment, which were ordered, and the amendment was lost by a tie vote.

Yeas.. 36
Nays.. 36

Those voting in the affirmative are:

Messrs. Bate, Blackburn, Branson, Brandon, Britton, Brooks, Brown of Davidson, Byrne, Campbell, Carter, Chowning, Coffin, Cypert, Deaderick, Dromgoole, Fentress, Fielder, Finley, Fulkerson, Gardner, Gaut, Gibbs, Gibson, Gordon, Hill of Gibson, Jones of Giles, Kirkpatrick, Kyle, McNabb, Martin, Parker, Porter of Haywood, Shepard, Stephens, Thompson of Davidson, and Wright—36.

Those voting in the negative are:.

Messrs. Baxter, Blizard, Brown of Henry, etc., Burkett, Burton, Cummings, Deavenport, Dibbrell, Doherty, Garner, Heiskell, Henderson, Hill of Warren, House of Williamson, House of Montgomery, etc., Ivie, Jones of Lincoln, Kennedy, Key, Mabry, McDougal, Morris, Meeks, Netherland, Nicholson, Porter of Henry, Sample, Seay, Shelton, Staley, Taylor, Thompson of Maury, Turner, Walters, Warner and Williamson—36.

(Previous to the offering of and action of the Convention on the amendments of Messrs. GIBSON and FENTRESS, Section 6 was, on motion of Mr. Jones, of Lincoln, amended by striking out the words "elected to each House," and inserting "*to which each House shall be entitled,*" which was adopted by the Convention.)

The Convention took a recess to 2½ o'clock P. M.

AFTERNOON SESSION.

Mr. HEISKELL demanded the yeas and nays upon the adoption of Section 6, which were ordered, and the section was adopted.

Yeas... 38
Nays... 29

Those voting in the affirmative are:

Messrs. Allen, Baxter, Blizard, Brandon, Britton, Brooks, Brown of Henry, etc., Burkett, Burton, Byrne, Carter, Chowning, Coffin, Cummings, Deaderick, Fielder, Garner, Gaut, Gibson, Heiskell, Henderson, Hill of Warren, House of Montgomery, etc., Ivie, Kennedy, Key, Kirkpatrick, Kyle, Mabry, McDougal, McNabb, Meeks, Nicholson, Staley, Taylor, Thompson of Maury, Warner and Wright—38.

Those voting in the negative are:

Messrs. Bate, Branson, Brown of Davidson, Campbell, Cypert, Dibbrell, Doherty, Dromgoole, Fentress, Fulkerson, Garner, Gibbs, Hill of Gibson, Jones of Lincoln, Jones of Giles, Martin, Morris, Parker, Porter of Haywood, Porter of Henry, Sample, Seay, Shepard, Shelton, Stephens, Thompson of Davidson, Turner, Walters and Williamson—29.

Mr. HEISKELL moved to reconsider the vote adopting Section 6, and further moved to lay the motion to reconsider on the table.

Mr. TAYLOR demanded the yeas and nays on the motion to lay

the motion to reconsider on the table, which were ordered, and the motion to lay on the table rejected.

Yeas.. 34
Nays.. 39

Those voting in the affirmative are:

Messrs. Allen, Arledge, Baxter, Blizard, Brandon, Britton, Burkett, Burton, Byrne, Carter, Chowning, Cummings, Deaderick, Dibbrell, Doherty, Fielder, Gaut, Gordon, Heiskell, Henderson, Hill of Warren, House of Montgomery, etc., Ivie, Kennedy, Key, Kirkpatrick, Kyle, Mabry, McNabb, Netherland, Nicholson, Porter, Staley and Wright—34.

Those voting in the negative are:

Messrs. Bate, Blackburn, Branson, Brooks, Brown of Davidson, Brown of Henry, etc., Campbell, Coffin, Cypert, Dromgoole, Fentress, Finley, Fulkerson, Gardner, Garner, Gibbs, Gibson, Hill of Gibson, House of Williamson, Jones of Lincoln, Jones of Giles, McDougal, Martin, Morris, Meeks, Parker, Porter of Haywood, Sample, Seay, Shepard, Shelton, Stephens, Taylor, Thompson of Davidson, Thompson of Maury, Turner, Walters, Warner and Williamson—39.

Mr. HEISKELL withdrew his motion to reconsider.

Mr. THOMPSON, of Maury, renewed the motion to reconsider.

Mr. BAXTER demanded the yeas and nays, which were ordered, and the motion to reconsider was sustained.

Yeas.. 37
Nays.. 36

Those voting in the affirmative are:

Messrs. Bate, Blackburn, Branson, Brown of Davidson, Brown of Henry, etc., Campbell, Chowning, Coffin, Cypert, Dromgoole, Fentress, Finley, Fulkerson, Gardner, Garner, Gibbs, Gibson, Hill of Gibson, House of Williamson, Jones, of Lincoln, Jones of Giles, Martin, Morris, Meeks, Parker, Porter of Haywood, Sample, Seay, Shepard, Shelton, Stephens, Taylor, Thompson of Davidson, Turner, Walters, Warner and Williamson—37.

Those voting in the negative are:

Messrs. Allen, Arledge, Baxter, Blizard, Brandon, Britton, Brooks, Burkett, Burton, Byrne, Carter, Cummings, Deaderick, Dibbrell, Doherty, Fielder, Gaut, Gordon, Heiskell, Henderson, Hill of Warren, House of Montgomery, etc., Ivie, Kennedy, Key, Kirkpatrick, Kyle, Mabry, McDougal, McNabb, Netherland, Nicholson, Porter of Henry, Staley, Thompson of Maury, and Wright—36.

Mr. PORTER, of Haywood, moved to strike out the whole of Section 6.

Mr. HEISKELL demanded the previous question on the motion to strike out.

Mr. TURNER demanded the yeas and nays, which were ordered, and the demand for the previous question was rejected.

Yeas.. 29
Nays.. 43

Those voting in the affirmative are:

Messrs. Baxter, Blackburn, Blizard, Brandon, Britton, Burkett, Burton, Byrne, Carter, Deaderick, Doherty, Gaut, Heiskell, Henderson, Hill of Warren, Ivie, Jones of Lincoln, Kennedy, Key, Kirkpatrick, Kyle, Mabry, McNabb, Netherland, Nicholson, Porter of Henry, Shelton, Staley and Wright—29.

Those voting in the negative are:

Messrs. Allen, Arledge, Branson, Brooks, Brown of Davidson, Brown of Henry, etc., Campbell, Chowning, Coffin, Cummings, Cypert, Dibbrell, Dromgoole, Fentress, Fielder, Finley, Fulkerson, Gardner, Garner, Gibbs, Gibson, Gordon, Hill of Gibson, House of Williamson, House of Montgomery, etc., Jones of Giles, McDougal, Martin, Morris, Meeks, Parker, Porter of Haywood, Sample, Seay, Shepard, Stephens, Taylor, Thompson of Davidson, Thompson of Maury, Turner, Walters, Warner and Williamson—43.

Mr. TURNER offered the following amendment:

Add at the end of line 8th; "*Provided*, The causes of his removal are such as are prescribed by a general law of the land, passed by a Legislature prior to the one taking action thereon."

Mr. FENTRESS offered the following in lieu of Mr. Turner's.

Article VI, Section 6, insert after the word "State" in the first line the following: "For official corruption or for continued neglect of duty, or incapacity of any kind to perform the duties of his office."

Mr. GIBSON moved that Section 6, and all the pending amendments be committed to a Select Committee of seven to be appointed by the President.

Mr. BLIZARD demanded the Previous Question.

Mr. TURNER demanded "*The Question*" which was sustained.

A vote was taken upon Mr. GIBSON's motion to commit, and was rejected.

Mr. FENTRESS's amendment was rejected.

Mr. TURNER's amendment was rejected.

A vote was taken on Mr. PORTER'S (of Haywood) motion to strike out the 6th Section, and it was rejected.

Section 6, as amended, was again adopted by the Convention.

Mr. KENNEDY moved to reconsider the vote adopting Section 6, and further moved to lay the motion to reconsider on the table.

Which latter motion was adopted.

Mr. HOUSE, of Montgomery, etc., offered the following amendment to Section 7:

The salary of a Supreme Judge shall not be less than forty-five hundred dollars per annum, and that of a Chuncellor or Circuit Judge not less than three thousand dollars per annum.

Mr. SAMPLE offered the following amendment to Mr. House's amendment:

"That the salaries of the Judges be left with the Legislature."

On motion of Mr. BROOKS the amendments were laid on the table.

Section 7, as recommended by the Committee was adopted by the Convention.

Section 8, was taken up, when Mr. TAYLOR proposed the following amendment:

Amend Section 8, by adding after "Legislature" in second line the following: "And their organization shall be uniform throughout the State."

Mr. TAYLOR subsequently withdrew his amendment.

Section 8, as recommended by the Committee, was adopted by the Convention.

Section 9, as reported by the Committee was adopted by the Convention.

Mr. HILL, of Gibson, offered the following in lieu of Section 10:

The Judges, Chancellors or Justices of the inferior courts of Law and Equity shall have power in all civil cases, to issue writs of *certiorari* to remove any cause or the transcript *of the record thereof*, from any inferior jurisdiction into such Courts of Law, on sufficient cause supported by oath or affirmation.

Which was adopted in lieu, and the Section as thus amended was adopted by the Convention.

Sections 11 and 12, were adopted as recommended by the Committee without amendment.

Mr. STEPHENS move to reconsider the vote adopting his amendment to Section 13 on Tuesday last.

Mr. JONES, of Lincoln, demanded the yeas and nays, which were ordered, and the motion to reconsider was adopted:

Yeas.. 37
Nays.. 34

Those voting in the affirmative are:

Messrs. Bate, Baxter, Brandon, Brown of Davidson, Brown of Henry, etc., Burton, Campbell, Carter, Deaderick, Fentress, Gardner, Garner, Gibbs, Gordon, Heiskell, Henderson, Hill of Gibson, House of Williamson, House of Montgomery, etc., Jones of Giles, Kennedy, Key, Kirkpatrick, Kyle, Martin, Netherland, Nicholson, Seay, Shepard, Shelton, Staley, Stephens, Taylor, Thompson of Davidson, Thompson of Maury, Turner and Williamson—37.

Those voting in the negative are:

Messrs. Allen, Arledge, Blizard, Branson, Britton, Brooks, Burkett, Byrne, Chowning, Coffin, Cummings, Cypert, Dibbrell, Doherty, Dromgoole, Fielder, Finley, Gaut, Gibson, Hill of Warren, Ivie, Jones of Lincoln, Mabry, McDougal, McNabb, Morris, Meeks, Parker, Porter of Haywood, Porter of Henry, Sample, Walters, Warner, and Wright—34.

Mr. JONES, of Lincoln, offered the following in lieu of Section 13:

Clerks of the Supreme Court shall be elected, each for the term of six years, by the qualified voters of the respective grand divisions of the State, in which said Court is required to be held.

Clerks and Masters of the Chancery Courts shall be elected, each for the term of six years, by the qualified voters of the respective counties, districts or divisions in which such Courts shall be required to be held.

Clerks of the Circuit Courts, and Clerks of such inferior courts as may be hereafter established, shall be elected, each for the term of four years, by the qualified voters of the respective counties in and for which said Courts shall be required to be held.

The Clerks provided for in this Section shall be removed from office for malfeasance, incompetency, or neglect of duty, in such manner as may be prescribed by law.

The consideration of said amendment was posponed until tomorrow.

VISIT OF RESPECT TO MRS. POLK.

Mr. Burton offered the following resolution, which was adopted by the Convention:

Resolved, That a committee of three be appointed to wait on Mrs. POLK, the late widow of President JAMES K. POLK, and ascertain when it would suit her convenience to receive a visit of respect from this body.

On motion of Mr. JONES, of Lincoln, the Convention adjourned until to-morrow at 9½ o'clock, A. M.

FRIDAY MORNING, FEBRUARY 4, 1870.

The Convention met pursuant to adjournment, Mr. President BROWN in the Chair.

Prayer by the Rev. Mr. SAMPLE, a member of the Convention.

The Journal of yesterday was read, and approved.

The roll was called for memorials and petitions.

MEMORIALS.

Mr. DEADERICK presented a memorial from sundry citizens of Roane, Monroe and Blount counties, praying the creation of a new county out of portions of said counties, which, without being read, was referred to the Committee on New Counties and County Lines.

Mr. TAYLOR presented a memorial from citizens of the counties of Henderson, Madison, McNairy and Hardeman, praying the creation of a new county out of portions of said counties, which, without being read, was referred to the Committee on New Counties and County Lines.

AMENDMENTS PROPOSED.

Mr. SAMPLE offered the following resolution, which was read and referred to the Committee on Miscellaneous Provisions:

Resolved, That the Legislature shall have power, after the ratification of this Constitution, every eight years thereafter, to offer to the people an amendment to the Constitution, and after due notice if the people by a majority of the popular vote, ratify the said amendment then, it shall become a part of the organic law of the State, and the Governor shall declare the same by proclamation.

Mr. BROOKS offered the following resolution, which was read and referred to the Committee on the Judiciary:

Resolved, That the salary of the Supreme Court Judges be three thousand dollars per annum.

Be it further resolved, That the Judges of the Circuit and Chancery Courts shall receive a salary of two thousand dollars per annum.

CHANGE OF RULES.

Mr. BROWN, of Davidson, offered the following resolution:

Resolved, That the rule of this Convention authorizing the Previous Question, be and the same is repealed, and no member who speaks upon a pending question shall be allowed at the close of his speech to make a motion to lay on the table.

Mr. BROWN moved to suspend the rules and take up the resolution, which motion was rejected and the resolution lies over under the rule.

REPORT ON MISCELLANEOUS BUSINESS.

Mr. TURNER, from the Committee on Miscellaneous Provisions, made the following report:

MR. PRESIDENT:

The Committee on Miscellaneous Provisions having had under consideration several subjects beg leave to submit for the consideration of the Convention the two following Sections as amendments to the Constitution.

Section —— "The General Assembly shall have power to enact laws for the protection and preservation of game and fish within the State, and such laws may be enacted for, and applied and enforced, in particular counties or geographical districts designated by the General Assembly."

Sec. ——. "The due coupons of the Bonds of the State, legally issued, and all Treasury Warrants shall be received at par after January 1, 1871, for all taxes or other dues to the State; *Provided,* that this Section shall not apply during a rebellion or invasion of the State."

All of which is respectfully submitted,

JAMES J. TURNER,
Chairman.

On motion of Mr. TAYLOR it was ordered that the report be

laid on the table, and 100 copies printed for the use of the Convention.

COMMITTEE TO WAIT ON MRS. POLK.

The President announced the following Committee to wait on Mrs. Polk, in accordance with Mr. BURTON's resolution:

Messrs. Burton, Netherland and Campbell.

LEAVE OF ABSENCE.

Mr. NETHERLAND asked and obtained leave of absence for Mr Martin, on account of sickness.

REPORT ON JUDICIARY FURTHER CONSIDERED.

The Convention resumed the consideration of the unfinished business of yesterday.

Mr. MORRIS offered the following amendment:

Strike out line 1, of Section 13, and insert in lieu thereof:

Section 13. Judges of the Supreme Courts shall appoint their clerks, who shall hold their offices for eight years.

Which was rejected by the Convention.

Mr. MORRIS submitted the following amendment:

Strike out of lines 2 and 3, of Section 13, the words "Chancellors (if Chancery Courts shall be established,) shall appoint their Clerks and Masters, who shall hold their offices for the period of six years," and insert in lieu thereof, "The Clerks and Masters of the Chancery Courts shall be elected by the qualified voters of the county or counties or districts for which a Chancery Court is held, and shall hold their offices for eight years. Clerks of the Circuit Courts shall be elected by the qualified voters of the respective counties for which Circuit Courts are held, and shall hold their offices for eight years."

Mr. SAMPLE moved to amend the amendment of Mr. Morris by striking out the word "eight" and inserting "six."

Mr. BLIZARD demanded the previous question, which demand was sustained.

Mr. SAMPLE's amendment to Mr. Morris' amendment was adopted.

Mr. MORRIS demanded the yeas and nays on the adoption of his amendment as amended, which were ordered, and the amendment adopted.

Yeas...37
Nays...35

Those voting in the affirmative are:

Messrs. Arledge, Blackburn, Blizard, Branson, Brandon, Britton, Brooks, Burkett, Chowning, Cypert, Deavenport, Dibbrell, Doherty, Dromgoole, Fentress, Fielder, Finley, Gaut, Gibson, Hill of Warren, Hill of Gibson, Ivie, Jones of Lincoln, Mabry, McNabb, Morris, Parker, Porter of Haywood, Sample, Shepard, Stephens, Taylor, Thompson of Maury, Walters, Warner, Williamson and Wright—37.

Those voting in the negative are:

Messrs. Bate, Baxter, Brown of Davidson, Brown of Henry, etc., Burton, Byrne, Campbell, Carter, Coffin, Cummings, Deaderick, Fulkerson, Gardner, Garner, Gibbs, Gordon, Heiskell, Henderson, House of Williamson, House of Montgomery, etc., Jones of Giles, Kennedy, Key, Kirkpatrick, Kyle, McDougal, Meeks, Netherland, Nicholson, Porter of Henry, Seay, Shelton, Staley, Thompson of Davidson, and Turner—35.

Mr. Stephens withdrew his amendment.

Mr. Dibbrell demanded the yeas and nays on the adoption of the amendment of Mr. Jones, of Lincoln, in lieu of the 13th Section, which were ordered, and the amendment was rejected.

Yeas...28
Nays...44

Those voting in the affirmative are:

Messrs. Arledge, Blackburn, Branson, Britton, Brooks, Chowning, Cypert, Deavenport, Dibbrell, Doherty, Fentress, Fielder, Finley, Gibson, Hill of Warren, Hill of Gibson, Jones of Lincoln, Mabry, McDougal, McNabb, Meeks, Parker, Porter of Haywood, Sample, Stephens, Taylor, Walters and Warner—28.

Those voting in the negative are:

Messrs. Baxter, Blizard, Brandon, Brown of Davidson, Brown of Henry, etc., Burkett, Burton, Byrne, Campbell, Carter, Coffin, Cummings, Deaderick, Dromgoole, Fulkerson, Gardner, Garner, Gaut, Gibbs, Gordon, Heiskell, Henderson, House of Williamson, House of Montgomery, etc., Ivie, Jones of Giles, Kennedy, Key, Kirkpatrick, Kyle, Morris, Netherland, Nicholson, Porter of Henry, Seay, Shepard, Shelton, Staley, Thompson of Davidson, Thompson of Maury, Turner, Williamson, Wright and President Brown—44.

By unanimous consent, the word "*they*," in the fifth line, was stricken out, and "*these Clerks*" inserted.

Mr. KENNEDY demanded the yeas and nays on the adoption of Section 13, as amended, which were ordered, and the section was adopted by the Convention.

Yeas..42
Nays..29

Those voting in the affirmative are:

Messrs. Arledge, Blackburn, Blizard, Branson, Brandon, Britton, Brooks, Brown of Davidson, Brown of Henry, etc., Burkett, Byrne, Chowning, Coffin, Deavenport, Dibbrell, Doherty, Dromgoole, Fielder, Finley, Gaut, Gibson, Heiskell, Hill of Warren, Hill of Gibson, Ivie, Jones of Lincoln, Key, Mabry, McNabb, Morris, Parker, Porter of Haywood, Sample, Seay, Shepard, Stephens, Thompson of Maury, Turner, Walters, Warner, Williamson and Wright—42.

Those voting in the negative are:

Messrs. Allen, Baxter, Burton, Campbell, Carter, Cummings, Deaderick, Fentress, Fulkerson, Gardner, Garner, Gibbs, Gordon, Henderson, House of Williamson, House of Montgomery, etc., Jones of Giles, Kennedy, Kirkpatrick, Kyle, McDougal, Meeks, Netherland, Nicholson, Porter of Henry, Shelton, Staley, Taylor and Thompson of Davidson—29.

Mr. JONES, of Lincoln, moved to reconsider the vote adopting Section 13, and further moved to lay the motion to reconsider on the table, which latter motion was adopted.

Section 14 was adopted as recommended by the Committee.

Mr. BURKETT offered the following amendment to Section 15:

Resolved, That Section 15 be amended by striking out "two," in the third line, and inserting in lieu thereof "one;" and in the fifth line, by striking out "three" and inserting in lieu thereof "two."

Mr. JONES, of Lincoln, demanded the previous question, which demand was sustained.

Mr. BURKETT demanded the yeas and nays on the adoption of his amendment, which were ordered, and the amendment was rejected.

Yeas..14
Nays..55

Those voting in the affirmative are:

Messrs. Blizard, Branson, Burkett, Cypert, Fulkerson, Gaut,

Heiskell, House of Montgomery, etc., Kennedy, Key, Kirkpatrick, Kyle, Parker and Williamson—14.

Those voting in the negative are:

Messrs. Arledge, Baxter, Blackburn, Brandon, Britton, Brooks, Brown of Davidson, Brown of Henry, etc., Burton, Byrne, Campbell, Carter, Chowning, Coffin, Cummings, Deavenport, Dibbrell, Doherty, Dromgoole, Fentress, Fielder, Finley, Gardner, Garner, Gibbs, Gibson, Gordon, Henderson, Hill of Warren, Hill of Gibson, House of Williamson, Ivie, Jones of Lincoln, Jones of Giles, Mabry, McDougal, McNabb, Morris, Meeks, Netherland, Nicholson, Porter of Henry, Sample, Seay, Shepard, Shelton, Staley, Stephens, Taylor, Thompson of Davidson, Thompson of Maury, Turner, Walters, Warner and Wright—55.

Section 15, as recommended by the Committee, was then adopted by the Convention.

Mr. Kennedy offered the following as an independent section:

If at any election for Chancery Court Clerk, no candidate shall receive a majority of all the votes cast, then the Chancellor shall appoint the Clerk.

Which was rejected by the Convention.

Mr. Gibson offered the following as an independent section:

Section —. The Legislature shall, from time to time, by a general law, divide the State into Judicial Circuits and Chancery Districts or Divisions, so that the number of Circuits shall not exceed one for every sixty thousand inhabitants, and the number of Chancery Districts or Divisions shall not exceed one for every seventy-five thousand inhabitants: *Provided*, that territory and population shall be so equalized as to equalize the labors of the several Judges and of the several Chancellors as nearly as possible. And no Circuit, District or Division shall be created otherwise than by a general law re-circuiting or re-districting the entire State.

Pending which, the Convention took a recess until 2½ o'clock P. M.

AFTERNOON SESSION.

Mr. PORTER, of Henry, moved to lay the amendment of Mr. Gibson on the table.

Mr. GIBSON demanded the yeas and nays, which were ordered, and the motion to lay on the table sustained.

Yeas..42
Nays..19

Those voting in the affirmative are:

Messrs. Bate, Baxter, Brown of Davidson, Brown of Henry, etc., Burkett, Burton, Byrne, Campbell, Carter, Cummings, Cypert, Deaderick, Doherty, Dromgoole, Fentress, Fielder, Gardner, Garner, Gaut, Gibbs, Heiskell, Henderson, Hill of Gibson, House of Williamson, Jones of Giles, Kennedy, Key, Kirkpatrick, Mabry, McDougal, Morris, Meeks, Netherland, Porter of Haywood, Porter of Henry, Shepard, Shelton, Stephens, Taylor, Thompson of Davidson, Thompson of Maury, and Wright—42.

Those voting in the negative are:

Messrs. Blackburn, Blizard, Branson, Brandon, Britton, Brooks, Chowning, Fulkerson, Gibson, Hill of Warren, Kyle, McNabb, Nicholson, Parker, Sample, Seay, Turner, Warner and Williamson —19.

TERM OF OFFICE AND VACANCIES.

Mr. GIBSON offered the following resolution:

Section —. All officers authorized by this Constitution or by the Legislature, shall hold their offices until their successors shall be elected or appointed and qualified; and whenever a vacancy occurs in any office, the officer elected or appointed to fill the vacancy, shall hold office only for the unexpired term of his predecessor, and until his successor is elected or appointed and qualified.

On motion of Mr. FENTRESS, the resolution was referred to the Committee on Elections.

SCHEDULE.

The 1st section of the Schedule was, by unanimous consent, amended by inserting "and Reporter" after the word general, in the second line.

Mr. SEAY moved to amend Section 1 of the Schedule by inserting, after the word "State" in the second line, the words "Attorneys for the State for the several circuits or districts," and after the word "courts," in the same line, insert the words, "Justices of the Peace."

Mr. KEY offered the following in lieu of the first paragraph of Section 1 of the Schedule, and Mr. Seay's amendment:

That no inconvenience may arise from a change of the Constitution, it is declared that all civil officers shall hold their offices until the first day of November, 1871, unless their term of service previously expires.

Mr. DROMGOOLE proposed to amend the Schedule by inserting after the word Judges, in the second line, "and Clerks and County Registers," so that the same will read:

That no inconvenience may arise from a change of the Constitution, it is declared that all civil officers, except the Attorney General and Reporter for the State, and the Judges and Clerks of the several courts, and County Registers, shall hold their offices until the expiration of their present term of service.

THE VISIT TO MRS. POLK.

Mr. BURTON, from the Committee appointed to wait on Mrs. Polk, reported that they had performed that duty, and that Mrs. Polk had expressed a readiness to receive the committee to-morrow afternoon.

On motion of Mr. THOMPSON, of Davidson, the Convention adjourned until to-morrow morning, at 9½ o'clock.

SATURDAY MORNING, FEBRUARY 5, 1870.

The Convention met pursuant to adjournment, Mr. President BROWN in the Chair.

Prayer by the Rev. Dr. YOUNG.

The Journal of yesterday was read, corrected and approved.

THE JUDICIARY FURTHER CONSIDERED.

Mr. JONES, of Lincoln, moved to reconsider the vote adopting Section 13, which being objected to, as a motion had been made to reconsider that vote, and the motion to reconsider had been laid on the table:

Mr. JONES then moved to take from the table the motion to reconsider, which was adopted, and the motion to reconsider was then adopted.

Mr. JONES, of Lincoln, proposed the following amendment to Section 13:

Strike out "six" where it applies to the Circuit Court Clerks, and insert "four."

Mr. JONES demanded the previous question.

Objection was made to entertaining Mr. JONES' amendment, as it was not reduced to writing The objection was sustained by the Chair.

Mr. JONES proceeded to write out his amendment; whereupon Mr. Kennedy claimed the floor, and he was recognized by the Chair.

Mr. Kennedy then offered the following in lieu of Section 13:

Judges of the Supreme Court shall appoint their Clerks, who shall hold their office for six years; Chancellors shall appoint their Clerks and Masters, who shall hold their offices for six years. Clerks of such inferior courts as may be hereafter established, which shall be required to be holden in the respective counties of this State, shall be elected by the qualified voters thereof, for the term of four years. They shall be removed from office for malfeasance, incompetency, or neglect of duty, in such manner as may be prescribed by law.

Mr. JONES presented his amendment, as above, in writing, which was reported by the Secretary, and again demanded the previous question, which was sustained.

Mr. JONES amendment was then adopted.

Mr. KENNEDY demanded the yeas and nays on the adoption of his amendment in lieu, which were ordered, and the amendment adopted.

Yeas..36
Nays..34

Those voting in the affirmative are:

Messrs. Allen, Bate, Baxter, Brown of Davidson, Brown of

Henry, etc., Burton, Byrne, Campbell, Carter, Coffin, Deaderick, Doherty, Fentress, Fulkerson, Gardner, Garner, Gibbs, Gordon, Heiskell, Henderson, House of Williamson, House of Montgomery, etc., Jones of Giles, Kennedy, Key, Kirkpatrick, Kyle, Netherland, Porter of Henry, Seay, Shelton, Staley, Thompson of Davidson, Turner, Wright and President Brown.

Those voting in the negative are:

Messrs. Arledge, Blackburn, Blizard, Brandon, Branson, Britton, Brooks, Burkett, Chowning, Cummings, Deavenport, Dibbrell, Dromgoole, Fielder, Finley, Gaut, Gibson, Hill of Warren, Hill of Gibson, Ivie, Jones of Lincoln, McDougal, McNabb, Meeks, Morris, Parker, Porter of Haywood, Sample, Shepard, Stephens, Taylor, Thompson of Maury, Walters and Warner—34.

Mr. BURKETT demanded the yeas and nays on the adoption of the 13th Section as amended, which were ordered, and the section, as amended, was adopted.

Yeas..38
Nays..33

Those voting in the affirmative are:

Messrs. Allen, Bate, Baxter, Branson, Brown of Davidson, Brown of Henry, etc., Burton, Byrne, Campbell, Carter, Coffin, Deaderick, Doherty, Fentress, Fulkerson, Gardner, Garner, Gibbs, Gordon, Heiskell, Henderson, House of Williamson, House of Montgomery, etc., Jones of Giles, Kennedy, Key, Kirkpatrick, Kyle, McDougal, Netherland, Porter of Henry, Seay, Shelton, Staley, Thompson of Davidson, Turner, Wright and President Brown—38.

Those voting in the negative are:

Messrs. Arledge, Blackburn, Blizard, Brandon, Britton, Brooks, Burkett, Chowning, Cummings, Deavenport, Dibbrell, Dromgoole, Fielder, Finley, Gaut, Gibson, Hill of Warren, Hill of Gibson, Jones of Lincoln, Ivie, Mabry, McNabb, Morris, Meeks, Parker, Porter of Haywood, Sample, Shepard, Stephens, Taylor, Thompson of Maury, Walters and Warner—33.

Mr. WILLIAMSON stated, when his name was called, that he had *paired off* with Mr. Nicholson, and was, in consequence, excused from voting.

LEAVE OF ABSENCE

Mr. TURNER asked and obtained leave of absence for Mr. Cypert.

Mr. NETHERLAND asked and obtained leave of absence for Mr. Ivie on account of sickness.

On motion of Mr. WILLIAMSON, leave of absence was granted Mr. Blackburn for four days of next week.

Mr. CAMPBELL offered the following resolution:

Resolved, That when this Convention adjourn for recess this day, the Delegates proceed in a body to the residence of Mrs. President Polk for the purpose of paying their respects to her.

On motion of Mr. JONES, of Lincoln, the rules were suspended, and the resolution adopted.

TO CHANGE THE RULES.

Mr. FENTRESS called up the resolution of Mr. Brown, of Davidson, in relation to the previous question.

On motion of Mr. McDOUGAL, the resolution was amended by striking out the words: "The rule authorizing the previous question be and the same is hereby repealed."

On motion of Mr. HOUSE, of Williamson, the resolution was further amended by adding the words "table," "or call for the previous question." And the resolution, as thus amended, was adopted by the Convention.

THE SCHEDULE FURTHER CONSIDERED.

The Convention proceeded to the consideration of the unfinished business of yesterday,—the schedule proposed by the Judiciary Committee, and the proposed amendment thereto—and at 1 o'clock took a recess until 2½ o'clock P. M.

AFTERNOON SESSION.

The President called the Convention to order at 2½ o'clock P. M.

NO QUORUM.

Mr. BROWN, of Davidson, moved for a call of the Convention, when the following Delegates were found to be absent:

Messrs. Allen, Arledge, Bate, Blackburn, Brooks, Burton, Campbell, Carter, Chowning, Cypert, Doherty, Fentress, Fielder, Garner, Gaut, Hill of Gibson, House of Williamson, House of Montgomery, Ivie, Jones of Giles, Kennedy, Key, Mabry, McDougal, Martin, Meeks, Netherland, Nicholson, Porter of Henry, Seay, Shepard, Shelton, Stephens, Taylor, Thompson of Davidson, Thompson of Maury, Turner, Walters and Williamson—39.

There not being a quorum present, the Convention adjourned until Monday morning, at 9½ o'clock.

MONDAY MORNING, FEBRUARY 7, 1870.

The Convention met pursuant to adjournment, Mr. President BROWN in the Chair.

Prayer by the Rev. Dr. SUMMERS.

The Journal of Saturday was read, corrected and approved.

MEMORIALS AND PETITIONS.

Mr. BROWN, of Davidson, presented a memorial in favor of erecting a new county out of portions of Madison, Henderson, Hardeman and McNairy counties, which, without being read, was referred to the Committee on new Counties and County Lines.

Mr. FINLEY presented a remonstrance against the formation of a new county out of portions of the counties of Blount, Roane and Monroe, which, without being read, was referred to the Committee on New Counties and County Lines.

Mr. GIBSON presented a memorial signed by seventy-six members of the General Assembly and by a large number of citizens, praying the creation of a new county out of portions of the counties of Roane, Monroe and Blount, which, without being read, was referred to the Committee on New Counties and County Lines.

Mr. NETHERLAND presented a memorial from a large number of citizens, praying an amendment to the Constitution, giving the qualified voters of civil districts and towns the right to say whether spirituous liquors shall be manufactured and sold in their limits, which, without being read, was referred to the Committee on Miscellaneous Provisions.

Mr. TAYLOR presented a memorial from sundry citizens, praying the creation of a new county out of portions of the counties of Henderson, Hardeman, Madison and McNairy, which, without being read, was referred to the Committee on New Counties and County Lines.

LEAVE TO VOTE.

Messrs. ARLEDGE and IVIE asked and obtained leave to record their votes against the amendment conferring the appointment of Clerks and Masters on the Chancellors.

THE SCHEDULE FURTHER CONSIDERED.

The Convention proceeded to the consideration of the unfinished business of Saturday.

On motion of Mr. BROWN, of Henry, etc., the amendment of Mr. Dromgoole to the Schedule was laid on the table.

Mr. BROWN, of Henry, etc., moved to lay the amendment of Mr. Key, offered in lieu of Mr. Seay's amendment to the Schedule on the table.

Mr. KEY demanded the yeas and nays, which were ordered, and the motion to lay on the table sustained.

Yeas...54
Nays...11

Those voting in the affirmative are:

Messrs. Arledge, Baxter, Blizard, Brandon, Branson, Britton, Brown of Henry, etc., Burton, Byrne, Campbell, Carter, Chowning, Cummings, Deaderick, Deavenport, Dibbrell, Doherty, Dromgoole, Fentress, Fielder, Finley, Gardner, Garner, Gaut, Gibbs, Gibson, Gordon, Heiskell, Henderson, Hill of Warren, Hill of Gibson, Ivie, Kyle, Mabry, McDougal, McNabb, Meeks, Morris, Netherland, Nicholson, Parker, Porter of Henry, Sample, Seay, Shelton, Staley, Stephens, Taylor, Thompson of Davidson, Thompson of Maury, Walters, Warner, Williamson and Wright—54.

Those voting in the negative are:

Messrs. Bate, Brooks, Brown of Davidson, Coffin, House of

Montgomery, etc., Jones of Lincoln, Kennedy, Key, Kirkpatrick, Porter of Haywood, and Turner—11.

Mr. PORTER, of Henry, offered the following in lieu of Mr. Seay's:

Section 1. That no inconvenience may arise from a change of the Constitution, it is declared that the Governor of the State and members of the General Assembly shall hold their offices until the expiration of their present term of service; all other officers except those elected at the general election of March, 1870, shall vacate their places on the ratification of this Constitution; *Provided*, That the last-named officers be elected for the constitutional term from the day of the general election of civil officers fixed in this Constitution.

Mr. SEAY demanded the yeas and nays on the adoption of Mr. Porter's amendment in lieu, which were ordered, and Mr. Porter's amendment was adopted in lieu of Mr. Seay's.

Yeas.. 45
Nays.. 24

Those voting in the affirmative are:

Messrs. Allen, Arledge, Baxter, Blizard, Brandon, Britton, Brown of Henry, etc., Burton, Campbell, Carter, Chowning, Cummings, Deaderick, Deavenport, Dibbrell, Doherty, Dromgoole, Fentress, Fielder, Fulkerson, Gardner, Gaut, Gibbs, Gordon, Heiskell, Henderson, Hill of Warren, Hill of Gibson, Ivie, Kyle, McDougal, McNabb, Meeks, Netherland, Nicholson, Porter of Henry, Shelton, Stephens, Taylor, Thompson of Davidson, Thompson of Maury, Walters, Warner, Williamson and Wright—45.

Those voting in the negative are:

Messrs. Bate, Branson, Brooks, Brown of Davidson, Byrne, Coffin, Finley, Garner, Gibson, House of Williamson, House of Montgomery, etc., Jones of Lincoln, Kennedy, Key, Kirkpatrick, Mabry, Morris, Parker, Porter of Haywood, Sample, Seay, Shepard, Staley and Turner—24.

Mr. GARNER proposed the following amendment to Mr. Porter's amendment:

After the word "*Assembly*" in the 6th line, insert the words "except the Executive officers who may be elected by the present General Assembly."

Which was adopted by the Convention.

Mr. GARDNER submitted the following amendment to Mr. Porter's amendment:

After the word "places" in the 12th line, strike out the words "the ratification of this Constitution" and insert the following words, "thirty days after the day of the general election of civil officers under this Constitution."

Which was adopted by the Convention.

Mr. IVIE proposed to amend Mr. Porter's amendment by inserting after the words "General Assembly," "County and Circuit Court Clerks and Justices of the Peace."

Mr. PORTER, of Henry, moved to lay the amendment of Mr. Ivie on the table.

Mr. IVIE modified his amendment so as to except Justices of the Peace only, and demanded the yeas and nays, which were ordered, but the hour of recess having arrived, the vote was postponed, and the Convention took a recess until 2½ o'clock.

AFTERNOON SESSION.

A vote was taken upon Mr. PORTER's motion to lay Mr. Ivie's amendment on the table, and the motion sustained.

Yeas..38
Nays 20

Those voting in the affirmative are:

Messrs. Allen, Baxter, Blizard, Britton, Brown of Henry, etc., Burkett, Burton, Campbell, Cummings, Deavenport, Dibbrell, Dromgoole, Fentress, Fielder, Fulkerson, Gardner, Garner, Gaut, Gibbs, Heiskell, Henderson, Hill of Warren, House of Williamson, Kyle, McDougal, McNabb, Meeks, Morris, Netherland, Nicholson, Porter of Henry, Seay, Shelton, Stephens, Taylor, Thompson of Maury, Walters, Williamson and Wright—38.

Those voting in the negative are:

Messrs. Brandon, Branson, Brooks, Brown of Davidson, Byrne, Doherty, Gibson, Hill of Gibson, House of Montgomery, etc., Ivie, Jones of Lincoln, Kennedy, Key, Kirkpatrick, Parker, Porter of Haywood, Sample, Turner and Warner—20.

Mr. IVIE offered to amend by inserting after the words "General Assembly" "County and Circuit Court Clerks."

Mr. BURKETT moved to lay the amendment on the table.

Mr. IVIE demanded the yeas and nays, which were ordered, and the motion to lay on the table sustained.

Yeas.. 37
Nays.. 27

Those voting in the affimative are:

Messrs. Bate, Baxter, Blizard, Brown of Henry, etc., Burkett, Burton, Campbell, Carter, Cummings, Deavenport, Dibbrell, Dromgoole, Fentress, Fielder, Fulkerson, Gardner, Gaut, Gibbs, Heiskell, Hill of Warren, Hill of Gibson, Kyle, Mabry, McDougal, McNabb, Meeks, Morris, Netherland, Nicholson, Porter of Henry, Seay, Shelton, Stephens, Taylor, Thompson of Davidson, Walters and Wright—37.

Those voting in the negative are:

Messrs. Brandon, Branson, Britton, Brooks, Brown of Davidson, Byrne, Coffin, Doherty, Finley, Garner, Gibson, House of Montgomery, etc., Ivie, Jones of Lincoln, Kennedy, Key, Kirkpatrick, Parker, Porter of Haywood, Sample, Shepard, Staley, Thompson of Maury, Turner, Warner, Williamson and President Brown —27.

The first clause of Section 1 of the schedule was adopted.

Mr. WRIGHT moved to reconsider the vote adopting the clause, and further moved to lay the motion to reconsider on the table, which latter motion was rejected by the Convention.

Mr. WRIGHT then withdrew his motion to reconsider.

Mr. HOUSE, of Montgomery, etc., offered the following in lieu of the 2nd, 3rd and 4th clauses of the 1st Section of Schedule.

So much of this Constitution as provides for the election of permanent Judges of the Supreme Court, shall not go into operation until the first Saturday in March, 1871. Immediately after the ratification of this Constitution the Legislature shall, by joint ballot, elect nine temporary Judges, three from each Grand Division of the State, who shall constitute the Supreme Court, until the first Saturday in March, 1871, and until the election and qualification of the permanent Supreme Court provided for in the Constitution.

The compensation of each of said temporary Judges shall be four thousand dollars for their entire term of service. Said Judges shall sit in three sections of three each, and shall hear and determine causes at the same time; but they shall not sit in different grand divisions at the same time.

Mr. FENTRESS offered the following in lieu of Mr. House's amendment, and of paragraphs 2, 3 and 4 of the Schedule:

In order to dispose of the accumulated business, there shall be elected three Judges by the qualified voters of each grand division of the State, who shall hold their offices until the first day of January, 1872, unless the business is sooner disposed of; three of whom shall sit in Jackson, three in Nashville, and three in Knoxville, and hear causes and deliver their opinions in the same manner as the Supreme Court now does; and the Clerks of each of these Courts shall, within ten days after the decision of each case, in which a written opinion is delivered, transmit the record and briefs and opinion therein, to the regular Judges of the Supreme Court at Nashville, who, until the first of January, 1872, shall act as a revising Court, approving the decisions of the temporary Courts, hereinbefore provided for, or disapproving them, and rendering such judgment as should have been rendered; *Provided*, that no argument shall be made before the revising Court, nor shall any other brief be presented or read save such as were presented to the temporary Court on the trial; and that on the first day of January, 1872, or as soon as the business of the three temporary Courts herein established shall cease, and the regular Supreme Judges shall resume their proper duties, holding their Courts at Knoxville, Nashville and Jackson, as the Supreme Court of Tennessee.

Mr. FENTRESS subsequently withdrew his amendment.

Mr. HEISKELL offered the following in lieu of Mr. House's amendment, and of the second, third and fourth paragraphs of the Schedule:

At the first election of Judges under this Constitution, there shall be elected two Judges of the Supreme Court from each grand division of the State, who shall hold their offices for the term herein prescribed. In the event, however, that at any time after the first day of January, 1873, if any vacancy shall occur in the office of Supreme Judge, it shall remain unfilled, and the Court shall from that time be constituted of five Judges.

While the Court shall consist of six Judges, they may sit in two sections, and hear and determine causes in each at the same time, but not in different grand divisions at the same time. In each section two Judges shall be necessary to a decision; *Provided*, that the office of the sixth Judge may be vacated after January 1, 1873, in such manner and at such time as shall be determined by the Legislature.

Mr. HOUSE's amendment was laid on the table.

Mr. HEISKELL's amendment was then adopted by the Convention.

On motion of Mr. BURTON, the amendment of Mr. Heiskell was amended by striking out the proviso.

Mr. BROOKS demanded the yeas and nays upon the adoption of Mr. Heiskell's amendment to the Schedule, which were ordered, and the amendment adopted.

Yeas..52
Nays..18

Those voting in the affirmative are:

Messrs. Allen, Arledge, Bate, Baxter, Blizard, Britton, Brown of Davidson, Brown of Henry, etc., Burkett, Burton, Byrne, Campbell, Chowning, Coffin, Cypert, Deaderick, Doherty, Dromgoole, Fentress, Fielder, Fulkerson, Gardner, Gaut, Gibbs, Gordon, Heiskell, Henderson, Hill of Warren, Hill of Gibson, House of Montgomery, etc., Ivie, Kirkpatrick, Mabry, McDougal, McNabb, Morris, Netherland, Nicholson, Porter of Haywood, Porter of Henry, Seay, Shepard, Shelton, Stephens, Taylor, Thompson of Davidson, Thompson of Maury, Turner, Walters, Williamson, Wright and President Brown—52.

Those voting in the negative are:

Messrs. Brandon, Branson, Brooks, Cummings, Deavenport, Dibbrell, Finley, Garner, Gibson, House of Williamson, Kennedy, Key, Kyle, Meeks, Parker, Sample, Staley and Warner—18.

Mr. DIBBRELL offered the following amendment to the Schedule:

The first election for Judges of the Supreme Court, Chancellors, Circuit and other Judges and District Attorneys, after the ratification of this Constitution, shall be held on the last Thursday in July, 1870.

Mr. GIBSON demanded the yeas and nays upon the adoption of the amendment, which were ordered, and the amendment adopted.

Yeas..50
Nays..17

Those voting in the affirmative are:

Messrs. Allen, Arledge, Bate, Baxter, Blizard, Brandon, Britton, Brooks, Brown of Henry, etc., Burkett, Burton, Byrne, Campbell, Chowning, Cummings, Deaderick, Deavenport, Dibbrell, Doherty, Dromgoole, Fielder, Fulkerson, Gardner, Gaut, Gibbs, Gordon, Henderson, Hill of Warren, Hill of Gibson, House of Williamson, Kirkpatrick, Kyle, McDougal, McNabb, Meeks,

Netherland, Nicholson, Porter of Haywood, Porter of Henry, Seay, Shepard, Shelton, Stephens, Taylor, Thompson of Davidson, Thompson of Maury, Walters, Warner, Williamson and Wright —50.

Those voting in the negative are:

Messrs. Branson, Brown of Davidson, Coffin, Cypert, Fentress, Garner, Gibson, Heiskell, House of Montgomery, etc., Ivie, Kennedy, Key, Mabry, Morris, Sample, Staley and Turner—17.

Mr. Burton entered a motion to reconsider the vote adopting the amendment; which lies over.

On motion of Mr. Nicholson, the Schedule and the amendments adopted thereto were re-committed to the Committee on the Judiciary.

On motion of Mr. Thompson, of Maury, the Convention adjourned until to-morrow morning at 9½ o'clock.

TUESDAY MORNING, FEBRUARY 8, 1870.

The Convention met pursuant to adjournment, Mr. President Brown in the Chair.

The Journal of yesterday was read and approved.

MEMORIALS AND PETITIONS.

Mr. Ivie presented a memorial from a number of citizens of Bedford County, praying that the Constitution be so amended, that towns and civil districts shall have power, by vote, to prevent the sale of spirituous liquors in their limits, which was read and referred to the Committee on Miscellaneous Provisions.

Mr. Brandon presented a memorial from sundry citizens of Stewart County, praying that the Constitution be so amended that old counties, in the formation of new ones, may be reduced to four hundred square miles, which, without being read, was referred to the Committee on New Counties and County Lines.

Mr. THOMPSON, of Maury, presented the following memorial:

Your memorialist states that the Bank of Tennessee is the holder of two notes drawn by Isaac M. Jamieson; the first, dated January 16, 1862, for two hundred dollars, and payable at four months; the second is dated February 12, 1862, for two hundred dollars, and also payable at four months. The Bank of Tennessee assigned these notes after they had become due, and when said Bank was insolvent, to Samuel Watson, in trust for the benefit of its creditors. Subsequent to said assignment the said Watson instituted separate suits upon said notes in the Circuit Court of Maury County, where the same are now pending. The said Isaac M. Jamieson hath since the institution of said suits departed this life intestate, and your memorialist is his administrator. Your memorialist now states that since his appointment he has tendered to the attorney and agent of said Bank, and said Watson, payment of said notes, and the legal interest thereon to date of tender, in the bills and notes of said Bank issued prior to the assignment made to the said Watson, and said Watson and said agent refuses to accept the tender so made, alleging that the bills and notes so tendered by your memorialist were issued by the Bank after the 6th day of May, 1861, and that being so issued they have been declared by the amendment made to the Constitution of the State, and adopted in February, 1865, to be illegal and void. Your memorialist states that he has been informed and believes that the Judges of the courts of Tennessee believe and hold that said amended Constitution is a law unto them which they are not at liberty to disregard.

Your memorialist is informed that Section 6, of the schedule adopted as a part of the Constitution of the State, in February, 1865, and to which said agent of the Bank, in refusing to accept the tender aforesaid referred is in violation of Section 10, Article I, of the Constitution of the United States; and is also in conflict with Section 20, of the Bill of Rights of the Constitution of the State, said Section 6, does "*impair the obligation of a contract*" as must be evident to the mind of every one. It takes away the rights and equities secured to the holders of the bills and notes of the Bank under the general Banking law of the State, adopted by the General Assembly in 1857–8. The rights that belonged to the holder of the note of the Bank as a payee, and the rights and equities that belonged to him as debtor of the Bank were vested and perfect prior to the adoption of said amendment. Yet, as your body well knows, your memorialist cannot test the question involved herein (if at all) in the Courts of the United States without great expense to himself and his estate. His condition in this regard is that of hundreds of other citizens of Tennessee, who are debtors to the Bank. Your memorialist is informed that said Section 6, of the amended Constitution, was adopted under the belief that the issue made by the Bank, after May 6, 1861, was made with a view of aiding the rebellion. But your memorialist is informed and so believes, that the issue was made for no such purpose, and was in fact not so used or circulated. On the contrary, the issue was made to meet the wants and necessities of the people of Tennessee, owing to the suspension and insolvency of the Banks of neighboring States that had previous thereto supplied a large portion of the currency of the State. Your memorialist is informed, and so believes, that this alledged new issue was paid out by the Bank to its customers without regard to date of issue and in payment of its debts to depositors and other creditors, and not otherwise.

Under these facts your memorialist submits to the Convention that inasmuch as the faith of the State was pledged to make good any of the deficiencies, or losses, made by said Bank, and inasmuch as great injustice is done him, and others in like condition, by said amendment; that it is equitable, legal and in obedience to the Constitution of the United States that said amendment should be stricken out, and if no more be done, that at least your memorialist should be left unembarrassed by such provision to litigate his rights before the Courts of the State. It is submitted that it must be apparent that the State (the State being the ultimate party to be benefitted under the guarantees as contained in the charter of said Bank) is seeking, by the collection of the notes given by your memorialist's intestate, to avail itself of the acts of the officers of said Bank after May 6, 1861, where it is to be benefitted, and that it seeks to repudiate the acts of said officers where it is likely to be injured. Your memorialist feels assured that such a position is not a just one to the State; wherefore, he prays that said amendment, repugnant, as aforesaid, to the Constitution of the United States be stricken from the Constitution of the State of Tennessee.

R. H. JAMIESON,
Administrator.

Which was read and referred to the Committee on the Judiciary.

RESPECT TO MRS. JUDGE CATRON.

Mr. NETHERLAND offered the following resolution:

Resolved, That a committee of three be appointed to wait on Mrs. Catron, the widow of the late Chief Justice, and ascertain and report when it would suit her convenience to receive a visit of respect from this body.

On motion of Mr. NETHERLAND the rules were suspended and the resolution adopted.

PROTEST:

Mr. GIBSON presented the following

The undersigned cannot consent to the removal of all the Judges, Chancellors, Attorneys for the State. Justices of the Peace, Supreme, Chancery, Circuit and County Court Clerks and Règisters without entering a respectful, yet decided protest:

The undersigned do not subscribe to the doctrine, here dogmatically promulgated, that the amending of a Constitution, *ipso facto*, vacates every office in the State not expressly allowed to remain filled. The undersigned admit that, if there be any office incompatible with the Constitution as amended, or if there be any office the tenure or duties whereof, or the qualifications wherefor, are fundamentally, changed, *then* would such office be abolished or vacated; but the undersigned go no further, and the undersigned maintain that this is the true doctrine: Where the amendments to a Constitution do not materially change the duties or tenure of an office, or the manner of filling the same, or the qualifications therefor, that then such office continues undisturbed, and its occupant is neither necessarily nor impliedly ousted. In other words, where the office is, in all its essentials, precisely the same in the old as in the amended Constitution, there the office and its incumbent remain precisely the same as though the old Constitution was still in full force. Because, by ratifying the amendments the people do not thereby make a new Constitution: they merely accept the old Constitution as *amended*. Their ratification vitalizes the amendments *only*: for the body of the Constitution was already vitalized and the amendments are merely *engrafted* on this already vitalized body. Suppose this Convention had done nothing but make every man a voter and liable to poll tax and military duty, would any one have maintained that the adoption of these amendments would *ipso facto* vacate every office in Tennessee?

Having disposed of the political heresy that the adoption of this amended Constitution, *ipso facto*, vacates all the offices in the State, the undersigned would enumerate the following additional reasons for their vote against the removal of said officers:

1st. The vacation of said offices was not an *issue* before the people when the delegates where elected: and to vacate these offices is no part of the *professed* object of this Convention.

2nd. The vacation of the offices of Judge, Chancellor and States Attorney is a direct violation of political *faith*, said offices having been recently filled by a popular election demanded and brought on *by the very men* who now seek to empty them again, seek indeed to empty them before fully warmed by their new occupants!

3rd. The vacation of the offices of Justice, Court Clerks and Register is an act of *littleness*, of *petty* persecution, utterly unworthy the dignity of a Constitutional Convention, especially when that Convention *in no single particular* changes the term or tenure of said offices, the method of filling the same, or the qualifications therefor.

4th. The vacation of all of said offices will be construed by the Republicans as a direct partisan blow at *them*, and as an exhibition of political malice, prompted only by a desire for *party vengeance*. And thus will strife be perpetuated in Tennessee.

5th. The vacation of said offices is the *basest ingratitude* to those members of the Republican party, who made this Convention *possible*, by putting the ballot in the hands of the disfranchised. But those Republicans never dreamed that the *weapon* they restored would be used to strike down *those* who restored it. It sounds like the old story of the viper stinging the bosom that had warmed it into life.

6th. The vacation of said offices is in violation of all good precedents, is not required by the necessities of the times, is an ingenious device to put *out "the ins"* and to put *in* "the outs," it is a *beginning* that may be dangerous in its *ending*, and as a political invention may yet "torment the inventor."

7th. The vacation of said offices is a summary and ex-parte judgement of condemnation pronounced alike on the just and the unjust, the worthy and the unworthy. If any of the incumbents of said offices deserve removal, the amplest power to remove already exists. This summary removal is an act of tyranny, an d, as made, is inviolation of the Constitution of the United States.

8th. The vacation of said offices will make the North distrust the South, will be deemed a proclamation of war against Union men, will discourage immigration to the State, will prevent the investment of capital and the development of our resources, will postpone the general removal of Constitutional disabilities by Congress, will give additional reasons for federal intervention, and will delay the return of peace and harmony and the ultimate restoration of the Union.

The undersigned therefore protest against the vacation of said offices, or any of them, and ask that this, their protest be spread upon the Journal.

HENRY R. GIBSON,
JAS. W. BRANSON,
W. B. STALEY,
J. C. PARKER,
W. H. FINLEY,
JOS. H. BLACKBURN.

COUNTY SUBSCRIPTION.

Mr. NETHERLAND offered the following resolution:

Resolved, That the Counties of Grainger, Hawkins, Hancock, Union, Campbell, Scott, Morgan, Grundy, Sumner, Smith, Fentress, VanBuren, White, Putnam, Overton, Jackson, Cumberland, Coffee, Cocke, Macon, Anderson, Henderson, Roane, Wayne and Marshall, be excepted out of the provisions of Article II, Section 29, of the Constitution, and that the assent of a majority of the qualified voters of either of said counties, voting on the question, shall be sufficient when the credit of said county is given or loaned to any person, association, or corporation.

Mr. BROWN, of Davidson, offered the following amendment to Mr. Netherland's resolution:

Provided, That the exception of the counties, above named, shall not be in force beyond the year 1880, and after that period they shall be subject to the three-fourths majority applicable to the other counties of the State.

Which was accepted by Mr. NETHERLAND.

Mr. HOUSE, of Montgomery, moved to lay the resolution on the table.

Mr. JONES, of Lincoln, demanded the yeas and nays, which were ordered, and the motion to lay on the table rejected.

Yeas 18
Nays..54

Those voting in the affirmative are:

Messrs. Arledge, Bate, Blizard, Burkett, Carter, Doherty, Dromgoole, Fentress, Fielder, Hill of Warren, Hill of Gibson, House of Montgomery, etc., Jones of Lincoln, Kennedy, Morris, Porter of Henry, Shelton and Stephens—18.

Those voting in the negative are:

Messrs. Allen, Baxter, Brandon, Branson, Britton, Brooks, Brown of Davidson, Brown of Henry, etc., Burton, Byrne, Campbell, Chowning, Coffin, Cummings, Cypert, Deaderick, Deavenport, Dibbrell, Finley, Fulkerson, Gardner, Garner, Gaut, Gibbs, Gibson, Gordon, Heiskell, Henderson, House of Williamson, Ivie, Jones of Giles, Key, Kirkpatrick, Kyle, Mabry, McDougal, McNabb, Meeks, Netherland, Nicholson, Parker, Porter of Haywood, Sample, Seay, Shepard, Staley, Taylor, Thompson of Davidson, Thompson of Maury, Turner, Walters, Warner, Williamson and Wright—54.

Mr. GORDON moved to refer the resolutions to the Judiciary

Committee, with instructions to report a provision that, under the authority of an act of the Legislature, the excepted counties, by a vote of the majority of the freehold and personal property tax-payers thereof, may loan their credit to railroad companies.

Mr. GARNER demanded the yeas and nays on the adoption of Mr. Gordon's resolution, which were ordered, and the resolution rejected.

Yeas.. 9
Nays..61

Those voting in the affirmative are:

Messrs. Allen, Arledge, Gibbs, Gordon, House of Montgomery, etc., Jones of Lincoln, Kennedy, McDougal and Meeks—9.

Those voting in the negative are:

Messrs. Bate, Baxter, Blizard, Brandon, Branson, Britton, Brooks, Brown of Davidson, Brown of Henry, etc., Burkett, Burton, Byrne, Campbell, Carter, Chowning, Coffin, Cummings, Cypert, Deaderick, Deavenport, Dibbrell, Doherty, Dromgoole, Fentress, Fielder, Finley, Fulkerson, Gardner, Garner, Gaut, Gibson, Heiskell, Henderson, Hill of Warren, Hill of Gibson, House of Williamson, Ivie, Key, Kirkpatrick, Kyle, Mabry, McNabb, Morris, Netherland, Nicholson, Parker, Porter of Haywood, Porter of Henry, Sample, Seay, Shepard, Shelton, Staley, Taylor, Thompson of Davidson, Thompson of Maury, Turner, Walters, Warner, Williamson and Wright—61.

Mr. SHEPARD demanded the yeas and nays on the adoption of Mr. Netherland's resolution, which were ordered, and the resolution adopted.

Yeas..48
Nays..26

Those voting in the affirmative are:

Messrs. Allen, Bate, Baxter, Brandon, Branson, Britton, Brooks, Brown of Davidson, Byrne, Campbell, Chowning, Coffin, Cummings, Cypert, Deaderick, Dibbrell, Fentress, Finley, Fulkerson, Gardner, Garner, Gaut, Gibbs, Gibson, Gordon, Heiskell, Ivie, Jones of Giles, Key, Kirkpatrick, Kyle, Mabry, McDougal, McNabb, Netherland, Nicholson, Parker, Seay, Shepard, Staley, Taylor, Thompson of Davidson, Thompson of Maury, Turner, Walters, Warner, Williamson and Wright—48.

Those voting in the negative are:

Messrs. Arledge, Blizard, Brown of Henry, etc., Burkett, Burton, Carter, Deavenport, Doherty, Dromgoole, Fielder, Henderson, Hill of Warren, Hill of Gibson, House of Williamson, House of Montgomery, etc., Jones of Lincoln, Kennedy, Meeks, Morris, Porter of Haywood, Porter of Henry, Sample, Shelton and Stephens—26.

The resolution was ordered to be referred to the Committee on Revision.

REPORT OF COMMITTEE ON ELECTIONS.

Mr. NICHOLSON, from the Committee on Elections and Suffrage, made the following report:

The Committee on Elections and Suffrage have considered the propositions of Messrs. Gordon and Gibson as to filling vacancies in office, and have agreed, in pursuance of said propositions, to recommend the Convention to adopt the following as Section 5, of Article IV, of the Constitution.

ARTICLE IV.

Sec. 5. In filling vacancies in all offices under this Constitution, or in those created by the Legislature, the appointment or election shall be made for the unexpired term. And all officers, appointed or elected, shall hold until their successors are appointed, or elected and qualified.

All of which is respectfully submitted.

A. O. P. NICHOLSON, Chairman.

The amendment, recommended by the Committee on Elections and Suffrage, was adopted, and ordered to be referred to the Committee on Revision.

REPORT ON FINANCE, ETC.

Mr. GARDNER, from the Committee on Finance, Internal Improvements and Corporations, made the following report:

The Committee have reconsidered their report, heretofore made on the subject of interest, and have instructed me to ask leave to withdraw the previous report on this subject, and submit the following in lieu:

INTEREST.

The legal rate of interest in this State shall be six per centum per annum, and shall be equal and uniform throughout the State; but any rate of interest shall be lawful which may be agreed upon by the parties, and inserted in a written contract, not exceeding ten per centum per annum.

All of which is respectfully submitted.

JOHN A. GARDNER, Chairman.

On motion of Mr. HEISKELL, it was ordered that the report be laid on the table for the present.

RESPECT TO MRS. CATRON.

The PRESIDENT announced the Committee to wait on Mrs. Catron, to be: Messrs. Netherland, Jones of Lincoln and Gardner.

REPORT ON LEGISLATIVE DEPARTMENT FURTHER CONSIDERED.

The Convention resumed the consideration of the report of the Committee on the Legislative Department.

Mr. KENNEDY offered the following amendment to Section 31, as reported by the Committee:

"Nor shall any Bank be owned in whole or in part by the State."

Mr. MABRY demanded the yeas and nays on the adoption of Mr. Kennedy's amendment, which were ordered, and the amendment adopted.

Yeas..45
Nays..23

Those voting in the affirmative are:

Messrs. Arledge, Bate, Baxter, Brandon, Branson, Britton, Brooks, Brown of Davidson, Brown of Henry, etc., Byrne, Campbell, Carter, Coffin, Cummings, Deaderick, Doherty, Fentress, Fielder, Finley, Fulkerson, Garner, Gaut, Gibson, Gordon, Hill of Warren, Hill of Gibson, House of Williamson, House of Montgomery, etc., Jones of Lincoln, Kennedy, Key, Kirkpatrick, McNabb, Morris, Parker, Porter of Haywood, Porter of Henry, Sample, Seay, Staley, Stephens, Turner, Walters, Warner and Williamson—45.

Those voting in the negative are:

Messrs. Allen, Blizard, Burkett, Cypert, Deavenport, Dibbrell, Dromgoole, Gardner, Gibbs, Heiskell, Henderson, Ivie, Jones of Giles, Kyle, Mabry, McDougal, Meeks, Netherland, Nicholson, Taylor, Thompson of Davidson, Thompson of Maury and Wright—23.

The Convention took a recess until 2½ o'clock.

AFTERNOON SESSION.

The Convention resumed the consideration of the report of the Committee on the Legislative Department.

Mr. KENNEDY offered the following as an independent section:

No bonds of the State shall be issued to any railroad company that has failed to pay and is now in default of paying the interest upon bonds already issued to it, or that shall at any time before application for such bonds, be in default of such payment, or that has sold or absolutely disposed of any bonds issued to it for less than par.

On motion of Mr. FENTRESS, it was ordered that 100 copies be printed for the use of the Convention, and that it be referred to the Committee on Finance.

Mr. GIBSON offered the following amendment to Section 28:

Insert the word "exclusively" after the word "used," in the second line; and insert the words "and used" after the word "held" in the same line.

Which was adopted by the Convention.

Mr. GIBSON offered the following amendment to Seection 28:

Strike out the words "*one thousand*" after the word "except" in the third line, and insert "five hundred."

Mr. MORRIS demanded the yeas and nays upon the adoption of the amendment, which were ordered and the amendment rejected.

Yeas....................................a........................ 22
Nays.. 49

Those voting in the affirmative are:

Messrs. Brandon, Brooks, Brown of Davidson, Burkett, Burton, Byrne, Chowning, Cypert, Fentress, Finley, Garner, Gibbs, Gibson, Hill of Warren, Ivie, Mabry, Nicholson, Parker, Porter of Haywood, Turner, Williamson and Wright—22.

Those voting in the negative are:

Messrs. Allen, Arledge, Bate, Baxter, Blizard, Brandon, Britton, Brown of Henry, etc., Campbell, Carter, Coffin, Cummings, Deaderick, Deavenport, Dibbrell, Doherty, Dromgoole, Fielder, Gardner, Gaut, Gordon, Heiskell, Henderson, Hill of Gibson, House of Williamson, House of Montgomery, etc., Jones of Lincoln, Jones of Giles, Kennedy, Key, Kirkpatrick, Kyle, McDougal, McNabb, Meeks, Morris, Netherland, Porter of Henry, Sample, Seay, Shepard, Shelton, Staley, Stephens, Taylor, Thompson of Davidson, Thompson of Maury, Walters and Warner—49.

Mr. CARTER offered the following in lieu of Section 28:

Article II, Section 28. All lands held by deed, grant or entry, town lots, bank stocks, and such other property as the Legislature may deem, from time to time, expedient, shall be taxable, except such as may be held by the State, by counties, cities or towns, and used for public or corporation purposes, and such as may be held for purposes purely religious, charitable, scientific, literary or educational. All property shall be taxed according to its value, that value to be ascertained in such manner as the Legislature shall direct, so that the sum shall be equal and uniform throughout the State.

No one species of property, from which a tax may be collected, shall be taxed higher than any other species of property of equal value. But the Legislature shall have power to tax merchants, peddlers and privileges, in such manner as they may, from time to time, direct.

The Legislature shall levy a special tax upon incomes derived from stocks and bonds exempted by the laws of the United States from taxation.

All male citizens over the age of twenty-one years shall be liable to a poll-tax of not less than fifty cents nor more than one dollar per annum, until such age as may be fixed by law.

Mr. THOMPSON, of Davidson, offered the following amendment to Section 28:

Be it resolved, That between the words "*taxed*" and "*except*" in the first line of Section 28, be inserted the words "*but the Legislature may*," so that the section shall read: *All property, real, personal or mixed, shall be taxed*, but the *Legislature may except*, etc.

Mr. THOMPSON, of Maury, offered the following as an amendment to Mr. Thompson's of Davidson:

In third line insert between the words "and" and "except" the words "the Legislature may," so that the section will then read, "and the Legislature may except personal property to the amount of," etc.

Which was decided to be out of order, as it was not germain to the amendment it was intended to amend.

The amendment of Mr. THOMPSON, of Davidson, was adopted.

Mr. JONES, of Lincoln, offered the following in lieu of paragraph 1, Section 28:

All real estate and such personal property as the General Assembly shall designate, shall be taxed according to its value, except such as may be held by the State, by a county, a city or town, and used for State, county, city or town purposes, and such as may be held for purposes purely religious, charitable, scientific, literary or educational.

Mr. THOMPSON, of Maury, again presented his amendment.

Mr. FENTRESS offered the following amendment:

Strike out of Section 28, lines three and four, the words "and except one thousand dollars' worth of personal property in the hands of each tax-payer."

The further consideration of the question was postponed until to-morrow.

MERCHANTS' BANQUET.

Mr. STEPHENS presented and read the following letter

NASHVILLE, Feb. 8, 1870.

HON. JOHN C. BROWN, President, etc.

Dear Sir: The merchants of Nashville desirous of testifying their high appreciation of the manly, conservative and patriotic action of your honorable body upon all questions of public interest upon which you have been called to deliberate, have unanimously resolved to tender to you and through you to the members of the Constitutional Convention, a complimentary dinner. You are, therefore, most cordially invited to be present at the merchants' banquet, to be given in this city on next Tuesday. The exact time and place will be indicated in the cards of invitation, which will be presented to each member of the Convention as soon as they can be prepared.

We have the honor to be, very respectfully, your obedient servants,

MATTHEW McCLUNG,
JOHN P. WHITE,
JOSEPH B. O'BRYAN.
Committee of Invitation.

Mr. STEPHENS presented the following preamble and resolutions:

WHEREAS, The merchants of Nashville have tendered to the members of this Convention an invitation to a complimentary dinner to be given by them; therefore,

Resolved 1, That the Convention return their thanks for the in vitation so kindly given, and will accept the same as tendered.

Resolved 2, That the Secretary of the Convention furnish a copy these proceenings to the Committee of Invitation.

The resolutions were adopted.

On motion of Mr. JONES, of Giles, the Convention adjourned until to-morrow morning at 9½ o'clock.

WEDNESDAY MORNING, FEBRUARY 9, 1870.

The Convention met pursuant to adjournment, Mr. President BROWN in the Chair.

Prayer by the Rev. Mr. WELCHSLER.

The Journal of yesterday was read, corrected and approved.

MEMORIALS AND PETITIONS.

Mr. THOMPSON, of Davidson, presented the following memorial:

To the Constitutional Convention of the State of Tennessee, now sitting at Nashville:

Your memorialists would respectfully represent to your honorable body that circumstances have led them to examine the municipal laws of the State in comparison with other States on the subject of taxation and the sources of municipal revenue. We are satisfied that municipal corporations ought to have the power to discriminate in the selection of the species of property to be taxed, and should have authority to exempt certain property taxed by the State, from taxation by themselves and also with priviliges. But by Section 28 of the Constitution, Article II, all property is to be taxed according to its value, and no species of property from which tax may be collected, shall be taxed higher than any other species of property of equal value. The consequence is that every species of property the State taxes, the Corporation taxes. By Section 1359 of the Code, Sub-Section 17, it will be seen that all property and priviliges within its limits which are subject to taxation by the

State, must be taxed by the Corporation; and so it is the case in all municipal corporations granted since the adoption of the Constitution.

Now, what we desire is that the existing Corporations shall have the power to discriminate to tax one species of property, exempt another, or put a lower rate on the one than another, and that the Legislature should be empowered .to grant charters allowing such discriminations. That existing municipal corporations shall have the power to levy a general tax on the city or town for corporation purposes, and make a special assessment upon the property fronting on a street for the improvement of the street, and shall have the power to issue bonds for any particular purposes; *Provided*, They are authorized to do so by a majority of two-thirds of the voters of said corporation at the election held for that purpose, and that they may levy a tax on priviliges or not as they may see proper.

And that in all municipal elections, a receipt for his poll tax shall be exhibited and shown to the Judges of said election by the voters to entitle them to vote.

K. J. MORRIS,
Mayor of Nashville,
J. B. WHITE,
Mayor of Edgefield.

Which was read and referred to the Committee on Finance and Corporations.

Mr. DIBBRELL presented a memorial from citizens of Sequatchie county praying that said county be declared a Constitutional county, which, without being read, was referred to the Committee on New Counties and County Lines.

Mr. MARTIN presented a memorial from citizens of Grundy county, praying to be attached to the county of Coffee, which, without being read, was referred to the Committee on New Counties and County Lines.

REPORT OF COMMITTEE.

Mr. NETHERLAND, from the Special Committee to wait on Mrs. Catron, made the following report:

The Committee appointed to wait on Mrs. Judge Catron, to ascertain when it would be convenient for her to receive a visit of respect from this Convention, report: That they have performed the duty assigned them, and that it will be convenient and agreeable to Mrs. Catron to receive the delegates of the Convention on Friday, 11th instant, at 1½ o'clock, P. M.

The Committee, therefore, recommend the adoption of the following resolution:

Resolved, That the Convention, in a body, call on Mrs. Catron at the time indicated in the report.

Which is respectfully submitted,

JOHN NETHERLAND.

Mr. SEAY, from the Committee on New Counties and County Lines, made the following

REPORT:

Which was read, and on motion of Mr. Taylor, it was ordered that it be laid on the table, and 100 copies be printed for the use of the Convention:

REPORT OF COMMITTEE ON NEW COUNTIES AND COUNTY LINES.

The Committee on New Counties and County Lines, to whom were referred sundry propositions and memorials for the amendment of the existing Constitution relating to said subjects, have had the same under consideration, and have unanimously instructed me to report the following amendments and recommend their adoption.

Taking up Article X, I am instructed to recommend that said article be amended as follows:

Sec. 4. Strike out the words "three hundred and fifty" in the second line, and insert the words "two hundred and fifty." Strike out all of said section, after the word "miles," in the twelfth line, and insert the following in lieu thereof: *Provided,* however, that the following exceptions be made to the foregoing provisions, viz: New counties may be established by the present, or any succeeding, Legislature, out of the following territory, to-wit:

Out of that portion of Obion county which lies west of low water mark of Reel Foot Lake:

Out of territory made up of fractions of Sumner, Macon and Smith counties; but no line of such county shall approach the Court-house of Sumner county, nearer than nine and a half miles, nor of Smith county, nearer than ten miles; nor shall any line thereof include any territory of Macon county lying within nine and a half miles of the Court-house of Macon county, nor shall more than twenty square miles be taken from Macon county; nor shall the area of Sumner or Smith counties be reduced below four hundred square miles, in the formation of said new county:

Out of territory made up of fractions of Jackson and Overton counties; but no line of such county shall approach the Court-house of Jackson county, or of Overton county, nearer than ten miles:

Out of territory made up of fractions of Grainger and Jefferson counties; but no line of such county shall approach the Court-house of Grainger county, nearer than the Holston River, at the point nearest said Court-house, nor shall any line thereof approach the Court-house of Jefferson county nearer than eleven miles:

Out of territory made up of fractions of Roane, Monroe and Blount counties; but no line of such new county shall approach the towns of Maryville, Kingston or Madisonville, nearer than eleven miles:

"The counties of Cheatham and Sequatchie, as now established by Legislative enactments, are hereby declared to be Counstitutional counties. *Provided,* That no other territory of Bledsoe county shall be taken to form a new county, or any part thereof, or attached to any adjoining county.

The Committee further instruct me to report that, in the opinion of the Committee, the memorials from the counties of Dyer, Gibson, Haywood and Madison; and Fayette, Hardeman and McNairy; and of Henderson, Madison, Carroll and Gibson; and of Maury, Williamson, Rutherford, Marshall and Bedford, are reasonable, and entitled to favorable consideration by this body; these, together with the memorials from the counties of Benton, Decatur, Henderson and Carroll; and Obion, Dyer, Carroll and Weakley; and Hardeman, Madison, McNairy and Henderson; and Weakley, Carroll and Henry; and Lincoln, Bedford and Franklin counties, and the memorial from citizens of Marion county, asking to be attached to Grundy county, have each been fully and fairly investigated by the Committee, and the Committee have instructed me to report said memorials back, and recommend them to the respectful consideration of the Convention, believing them to be entitled to such by this body.

The Committee recommend no amendment to Section 5, of said Article.

A majority of the Committee have instructed me to report that they recommend no other amendments to Section 4, of said Article, than those above specified, from which instruction a minority of the Committee have dissented. Below will be found the Majority Report of the Committee, which they recommend as a substitute for the 4th and 5th Sections of Article X, of the present Constitution.

The Committee ask to be discharged from the further consideration of the matters referred.

All of which is respectfully submitted,

GEORGE E. SEAY,
Chairman.

Feb. 9th, 1870.

MAJORITY REPORT OF THE COMMITTEE ON NEW COUNTIES AND COUNTY LINES.

Section 4. New counties may be established by the Legislature to consist of not less than *two hundred and fifty* square miles, and which shall contain a population of four hundred and fifty qualified voters. No line of such county shall approach the Court-house of any old county, from which it may be taken, nearer than twelve miles. No part of a county shall be taken off to form a new county, or a part thereof, without the consent of a majority of the qualified voters in such part taken off. And in all cases where an old county may be reduced for the purpose of forming a new one, the seat of justice in said old county shall not be removed without the concurrence of two-thirds of both branches of the Legislature, nor shall said old county be reduced to less than six hundred and twenty-five square miles: *Provided,* however, that the following exceptions be made to the foregoing provisions, viz: New counties may be established by the present, or any succeeding Legislature, out of the following territory, to-wit:

Out of that portion of Obion county wich lies west of low water mark of Reel Foot Lake:

Out of territory made up of fractions of Sumner, Macon and Smith counties; but no line of such county shall approach the Court-house of Sumner county, nearer than nine and a half miles, nor of Smith county, nearer than ten miles; nor shall any line thereof include any territory of Macon county lying within nine and a half miles of the Court-house of Macon county, nor shall more than twenty square miles be taken from Macon county; nor shall the area of Sumner or Smith counties be reduced below four hundred square miles, in the formation of said new county:

Out of territory made up of fractions of Jackson and Overton counties; but no line of such county shall approach the Court-house of Jackson county, or of Overton county, nearer than ten miles:

Out of territory made up of fractions of Grainger and Jefferson counties; but no line of such county shall approach the Court-house of Grainger county, nearer than the Holston River, at the point nearest said Court-house, nor shall any line thereof approach the Court-house of Jefferson county nearer than eleven miles:

Out of territory made up of fractions of Roane, Monroe and Blount counties, but no line of such new county shall approach the towns of Maryville, Kingston or Madisonville, nearer than eleven miles.

The counties of Cheatham and Sequatchie, as now established by Legislative enactments, are hereby declared to be Constitutional counties. *Provided,* That no other territory of Bledsoe county shall be taken to form a new county, or any part thereof, or attached to any adjoining county.

Sec. 5. The citizens who may be included in any new county, shall vote with the county or counties from which they may have been stricken off, for members of Congress, for Governor and for members of the General Assembly, until the next apportionment of members to the General Assembly after the establishment of such new county.

Mr. GIBBS, from the minority of the Committee on New Counties and County Lines, made the following report, which, on motion of Mr. TAYLOR, was ordered to be laid on the table, and 100 copies printed for the use of the Convention :

REPORT OF THE MINORITY OF THE COMMITTEE ON NEW COUNTIES AND COUNTY LINES.

The undersigned, a minority of the Committee to which was referred the consideration of New Counties and County Lines, beg leave to submit the following report:

That, while agreeing to that portion of the Majority Report recommending the establishment of New Counties with an area of 250 square miles, they cannot concur in the opinion that no old county shall be reduced below an area of 625 square miles, prescribed by the Constitution of 1834.

They believe that many counties, now rapidly filling up with a thrifty and industrious population, and capable of sustaining an immense number of people, will very soon, if they do not now, demand a change in the present order.

While they believe that the framers of the Old Constitution acted for the best, and acted wisely in the then existing condition of affairs, they do not think it was intended by them, in all time to come, to inconvenience the many for the benefit of the few, but that the sparse population of the then unsettled country, was a material consideration with the wise men who framed the Old Constitution, and with the passing away of that reason, has passed away all reason why counties shall be so large.

They hold that the subdivision of counties, within reasonable limits, should depend upon the wants of the people and subserve their convenience, and that true statesmanship should secure to those who actually need it, a convenient and accessible point for the transaction of their legal, police and registration business.

They believe that the present Convention should provide against the annoyance and inconvenience which will result to a very large portion of the tax-payers of Tennessee from a forty years' continuance of the present system, and common prudence should dictate to us to provide, while we can, a remedy for the evil.

They believe that in those cases, where a whole community are deliberately willing to go to themselves, and asking no aid from the counties they leave, build for themselves Court-houses and jails, they should be allowed to do so, especially by the old counties to which they have been tributary, and which retain the buildings erected by their joint efforts. Their willingness to undertake the cost is the best evidence of the utility of the movement.

The State will lose nothing, for where now centres of business, trade, education and religion are found in districts before remote and inacessible, property will be in enhanced in value proportionate to the increased advantages, and furnish a proportionate increase to her revenue. No longer time will be required to transact the legal business of the section than when it was tied on to the old county, and, therefore, no added cost or labor to the judicial officers; and indeed there will be added no cost to any save themselves, and this will be amply recompensed to them in the saving of time, expense, and travel incurred in attending distant courts, oft-times imperiling their lives by swimming swollen streams which they must cross under subpœna, recompensed to them by being permitted to return to their families after the daily adjournment of courts, instead of camping about the village where courts are usually held, and which seldom have acommodations for the miserable throng of litigants, jurors and witnesses, too far off to go home, and sometimes too poor to pay for good lodging if procurable.

And, besides, the labor system of the country is so changed, its lands being divided into small parcels, and every man becoming his own servant to do his work, that considerations of public convenience require that his compelled absence at court shall not be a journey of days, but shall permit him to chop wood for his shivering children, and feed his famished stock.

The day is past when a gentleman can go to court in his carriage, leaving a host of servants to wait upon his household.

These and many other considerations, which will readily present themselves to the Convention, have induced the undersigned to offer, in lieu of so much of the majority report as re-establishes the old constitutional limits of 625 square miles, and requires a limit of 12 miles from county seats, the following:

Provided, That no old county shall be reduced in forming a new county to a less territory than 450 square miles, and no section of an old county shall be taken off to form a new one, or to be transferred to another, without a majority of the voters of said section voting therefor.

All of which is respectfully submitted.

C. N. GIBBS,
GEORGE E. SEAY,
RICHARD WARNER, Jr.

REPORT ON LEGISLATIVE DEPARTMENT FURTHER CONSIDERED.

The Convention resumed the consideration of the unfinished business of yesterday—the report of the Committee on the Legislative Department.

The question recurring on the amendment of Mr. Thompson of

Maury, Mr. Jones, of Lincoln, demanded the yeas and nays on the adoption of the amendment, which were ordered, and the amendment rejected.

Yeas..31
Nays..36

Those voting in the affirmative are:

Messrs. Allen, Arledge, Baxter, Blizard, Branson, Britton, Brown of Henry, etc., Byrne, Campbell, Chowning, Cypert, Deaderick, Doherty, Dromgoole, Finley, Garner, Gaut, Gibbs, Gibson, Gordon, McDougal, Meeks, Nicholson, Parker, Porter of Henry, Sample, Seay, Thompson of Davidson, Thompson of Maury, Turner and Warner—31.

Those voting in the negative are:

Messrs. Bate, Brandon, Brooks, Brown of Davidson, Coffin, Cummings, Deavenport, Dibbrell, Fentress, Fielder, Fulkerson, Gardner, Heiskell, Henderson, Hill of Warren, Hill of Gibson, House of Williamson, House of Montgomery, etc., Ivie, Jones of Lincoln, Jones of Giles, Kennedy, Key, Kirkpatrick, Kyle, McNabb, Morris, Netherland, Porter of Haywood, Shepard, Shelton, Stephens, Taylor, Walters, Williamson and Wright—36.

Mr. JONES, of Lincoln, demanded the yeas and nays on the adoption of Mr. Fentress' amendment, which were ordered, and the amendment was rejected.

Yeas..10
Nays..59

Those voting in the affirmative are:

Messrs. Burkett, Campbell, Fentress, Garner, Gaut, Nicholson, Thompson of Davidson, Williamson and Wright—10.

Those voting in the negative are:

Messrs. Allen, Arledge, Bate, Baxter, Blizard, Brandon, Branson, Britton, Brooks, Brown of Davidson, Brown of Henry, etc., Byrne, Chowning, Coffin, Cummings, Cypert, Deaderick, Deavenport, Dibbrell, Doherty, Dromgoole, Fielder, Finley, Fulkerson, Gardner, Gibbs, Gibson, Gordon, Heiskell, Henderson, Hill of Warren, Hill of Gibson, House of Williamson, House of Montgomery, etc., Ivie, Jones of Lincoln, Jones of Giles, Kennedy, Key, Kirkpatrick, Kyle, McDougal, McNabb, Martin, Meeks, Morris, Netherland, Parker, Porter of Haywood, Porter of Henry, Sample, Seay, Shepard, Shelton, Stephens, Taylor, Turner, Walters and Warner—59.

Mr. PORTER, of Haywood, offered the following amendment:

After the word "educational," in Section 28, line 3, insert the following: There shall be exempted $500 worth of real estate, and $500 worth of personal property, in the hands of each tax-payer, and the direct product of the soil in the hands of the producer.

Mr. NETHERLAND moved to lay the pending amendments on the table.

Mr. WILLIAMSON demanded the yeas and nays, which were ordered, and the motion to lay on the table adopted.

Yeas..51
Nays..16

Those voting in the affirmative are:

Messrs. Allen, Arledge, Bate, Baxter, Blizard, Brandon, Branson, Britton, Brooks, Brown of Davidson, Brown of Henry, etc., Byrne, Chowning, Coffin, Cummings, Deaderick, Doherty, Dromgoole, Fielder, Finley, Gardner, Garner, Gaut, Gibbs, Henderson, Hill of Gibson, House of Williamson, House of Davidson, etc., Ivie, Jones of Lincoln, Kennedy, Kirkpatrick, Kyle, Mabry, McDougal, McNabb, Martin, Meeks, Morris, Netherland, Nicholson, Porter of Henry, Sample, Seay, Shepard, Stephens, Taylor, Thompson of Davidson, Walters, Warner and Wright—51.

Those voting in the negative are:

Messrs. Burkett, Campbell, Deavenport, Dibbrell, Fentress, Fulkerson, Gibson, Gordon, Heiskell, Hill of Warren, Jones of Giles, Key, Parker, Porter of Haywood, Thompson of Maury, and Williamson—16.

Mr. FENTRESS moved to amend by striking out the word "personal" in the 4th line, so that it shall read: "And except one thousand dollars worth of property in the hands of each tax-payer, and the direct products of the soil in the hands of the producer."

On motion of Mr. IVIE, the amendment was laid on the table.

Mr. STEPHENS offered the following, in lieu of the first four lines of Section 28, Article II, as reported by the Committee:

All property shall be taxed except such as may be owned by the State, and except such as may be owned by counties, cities, or towns, or agricultural fairs, chartered by the State, and used exclusively for public or corporation purposes; and except such real estate as may be held and used exclusively for the purpose of religious worship, or held and used exclusively as public schools, academies, colleges, cemeteries, asylums for the insane, for orphans, or for the indigent. *Provided*, That so much only of such real estate as shall be used exclusively for such purposes, or for any two or more of them, shall be exempted.

There shall also be exempted one thousand dollars worth of personal property in the hands of each tax-payer, and the direct products of the soil in the hands of the producer.

Mr. HILL, of Gibson, moved to amend the amendment by striking out "shall" and inserting "may" in the first line.

Mr. IVIE moved to lay the amendment on the table.

Mr. HOUSE, of Williamson, demanded the yeas and nays, which were ordered, and the motion to lay on the table rejected.

Yeas.. 25
Nays.. 43

Those voting in the affirmative are:

Messrs. Arledge, Bate, Branson, Burkett, Deaderick, Dromgoole, Fulkerson, Garner, Gaut, Gibson, Heiskell, Henderson, Hill of Gibson, Ivie, Jones of Giles, Kirkpatrick, Kyle, Mabry, Martin, Netherland, Nicholson, Parker, Sample, Thompson of Davidson, and Thompson of Maury—25.

Those voting in the negative are:

Messrs. Allen, Baxter, Blizard, Brandon, Britton, Brooks, Brown of Davidson, Brown of Henry, etc., Byrne, Campbell, Chowning, Coffin, Cummings, Cypert, Deavenport, Dibbrell, Doherty, Fentress, Fielder, Finley, Gardner, Gibbs, Gordon, Hill of Warren, House of Williamson, House of Davidson, etc., Jones of Lincoln, Kennedy, Key, McDougal, McNabb, Meeks, Morris, Porter of Haywood, Porter of Henry, Seay, Shepard, Shelton, Stephens, Turner, Warner, Williamson and Wright—43.

Mr. FIELDER demanded the yeas and nays upon the adoption of Mr. Stephens' amendment, which were ordered, and the amendment rejected.

Yeas..16
Nays..53

Those voting in the affirmative are:

Messrs. Allen, Baxter, Brandon, Brooks, Brown of Henry, etc., Chowning, Dibbrell, Doherty, Finley, Morris, Seay, Shepard, Stephens, Turner, Walters and Williamson—16.

Those voting in the negative are:

Messrs. Arledge, Bate, Blizard, Branson, Britton, Brown of Davidson, Burkett, Byrne, Campbell, Coffin, Cummings, Cypert, Deaderick, Deavenport, Fentress, Fielder, Fulkerson, Gardner, Garner, Gaut, Gibbs, Gibson, Gordon, Heiskell, Henderson, Hill of Warren, Hill of Gibson, House of Williamson, House of Montgomery, etc., Ivie, Jones of Lincoln, Jones of Giles, Kennedy, Key, Kirpatrick, Kyle, McDougal, McNabb, Martin, Meeks, Netherland, Nicholson, Parker, Porter of Haywood, Porter of Henry, Sample, Shelton, Taylor, Thompson of Davidson, Thompson of Maury, Warner and Wright—53.

Mr. IVIE offered the following in lieu of the first four lines of Section 28, as reported by the Committee:

All lands held by deed, grant, or entry, town lots, bank stock, and such other property as the Legislature may from time to time deem expedient, shall be taxable.

Mr. HOUSE, of Williamson, demanded the yeas and nays on the adoption of Mr. Ivie's amendment, which were ordered, and the amendment adopted.

Yeas... 36
Nays... 33

Those voting in the affirmative are:

Messrs. Arledge, Bate, Branson, Britton, Brooks, Chowning, Cummings, Deaderick, Dromgoole, Fentress, Fulkerson, Garner, Gaut, Gibson, Gordon, Henderson, Hill of Warren, Hill of Gibson, Ivie, Jones of Lincoln, Jones of Giles, Kirkpatrick, Kyle, McDougal, McNabb, Martin, Meeks, Netherland, Nicholson, Parker, Sample, Taylor, Thompson of Davidson, Thompson of Maury, Walters and Warner—36.

Those voting in the negative are:

Messrs. Allen, Baxter, Blizard, Brandon, Brown of Davidson, Brown of Henry, etc., Burkett, Byrne, Campbell, Coffin, Cypert, Deavenport, Dibbrell, Doherty, Fielder, Finley, Gardner, Gibbs, Heiskell, House of Williamson, House of Montgomery, etc., Kennedy, Key, Morris, Porter of Haywood, Porter of Henry, Seay, Shepard, Shelton, Stephens, Turner, Williamson and Wright—33.

Mr. HEISKELL offered the following amendment after first clause:

Property used for manufacturing purposes may be temporarily exempted by law from taxation, but not for a period greater than ten years from the establishment of such manufactory. But in such case of temporary exemption, profits realized by such establishment shall be subject to a special tax.

Mr. JONES, of Lincoln, submitted the following in lieu of Mr. Heiskell's amendment:

"The General Assembly shall have no power to exempt from taxation the property or capital of incorporated companies."

The Convention took a recess until 2½ o'clock P. M.

AFTERNOON SESSION.

Mr. JONES, of Lincoln, demanded the yeas and nays on the adoption of his amendment in lieu, which were ordered, and the amendment rejected.

Yeas...33
Nays...38

Those voting in the affirmative are:

Messrs. Allen, Arledge, Bate, Blizard, Brandon, Britton, Brooks, Burkett, Chowning, Deaderick, Dromgoole, Fentress, Fielder, Finley, Garner, Gaut, Gordon, Hill of Warren, Ivie, Jones of Lincoln, Jones of Giles, Kyle, Martin, Meeks, Morris, Porter of Henry, Sample, Staley, Taylor, Thompson of Maury, Walters, Warner and Williamson—33.

Those voting in the negative are:

Messrs. Baxter, Branson, Brown of Davidson, Brown of Henry, etc., Burton, Byrne, Campbell, Carter, Coffin, Cummings, Cypert, Dibbrell, Doherty, Fulkerson, Gardner, Garner, Gibbs, Gibson, Heiskell, Henderson, Hill of Gibson, House of Williamson, House Montgomery, etc., Kennedy, Key, Kirkpatrick, McDougal, McNabb, Netherland, Nicholson, Parker, Porter of Haywood, Seay, Shepard, Shelton, Stephens, Thompson of Davidson, and Wright—38.

On motion of Mr. BROWN, of Henry, etc., the amendment of Mr. Heiskell was amended by striking out "ten" and inserting "five."

Mr. THOMPSON, of Maury, offered the following amendment:

The General Assembly shall have no power to exempt from taxation the property of any person, partnership or corporation engaged in mining, manufacturing or any other branch of industry.

Mr. GARNER moved to lay the amendment of Mr. Thompson on the table.

Mr. JONES, of Lincoln, demanded the yeas and nays, which were ordered, and the amendment was laid on the table.

Yeas...51
Nays...14

Those voting in the affirmative are:

Messrs. Baxter, Blizard, Brandon, Branson, Britton, Brooks,

Brown of Davidson, Brown of Henry, etc., Burkett, Burton, Bryne, Campbell, Carter, Coffin, Cummings, Cypert, Deaderick, Dibbrell, Doherty, Dromgoole, Fielder, Fulkerson, Gardner, Garner, Gibbs, Gibson, House of Williamson, House of Montgomery, etc., Ivie, Kennedy, Key, Kirkpatrick, Kyle, McDougal, McNabb, Meeks, Morris, Netherland, Nicholson, Parker, Porter of Haywood, Sample, Seay, Shepard, Staley, Stephens, Taylor, Thompson of Davidson, Williamson and Wright—51.

Those voting in the negative are:

Messrs. Allen, Arledge, Chowning, Fentress, Finley, Gordon, Jones of Lincoln, Jones of Giles, Martin, Porter of Henry, Thompson of Maury, Turner, Walters and Warner—14.

Mr. Baxter demanded the yeas and nays on the adoption of Mr. Heiskell's amendment as amended, which were ordered, and the amendment rejected.

Yeas...27
Nays...44

Those voting in the affirmative are:

Messrs. Bate, Brown of Davidson, Brown of Henry, etc., Burton, Byrne, Campbell, Carter, Coffin, Cummings, Cypert, Doherty, Fulkerson, Gardner, Gibbs, Heiskell, House of Williamson, House of Montgomery, etc., Kennedy, Key, McDougal, Nicholson, Porter of Haywood, Shepard, Taylor, Thompson of Davidson, Turner and Wright—27.

Those voting in the negative are:

Messrs. Allen, Arledge, Baxter, Blizard, Brandon, Branson, Britton, Brooks, Burkett, Chowning, Deaderick, Deavenport, Dibbrell, Dromgoole, Fentress, Fielder, Finley, Garner, Gibson, Gordon, Henderson, Hill of Warren, Hill of Gibson, Ivie, Jones of Lincoln, Jones of Giles, Kirkpatrick, Kyle, McNabb, Martin, Meeks, Morris, Netherland, Parker, Porter of Henry, Sample, Seay, Shelton, Staley, Stephens, Thompson, Walters, Warner and Williamson—44.

Mr. Ivie offered the following amendment to Section 28:

But in no case shall the property of the State be taxed. The Legislature may except property held by counties, cities, towns, villages or corporations, and by them used for strictly religious, scientific, literary or educational purposes.

Mr. Cummings demanded the yeas and nays on the adoption of the amendment, which were ordered, and the amendment rejected.

Yeas...27
Nays...44

Those voting in the affirmative are:

Messrs. Arledge, Baxter, Britton, Carter, Cypert, Deaderick, Dibbrell, Gordon, Hill of Gibson, Ivie, Jones of Lincoln, Jones of Giles, Kirkpatrick, Kyle, McDougal, Martin, Meeks, Netherland, Nicholson, Seay, Taylor, Thompson of Davidson, Thompson of Maury, Turner, Walters and Warner—27.

Those voting in the negative are:

Messrs. Allen, Bate, Blizard, Brandon, Branson, Brooks, Brown of Davidson, Brown of Henry, etc., Burkett, Burton, Byrne, Campbell, Chowning, Coffin, Cummings, Deavenport, Doherty, Dromgoole, Fentress, Fielder, Finley, Fulkerson, Gardner, Garner, Gibbs, Gibson, Heiskell, Henderson, Hill of Warren, House of Williamson, Kennedy, Key, McNabb, Morris, Parker, Porter of Haywood, Porter of Henry, Sample, Shepard, Shelton, Staley, Stephens, Williamson and Wright—44.

Mr. FENTRESS moved to reconsider the vote by which Mr. Ivie's amendment in lieu of the first four lines of Section 28 was adopted.

Mr. WALTERS moved to lay the motion to reconsider on the table, and demanded the yeas and nays, which were ordered, and the motion to lay on the table rejected.

Yeas	29
Nays	42

Those voting in the affirmative are:

Messrs. Arledge, Britton, Brown of Davidson, Carter, Cummings, Deaderick, Dromgoole, Fielder, Fulkerson, Garner, Gordon, Henderson, Hill of Warren, Hill of Gibson, Ivie, Jones of Lincoln, Jones of Giles, Kirkpatrick, Kyle, McDougal, McNabb, Meeks, Netherland, Nicholson, Taylor, Thompson of Davidson, Turner and Walters —29.

Those voting in the negative are:

Messrs. Allen, Bate, Baxter, Blizard, Brandon, Branson, Brooks Brown of Henry, etc., Burkett, Burton, Byrne, Campbell, Chowning, Coffin, Cypert, Deavenport, Dibbrell, Doherty, Fentress, Finley, Gardner, Gibbs, Gibson, Heiskell, House of Williamson, House of Montgomery, etc., Kennedy, Key, Martin, Morris, Parker, Porter of Haywood, Porter of Henry, Sample, Seay, Shepard, Shelton, Staley, Stephens, Warner, Williamson and Wright—42.

The further consideration of the subject was postponed until tomorrow.

LEAVES OF ABSENCE.

On motion of Mr. NETHERLAND, indefinite leave of absence was granted to Mr. Carter, delegate from Carter and Johnson, on account of ill-health.

On motion of Mr. BURTON, leave of absence was granted Mr. Cummings for the remainder of the week.

On motion of Mr. JONES, of Giles, the Convention adjourned until to-morrow morning at 9½ o'clock.

THURSDAY MORNING, FEBRUARY 10, 1870.

The Convention met pursuant to adjournment, Mr. President BROWN in the Chair.

Prayer by the Rev. Mr. INMAN.

The Journal of yesterday was read and approved.

MEMORIALS AND PETITIONS.

Mr. SHEPARD presented a memorial from citizens of Wilson, Smith, DeKalb, Cannon and Rutherford Counties, praying the creation of a new county out of portions of said counties, which, without being read, was referred to the Committee on New Counties and County Lines.

REPORTS OF COMMITTEES.

Mr. GARDNER, from the Committee on Finance, reported back the resolution of Mr. Thompson, of Davidson, in relation to rechartering the Bank of Tennessee, and asked that the Committee be discharged from its further consideration, and it was so ordered by the Convention.

REPORT ON LEGISLATIVE DEPARTMENT FURTHER CONSIDERED.

The Convention resumed the consideration of the unfinished business of yesterday, the pending question being Mr. FENTRESS' motion to reconsider the vote adopting Mr. Ivie's amendment to Section 28 of the Legislative Report.

Mr. CYPERT demanded the yeas and nays on the motion to reconsider, which were ordered, and the motion to reconsider adopted.

Yeas.. 39
Nays.. 33

Those voting in the affirmative are:

Messrs. Allen, Bate, Baxter, Blizard, Brandon, Brown of Davidson, Brown of Henry, etc., Burkett, Burton, Byrne, Campbell, Chowning, Coffin, Deavenport, Dibbrell, Doherty, Fentress, Finley, Gardner, Gaut, Gordon, Heiskell, House of Williamson, House of Montgomery, etc., Kennedy, Key, McDougal, Meeks, Morris, Porter of Haywood, Porter of Henry, Sample, Seay, Shepard, Shelton, Stephens, Turner, Williamson and Wright—39.

Those voting in the negative are:

Messrs. Arledge, Branson, Britton, Brooks, Carter, Cypert, Deaderick, Dromgoole, Fielder, Fulkerson, Garner, Gibbs, Gibson, Henderson, Hill of Warren, Hill of Gibson, Ivie, Jones of Lincoln, Jones of Giles, Kirkpatrick, Kyle, Mabry, McNabb, Martin, Netherland, Nicholson, Taylor, Thompson of Davidson, Thompson of Maury, Walters and Warner—33.

Mr. FENTRESS offered the following amendment in lieu of the amendment in lieu of Mr. Ivie:

All property, real, personal and mixed, shall be taxed except such as may be held by the State and counties; *Provided*, The Legislature shall have power to exempt such property as may be held by the cities or towns exclusively for corporation purposes, and also such property as may be held or used for purposes purely and exclusively religious, charitable, scientific, literary or educational, and also household and kitchen furniture and farming implements to the value of five hundred dollars.

Mr. JONES, of Lincoln, demanded the yeas and nays on the adopion of the amendment in lieu, which were ordered, and the amendment rejected.

Yeas.. 22
Nays.. 50

Those voting in the affirmative are:

Messrs. Blizard, Britton, Brooks, Brown of Henry, etc., Burkett, Burton, Campbell, Chowning, Fentress, Gardner, Gaut, Gordon, House of Williamson, Key, McDougal, McNabb, Porter of Haywood, Shepard, Thompson of Davidson, Thompson of Maury, Turner and Williamson—22.

Those voting in the negative are:

Messrs. Allen, Arledge, Bate, Baxter, Brandon, Branson, Brown of Davidson, Byrne, Carter, Coffin, Cypert, Deaderick, Deavenport, Dibbrell, Doherty, Dromgoole, Fielder, Finley, Fulkerson, Garner, Gibbs, Gibson, Heiskell, Henderson, Hill of Warren, Hill of Gibson, House of Montgomery, etc., Ivie, Jones of Lincoln, Jones of Giles, Kennedy, Kirkpatrick, Kyle, Mabry, Martin, Meeks, Morris, Netherland, Nicholson, Parker, Porter of Henry, Sample, Seay, Shelton, Staley, Stephens, Taylor, Walters, Warner and Wright—50.

Mr. Allen offered the following in lieu of Mr. Ivie's:

Resolved, That all property, personal, real or mixed, shall be taxed, except that the Legislature may exempt such as may be held by the State, by counties, cities or towns, and used for public or corporation purposes, or such as may be held for purposes purely religious, charitable, scientific, literary or educational, and except three hundred dollars' worth of personal property in the hands of each tax-payer.

Mr. Blizard moved to lay the amendment of Mr. Allen on the table.

Mr. Cypert demanded the yeas and nays, which were ordered, and the motion to lay on the table sustained.

Yeas..61
Nays..11

Those voting in the affirmative are:

Messrs. Arledge, Bate, Baxter, Blizard, Brandon, Branson, Britton, Brown of Davidson, Brown of Henry, etc., Burton, Byrne, Carter, Chowning, Coffin, Cypert, Deaderick, Deavenport, Dibbrell, Doherty, Dromgoole, Fielder, Finley, Fulkerson, Gardner, Gaut, Gibbs, Gibson, Gordon, Heiskell, Hill of Warren, Hill of Gibson, House of Williamson, House of Montgomery, etc., Ivie, Jones of Lincoln, Jones of Giles, Kennedy, Kirkpatrick, Kyle, Mabry, McDougal, McNabb, Martin, Meeks, Morris, Netherland, Nicholson, Parker, Sample, Seay, Shepard, Shelton, Staley, Stephens, Taylor, Thompson of Davidson, Walters, Warner, Williamson and Wright—61.

Those voting in the negative are:

Messrs. Allen, Brooks, Burkett, Campbell, Fentress, Henderson, Key, Porterof Haywood, Porter of Henry, Thompson of Maury, and Turner—11.

Mr. GIBSON offered the following in lieu of Mr. Ivie's amendment:

Section 28. All property, real, personal or mixed, shall be taxable except eight hundred dollars' worth of personal property in the hands of each tax-payer, and the direct product of the soil in the hands of the producer, but the Legislature may exempt such property as may be held by the State, by counties, cities or towns, and used exclusively for public or corporation purposes, and such as may be held and used for purposes exclusively religious, charitable or educational.

Mr. HOUSE, of Montgomery, etc., moved to lay the amendments of Messrs. Gibson and Ivie on the table.

Mr. JONES, of Lincoln, demanded the yeas and nays, which were ordered, and the motion to lay on the table sustained.

Yeas... 39
Nays... 33

Those voting in the affirmative are:

Messrs. Allen, Bate, Baxter, Blizard, Brandon, Brown of Davidson, Brown of Henry, etc., Burkett, Burton, Campbell, Chowning, Coffin, Deavenport, Dibbrell, Doherty, Fentress, Gardner, Gaut, Gordon, Heiskell, House of Williamson, House of Montgomery, etc., Kennedy, Key, Kirkpatrick, McDougal, Meeks, Morris, Porter of Haywood, Porter of Henry, Seay, Shepard, Shelton, Staley, Stephens, Turner, Walters, Williamson and Wright—39.

Those voting in the negative are:

Messrs. Arledge, Branson, Britton, Brooks, Byrne, Carter, Cypert, Deaderick, Dromgoole, Fielder, Finley, Fulkerson, Garner, Gibbs, Gibson, Henderson, Hill of Warren, Hill of Gibson, Ivie, Jones of Lincoln, Jones of Giles, Kyle, Mabry, McNabb, Martin, Netherland, Nicholson, Parker, Sample, Taylor, Thompson of Davidson, Thompson of Maury, and Warner—33.

Mr. KIRKPATRICK moved to reconsider the vote laying the amendments on the table.

Mr. KEY moved to lay the motion to reconsider on the table.

Mr. HOUSE, of Montgomery, etc., demanded the yeas and nays, which were ordered, and the motion to lay on the table sustained.

Yeas...41
Nays...30

Those voting in the affirmative are:

Messrs. Allen, Bate, Baxter, Blizard, Brandon, Brown of Davidson, Brown of Henry, etc., Burkett, Burton, Campbell, Chowning, Coffin, Cypert, Deavenport, Dibbrell, Doherty, Fentress, Finley, Gardner, Gaut, Gordon, Heiskell, House of Williamson, House of Montgomery, etc., Kennedy, Key, McDougal, Meeks, Morris, Porter of Haywood, Porter of Henry, Seay, Shepard, Shelton, Staley, Stephens, Turner, Walters, Williamson and Wright—41.

Those voting in the negative are:

Messrs. Arledge, Branson, Britton, Brooks, Carter, Deaderick, Dromgoole, Fielder, Fulkerson, Garner, Gibbs, Gibson, Henderson, Hill of Warren, Hill of Gibson, Ivie, Jones of Lincoln, Jones of Giles, Kirkpatrick, Kyle, Mabry, McNabb, Martin, Netherland, Nicholson, Parker, Sample, Taylor, Thompson of Davidson, Thompson of Maury, and Warner—30.

Mr. DROMGOOLE offered the following amendment to Section 28:

All lands held by deed, grant or entry, town lots, bank stock, State bonds and government securities of any kind, and such other property as the Legislature may, from time to time, deem expedient shall be taxable, except property held by the State, by counties, towns or cities, and used exclusively for public purposes, and all buildings used purely for religious, charitable or educational purposes, together with $500, and the direct produce of the soil in the hands of the producer, which shall be exempt from taxation.

Mr. KENNEDY demanded the question.

The yeas and nays were ordered, and the demand sustained.

Yeas.. 40
Nays.. 31

Those voting in the affirmative are:

Messrs. Allen, Bate, Baxter, Blizard, Brandon, Brooks, Brown of Davidson, Brown of Henry, etc., Burkett, Burton, Byrne, Campbell, Chowning, Deavenport, Dibbrell, Doherty, Fulkerson, Gardner, Gaut, Gordon, Heiskell, House of Williamson, House of Montgomery, etc., Kennedy, Key, McDougal, McNabb, Meeks, Morris, Porter of Haywood, Porter of Henry, Sample, Seay, Shepard, Shelton, Stephens, Turner, Walters, Williamson and Wright—40.

Those voting in the negative are;

Messrs. Arledge, Branson, Britton, Carter, Coffin, Cypert, Deaderick, Dromgoole, Fentress, Fielder, Finley, Garner, Gibbs, Gibson, Henderson, Hill of Warren, Hill of Gibson, Ivie, Jones of Lincoln, Jones of Giles, Kirkpatrick, Kyle, Mabry, Martin, Netherland, Nicholson, Parker, Staley, Taylor, Thompson of Davidson, Thompson of Maury and Warner—31.

The question recurring upon the adoption of the first paragraph of Section 28, as amended, Mr. JONES, of Lincoln, demanded the yeas and nays, which were ordered, and the paragraph adopted.

Yeas..39
Nays..33

Those voting in the affirmative are:

Messrs. Allen, Bate, Baxter, Blizard, Brandon, Brooks, Brown of Davidson, Brown of Henry, etc., Burkett, Burton, Byrne, Campbell, Chowning, Deavenport, Dibbrell, Doherty, Gardner, Gaut, Gordon, Heiskell, House of Williamson, House of Davidson, etc., Kennedy, Key, McDougal, McNabb, Meeks, Morris, Porter of Haywood, Porter of Henry, Sample, Seay, Shepard, Shelton, Stephens, Turner, Walters, Williamson and Wright—39.

Those voting in the negative are:

Messrs. Arledge, Branson, Britton, Carter, Coffin, Cypert, Deaderick, Dromgoole, Fentress, Fielder, Finley, Eulkerson, Garner, Gibbs, Gibson, Henderson, Hill of Warren, Hill of Gibson, Ivie, Jones of Giles, Jones of Lincoln, Kirkpatrick, Kyle, Mabry, Martin, Netherland, Nicholson, Parker, Staley, Taylor, Thompson of Davidson, Thompson of Maury and Warner—33.

Mr. GARDNER moved to reconsider the vote adopting the paragraph, and further moved to lay the motion to reconsider on the table, which latter motion was adopted.

The Convention took a recess until 2½ o'clock P. M.

AFTERNOON SESSION.

Mr. GARDNER offered the following amendment:

Section 28, Paragraph 2. After the words "to its" in the first line, insert the words "cash market," and after the words "so that the" in the second line, insert the following, "manner shall be uniform, and rate of valuation;" and in the second line strike out the words "and uniform," so as to make the paragraph read:

All property shall be taxed according to its cash market value, that value to be ascertained in such manner as the Legislature shall direct, so that the manner shall be uniform, and the rate of valuation shall be equal throughout the State. No one species of property, from which a tax may be collected, shall be taxed higher than any other species of property of the same value.

Mr. GARNER demanded the previous question, which was sustained.

Mr. JONES, of Lincoln, demanded the yeas and nays on the adoption of Mr. Gardner's amendment, which were ordered, and the amendment adopted.

Yeas..36
Nays..33

Those voting in the affirmative are:

Messrs. Bate, Baxter, Brandon, Brown of Davidson, Brown of Henry, etc., Burkett, Burton, Byrne, Campbell, Coffin, Cypért, Deavenport, Doherty, Fentress, Gardner, Gaut, Gordon, Heiskell, House of Williamson, House of Davidson, etc., Ivie, Kyle, McDougal, Meeks, Nicholson, Porter of Haywood, Porter of Henry, Seay, Shepard, Shelton, Stephens, Taylor, Thompson of Maury, Turner and Wright—36.

Those voting in the negative are:

Messrs. Allen, Arledge, Branson, Britton, Brooks, Carter, Chowning, Deaderick, Dibbrell, Dromgoole, Fielder, Finley, Fulkerson, Garner, Gibbs, Gibson, Henderson, Hill of Warren, Hill of Gibson, Jones of Lincoln, Jones of Giles, Kennedy, Key, Kirpatrick, Martin, Morris, Netherland, Parker, Sample, Thompson of Davidson, Walters, Warner and Williamson—33.

Mr. JONES, of Lincoln, demanded the yeas and nays on the adoption of the paragraph as amended, which were ordered, and the paragraph adopted.

Yeas..42
Nays..28

Those voting in the affirmative are:

Messrs. Bate, Baxter, Brandon, Brooks, Brown of Davidson, Brown of Henry, etc., Burton, Byrne, Campbell, Coffin, Cypert, Deavenport, Dibbrell, Doherty, Fentress, Finley, Gardner, Gaut, Gordon, Heiskell, House of Williamson, House of Montgomery, etc., Ivie, Kennedy, Key, McDougal, McNabb, Meeks, Nicholson, Porter of Haywood, Porter of Henry, Seay, Shepard, Shelton, Staley, Stephens, Taylor, Thompson of Maury, Turner, Walters, Williamson and Wright—42.

Those voting in the negative are:

Messrs. Arledge, Blizard, Branson, Britton, Burkett, Carter,

Chowning, Deaderick, Dromgoole, Fielder, Fulkerson, Garner, Gibbs, Gibson, Henderson, Hill of Warren, Hill of Gibson, Jones of Lincoln, Jones of Giles, Kirkpatrick, Kyle, Martin, Morris, Netherland, Parker, Sample, Thompson of Davidson and Warner—28.

On motion of Mr. WILLIAMSON, the vote adopting the paragraph was reconsidered.

Mr. GARDNER, stating that his amendment was not in lieu of paragraph 2, but as an amendment thereto, it was ruled out of order by the Chair, as it proposed more than one amendment, and to different portions of the section.

Mr. WILLIAMSON offered the following amendment:

Strike out the words "the same" in second line, Paragraph 2, Section 28, and insert "taxes."

Mr. BAXTER proposed the following amendment:

Strike out of the 6th line the following words, "so that the same shall be equal and uniform throughout the State," so that the sentence will read as follows:

All property shall be taxed according to its value, that value to be ascertained in such manner as the Legislature may direct.

Mr. BAXTER subsequently withdrew his amendment.

Mr. WILLIAMSON'S amendment was then adopted, and the paragraph, as thus amended, was adopted by the Convention.

Mr. JONES, of Lincoln, offered the following amendment to paragraph 3, of Section 28:

Strike out of lines ten and eleven the words, "five hundred dollars per annum to be graduated as the Legislature shall direct," and insert, "which shall not exceed the *ad valorem* tax."

Mr. STEPHENS proposed the following in lieu of Mr. Jones' amendment:

After the words "per annum" in tenth line, insert, "and which shall in no case exceed the *ad valorem* tax assessed upon the same person."

Which was accepted Mr. JONES.

Mr. JONES, of Lincoln, demanded the yeas and nays upon the adoption of the amendment, which were ordered, and the amendment rejected.

Yeas..33
Nays..37

Those voting in the affirmative are:

Messrs. Allen, Arledge, Bate, Blizard, Brooks, Brown of Davidson, Campbell, Carter, Chowning, Coffin, Dibbrell, Doherty, Finley, Garner, Gaut, Gibbs, Heiskell, Ivie, Jones of Lincoln, Key, Kyle, McNabb, Meeks, Morris, Porter of Haywood, Shepard, Staley, Stephens, Taylor, Thompson of Davidson, Thompson of Maury, Turner and Warner—33.

Those voting in the negative are:

Messrs. Baxter, Brandon, Branson, Britton, Brown of Henry, etc., Burton, Byrne, Cypert, Deaderick, Deavenport, Dromgoole, Fentress, Fielder, Fulkerson, Gardner, Gibson, Gordon, Henderson, Hill of Warren, Hill of Gibson, House of Williamson, House of Montgomery, etc., Jones of Giles, Kennedy, Kirkpatrick, McDougal, Martin, Netherland, Nicholson, Parker, Porter of Henry, Sample, Seay, Shelton, Walters, Williamson and Wright—37.

Mr. BROWN, of Davidson, offered the following amendment to paragraph 3:

Strike out the word "privileges," and insert, "such occupations as are not permanent in their character, or one special in their nature."

Mr. CARTER offered the following in lieu of the paragraph (3) reported by the Committee:

But the Legislature shall have power to tax merchants, peddlers and privileges, in such manner as they may from time to time direct.

The further consideration of the amendments was postponed until to-morrow.

On motion of Mr. THOMPSON, of Davidson, the Convention adjourned until 9½ o'clock to-morrow morning.

FRIDAY MORNING, FEBRUARY 11, 1870.

The Convention met pursuant to adjournment, Mr. President BROWN in the Chair.

Prayer by the Rev. Dr. KELLY.

The Journal of yesterday was read, corrected and approved.

MEMORIALS AND PETITIONS.

Mr. MEEKS presented a memorial in favor of the formation of a new county out of portions of Hardin and McNairy counties, which, without being read, was referred to the Committee on New Counties and County Lines.

Mr. MARTIN presented a memorial from a large number of citizens of Coffee, Bedford, Lincoln and Franklin counties, praying the formation of a new county out of portions of said counties, which, without being read, was referred to the Committee on New Counties and County Lines.

RECOMMITTED.

On motion of Mr. COFFIN that portion of the report of the Majority of the Committee on New Counties, which refers to the formation of a new county out of portions of Roane, Blount and Monroe, and all papers referring thereto, were ordered to be recommitted to the Committee.

REPORT OF THE COMMITTEE ON THE JUDICIARY.

Mr. HEISKELL, from the Committee on the Judiciary, made the following report, which, on his motion, was ordered to be laid on the table, and 100 copies ordered to be printed for the use of the Convention:

The Judiciary Committee to which has been recommitted the schedule heretofore reported, with the amendments made in the House, have reconsidered these matters with others committed to them and submit the following report:

They have redrawn the schedule so far as it relates to the matters submitted and submit the same herewith.

They also find it necessary to suggest certain changes in other portions of the Constitution connected with the subject referred.

They recommend that the elections of Judges and other civil officers be brought on at the same time, and since political elections are, by our action, changed from the 1st Thursday in August, every two years, and that has been found by experience to be a convenient and suitable time for elections, they suggest that this day be appropriated to the general election for Judicial and civil officers.

They also suggest certain verbal amendments.

Section 1. That no inconvenience may arise from a change of the Constitution, it is declared that the Governor of the State, the members of the General Assembly and all officers, elected at or after the general election of March, 1870, shall hold their offices for the terms prescribed in this Constitution.

All other officers shall vacate their places, thirty days after the day fixed for the election of their successors under this Constitution.

The Secretary of State, Comptroller and Treasurer shall hold their offices until the first session of the present General Assembly occurring after the ratification of this Constitution and until their successors are elected and qualified.

The officers then elected shall hold their offices until the 15th day of January, 1873.

At the first election of Judges under this Constitution there shall be elected six Judges of the Supreme Court, two from each grand division of the State, who shall hold their offices for the term herein prescribed.

In the event any vacancy shall occur in the office of either of said Judges at any time after the first day of January, 1873, it shall remain unfilled and the Court shall from that time be constituted of five Judges.

While the Court shall consist of six judges they may sit in two sections and may hear and determine causes in each at the same time but not in different grand divisions at the same time.

When so sitting the concurrence of two judges shall be necessary to a decision.

The Attorney General and Reporter for the State shall be appointed after the election and qualification of the Judges of the Supreme Court herein provided for.

ARTICLE VII.

In Section 3, insert after the word "*Treasurers,*" "and a Comptroller of the Treasury," and strike out "his or."

In Section 4, strike out the words "that may happen by death, resignation or removal."

Strike out Section 5, and substitute: Elections for Judicial and other civil officers shall be held on the first Thursday in August, 1870, and forever thereafter on the first Thursday in August next preceding the expiration of their respective terms of service.

The term of each officer so elected shall be computed from the first day of September next succeeding his election.

The term of office of the Governor and of other executive officers shall be computed from the 15th of January next after the election of the Governor.

No appointment or election to fill a vacancy shall be made for a period extending beyond the unexpired term.

Every officer shall hold his office until his successor is elected or appointed and qualified.

No special election shall be held to fill a vacancy in the office of Judge or District Attorney, but at the time herein fixed for the general elections of civil officers.

REPORTED BACK.

Mr. HEISKELL, from the Judiciary Committee reported back the resolution of Mr. McDougal in relation to the election of Judges and Attorneys General, and asked to be discharged from its further consideraiion, as the subject of it was embraced in the report heretofore submitted, and the committee was accordingly discharged.

LEAVE OF ABSENCE.

On motion of Mr. PORTER, of Henry, leave of absence was granted Mr. Brown, of Henry, etc., on account of sickness.

REPORT ON LEGISLATIVE DEPARTMENT FURTHER CONSIDERED.

The Convention resumed the consideration of the unfinished business of yesterday, the pending question being Mr. Brown's (of Davidson) amendment.

Mr. BROWN, of Davidson, withdrew his amendment and offered the following in lieu of the same:

Provided, that the business of farming, mechanical and manufacturing pursuits and the learned professions shall not be considered privileges under this Constitution.

Mr. GORDON demanded the yeas and nays on the adoption of the amendment, which were ordered, and the amendment rejected:

Yeas..18
Nays..45

Those voting in the affirmative are:

Messrs. Bate, Blizard, Brown of Davidson, Burkett, Chowning, Coffin, Cypert, Deavenport, Doherty, Gardner, Henderson, House of Williamson, Kirkpatrick, Porter of Haywood, Sample, Taylor, Thompson of Davidson and Walters—18.

Those voting in the negative are:

Messrs. Allen, Arledge, Baxter, Brandon, Branson, Britton, Brooks, Byrne, Campbell, Carter, Deaderick, Dibbrell, Dromgoole, Fentress, Fielder, Fulkerson, Garner, Gaut, Gibbs, Gibson, Heiskell, Hill of Warren, Hill of Gibson, House of Montgomery, etc., Ivie, Jones of Lincoln, Kennedy, Key, Kyle, McDougal, McNabb, Martin, Meeks, Morris, Netherland, Nicholson, Parker, Porter of Henry, Seay, Shepard, Stephens, Thompson of Maury, Turner, Warner Williamson and Wright—45.

The Convention took a recess until 2½ o'clock P. M.

AFTERNOON SESSION.

Mr. HOUSE, of Williamson, offered the following amendment to paragraph 3, of Section 28: "After the word "specific" insert the words "*or privileges*," which was adopted by the Convention.

Mr. SAMPLE offered the following amendment:

That capital invested in the buying and selling of merchandise, shall be estimated and taxed according to the capital invested during the fiscal year. And merchants shall pay in addition to an *ad valorem* tax thereupon, a specific tax which the Legislature shall regulate by law.

Mr. JONES, of Lincoln, moved that the Convention adjourn until to-morrow morning 9½ o'clock, and demanded the yeas and nays, which were ordered and the motion to adjourn rejected:

Yeas..16
Nays..47

Those voting in the affirmative are:

Messrs. Arledge, Bate, Brooks, Dromgoole, Fentress, Finley, Jones of Lincoln, Mabry, Martin, Meeks, Morris, Parker, Sample, Staley, Stephens and Thompson of Davidson—16.

Those voting in the negative are:

Messrs. Allen, Baxter, Blizard, Brandon, Branson, Britton, Brown of Davidson, Burton, Byrne, Campbell, Carter, Coffin, Deaderick, Deavenport, Dibbrell, Doherty, Fielder, Fulkerson, Gardner, Garner, Gaut, Gibbs, Gibson, Heiskell, Henderson, Hill of Warren, Hill of Gibson, House of Williamson, House of Montgomery, etc., Ivie, Kennedy, Key, Kyle, McNabb, Nicholson, Porter of Haywood,

Porter of Henry, Seay, Shepard, Shelton, Taylor, Thompson of Maury, Turner, Walters, Warner, Williamson, Wright and President Brown—47.

Mr. PORTER, of Henry, demanded the previous question.

Mr. FENTRESS called for the yeas and nays, which were ordered and the demand for the previous question sustained:

Yeas..41
Nays..26

Those voting in the affirmative are:

Messrs. Allen, Arledge, Baxter, Blizard, Brandon, Branson, Burkett, Byrne, Campbell, Carter, Coffin, Cypert, Deaderick, Dibbrell, Doherty, Dromgoole, Fielder, Fulkerson, Gardner, Garner, Gaut, Gibbs, Gibson, Henderson, House of Williamson, House of Montgomery, etc., Ivie, Kennedy, Key, Kirkpatrick, Kyle, Martin, Morris, Porter of Haywood, Porter of Henry, Shepard, Shelton, Stephens, Turner, Walters, Wright and President Brown—41.

Those voting in the negative are:

Messrs. Bate, Britton, Brooks, Brown of Davidson, Burton, Deavenport, Fentress, Finley, Heiskell, Hill of Warren, Hill of Gibson, Jones of Giles, Mabry, McNabb, Meeks, Netherland, Nicholson, Parker, Sample, Seay, Staley, Taylor, Thompson of Davidson, Thompson of Maury, Warner and Williamson—26.

At 5 o'clock P. M., Mr. MABRY moved that the Convention adjourn.

Mr. BAXTER demanded the yeas and nays, which were ordered and the motion to adjourn rejected.

Yeas..28
Nays..40

Those voting in the affirmative are:

Messrs. Arledge, Bate, Brandon, Branson, Brooks, Burton, Carter, Cypert, Deavenport, Dromgoole, Fentress, Finley, Hill of Gibson, Ivie, Jones of Giles, Mabry, McNabb, Martin, Meeks, Netherland, Nicholson, Parker, Sample, Seay, Staley, Taylor, Thompson of Davidson, and Williamson—28.

Those voting in the negative are:

Messrs. Allen, Baxter, Blizard, Britton, Brown of Davidson, Burkett, Byrne, Campbell, Coffin, Deaderick, Dibbrell, Doherty, Fielder, Fulkerson, Gardner, Garner, Gaut, Gibbs, Gibson, Heiskell, Henderson, Hill of Warren, House of Williamson, House of Montgomery, etc., Kennedy, Key, Kirkpatrick, Kyle, Morris, Porter of Haywood, Porter of Henry, Shepard, Shelton, Stephens, Thompson of Maury, Turner, Walters, Warner, Wright and President Brown—40.

Mr. MORRIS demanded the yeas and nays upon the adoption of Mr. Sample's amendment, which were ordered, and the amendment rejected.

Yeas..10
Nays..55

Those voting in the affirmative are:

Messrs. Brandon, Dromgoole, Fulkerson, Hill of Warren, Hill of Gibson, Ivie, Key, Martin, Netherland and Sample—10.

Those voting in the negative are:

Messrs. Arledge, Bate, Baxter, Blizard, Branson, Britton, Brooks, Brown of Davidson, Burkett, Burton, Byrne, Campbell, Carter, Coffin, Deaderick, Deavenport, Dibbrell, Doherty, Fentress, Fielder, Finley, Gardner, Garner, Gaut, Gibbs, Gibson, Heiskell, Henderson, House of Williamson, House of Montgomery, etc., Jones of Giles, Kennedy, Kirkpatrick, Kyle, Mabry, McNabb, Meeks, Morris, Nicholson, Parker, Porter of Haywood, Porter of Henry, Shepard, Stephens, Taylor, Thompson of Davidson, Thompson of Maury, Turner, Walters, Williamson, Wright and President Brown—55.

Mr. JONES, of Giles, moved that the Convention adjourn until the regular hour of meeting to-morrow morning.

Mr. MORRIS demanded the yeas and nays, which were ordered, and the motion to adjourn sustained.

Yeas.. 46
Nays.. 19

Those voting in the affirmative are:

Messrs. Allen, Bate, Baxter, Brandon, Branson, Britton, Brooks, Brown of Davidson, Byrne, Carter, Cypert, Deaderick, Deavenport, Dibbrell, Dromgoole, Finley, Gardner, Gibbs, Heiskell, Henderson, Hill of Warren, Hill of Gibson, House of Williamson, House of Montgomery, etc., Ivie, Jones of Giles, Key, Kyle, Mabry, McNabb, Meeks, Netherland, Nicholson, Parker, Porter of Haywood, Sample, Seay, Shepard, Staley, Stephens, Taylor, Thompson of Davidson, Thompson of Maury, Walters, Warner and Williamson—46.

Those voting in the negative are:

Messrs. Blizard, Burkett, Campbell, Doherty, Fentress, Fielder, Fulkerson, Garner, Gaut, Gibson, Kennedy, Kirkpatrick, Martin, Morris, Porter of Henry, Turner, Wright and President Brown —19.

SATURDAY MORNING FEBRUARY 12, 1870.

The Convention met pursuant to adjournment, Mr. President BROWN in the Chair.

The Journal of yesterday was read and approved.

LEAVE OF ABSENCE.

On motion of Mr. WALTERS, leave of absence was granted Mr. McDougal on account of sickness.

REPORTS OF COMMITTEES.

Mr. GARDNER, from the Committee on Finance, Internal Improvements and Corporations, made the following report:

The Committee have had under consideration the proposition of the delegate from Montgomery (Mr. Kennedy) on the subject of the further issue of State bonds, and a majority of said Committee have instructed me to report the following in lieu of the original proposition, and to recommend its adoption:

"No bonds of the State shall be issued to any railroad company, which, at the time of its application for the same, shall be in default in paying the interest upon State bonds previously loaned to it; or that shall hereafter, and before such application, sell, or absolutely dispose of any State bonds loaned to it for less than par.

All of which is respectfully submitted.

JOHN A. GARDNER,
Chairman.

MINORITY REPORT.

Mr. SEAY, from the minority of the Committee on Finance, etc., made the following report on the proposition of Mr. Kennedy:

" The undersigned cannot concur with the report of the majority of the Committee on said proposition, and beg leave to submit the following reasons:

1st. Because we believe the subject matter of said proposition to be more properly matter for legislation, and should be left to be regulated and controlled by the Legislature and not embodied in the organic law of the State. We believe that the Legislature, coming fresh from the people every two years, will be enabled to legislate in regard to such matters so as best to promote the interests of the Commonwealth and of the people, and in a republican form of government can be safely trusted to protect the interests of the State and citizens in such matters.

2nd. Because we insist that said proposition not only trenches upon what is more properly a subject for the Legislature to control, but one which should be left to be passed upon by the Judiciary, should a necessity therefor ever arise, and can be safely trusted in their hands.

3rd. We believe it to be in violation of the spirit of the Constitution of the United States, which declares that "no State shall pass any law impairing the obligation of contracts."

All of which is respectfully submitted.

GEO. E. SEAY,
G. G. DIBBRELL,
JOS. A. MABRY.

On motion of Mr. PORTER, of Haywood, it was ordered that the reports be laid on the table, and 100 copies be printed for the use of the Convention.

MEMORIAL.

Mr. KENNEDY presented a memorial from the County Court of Montgomery County, praying for a provision to be made to compel the property-holders of the fractions of said county which have been attached to other counties to pay their proportion of the railroad tax; which, without being read, was referred to the Committee on New Counties and County Lines.

REPORT ON LEGISLATIVE DEPARTMENT FURTHER CONSIDERED.

The Convention resumed the consideration of the unfinished business of yesterday.

Mr. GIBSON demanded the yeas and nays upon the adoption of Mr. Carter's amendment in lieu of paragraph 3, of Section 28, which were ordered, and the amendment adopted.

Yeas.. 41
Nays.. 30

Those voting in the affirmative are:

Messrs. Allen, Brandon, Branson, Britton, Brooks, Burton, Carter, Chowning, Cypert, Deaderick, Dromgoole, Fentress, Fielder, Finley, Fulkerson, Garner, Gibson, Gordon, Henderson, Hill of Warren, Hill of Gibson, Ivie, Jones of Lincoln, Jones of Giles, Key, Kirkpatrick, Kyle, Mabry, McNabb, Martin, Meeks, Morris, Netherland, Nicholson, Parker, Sample, Taylor, Thompson of Maury, Walters and Warner—41.

Those voting in the negative are:

Messrs. Bate, Baxter, Blizard, Brown of Davidson, Brown of Henry, etc., Burkett, Byrne, Campbell, Coffin, Deavenport, Dibbrell, Doherty, Gardner, Gaut, Gibbs, Heiskell, House of Williamson, House of Montgomery, etc., Kennedy, Porter of Haywood, Porter of Henry, Seay, Shepard, Shelton, Stephens, Thompson of Davidson, Turner, Williamson, Wright and President Brown—30.

Mr. HEISKELL demanded the yeas and nays on the adoption of paragraph 3, Section 28, as thus amended, which were ordered, and the paragraph adopted.

Yeas.. 41
Nays.. 30

Those voting in the affirmative are:

Messrs. Allen, Baxter, Brandon, Branson, Britton, Brooks, Burkett, Carter, Chowning, Cypert, Deaderick, Dromgoole, Fentress, Fielder, Finley, Fulkerson, Garner, Gibson, Gordon, Henderson, Hill of Warren, Hill of Gibson, Ivie, Jones of Lincoln, Jones of Giles, Key, Kirkpatrick, Kyle, Mabry, McNabb, Martin, Meeks, Morris, Netherland, Nicholson, Parker, Sample, Staley, Thompson of Maury, Walters and Warner—41.

Those voting in the negative are:

Messrs. Bate, Blizard, Brown of Davidson, Brown of Henry, etc., Burton, Byrne, Campbell, Coffin, Deavenport, Dibbrell, Doherty, Gardner, Gaut, Gibbs, Heiskell, House of Williamson, House of Montgomery, etc., Kennedy, Porter of Haywood, Porter of Henry, Seay, Shepard, Shelton, Stephens, Taylor, Thompson of Davidson, Turner, Williamson, Wright and President Brown—30.

Mr. GARNER moved to reconsider the vote adopting the paragraph, and further moved to lay the motion to reconsider on the table, which latter motion was adopted.

Mr. JONES, of Lincoln, moved to amend by striking out the fourth paragraph.

Mr. KENNEDY offered the following in lieu of paragraph 4:

"The Legislature shall have power to levy a tax upon incomes derived from stocks and bonds that are not taxed *ad valorem*."

Mr. BAXTER demanded the previous question, which was sustained.

Mr. JONES, of Lincoln, demanded the yeas and nays on his motion to strike out, which were ordered, and the motion to strike out rejected.

Yeas...14
Nays...53

Those voting in the affirmative are:

Messrs. Branson, Coffin, Dromgoole, Finley, Garner, Gibson, Jones of Lincoln, Kyle, Nicholson, Parker, Sample, Staley, Thompson of Maury and Williamson—14.

Those voting in the negative are:

Messrs. Allen, Bate, Baxter, Blizard, Brandon, Britton, Brooks, Brown of Davidson, Brown of Henry, etc., Burkett, Byrne, Campbell, Carter, Chowning, Deaderick, Deavenport, Dibbrell, Doherty, Fentress, Fielder, Fulkerson, Gardner, Gibbs, Heiskell, Henderson, Hill of Warren, Hill of Gibson, House of Williamson, House of Montgomery, etc., Ivie, Jones of Giles, Kennedy, Key, Kirkpatrick, Mabry, McNabb, Martin, Meeks, Morris, Netherland, Porter of Haywood, Porter of Henry, Seay, Shepard, Shelton, Stephens, Taylor, Thompson of Davidson, Turner, Walters, Warner, Wright and President Brown—53.

Mr. JONES, of Lincoln, demanded the yeas and nays on the adoption of Mr. Kennedy's amendment in lieu, which were orordered, and the amendment in lieu adopted.

Yeas...67
Nays... 2

Those voting in the affirmative are:

Messrs. Allen, Baxter, Blizard, Brandon, Branson, Britton, Brooks, Brown of Davidson, Brown of Henry, etc., Burkett, Byrne, Campbell, Carter, Chowning, Coffin, Cypert, Deaderick, Deavenport, Dibbrell, Doherty, Dromgoole, Fentress, Fielder, Finley, Fulkerson, Gardner, Garner, Gaut, Gibbs, Gibson, Gordon, Heiskell, Henderson, Hill of Warren, Hill of Gibson, House of Williamson, House of Montgomery, etc., Ivie, Jones of Giles, Kennedy, Key, Kirkpatrick, Kyle, Mabry, McNabb, Martin, Meeks, Morris, Netherland, Nicholson, Parker, Porter of Haywood, Porter of Henry, Sample, Seay, Shepard, Shelton, Staley, Stephens, Taylor, Thompson of Davidson, Thompson of Maury, Turner, Walters, Warner and President Brown—67.

Those voting in the negative are:

Messrs. Jones of Lincoln and Williamson—2.

Paragraph 4, as thus amended, was adopted by the Convention.

Mr. BAXTER offered the following amendment to paragraph 5:

Strike out the 15th and 16th lines, and insert:

"All male citizens of this State over the age of twenty-one years, except such persons as may be exempted by law on account of age or other infirmity, shall be liable to a poll-tax of not less than one, nor more than two dollars per annum."

Mr. GIBSON offered the following amendment to Mr. Baxter's amendment:

Add: "*Provided,* The Legislature shall have no power to levy a poll-tax, so long as the payment of such tax is a necessary qualification for voting."

Which was ruled out of order by the Chair, the matter having been acted on and decided by the Convention.

Mr. TURNER submitted the following amendment to Mr. Baxter's amendment:

Insert at the end of the section: "Nor shall any county or corporation levy a poll-tax exceeding the amount levied by the State.

Mr. BAXTER demanded the yeas and nays on the adoption of Mr. Turner's amendment, which were ordered, and the amendment adopted.

Yeas.. 46
Nays.. 18

Those voting in the affirmative are:

Messrs. Blizard, Brandon, Branson, Brooks, Brown of Davidson, Burkett, Byrne, Campbell, Carter, Coffin, Cypert, Daavenport, Doherty, Dromgoole, Fentress, Fielder, Finley, Gardner, Garner, Gibson, Gordon, Heiskell, Hill of Warren, Hill of Gibson, House of Williamson, House of Montgomery, etc., Jones of Giles, Kennedy, Key, Mabry, Martin, Morris, Parker, Porter of Haywood, Porter of Henry, Seay, Shepard, Shelton, Staley, Stephens, Taylor, Thompson of Davidson, Thompson of Maury, Turner, Williamson and President Brown—46.

Those voting in the negative are:

Messrs. Baxter, Britton, Deaderick, Fulkerson, Gaut, Gibbs, Henderson, Ivie, Jones of Lincoln, Kyle, McNabb, Meeks, Nicholson, Sample, Walters and Warner—18.

Mr. BAXTER offered to amend his amendment by striking out "one dollar" and inserting "fixty cents," and by striking out "two" and inserting "one dollar."

Mr. HEISKELL demanded the yeas and nays upon the adoption of the amendment, which were ordered, and the amendment was adopted.

Yeas.. 48
Nays.. 19

Those voting in the affirmative are:

Messrs. Allen, Baxter, Blizard, Branson, Burton, Byrne, Carter, Chowning, Coffin, Cypert, Deaderick, Deavenport, Dibbrell, Doherty, Fentress, Fielder, Finley, Fulkerrson, Gaut, Gibbs, Gibson, Henderson, Hill of Warren, Hill of Gibson, House of Williamson, Ivie, Jones of Lincoln, Kennedy, Key, Kirkpatrick, Kyle, McNabb, Martin, Meeks, Morris, Netherland, Nicholson, Parker, Porter of Henry, Sample, Seay, Staley, Thompson of Maury, Turner, Walters, Warner, Williamson and President Brown—48.

Those voting in the negative are:

Messrs. Bate, Brandon, Brooks, Brown of Davidson, Burkett, Campbell, Dromgoole, Gardner, Garner, Gordon, Heiskell, House of Montgomery, etc., Jones of Giles, Porter of Haywood, Shepard, Shelton, Stephens, Thompson of Davidson and Wright—19.

Mr. GARNER offered the following in lieu of Mr. Baxter's amendment:

Strike out lines 15 and 16 Section 28, and insert in lieu thereof:

A tax on polls shall be laid in such manner, and of such an amount, as may be prescribed by law.

Mr. FULKERSON moved to lay the amendment on the table.

Mr. GARNER demanded the yeas and nays, which were ordered, and the motion to lay on the table sustained.

Yeas.. 56
Nays.. 10

Those voting in the affirmative are:

Messrs. Allen, Baxter, Blizard, Branson, Britton, Brooks, Brown of Davidson, Burkett, Burton, Byrne, Campbell, Carter, Chowning, Coffin, Deaderick, Deavenport, Dibbrell, Doherty, Dromgoole, Finley, Fulkerson, Gardner, Gaut, Gibbs, Gibson, Gordon, Heiskell, Henderson, Hill of Warren, Hill of Gibson, House of Williamson, House of Davidson, etc., Ivie, Jones of Giles, Kennedy, Key, Kirkpatrick, Kyle, McNabb, Netherland, Nicholson, Parker, Porter of Haywood, Porter of Henry, Sample, Seay, Shepard, Shelton, Staley, Thompson of Maury, Turner, Walters, Warner, Williamson and Wright—56.

Those voting in the negative are:

Messrs. Cypert, Fentress, Fielder, Garner, Jones of Lincoln, Martin, Meeks, Morris, Stephens and Taylor—10.

Mr. HOUSE, of Montgomery, moved to lay the amendment of Mr. Baxter on the table.

Mr. FIELDER demanded the yeas and nays, which were ordered, and the motion to lay on the table rejected.

Yeas.. 24
Nays.. 41

Those voting in the affirmative are:

Messrs. Bate, Brandon, Brooks, Brown of Davidson, Burkett, Campbell, Cypert, Dibbrell, Dromgoole, Gardner, Garner, Gordon, Heiskell, House of Montgomery, etc., Jones of Giles, Kennedy, Porter of Haywood, Porter of Henry, Seay, Shepard, Shelton, Stephens, Thompson of Davidson, Williamson and Wright—24.

Those voting in the negative are:

Messrs. Baxter, Blizard, Branson, Britton, Burton, Byrne, Carter, Coffin, Deaderick, Deavenport, Doherty, Fentress, Fielder, Finley, Fulkerson, Gaut, Gibbs, Gibson, Henderson, Hill of Warren, Hill of Gibson, House of Williamson, Ivie, Jones of Lincoln, Key, Kyle, Mabry, McNabb, Martin, Meeks, Morris, Netherland, Nicholson, Parker, Sample, Staley, Taylor, Thompson of Maury, Turner, Walters and Warner—41.

Mr. JONES, of Lincoln, demanded the yeas and nays on Mr. Baxter's amendment, which were ordered, and the amendment adopted.

Yeas..56
Nays..11

Those voting in the affirmative are:

Messrs. Allen, Baxter, Blizard, Brandon, Branson, Britton, Brooks, Brown of Davidson, Brown of Henry, etc., Burkett, Burton, Byrne, Campbell, Chowning, Coffin, Cypert, Deaderick, Deavenport, Dibbrell, Doherty, Dromgoole, Fentress, Fielder, Finley, Fulkerson, Garner, Gaut, Gibbs, Gibson, Gordon, Henderson, Hill of Warren, Hill of Gibson, House of Williamson, Ivie, Jones of Giles, Kennedy, Key, Kirkpatrick, Kyle, McNabb, Martin, Meeks, Netherland, Nicholson, Parker, Porter of Haywood, Porter of Henry, Sample, Seay, Thompson of Davidson, Thompson of Maury, Turner, Walters, Warner, Williamson and President Brown—56.

Those voting in the negative are:

Messrs. Carter, Gardner, Heiskell, House of Davidson, etc., Jones of Lincoln, Morris, Shepard, Shelton, Stephens, Taylor, and Wright—11.

Mr. STEPHENS moved that when the Convention adjourn to-day, it adjourn until Monday morning at 10 o'clock.

Mr. FIELDER demanded the yeas and nays, which were ordered and the motion to adjourn over rejected:

Yeas..29
Nays..40

Those voting in the affirmative are:

Messrs. Allen, Bate, Blizard, Brooks, Burton, Campbell, Carter, Chowning, Coffin, Doherty, Dromgoole, Gibbs, Gordon, House of Williamson, House of Montgomery, etc., Ivie, Jones of Giles, Kennedy, Martin, Netherland, Parker, Pòrter of Haywood, Porter of Henry, Shelton, Stephens, Thompson of Davidson, Williamson, Wright and President Brown—29.

Those voting in the negative are:

Messrs. Baxter, Brandon, Branson, Britton, Brown of Davidson, Burkett, Byrne, Cypert, Deaderick, Deavenport, Dibbrell, Fentress, Fielder, Finley, Fulkerson, Gardner, Garner, Gaut, Gibson, Heiskell, Henderson, Hill of Warren, Hill of Gibson, Jones of Lincoln, Key, Kirkpatrick, Kyle, McNabb, Meeks, Morris, Nicholson, Sample, Seay, Shepard, Staley, Taylor, Thompson of Maury, Turner, Walters and Warner.—40.

The hour of recess having arrived the Convention took a recess until 2½ o'clock P. M.

AFTERNOON SESSION.

On motion of Mr. HILL, of Gibson, the roll was called and the following named delegates answered to their names, viz:

Messrs. Allen, Bate, Baxter, Blizard, Brandon, Britton, Brooks, Brown of Davidson, Burkett, Byrne, Campbell, Carter, Chowning, Coffin, Deaderick, Deavenport, Dibbrell, Doherty, Dromgoole, Fentress, Fielder, Fulkerson, Gardner, Garner, Gaut, Gibbs, Gibson, Gordon, Heiskell, Henderson, Hill of Warren, Hill of Gibson, Jones of Giles, Key, McNabb, Martin, Meeks, Morris, Nicholson, Netherland, Parker, Porter of Henry, Seay, Shepard, Shelton, Staley, Taylor, Walters and Warner—49.

It being announced that there was not a quorum present.

Mr. BATE moved to adjourn, whereupon a vote was taken and it appeared that there was not a quorum present.

Immediately after the announcement of the vote, a sufficient number of delegates appeared in the Hall to constitute a quorum and the motion to adjourn was withdrawn.

LEGISLATIVE DEPARTMENT FURTHER CONSIDERED.

Mr. GAUT offered the following resolution as an amendment to Section 32 of the report of the Committee on the Legislative Department:

Resolved, That the General Assembly may, by general law, authorize the inhabitants of cities, towns and civil districts within the State, by a vote of the majority of all the qualified voters of such cities, towns and civil districts as the General Assembly may prescribe, to prohibit the sale of intoxicating liquors within their respective limits.

Mr. COFFIN moved to amend the resolution by inserting, instead of "*a majority* of all the qualified voters"—"by a vote of two-thirds of all the qualified voters, etc."

Mr. GIBBS moved to lay the amendment of Mr. Gaut and all the amendments thereto on the table and called for the yeas and nays, which resulted as follows:

Yeas..21
Nays..33

Those voting in the affirmative are:

Messrs. Brandon, Brown of Davidson, Deavenport, Drongoole, Fulkerson, Gardner, Garner, Gibbs, Gibson, Gordon, Hill of Warren, Hill of Gibson, Key, Morris, Porter of Henry, Seay, Shelton, Thompson of Davidson, Williamson and Wright—19.

Those voting in the negative are:

Messrs. Allen, Bate, Baxter, Blizard, Branson, Brooks, Burkett, Byrne, Campbell, Carter, Chowning, Coffin, Deaderick, Dibbrell, Doherty, Fentress, Fielder, Gaut, Heiskell, Henderson, Jones of Giles, Kyle, McNabb, Martin, Meeks, Nicholson, Porter of Haywood, Sample, Shepard, Walters and President Brown—33.

Mr. GIBBS offered the following amendment to Mr. Gaut's: add after "liquors" "or tobacco," which was subsequently withdrawn.

Mr. GAUT's amendment was then rejected by a tie vote:

Yeas..29
Nays..29

Those voting in the affirmative are:

Messrs. Allen, Bate, Baxter, Blizard, Britton, Brooks, Burkett,

Byrne, Carter, Chowning, Coffin, Deaderick, Dibbrell, Doherty, Fentress, Gaut, Heiskell, Henderson, Jones of Giles, Kirkpatrick, Kyle, Mabry, Meeks, Netherland, Nicholson, Porter of Haywood, Sample, Shepard and Walters—29.

Those voting in the negative are:

Messrs. Brandon, Branson, Brown of Davidson, Campbell, Deavenport, Dromgoole, Fielder, Finley, Fulkerson, Garner, Gardner, Gibbs, Gibson, Gordon, Hill of Warren, Hill of Gibson, Key, Martin, Morris, Porter of Henry, Seay, Shelton, Staley, Thompson of Maury, Warner, Williamson and Wright—29.

Mr. GIBSON offered the following as an independent section:

"No law of a general nature shall take effect until the 60th day after its passage, unless the preamble to such law recite that the public welfare requires that the law take effect sooner."

Mr. BAXTER moved to lay the amendment of Mr. Gibson on the table, which was adopted, but the amendment was subsequently taken from the table and referred to the Committee on the Legislative Department.

Mr. DROMGOOLE offered the following resolution which was read and ordered to be laid upon the table until Tuesday:

"All the revenues of this State after defraying the current expenses of the Government shall be applied to the payment of the just debts of the State, and no other application of its revenues shall be made until the debts of the State are paid."

PROTEST.

Mr. HEISKELL offered the following protest, which was read and ordered to be spread upon the Journal:

The undersigned have voted against the proposition to except merchants from the protection of the Constitution, and from the rate of equal taxation guaranteed to other classes of the community, ask leave to enter a protest against what they regard as a declaration that the merchant is not entitled to the rights of a citizen.

We think that the principles of constitutional government require that every class of men shall be entitled to the same protection against oppression and against unequal burthens which are guaranteed to other classes. The provision inserted by the Convention, borrowed from the Constitution of 1834, declares that all men shall be taxed equally except merchants and peddlers. Why they should be singled out and subjected to a rule of taxation absolutely prohibited as to any other citizen, the subscribers cannot well perceive. They can see no good reason why merchants should not on the same principle be excluded from the protection of the Constitution as to trial by jury, or *habeas corpus*, or the clauses which give every man, for an injury done him in "his lands, goods, person or reputation," a remedy by due course of law.

It seems to us that such a proposition is no worse than this power expressly conferred on the Legislature to impose upon a small class of citizens all the burthens of the State.

If, for the period which has elapsed since the Constitution of 1834, this power had remained without exercise, or if the power had been exercised with any regard to principles of justice we might be less reluctant to submit to the violation of the principles of free and just government contained in this objectionable clause of the organic law.

But we know not only that existing power is contrary to just principles, but that it has been continually exercised to discriminate grievously against a portion of our citizens, to overrate them with burthens from which others are protected, by taxation amounting to from ten times to one hundred times the amount imposed on other citizens on the use of the same amount of property or capital. We have on this floor one member who, as a merchant, operating on a small capital, actually paid a tax of twenty-five cents on every dollar of his capital for the privilege of using it one year as a merchant. One-fourth of the whole of his capital taken in one year for taxes, while every other citizen, not of his class, paid at the same time twenty-five cents on every one hundred dollars of his capital, a tax actually one hundred times as much on this individual as upon his neighbors.

A departure from principles so odious, with known consequences so abhorrent to our sense of justice, and so calculated to depress the interests of trade and commerce, we cannot allow to pass without putting on record our *solemn protest* against it.

We respectfully submit this protest, and ask that it may be spread on the Journal.

W. H. STEPHENS,
NEIL S. BROWN,
ALEX. W. CAMPBELL,
S. G. SHEPARD,
W. M. WRIGHT,
J. C. THOMPSON,
H. R. BATE,
GEORGE C. PORTER,
T. M. BURKETT,
W. BYRNE,
G. G. DIBBRELL,
J. B. HEISKELL,
E. H. SHELTON.

Mr. BAXTER offered the following resolution as an amendment

in lieu of third amendment reported by the Committee on Finance, which was ordered to be laid over until Tuesday:

"Strike out the third amendment reported by the Committee on Finance, Internal Improvement and Corporations and insert:

"The rate of interest shall be fixed by law, and shall be uniform throughout the State, but the Legislature shall have power to provide by law for a conventional rate of interest."

REPORT ON CORPORATIONS CONSIDERED.

The Convention took up the report of the Committee on Corporations.

Mr. BAXTER offered the following amendment:

Insert after the word "no" in the first line the word "private."

Mr. BAXTER demanded the yeas and nays upon the adoption of his amendment, which were ordered, and the amendment rejected.

Yeas...12
Nays...44

Those voting in the affiative are:

Messrs. Bate, Baxter, Chowning, Campbell, Fielder, Finley, Jones of Giles, Netherland, Thompson of Davidson, Warner, Williamson and President Brown—12.

Those voting in the negative are:

Messrs. Allen, Blizard, Branson, Britton, Brooks, Brown of Davidson, Burkett, Byrne, Carter, Coffin, Cypert, Deaderick, Deavenport, Dibbrell, Doherty, Fentress, Fulkerson, Gardner, Garner, Gibson, Gordon, Heiskell, Henderson, Hill of Warren, Hill of Gibson, Key, Kyle, McNabb, Martin, Morris, Nicholson, Parker, Porter of Haywood, Porter of Henry, Sample, Seay, Shepard, Shelton, Staley, Taylor, Thompson of Maury, Walters and Wright—44.

Mr. NICHOLSON proposed to amend by adding at the end of the paragraph the following:

"But no such alteration or repeal shall interfere with or divest rights which have become vested."

On motion of Mr. BAXTER, the further consideration of the subject was postponed until Tuesday.

On motion of Mr. BAXTER, the Convention adjourned until Monday morning at 10 o'clock.

MONDAY MORNING, FEBRUARY 14, 1870.

The Convention met pursuant to adjournment, Mr. President BROWN in the Chair.

Prayer by the Rev. Dr. YOUNG.

The Journal of Saturday was read and approved.

REPORT ON CORPORATIONS FURTHER CONSIDERED.

Mr. JONES, of Lincoln, offered the following amendment to the report of the Committee on Incorporations, which was read and 100 copies ordered to be printed:

Add at the end of the Section on Corporations:

"Every stockholder in an incorporated Stock Company shall refund to the Company or its creditors, all dividends received by them respectively, in case it shall, at any time, be necessary to pay the liability of the Company."

THE FIFTEENTH AMENDMENT TO THE FEDERAL CONSTITUTION.

Mr. GIBSON offered the following preamble and resolution, which, under the rule, lies over one day.

WHEREAS, It is now settled in political science that suffrage is a *right* and not a privilege; and

WHEREAS, Three-fourths of the States have ratified, or soon will ratify, the proposed amendment to the Constitution of the United States, known as Article XV; and

WHEREAS, Upon such ratification universal suffrage will be the *supreme law* of the land, whether Tennessee *participates* in such ratification or not; and

WHEREAS, It is believed that such ratification by Tennessee will not only be in *fulfillment of the political pledges* of the last canvass for Governor and members of the Legislature, but will also accelerate the removal of disabilities now resting on many Tennesseeans by virtue of the XIV amendment to the United States Constitution; therefore,

Resolved, That it is the sense of this Convention that the Legislature of the State of Tennessee should, without delay, ratify said proposed amendment to the Constitution of the United States known as Article XV.

MANAGEMENT OF STATE FINANCES.

Mr. CARTER offered the following resolution, which, under the rule, was ordered to lie over:

Resolved, That a committee of five members be appointed to investigate and make report upon the management of the finances of the State, with power to send for persons and papers, and to examine parties and witnesses on oath.

EXPENSES OF THE CONVENTION.

Mr. WILLIAMSON offered the following resolution, which, under a suspension of the rules, was adopted:

Resolved, That a committee of three be appointed by the President to inquire into and audit the expenses of this Convention, and report the same at as early a day as practicable.

Whereupon the President appointed Messrs. WILLIAMSON, PORTER of Haywood, and BURKETT, to constitute said Committee.

REPORT OF COMMON SCHOOLS CONSIDERED.

Mr. JONES, of Lincoln, moved to strike out in line six of the Report of Committee on Common Schools the word "educational" and insert "*free or common schools,*" which was adopted.

Mr. NICHOLSON moved to insert in line three after "assessed," he words "by the State," which was adopted.

Mr. GORDON proposed to amend the report of the Committee by filling the blanks with five and sixteen years, which was rejected.

Mr. GIBSON moved to insert six instead of five, and eighteen instead of sixteen, which was adopted.

Mr. HEISKELL moved to insert 7 instead of 6, and 19 instead of 18, which was rejected:

Yeas..29
Nays..36

Those voting in the affirmative are:

Messrs. Baxter, Blackburn, Blizard, Brandon, Branson, Britton, Brown of Davidson, Burkett, Byrne, Chowning, Cypert, Deavenport, Finley, Fulkerson, Gibson, Gordon, Henderson, Key, Kirkpatrick, Kyle, McNabb, Meeks, Nicholson, Parker Sample, Staley, Thompson of Davidson, Thompson of Maury and Walters—29.

Those voting in the negative are:

Messrs. Allen, Bate, Brooks, Campbell, Carter, Coffin, Dibbrell, Doherty, Fentress, Fielder, Gardner, Garner, Gaut, Gibbs, Heiskell, Hill of Warren, Hill of Gibson, House of Williamson, House of Montgomery, etc., Jones of Lincoln, Jones of Giles, Kennedy, Mabry, Martin, Morris, Netherland, Porter of Haywood, Porter of Henry, Seay, Shepard, Shelton, Stephens, Taylor, Warner, Williamson and Wright—36.

Mr. WILLIAMSON moved to insert "twenty" instead of "nineteen," which was rejected.

Mr. PORTER, of Haywood, moved to lay the report of the Committee on the table.

Mr. BAXTER demanded the yeas and nays, which were ordered, and the motion to lay on the table rejected.

Yeas..21
Nays..44

Those voting in the affirmative are:

Messrs. Allen, Arledge, Bate, Campbell, Coffin, Dibbrell, Fentress, Fielder, Garner, Gaut, Gibbs, Heiskell, Hill of Warren, House of Montgomery, etc., Jones of Lincoln, Jones of Giles, Kennedy, Mabry, Porter of Haywood, Shepard and Shelton—21.

Those voting in the negative are:

Messrs. Baxter, Blackburn, Blizard, Branson, Brandon, Britton, Brooks, Brown of Davidson, Burkett, Byrne, Carter, Chowning, Cypert, Deaderick, Deavenport, Doherty, Finley, Fulkerson, Gardner, Gibson, Gordon, Henderson, Hill of Gibson, House of Williamson, Key, Kirkpatrick, Kyle, Martin, Morris, Meeks, Netherland, Nicholson, Parker, Porter of Henry, Sample, Seay, Staley, Taylor, Thompson of Davidson, Walters, Warner, Williamson, Wright and President Brown—44.

Mr. PORTER, of Haywood, offered the following amendment to the report of the Committee:

"The General Assembly may, by general law, provide for the establishment and maintenance of free schools for the gratuitous instruction of all the children of this State between the ages of—— and —— years, and shall have power to provide such ways and means for the maintenance and support of such schools as may be deemed expedient."

Mr. KIRKPATRICK moved to lay the amendment on the table.

Mr. GARNER demanded the yeas and nays, which resulted as follows:

Yeas..43
Nays..19

Those voting in the affirmative are:

Messrs. Baxter, Blackburn, Blizard, Brandon, Branson, Britton, Brooks, Brown of Davidson, Burkett, Byrne, Chowning, Cypert, Deaderick, Deavenport, Doherty, Finley, Gardner, Gaut, Gibbs, Gibson, Gordon, Henderson, Hill of Gibson, House of Williamson, Jones of Lincoln, Key, Kirkpatrick, Kyle, Mabry, McNabb, Martin, Meeks, Morris, Netherland, Nicholson, Sample, Shepard, Staley, Taylor, Thompson of Davidson, Walters, Warner and Wright—43.

Those voting in the negative are:

Messrs. Allen, Arledge, Bate, Campbell, Carter, Dibbrell, Fentress, Fielder, Fulkerson, Garner, Heiskell, Hill of Warren, Jones of Giles, Kennedy, Porter of Haywood, Porter of Henry, Seay, Shelton and Williamson—19.

INTOXICATING LIQUORS.

Mr. FIELDER moved to reconsider the vote by which Mr. Gaut's proposition in relation to the sale of intoxicating liquors was rejected.

Mr. JONES moved to lay the motion to reconsider on the table.

Mr. BURKETT demanded the yeas and nays, which were ordered, and the motion to lay on the table rejected.

Yeas..27
Nays..34

Those voting in the affirmative are:

Messrs. Arledge, Baxter, Blackburn, Brandon, Brown of Davidson, Campbell, Chowning, Cypert, Deavenport, Finley, Garner, Gibbs, Henderson, Hill of Warren, Hill of Gibson, Key, Martin, Morris, Meeks, Nicholson, Porter of Henry, Seay, Taylor, Thompson of Davidson, Warner, Williamson and Wright—27.

Those voting in the negative are:

Messrs. Bate, Blizard, Branson, Britton, Brooks, Burkett, Byrne, Carter, Coffin, Deaderick, Dibbrell, Doherty, Fentress, Fielder, Gardner, Gaut, Gibson, Gordon, Heiskell, House of Williamson, House of Davidson, etc., Jones of Giles, Kirkpatrick, Kyle,

Mabry, McNabb, Netherland, Parker, Porter of Haywood, Sample, Shepard, Staley and Walters—34.

The further consideration of the motion to reconsider was postponed to Wednesday next.

COMMON SCHOOLS FURTHER CONSIDERED.

The Convention proceeded to the consideration of the unfinished business of Saturday, the report of the Special Committee on Common Schools.

Mr. TAYLOR offered the following amendment:

Add to the end of paragraph after the word "purposes" the following:

"*Provided*, The Legislature shall have power to establish such a system throughout the State, so as to prevent the instruction of white children and negro children at the same institution or free school.

Mr. HEISKELL offered the following amendment:

Strike out in first line of report of Committee: "It shall be the duty of the General Assembly," and insert "the General Assembly may."

Mr. FENTRESS offered the following in lieu of the report of the Committee:

The General Assembly may authorize the County Courts of each county in this State to levy and collect a school tax for free common school purposes, for the children in such counties between the ages of six and eighteen years; *Provided*, That in case any county shall establish common schools within the limits thereof, there shall be separate schools for white and negro children.

The Convention took a recess until 2½ o'clock P. M.

AFTERNOON SESSION.

Mr. CAMPBELL offered the following in lieu of the report of the Committee on Common Schools:

"It shall be the duty of the General Assembly to provide for the establishment of free schools for the gratuitous instruction of all the children of this State between the ages of six and eighteen years. For this purpose, the ordinary tax assessed by the State on polls, under the provisions of this Constitution, shall never be applied to other than for free school purposes, ; and the General Assembly may, from time to time, provide such additional means as may be necessary for the support of a system of common schools."

Which amendment in lieu was, by the unanimous consent of his House, accepted by Mr. GORDON, the Chairman of the Committee.

Mr. TAYLOR demanded the yeas and nays on the adoption of the amendment, which were ordered, and the amendment adopted.

Yeas.. 60
Nays.. 11

Those voting in the affirmative are:

Messrs. Allen, Arledge, Bate, Brandon, Brooks, Brown of Davidson, Burkett, Burton, Byrne, Campbell, Carter, Chowning, Coffin, Cummings, Cypert, Deavenport, Dibbrell, Doherty, Dromgoole, Fentress, Fielder, Fulkerson, Gardner, Garner, Gibbs, Heiskell, Henderson, Hill of Warren, Hill of Gibson, House of Williamson, House of Montgomery, etc., Ivie, Jones of Lincoln, Jones of Giles, Kennedy, Kyle, Mabry, McDougal, McNabb, Martin, Morris, Meeks, Netherland, Nicholson, Porter of Haywood, Porter of Henry, Sample, Seay, Shepard, Shelton, Staley, Stephens, Taylor, Thompson of Davidson, Thompson of Maury, Turner, Walters, Warner, Williamson and Wright—60.

Those voting in the negative are:

Messrs. Baxter, Blackburn, Blizard, Branson, Britton, Finley, Gibson, Gordon, Key, Kirkpatrick and Parker—11.

Mr. TAYLOR moved to amend his amendment by striking out from the first line the words "have power," so that it will read:

"*Provided,* The Legislature shall establish such a system throughout the State, so as to prevent the instruction of white children and negro children at the same institution or free school."

Mr. BAXTER demanded the yeas and nays upon the adoption of the amendment, which were ordered, and the amendment adopted.

Yeas.. 72
Nays.. 1

Those voting in the affirmative are:

Messrs. Allen, Arledge, Bate, Baxter, Blizard, Branson, Brandon, Britton, Brooks, Brown of Davidson, Burkett, Burton, Byrne, Campbell, Carter, Chowning, Coffin, Cummings, Cypert, Deaderick, Deavenport, Dibbrell, Doherty, Dromgoole, Fentress, Fielder, Finley, Fulkerson, Gardner, Garner, Gaut, Gibbs, Gibson, Gordon, Heiskell, Henderson, Hill of Warren, Hill of Gibson, House of Williamson, House of Montgomery, etc., Ivie, Jones of Giles, Kennedy, Key, Kirkpatrick, Kyle, Mabry, McDougal, McNabb, Martin, Morris, Meeks, Netherland, Nicholson, Parker, Porter of Haywood, Porter of Henry, Sample, Seay, Shepard, Shelton, Staley, Taylor, Thompson of Davidson, Thompson of Maury, Turner, Walters, Warner, Williamson, Wright and President Brown—72.

Voting in the negative:

Mr. Jones of Lincoln—1.

Mr. BAXTER demanded the yeas and nays upon the adoption of Mr. Heiskell's amendment, which were ordered, and the amendment adopted.

Yeas.. 39
Nays.. 35

Those voting in the affirmative are:

Messrs. Allen, Arledge, Bate, Brooks, Coffin, Cummings, Dibbrell, Doherty, Dromgoole, Fentress, Fielder, Fulkerson, Gardner, Garner, Gaut, Gibbs, Heiskell, Hill of Warren, Hill of Gibson, House of Williamson, House of Montgomery, etc., Jones of Lincoln, Jones of Giles, Kennedy, Mabry, McDougal, Martin, Porter of Haywood, Porter of Henry, Seay, Shelton, Stephens, Taylor, Thompson of Davidson, Turner, Warner, Williamson, Wright and President Brown—39.

Those voting in the negative are:

Messrs. Baxter, Blackburn, Blizard, Branson, Brandon, Britton, Brown of Davidson, Burkett, Burton, Byrne, Campbell, Carter, Chowning, Cypert, Deaderick, Deavenport, Finley, Gibson, Gordon, Henderson, Ivie, Key, Kirkpatrick, Kyle, McNabb, Morris, Meeks, Netherland, Nicholson, Parker, Sample, Shelton, Staley, Thompson of Maury and Walters—35.

Mr. TAYLOR moved to reconsider the vote adopting the amendment.

Mr. HEISKELL moved to lay the motion to reconsider on the table.

The yeas and nays were ordered, and the motion to lay on the table rejected.

Yeas..33
Nays..40

Those voting in the affirmative are:

Messrs. Allen, Arledge, Bate, Brooks, Chowning, Coffin, Cummings, Dibbrell, Doherty, Dromgoole, Fentress, Fielder, Gardner, Garner, Gaut, Gibbs, Heiskell, Hill of Warren, Hill of Gibson,

House of Montgomery, etc., Jones of Lincoln, Jones of Giles, Kennedy, Mabry, McDougal, Martin, Porter of Haywood, Porter of Henry, Shelton, Stephens, Turner, Warner and Williamson—33.

Those voting in the negative are:

Messrs. Baxter, Blackburn, Blizard, Brandon, Branson, Britton, Brown of Davidson, Burkett, Byrne, Campbell, Carter, Cypert, Deaderick, Deavenport, Finley, Fulkerson, Gibson, Gordon, Henderson, House of Williamson, Ivie, Key, Kirkpatrick, Kyle, McNabb, Morris, Meeks, Netherland, Nicholson, Parker, Sample, Seay, Shepard, Staley, Taylor, Thompson of Davidson, Thompson of Maury, Walters and Wright—40.

The further consideration of the motion to reconsider was postponed until to-morrow.

LEAVE OF ABSENCE.

On motion of Mr. BAXTER, leave of absence was granted Mr. Fulkerson for the balance of the session of the Convention on account of sickness in his family.

On motion of Mr. PORTER, of Henry, the Convention adjourned until to-morrow morning, at 9½ o'clock.

TUESDAY MORNING, FEBRUARY 15, 1870.

The Convention met pursuant to adjournment, Mr. President BROWN in the Chair.

Prayer by the Rev. Mr. SAMPLE, a member of the Convention.

The Journal of yesterday was read, and approved.

HOURS OF MEETING AND ADJOURNMENT.

Mr. GAUT submitted the following resolution:

Resolved, That hereafter the Convention meet at 9 o'clock A. M., take a recess at 1 o'clock P. M., meet at 2 o'clock P. M., and adjourn at 7 o'clock P. M.

On motion of Mr. GAUT, the rules were suspended, and the resolution taken up.

Mr. PORTER, of Haywood, moved to amend the resolution by striking out "seven" and inserting "six."

Mr. JONES, of Lincoln, moved to amend Mr. Gaut's resolution by striking out, "and adjourn at 7 o'clock P. M.," which amendment was adopted.

Mr. THOMPSON, of Maury, offered the following in lieu of Mr. Gaut's amendment:

Resolved, That hereafter the Convention will meet at 9½ o'clock A. M., and adjourn to 3 o'clock P. M.

On motion of Mr. BAXTER, the resolution of Mr. GAUT, and the resolution in lieu, were laid on the table.

FREEDOM OF THE HALL.

Mr. THOMPSON, of Davidson, submitted the following resolution:

Be it resolved, That the freedom of the hall, during the sitting of the Convention, is tendered to the Hon. C. F. TRIGG, now holding an adjourned session of the United States District Court in Nashville.

The rules were suspended, and the resolution adopted.

COMMON SCHOOLS FURTHER CONSIDERED.

The Convention proceeded to the consideration of the unfinished business of yesterday, the pending question being Mr. TAYLOR'S motion to reconsider the vote adopting Mr. Heiskell's amendment.

Mr. TAYLOR demanded the yeas and nays upon the adoption of his motion, which were orderod, and the motion to reconsider adopted.

Yeas...... 37
Nays.. 34

Those voting in the affirmative are:

Messrs. Baxter, Blizard, Brandon, Branson, Britton, Brooks, Brown of Davidson, Burkett, Burton, Byrne, Campbell, Carter, Chowning, Cypert, Deaderick, Deavenport, Finley, Gibson, Gordon, Henderson, House of Williamson, Ivie, Key, Kirkpatrick, Kyle, Mabry,

McNabb, Morris, Meeks, Netherland, Nicholson, Parker, Samp'e, Shepard, Staley, Taylor and Walters—37.

Those voting in the negative are:

Messrs. Allen, Arledge, Bate, Coffin, Cummings, Dibbrell, Doherty, Dromgoole, Fentress, Fielder, Gardner, Garner, Gaut, Gibbs, Heiskell, Hill of Warren, Hill of Gibson, House of Montgomery, Jones of Lincoln, Jones of Giles, Kennedy, McDougal, Martin, Porter of Haywood, Porter of Henry, Seay, Shelton, Stephens, Thompson of Davidson, Thompson of Maury, Turner, Warner, Williamson and Wright—34.

Mr. GARNER demanded the previous question.

The question recurring on Mr. HEISKELL's amendment, Mr. Jones, of Lincoln, demanded the yeas and nays on its adoption, which were ordered, and the amendment rejected.

Yeas.. 30
Nays.. 40

Those voting in the affimative are:

Messrs. Allen, Arledge, Bate, Coffin, Cummings, Dibbrell, Doherty, Dromgoole, Fentress, Fielder, Gardner, Garner, Gaut, Gibbs, Heiskell, Hill of Warren, Hill of Gibson, House of Montgomery, etc., Jones of Lincoln, Jones of Giles, Kennedy, Porter of Haywood, Porter of Henry, Seay, Shelton, Stephens, Turner, Warner, Williamson and Wright—30.

Those voting in the negative are:

Messrs. Baxter, Blizard, Brandon, Branson, Britton, Brooks, Brown of Davidson, Burkett, Burton, Byrne, Campbell, Carter, Chowning, Cypert, Deaderick, Deavenport, Finley, Gibson, Gordon, Henderson, House of Williamson, Ivie, Key, Kirkpatrick, Kyle, Mabry, McDougal, McNabb, Morris, Meeks, Netherland, Nicholson, Parker, Sample, Shepard, Staley, Taylor, Thompson of Davidson, Thompson of Maury and Walters—40.

The question recurring on Mr. FENTRESS' amendment, Mr. Burton asked for a division of the question.

The Chair decided the question divisible.

Mr. HEISKELL demanded the yeas and nays on the adoption of the first clause of the amendment, which were ordered, and it was rejected.

Yeas.. 19
Nays.. 53

Those voting in the affirmative are:

Messrs. Arledge, Bate, Brooks, Fentress, Fielder, Gibbs, Heiskell, Hill of Warren, House of Montgomery, etc., Jones of Lincoln, Jones of Giles, Kennedy, Porter of Haywood, Porter of Henry, Seay, Shelton, Stephens, Taylor and Warner—19.

Those voting in the negative are:

Messrs. Allen, Baxter, Blizard, Brandon, Branson, Britton, Brown of Davidson, Burkett, Burton, Byrne, Campbell, Carter, Chowning, Coffin, Cummings, Cypert, Deaderick, Deavenport, Dibbrell, Doherty, Dromgoole, Finley, Gardner, Garner, Gaut, Gibson, Gordon, Hill of Gibson, House of Williamson, Ivie, Key, Kirkpatrick, Kyle, Mabry, McDougal, McNabb, Martin, Morris, Meeks, Netherland, Nicholson, Parker, Sample, Shepard, Staley, Thompson of Davidson, Thompson of Maury, Turner, Walters, Williamson, Wright and President Brown—53.

The remainder of the amendment of Mr. FENTRESS was ruled out of order by the Chair, it having been acted on by the Convention on yesterday.

The question recurring on Mr. Campbell's amendment, Mr. GARNER demanded the yeas and nays on its adoption, which were ordered, and the amendment adopted.

Yeas..52
Nays..17

Those voting in the affirmative are:

Messrs. Allen, Baxter, Blizard, Branson, Brandon, Britton, Brooks, Brown of Davidson, Burkett, Burton, Byrne, Campbell, Carter, Chowning, Coffin, Cummings, Cypert, Deaderick, Deavenport, Doherty, Finley, Gardner, Gaut, Gibson, Gordon, Henderson, House of Williamson, Ivie, Key, Kirkpatrick, Kyle, Mabry, McDougal, McNabb, Morris, Meeks, Netherland, Nicholson, Parker, Porter of Henry, Sample, Seay, Shepard, Staley, Taylor, Thompson of Davidson, Thompson of Maury, Walters, Warner, Williamson, Wright and President Browu—52.

Those voting in the negative are:

Messrs. Arledge, Bate, Dibbrell, Dromgoole, Fentress, Garner, Gibbs, Heiskell, Hill of Warren, Hill of Gibson, House of Montgomery, etc., Jones of Lincoln, Jones of Giles, Porter of Haywood, Shelton, Stephens and Turner—17.

Mr. JONES, of Lincoln, offered the following amendment:

Add to the Section the following:

"The whole amount of tax collected under this Section shall be paid over immediately by the Tax Collector to the County Trustee to be appropriated to, and expended in the counties from which the same shall be collected respectively."

Mr. THOMPSON, of Davidson, offered the following in lieu of Mr. Jones' amendment:

Be it resolved, That all State taxes on polls shall be paid over to the County Trustee by the Tax Collector, to be applied under the instructions of the County Courts for the purpose of Common Schools in which persons between the ages of six and eighteen may be taught to read and write without charge."

Mr. JONES, of Lincoln, subsequently withdrew his amendment and offered the following:

Add to the end of the Section:

The whole amount of taxes collected for Common Schools, under this Section, shall be paid over directly to the proper fiscal officer of the several counties of the State, in which the same may be collected and under the direction of the County Court, shall be expended for the support of Common Schools in the respective counties. The taxes appropriated under this Section shall be raised from poll taxes alone.

Mr. THOMPSON, of Davidson, withdrew his amendment in lieu.

Mr. KIRKPATRICK called for the previous question, which was sustained.

Mr. BAXTER demanded the yeas and nays on the adoption of Mr. Jones' amendment, which were ordered, and the amendment rejected.

Yeas..33
Nays..38

Those voting in the affirmative are:

Messrs. Arledge, Bate, Brooks, Cummings, Doherty, Dromgoole, Fentress, Fielder, Gardner, Garner, Gibbs, Heiskell, Hill of Warren, Hill of Gibson, House of Williamson, House of Davidson, etc., Ivie, Jones of Lincoln, Jones of Giles, Kennedy, Netherland, Porter of Haywood, Porter of Henry, Seay, Shepard, Shelton, Stephens, Taylor, Thompson of Davidson, Turner, Warner, Williamson and Wright—33.

Those voting in the negative are:

Messrs. Allen, Baxter, Blackburn, Blizard, Branson, Brandon, Britton, Brown of Davidson, Burkett, Byrne, Campbell, Carter, Chowning, Coffin, Cummings, Cypert, Deaderick, Deavenport, Dibbrell, Finley, Gaut, Gibson, Henderson, Key, Kirkpatrick, Kyle, Mabry, McDougal, McNabb, Martin, Morris, Meeks, Nicholson, Parker, Sample, Staley, Thompson of Maury and Walters—38.

Mr. HEISKELL offered the following amendment:

"But the Legislature shall not be required to levy a tax for the next ten years, of more than one million, five hundred thousand dollars, per annum, for school purposes."

Pending which the Convention took a recess.

AFTERNOON SESSION.

LEAVES OF ABSENCE.

On motion of Mr. WRIGHT leave of absence was granted Mr. Porter of Henry, for to-day and to-morrow on account of family affliction.

On motion of Mr. STEPHENS leave of absence was granted Mr. Dromgoole for the remainder of the day.

COMMON SCHOOLS FURTHER CONSIDERED.

Mr. CAMPBELL offered the following in lieu of Mr. Heiskell's amendment:

Add to the end of the Section the following:

"The whole amount of taxes collected for Common School purposes under this Section shall be paid over directly to the proper fiscal officer of the several counties of the State in which the same may be collected and under the direction of the County Court, shall be expended for the support of Common Schools in the respective counties; *Provided*, nothing herein shall be construed to prevent the several counties in this State from levying a tax for Common School purposes.

Mr. HEISKELL withdrew his amendment.

Mr. CAMPBELL then offered his amendment as an independent Section.

Mr. PORTER called for the previous question, which was sustained.

Mr. BROWN, of Davidson, moved that the amendment be laid on

the table for the present, and that the House proceed to the consideration of the special order of the day, which was rejected.

Mr. JONES, of Lincoln, demanded the yeas and nays on the adoption of Mr. Campbell's amendment, which were ordered, and the amendment adopted.

Yeas...41
Nays...31

Those voting in the affirmative are:

Messrs. Allen, Arledge, Bate, Brandon, Brooks, Brown of Henry, etc., Burton, Campbell, Cummings, Cypert, Doherty, Dromgoole, Fentress, Fielder, Gardner, Garner, Gibbs, Gordon, Heiskell, Hill of Warren, Hill of Gibson, House of Williamson, House of Montgomery, etc., Jones of Lincoln, Jones of Giles, Kennedy, Mabry, Porter of Haywood, Seay, Shepard, Shelton, Stephens, Taylor, Thompson of Davidson, Thompson of Maury, Turner, Warner, Williamson, Wright and President Brown—41.

Those voting in the negative are:

Messrs. Baxter, Blackburn, Blizard, Branson, Britton, Brown of Davidson, Burkett, Byrne, Carter, Chowning, Coffin, Deaderick, Deavenport, Dibbrell, Finley, Gibson, Henderson, Key, Kirkpatrick, Kyle, McDougal, McNabb, Martin, Morris, Meeks, Netherland, Nicholson, Parker, Sample, Staley, and Walters—31.

Mr. BAXTER moved that the Convention adjourn until to-morrow morning, and demanded the yeas and nays, which were ordered and the motion to adjourn rejected:

Yeas...14
Nays...56

Those voting in the affirmative are:

Messrs. Allen, Baxter, Blackburn, Blizzard, Branson, Britton, Deaderick, Doherty, Finley, Henderson, Kirkpatrick, Martin, Porter of Haywood and Staley—14.

Those voting in the negative are:

Messrs. Arledge, Bate, Brandon, Brooks, Brown of Davidson, Brown of Henry, etc., Burkett, Burton, Byrne, Campbell, Carter, Chowning, Coffin, Cummings, Cypert, Deavenport, Dibbrell, Fentress, Fielder, Gardner, Garner, Gibbs, Gibson, Gordon, Heiskell, Hill of Warren, Hill of Gibson, House of Williamson, House of Montgomery, etc., Jones of Lincoln, Jones of Giles, Kennedy, Key, Kyle, Mabry, McDougal, McNabb, Morris, Meeks, Netherland, Nicholson, Parker, Sample, Seay, Shepard, Shelton, Stephens, Tay-Thompson of Davidson, Thompson of Maury, Turner, Walters, Warner, Williamson, Wright and President Brown—56.

Mr. MEEKS moved to reconsider the vote adopting Mr. Campbell's amendment adopted in lieu of the report of the committee.

Mr. BAXTER demanded the yeas and nays, which were ordered and the motion to reconsider rejected:

Yeas..33
Nays..36

Those voting in the affirmative are:

Messrs. Arledge, Bate, Blizard, Brooks, Burkett, Byrne, Cummings, Dibbrell, Doherty, Fentress, Fielder, Garner, Gibbs, Heiskell, Hill of Warren, Hill of Gibson, House of Montgomery, etc., Jones of Lincoln, Jones of Giles, Kennedy, Mabry, McDougal, Meeks, Nicholson, Porter of Haywood, Shelton, Stephens, Taylor, Thompson of Maury, Turner, Warner, Williamson and Wright—33.

Those voting in the negative are:

Messrs. Allen, Baxter, Blackburn, Branson, Brandon, Britton, Brown of Davidson, Brown of Henry, etc., Burton, Campbell, Carter, Chowning, Coffin, Cypert, Deaderick, Deavenport, Finley Gardner, Gibson, Gordon, Henderson, House of Williamson, Key, Kirkpatrick, Kyle, McNabb, Martin, Morris, Netherland, Parker, Sample, Seay, Shepard, Staley, Thompson of Davidson and Walters—36.

On motion of Mr. HOUSE, of Montgomery, etc., the rules were suspended to allow another vote upon the proposition to reconsider the vote adopting Mr. Campbell's amendment.

Mr. WILLIAMSON demanded the yeas and nays, which were ordered, and the vote reconsidered:

Yeas..42
Nays..28

Those voting in the affirmative are:

Messrs. Allen, Arledge, Blizard, Brandon, Brooks, Burkett, Byrne, Carter, Chowning, Coffin, Cummings, Cypert, Deavenport, Dibbrell, Fielder, Garner, Gaut, Gibbs, Heiskell, Hill of Warren, Hill of Gibson, House of Williamson, House of Montgomery, etc., Jones of Lincoln, Jones of Giles, Kennedy, Key, Mabry, McDougal, Meeks, Netherland, Nicholson, Shepard, Stephens, Taylor, Thompson of Davidson, Turner, Walters, Warner and Wright—42.

Those voting in the negative are:

Messrs. Bate, Baxter, Blackburn, Branson, Britton, Brown of Davidson, Brown of Henry, etc., Burton, Campbell, Deaderick, Doherty, Fentress, Finley, Gardner, Gibson, Gordon, Henderson,

Ivie, Kirkpatrick, Kyle, McNabb, Martin, Parker, Porter of Haywood, Sample, Seay, Staley and Williamson—28.

Mr. House, of Mongomery, etc., moved to reconsider the vote by which the second amendment of Mr. Campbell was adopted.

Mr. FENTRESS demanded the yeas and nays which were ordered, and the motion to reconsider adopted:

Yeas 53
Nays..18

Those voting in the affirmative are:

Messrs. Allen, Arledge, Bate, Baxter, Blizard, Brandon, Britton, Brooks, Burkett, Burton, Byrne, Carter, Chowning, Coffin, Cummings, Cypert, Deaderick, Deavenport, Dibbrell, Fielder, Finley, Garner, Gaut, Gibbs, Heiskell, Henderson, Hill of Warren, Hill of Gibson, House of Williamson, House of Montgomery, etc., Ivie, Jones of Giles, Kennedy, Key, Kirkpatrick, Kyle, Mabry, McDougal, McNabb, Martin, Morris, Meeks, Netherland, Nicholson, Sample, Shepard, Shelton, Stephens, Taylor, Thompson of Davidson, Walters and Wright—53.

Those voting in the negative are:

Messrs. Blackburn, Branson, Brown of Davidson, Brown of Henry, etc., Campbell, Doherty, Fentress, Gardner, Gibson, Gordon, Jones of Lincoln, Parker, Porter of Haywood, Seay, Staley, Thompson of Maury, Turner and Williamson—18.

Mr. JONES, of Giles, offered Section 10, of Article XI, of the the Constitution of 1834, in lieu of the report of the Committee and all pending amendments, and demanded the previous question, which was sustained.

Mr. GIBSON demanded the yeas and nays upon the adoption of the amendment, which were ordered, and the amendment adopted.

Yeas..49
Nays..22

Those voting in the affirmative are:

Messrs. Allen, Arledge, Bate, Blizard, Brandon, Brooks, Burkett, Byrne, Carter, Chowning, Coffin, Cummings, Cypert, Deaderick, Deavenport, Dibbrell, Doherty, Dromgoole, Fielder, Garner, Gaut, Gibbs, Heiskell, Hill of Warren, Hill of Gibson, House of Williamson, House of Montgomery etc., Jones of Lincoln, Jones of Giles, Kennedy, Mabry, McDougal, Martin, McNabb, Meeks, Netherland, Nicholson, Porter of Haywood, Sample, Shepard, Shelton, Stephens,

Taylor, Thompson of Davidson, Thompson of Maury, Turner, Walters, Warner and Wright—49.

Those voting in the negative are:

Messrs. Baxter, Blackburn, Branson, Britton, Brown of Davidson, Brown of Henry, etc., Burton, Campbell, Fentress, Finley, Gardner, Gibson, Gordon, Henderson, Ivie, Key, Kirkpatrick, Kyle, Parker, Seay, Staley and Williamson—22.

Mr. KIRKPATRICK entered a motion to take from the table the motion to reconsider the vote adopting Section 1, Article IV.

CORPORATIONS FURTHER CONSIDERED.

The Convention proceeded to the consideration of the special order of the day, the report of the Committee on Finance, Internal Improvements and Corporations.

Mr. HOUSE, of Williamson, moved to lay the amendment of Mr. Jones, of Lincoln, heretofore offered, on the table.

Mr. JONES demanded the yeas and nays, which were ordered, and the motion to lay on the table sustained.

Yeas..53
Nays..13

Those voting in the affirmative are:

Messrs. Allen, Baxter, Blizard, Branson, Brandon, Britton, Brooks, Brown of Davidson, Brown of Henry, etc., Burton, Byrne, Campbell, Carter, Chowning, Coffin, Cypert, Deaderick, Dibbrell, Doherty, Finley, Gardner, Garner, Gaut, Gibbs, Gibson, Gordon, Heiskell, Henderson, Hill of Gibson, House of Williamson, House of Montgomery, etc., Jones of Giles, Kennedy, Key, Kirkpatrick, Mabry, McDougal, McNabb, Meeks, Netherland, Nicholson, Parker, Porter of Haywood, Sample, Seay, Shepard, Shelton, Staley, Stephens, Thompson of Davidson, Walters and Wright—53.

Those voting in the negative are:

Messrs. Bate, Cummings, Deavenport, Fentress, Fielder, Hill of Warren, Ivie, Jones of Lincoln, Morris, Thompson of Maury, Turner, Warner and Williamson—13

Mr. GIBSON offered the following amendment:

"Insert the words "or its powers increased or diminished" between the words "created" and "by," in the first line, so that the first clause will read "no corporation shall be created, or its powers increased or diminished by special laws."

Mr. NICHOLSON's amendment, heretofore offered, to-wit: "But no such alteration or repeal shall interfere with or divest rights which have become vested" was adopted by the Convention.

Mr. GIBSON's amendment was then adopted.

Mr. THOMPSON, of Maury, offered the following amendment:

In 1st line, between the word "corporation" and "shall" insert the words "except Banking Companies, Railroad Companies, Navigation Companies and Insurance Companies;" add to said section the words, "and all companies incorporated by the General Assembly shall each pay into the Treasury of the State one hundred dollars before the Act of Incorporation shall take effect or be in force."

Mr. BURTON demanded a division of the question, which was ordered, and the first clause of the amendment was rejected.

Mr. THOMPSON demanded the yeas and nays upon the adoption of the second clause of his amendment.

The Chair declared the rejection of the first clause disposed of the amendment.

Mr. JONES, of Giles, offered the following amendment:

Provided, That no charter incorporating a railroad, a bank, or town or city, where the number of inhabitants shall exceed two hundred and fifty, shall go into operation until the same shall be approved by a vote of the majority of each House of the Legislature.

Mr. TURNER demanded the previous question, which was sustained, and Mr. Jones', of Giles, amendment rejected, and Section 7, Article XI, as amended was adopted.

Mr. TURNER moved to reconsider the vote adopting the Section, and further moved to lay the motion to reconsider on the table.

Mr. BAXTER demanded the yeas and nays on the the motion to lay the motion to reconsider on the table, which were ordered, and the motion to lay on the table sustained.

Yeas..49
Nays..15

Those voting in the affirmative are:

Messrs. Brandon, Branson, Britton, Brown of Henry, etc., Burton, Byrne, Coffin, Cummings, Cypert, Deaderick, Deavenport, Dibbrell, Doherty, Fielder, Gardner, Garner, Gaut, Gibson, Heiskell, Henderson, Hill of Waren, Hill of Gibson, House of Williamson, Ivie, Jones of Lincoln, Kennedy, Key, Kirkpatrick, Mabry, McDougal, McNabb, Morris, Meeks, Netherland, Nicholson, Parker, Porter of Haywood, Sample, Seay, Shepard, Shelton, Staley, Stephens, Thompson of Davidson, Turner, Walters, Warner, Williamson and Wright—49.

Those voting in the negative are:

Messrs. Allen, Bate, Baxter, Blizard, Brooks, Brown of Davidson, Campbell, Carter, Chowning, Fentress, Finley, Gibbs, Gordon, Jones of Giles and Thompson of Maury—15.

On motion, the Convention adjourned until to-morrow morning at 9½ o'clock.

WEDNESDAY MORNING, FEBRUARY 16, 1870.

The Convention met pursuant to adjournment, Mr. President BROWN in the Chair.

The Journal of yesterday was read and approved.

AMENDMENTS PROPOSED.

Mr. JONES, of Lincoln, offered the following resolution:

Resolved, That the Committee on the Judiciary Department be and are hereby instructed to report a provision to be inserted in Section 13, Article 6, providing that Clerks of the Chancery Courts shall be elected for the term of four years by the qualified voters of the counties, or districts, for which the several courts may be held and also providing that Clerks of the Circuit Courts shall be elected by the qualified voters of the several counties for the term of four years.

Which lies over under the rules.

FRAUDULENT BONDS.

Mr. CAMPBELL submitted the following preamble and resolution:

WHEREAS, It having been stated upon the floor of this Convention, that extensive frauds and irregularities have been committed in obtaining the bonds of the State, for internal improvements and other purposes; that a large number of the bonds of the State have been illegally issued and appropriated; that other securities of the State are now in circulation without legal authority; and that irregularities have been committed in disposing of the Agricultural School Scrip. It is therefore,

Resolved, That the Legislature, now in session, be requested to pass a law creating a commission of three discreet citizens of the State, to be called "The Board of Commissioners on Bond and Public Securities," whose duty it shall be to examine into and adjudicate upon the validity of all bonds, and other securities issued by, and now outstanding against the State, and to report upon any irregularities that may have been committed in the disposition of the Agricultural School Scrip. That said Board of Commissioners have conferred upon them all the power, authority and machinery necessary to carry out the object and purposes of this resolution.

Which lies over under the rule.

PRINTING THE NEW CONSTITUTION.

Mr. TURNER offered the following resolution:

Resolved, That the Committee on Revision and Enrollment be instructed to have printed ten thousand copies of the amended Constitution, at as an early day as practicable. The same to be so printed as to show the additions and amendments to the present Constitution.

Which lies over under the rule.

Mr. GIBSON presented the following

PROTEST:

The undersigned having voted against all the propositions that tended to deprive the children of Tennessee of the benefits of free schools, and having especially voted against the 10th Section, of Article XI of the Constitution, desire to present, by way of protest, the reasons for their vote:

1. Said Section while declaring that "knowledge, learning and virtue are *essential* to the preservation of Republican institutions," at the same time provides *no means* to make *operative* that great truth, and is therefore an acknowledgment that the Convention is either *unable* or *unwilling* to devise a method of general public instruction.

2. The consecration of the "Common School Fund" to the "support and encouragement of Common Schools" is a *horrid mockery*

inasmuch as there is not *one cent* of said "fund" in existence; and the very language sounds like Scripture in the mouth of an *infidel.*

2. Said section, though one of the *longest* in the Constitution, has the *least* in it. It literally means *nothing.* It is a monstrous conglomeration of uncommonly long sentences, and sounds like an antique epitaph upon Plato's Academy. Its true signification is "*hic jacet.*"

4. Said section says in substance that the children of Tennessee are entitled to common schools, and yet practically denies them schools. And this said section is an inimitable illustration of "how not to do it."

The undersigned believe that the education of her children is the *highest duty* of the State—a duty not to be *postponed* in order to pay debts of doubtful obligation, but a duty to be preferred to *all* others. Free schools and free States are inseparable, for education is the foundation of freedom.

The section, as adopted, is but the *dead corpse* of the section in the old Constitution. The same *body* is there, but the *life,* the *money* is gone—gone past resurrection, and all that remains is to bury the ghastly carcass of what was once a glory and a blessing to Tennessee, forever out of sight. Why keep the section like an *Egyptian mummy,* preserved for exhibition in the Constitution, a perpetual offence to the sight, an unpleasant reminder of past good, now vanished forever.

The undersigned, therefore, protest against the adoption of said section as a promise without a fulfillment, a right without enjoyment, a preamble without a resolution, a "glittering generality," a repudiation of a great moral duty, and a deadly blow at education given in the name of friendship, and asked to have this their protest entered on the Journal.

HENRY R. GIBSON,
JAMES C. PARKER,
J. W. BRANSON.

REPORT ON THE JUDICIARY.

Mr. HEISKELL, from the Committee on the Judiciary, made the following report:

The Committee on the Judicial Department have directed me to report: That they have considered the matter of the memorial of Robert H. Jameison, and that they recommend the adoption of the following clauses to be incorporated in the Constitution.

HEISKELL, Chairman.

ARTICLE XI.

Section 1, as heretofore. Add to it the following:

But ordinances contained in any former Constitution or Schedule thereto are hereby abrogated.

The time which has elapsed from the 6th day of May, 1861, until the 1st day of January, 1867, shall not be computed, in any case affected by the statutes of limitation, nor shall any writ of error be affected by such lapse of time.

On motion of Mr. HEISKELL, it was ordered that the report be laid on the table, and 100 copies be printed for the use of the Convention.

RATE OF INTEREST.

The Convention proceeded to the consideration of the Report of the Committee on Finance, Internal Improvements and Corporations—the question immediately pending being that of interest.

Mr. JONES, of Lincoln, offered the following as an amendment to the amendment of Mr. Baxter:

Add, "for loaned money not exceeding ten per centum per annum."

Mr. PORTER, of Haywood, offered the following in lieu of Mr. Baxter's and the Report of the Committee:

Strike out Article XI, Section 6, and insert the following:

"The legal rate of interest in this State shall be six per centum per annum, but the Legislature shall have power to provide by law for a conventional rate of interest."

Mr. HILL, of Gibson, demanded the previous question, which was sustained.

Mr. JONES, of Lincoln, demanded the yeas and nays upon the adoption of his amendment, which were ordered and the amendment rejected.

Yeas.. 29
Nays.. 40

Those voting in the affirmative are:

Messrs. Arledge, Branson, Britton, Brooks, Brown of Davidson, Deavenport, Dromgoole, Fielder, Garner, Gaut, Gibson, Hill of Warren, House of Montgomery, etc., Ivie, Jones of Lincoln, Jones of Giles, Key, McDougal, McNabb, Martin, Meeks, Netherland, Nicholson, Parker, Seay, Shepard, Thompson of Maury, Turner and Warner—29.

Those voting in the negative are:

Messrs. Allen, Baxter, Blackburn, Blizard, Brandon, Brown of Henry, etc., Burkett, Burton, Byrne, Campbell, Carter, Chowning, Coffin, Cummings, Cypert, Deaderick, Dibbrell, Fentress, Finley,

Gardner, Gibbs, Gordon, Heiskell, Henderson, Hill of Gibson, House of Williamson, Kennedy, Kyle, Mabry, Morris, Porter of Haywood, Sample, Staley, Stephens, Taylor, Thompson of Davidson, Walters, Williamson and Wright—40.

Mr. PORTER, of Haywood, demanded the yeas and nays on the adoption of his amendment in lieu, which were ordered and the amendment rejected.

Yeas..23
Nays..46

Those voting in the affirmative are:

Messrs. Branson, Britton, Brooks, Brown of Davidson, Carter, Chowning, Coffin, Cypert, Deavenport, Fielder, Gaut, Gibson, Henderson, House of Montgomery, etc., Ivie, McDougal, McNabb, Meeks, Parker, Porter of Haywood, Seay, Staley and Turner—23.

Those voting in the negative are:

Messrs. Allen, Arledge, Baxter, Blackburn, Blizard, Brandon, Brown of Henry, etc., Burkett, Burton, Byrne, Campbell, Cummings, Deaderick, Dibbrell, Doherty, Dromgoole, Fentress, Finley, Gardner, Garner, Gibbs, Gordon, Heiskell, Hill of Warren, Hill of Gibson, House of Williamson, Jones of Lincoln, Jones of Giles, Kennedy, Key, Kyle, Mabry, Martin, Morris, Netherland, Nicholson, Sample, Shepard, Stephens, Taylor, Thompson of Davidson, Thompson of Maury, Walters, Warner, Williamson and Wright—46.

Mr. JONES, of Lincoln, demanded the yeas and nays on the adoption of Mr. Baxter's amendment, which were ordered and the amendment rejected.

Yeas..34
Nays..38

Those voting in the affirmative are:

Messrs. Baxter, Blackburn, Blizard, Brandon, Branson, Brown of Davidson, Brown of Henry, etc., Burkett, Burton, Byrne, Carter, Chowning, Coffin, Dromgoole, Fentress, Finley, Gibbs, Gibson, Hill of Gibson, House of Williamson, House of Montgomery, etc., Ivie, Kennedy, Key, McNabb, Netherland, Nicholson, Parker, Sample, Seay, Shepard, Turner and Williamson—34.

Those voting in the negative are:

Messrs. Allen, Arledge, Bate, Britton, Brooks, Campbell, Cummings, Cypert, Deaderick, Deavenport, Dibbrell, Doherty, Fielder, Gardner, Garner, Gaut, Gordon, Heiskell, Henderson, Hill of Warren, Jones of Lincoln, Jones of Giles, Kyle, Mabry, McDougal, Martin, Morris, Meeks, Porter of Haywood, Staley, Stephens, Taylor, Thompson of Davidson, Thompson of Maury, Walters, Warner, Wright and President Brown—38.

Mr. BAXTER demanded the yeas and nays on the adoption of the Report of the Committee, which were ordered and the report rejected.

Yeas..27
Nays..44

Those voting in the affirmative are:

Messrs. Allen, Blackburn, Blizard, Brown of Davidson, Brown of Henry, etc., Byrne, Campbell, Cypert, Deavenport, Dibbrell, Doherty, Dromgoole, Fentress, Finley, Gardner, Gaut, Heiskell, House of Williamson, Mabry, Porter of Haywood, Stephens, Taylor, Thompson of Davidson, Thompson of Maury, Turner, Wright and President Brown—27.

Those voting in the negative are:

Messrs. Arledge, Bate, Baxter, Branson, Brandon, Britton, Brooks, Burkett, Burton, Carter, Chowning, Coffin, Cummings, Deaderick, Fielder, Garner, Gibbs, Gibson, Gordon, Henderson, Hill of Warren, Hill of Gibson, House of Montgomery, etc., Ivie, Jones of Lincoln, Jones of Giles, Kennedy, Key, Kyle, McDougal, McNabb, Martin, Morris, Meeks, Netherland, Nicholson, Parker, Sample, Seay, Shepard, Staley, Walters, Warner and Williamson—44.

Mr. JONES, of Giles, offered the 6th Section of Article II of the Constitution of 1834, in lieu of all pending propositions, and demanded the previous question, which was sustained.

Mr. JONES, of Giles, demanded the yeas and nays on his amendment, which were ordered and the amendment adopted.

Yeas..52
Nays..19

Those voting in the affirmative are:

Messrs. Allen, Arledge, Bate, Baxter, Blackburn, Branson, Brandon, Britton, Brooks, Burkett, Burton, Carter, Chowning, Coffin, Cummings, Cypert, Deaderick, Doherty, Dromgoole, Fielder, Finley, Garner, Gaut, Gibson, Gordon, Henderson, Hill of Warren, Hill of Gibson, House of Williamson, House of Montgomery, etc., Ivie, Jones of Lincoln, Jones of Giles, Kennedy, Key, Kyle, McDougal, McNabb, Martin, Morris, Meeks, Netherland, Nicholson, Parker, Sample, Seay, Staley, Taylor, Thompson of Maury, Walters, Warner and Williamson—52.

Those voting in the negative are:

Messrs. Blizard, Brown of Davidson, Brown of Henry, etc.,

Byrne, Campbell, Deavenport, Dibbrell, Fentress, Gardner, Gibbs, Heiskell, Mabry, Porter of Haywood, Shepard, Stephens, Thompson of Davidson, Turner, Wright and President Brown—19.

Mr. BATE moved to reconsider the vote adopting the 6th Section of Article XI, and further moved to lay the motion to reconsider on the table, and demanded the yeas and nays on the latter motion, which were ordered, and the motion to lay on the table adopted.

Yeas..38
Nays..31

Those voting in the affirmative are:

Messrs. Bate, Branson, Brandon, Britton, Brooks, Burton, Carter, Chowning, Coffin, Cypert, Deaderick, Doherty, Dromgoole, Fielder, Garner, Gaut, Gibson, Gordon, Henderson, Hill of Warren, Hill of Gibson, House of Montgomery, etc., Ivie, Jones of Lincoln, Jones of Giles, Kyle, McDougal, McNabb, Martin, Morris, Meeks, Netherland, Nicholson, Parker, Sample, Staley, Walters and Warner—38.

Those voting in the negative are:

Messrs. Arledge, Baxter, Blizard, Brown of Davidson, Brown of Henry, etc., Burkett, Byrne, Campbell, Cummings, Deavenport, Dibbrell, Fentress, Gardner, Gibbs, Heiskell, House of Williamson, Kennedy, Key, Mabry, Porter of Haywood, Seay, Shepard, Stephens, Taylor, Thompson of Davidson, Thompson of Maury, Turner, Williamson, Wright and President Brown—31.

Mr. GIBBS offered the following amendment to 6th Section, Article XI:

But the Legislature may provide for a conventional rate of interest.

Mr. BATE demanded the yeas and nays on the adoption of the amendment, which were ordered, and the amendment adopted.

Yeas..40
Nays..24

Those voting in the affirmative are:

Messrs. Allen, Baxter, Brown of Davidson, Brown of Henry, etc., Burkett, Burton, Byrne, Campbell, Coffin, Cummings, Cypert, Dibbrell, Doherty, Fentress, Fielder, Gardner, Gaut, Gibbs, Gibson, Gordon, Heiskell, Hill of Gibson, House of Williamson, House of Montgomery, etc., Kennedy, Key, Mabry, Nicholson, Parker, Porter of Haywood, Seay, Shepard, Stephens, Taylor, Thompson of Davidson, Thompson of Maury, Turner, Walters, Williamson, Wright and President Brown—40.

Those voting in the negative are:

Messrs. Arledge, Bate, Blizard, Brandon, Britton, Brooks, Carter,

Chowning, Deaderick, Deavenport, Dromgoole, Garner, Henderson, Hill of Warren, Ivie, Jones of Lincoln, Jones of Giles, Kyle, McDougal, McNabb, Martin, Meeks, Morris, Netherland, Sample, Staley and Warner—24.

Mr. Henderson offered the following proviso:

"But no person, company or corporation shall be held liable as security for another upon any debt, contract or undertaking bearing a higher rate of interest than six per cent. per annum."

Pending which the Convention took a recess.

AFTERNOON SESSION.

Mr. HENDERSON's amendment being the pending question, Mr. Jones, of Lincoln, called for the question, and demanded the yeas and nays on the adoption of Mr. Henderson's amendment, which were ordered, and the amendment rejected.

Yeas.......................................a......................... 20
Nays... 42

Those voting in the affirmative are:

Messrs. Branson, Britton, Brooks, Deavenport, Garner, Gibson, Gordon, Henderson, Hill of Warren, Jones of Lincoln, Jones of Giles, Key, Kyle, McNabb, Morris, Netherland, Sample, Staley, Walters and Warner—20.

Those voting in the negative are:

Messrs. Arledge, Baxter, Blizard, Brandon, Brown of Henry, etc., Burkett, Burton, Byrne, Campbell, Carter, Chowning, Coffin, Cummings, Cypert, Deaderick, Dibbrell, Doherty, Dromgoole, Fentress, Fielder, Gardner, Gaut, Gibbs, Heiskell, Hill of Gibson, House of Williamson, House of Montgomery, etc., Ivie, Kennedy, Kirkpatrick, McDougal, Martin, Porter of Haywood, Seay, Shepard, Stephens, Taylor, Thompson of Davidson, Turner, Williamson, Wright and President Brown—42.

Mr. CYPERT offered the following proviso, as an amendment to Section 6, Article XI:

Provided, The Legislature shall have no power to enact any law allowing a higher rate of interest than *ten per cent. per annum.*

Mr. GARNER demanded the yeas and nays upon the adoption of the amendment, which were ordered, and the amendment adopted.

Yeas..53
Nays..15

Those voting in the affirmative are:

Messrs. Allen, Bate, Blizard, Brandon, Branson, Britton, Brooks, Byrne, Carter, Chowning, Coffin, Cummings, Cypert, Deaderick, Deavenport, Dibbrell, Doherty, Dromgoole, Fielder, Gardner, Garner, Gaut, Gibson, Gordon, Henderson, Hill of Warren, House of Williamson, House of Montgomery, etc., Ivie, Jones of Lincoln, Jones of Giles, Key, Kirkpatrick, Kyle, McDougal, McNabb, Martin, Meeks, Morris, Netherland, Nicholson, Parker, Sample, Seay, Shepard, Shelton, Staley, Taylor, Thompson of Maury, Turner, Walters, Warner and Wright—53.

Those voting in the negative are:

Messrs. Arledge, Baxter, Brown of Henry, etc., Burkett, Burton, Campbell, Fentress, Gibbs, Heiskell, Hill of Gibson, Kennedy, Porter of Haywood, Stephens, Thompson of Davidson and Williamson—15.

On motion of Mr. FENTRESS, leave of absence was granted Mr. Campbell on account of sickness.

STATE AID TO RAILROADS.

The Convention proceeded to the consideration of the following report of the Committee on Finance:

"No bonds of the State shall be issued to any railroad company which, at the time of its application for the same, shall be in default in paying the interest upon State bonds previously loaned to it, or that shall hereafter, and before such application, sell, or absolutely dispose of, any State bonds loaned to it for less than par."

Mr. JONES, of Lincoln, demanded the yeas and nays on the adoption of the report of the Committee, which were ordered, and the report rejected by a tie vote.

Yeas..34
Nays..34

Those voting in the affirmative are:

Messrs. Arledge, Bate, Baxter, Blizard, Brown of Davidson,

Brown of Henry, etc., Burton, Carter, Deavenport, Doherty, Dromgoole, Fielder, Gardner, Garner, Gordon, Henderson, Hill of Warren, Hill of Gibson, House of Williamson, House of Montgomery, etc., Ivie, Jones of Lincoln, Jones of Giles, Kennedy, McDougal, Meeks, Morris, Shelton, Staley, Stephens, Thompson of Davidson, Thompson of Maury, Walters and Warner—34.

Those voting in the negative are:

Messrs. Allen, Brandon, Branson, Britton, Brooks, Byrne, Chowning, Coffin, Cummings, Cypert, Deaderick, Dibbrell, Fentress, Finley, Gibbs, Gibson, Heiskell, Key, Kirkpatrick, Kyle, Mabry, McNabb, Martin, Netherland, Nicholson, Parker, Porter of Haywood, Sample, Seay, Shepard, Taylor, Turner, Williamson and Wright—34.

INTOXICATING LIQUORS.

The Convention proceeded to the consideration of the special order of the day—the motion of Mr. FIELDER—to reconsider the vote rejecting Mr. Gaut's amendment in relation to the prohibition of the sale of spirituous liquors by a vote of the citizens of towns, cities, and civil districts.

Mr. CYPERT demanded the yeas and nays on the motion to reconsider, which were ordered, and the motion rejected.

Yeas.. 31
Nays.. 37

Those voting in the affirmative are:

Messrs. Allen, Bate, Blizard, Branson, Britton, Brooks, Brown of Henry, etc., Byrne, Carter, Coffin, Deaderick, Dibbrell, Doherty, Dromgoole, Fentress, Fielder, Gaut, Gibson, Heiskell, Ivie, Jones of Giles, Kirkpatrick, Kyle, Mabry, McNabb, Netherland, Parker, Sample, Shepard, Staley and Wright—31.

Those voting in the negative are:

Messrs. Arledge, Baxter, Brandon, Brown of Davidson, Burton, Chowning, Cummings, Cypert, Deavenport, Gardner, Garner, Gibbs, Gordon, Henderson, Hill of Warren, Hill of Gibson, House of Williamson, House of Montgomery, etc., Jones of Lincoln, Kennedy, Key, McDougal, Martin, Meeks, Morris, Nicholson, Porter of Haywood, Seay, Shelton, Stephens, Taylor, Thompson of Davidson, Thompson of Maury, Turner, Walters, Warner and Williamson—37.

ELECTIVE FRANCHISE.

Mr. KIRKPATRICK called up his motion, entered on yesterday, to take from the table the motion to reconsider the vote adopting Section 1, of Article IV.

Mr. CYPERT demanded the yeas and nays, which were ordered, and the motion to take from the table the motion to reconsider was adopted.

Yeas..43
Nays..25

Those voting in the affirmative are:

Messrs. Arledge, Blizard, Brandon, Branson, Britton, Brooks, Brown of Henry, etc., Byrne, Carter, Chowning, Coffin, Cummings, Cypert, Deaderick, Dibbrell, Doherty, Fentress, Fielder, Gibbs, Gibson, Henderson, Hill of Warren, Hill of Gibson, Ivie, Jones of Lincoln, Key, Kirkpatrick, Kyle, Mabry, McDougal, McNabb, Martin, Meeks, Morris, Netherland, Nicholson, Parker, Porter of Haywood, Sample, Taylor, Walters, Warner and Williamson—43.

Those voting in the negative are:

Messrs. Allen, Bate, Baxter, Brown of Davidson, Deavenport, Dromgoole, Finley, Gardner, Garner, Gaut, Gordon, Heiskell, House of Williamson, House of Montgomery, etc., Jones of Giles, Kennedy, Seay, Shepard, Shelton, Staley Stephens, Thompson of Davidson, Thompson of Maury, Turner and Wright—25.

Mr. KENNEDY demanded the yeas and nays on the motion to reconsider, which were ordered, and the motion adopted:

Yeas..38
Nays..33

Those voting in the affirmative are:

Messrs. Arledge, Blizard, Brandon, Branson, Britton, Brooks, Brown of Henry, etc., Carter, Chowning, Coffin, Cummings, Cypert, Deaderick, Doherty, Fentress, Finley, Gibbs, Gibson, Henderson, Hill of Warren, Ivie, Jones of Lincoln, Key, Kirkpatrick, Kyle, McDougal, McNabb, Martin, Meeks, Morris, Netherland Parker, Sample, Staley, Taylor, Walters, Warner, and Williamson—38.

Those voting in the negative are:

Messrs. Allen, Bate, Baxter, Brown of Davidson, Burkett, Burton, Byrne, Deavenport, Dibbrell, Dromgoole, Fielder, Gardner, Garner, Gaut, Gordon, Heiskell, Hill of Gibson, House of Williamson, House of Montgomery, etc., Jones of Giles, Kennedy, Mabry, Nicholson, Porter of Haywood, Seay, Shepard, Shelton, Stephens, Thompson of Davidson, Thompson of Maury, Turner Wright and President Brown—33.

Mr. FENTRESS offered the following in lieu of Section 1, Article VI.

The following persons shall be entitled to the exercise of the Elective Franchise in this State:

1. Every free white man of the age of twenty-one years, being a citizen of the United States and resident of this State for twelve months; and resident of the county wherein he may offer his vote sixth months next preceding the day of election.

2. And if at any time hereafter the right of the States to declare who shall not be voters is legally surrendered to the Government of the United States, then such other persons as the United States Government shall declare entitled to exercise the Elective Franchise in Tennessee shall by virtue of the same be so entitled, but no further or otherwise.

Provided, That the General Assembly shall have power to enact laws requiring voters to vote in the election precincts in which they may reside, and laws to secure the freedom of elections and purity of the ballot box.

All male persons of the State shall be subject to military duty within such ages as may be prescribed by law; but no one shall be subject to a poll tax who is not legally entitled to vote in this State.

Mr. THOMPSON, of Davidson, offered the following in lieu of Mr. Fentress' amendment:

"*Provided,* That every voter shall be required to vote in the Civil District or Ward in which he resides."

Mr. JONES, of Lincoln, moved to lay the amendment of Mr. Fentress on the table.

Mr. KENNEDY demanded the previous question.

Mr. CYPERT demanded the yeas and nays on Mr. Jones' motion to lay Mr. Fentress' amendment on the table, which were ordered, and the motion to lay on the table sustained.

Yeas.. 55
Nays.. 17

Those voting in the affirmative are:

Messrs. Allen, Baxter, Blizard, Brandon, Branson, Britton, Brooks, Brown of Davidson, Burkett, Burton, Byrne, Chowning, Coffin, Cypert, Deaderick, Dibbrell, Doherty, Dromgoole, Fielder, Finley, Gardner, Garner, Gaut, Gibbs, Gibson, Henderson, Hill of Warren, Hill of Gibson, House of Williamson, House of Davidson, etc., Ivie, Jones of Lincoln, Kennedy, Key, Kirkpatrick, Kyle, McDougal, McNabb, Martin, Meeks, Morris, Netherland, Nicholson, Parker, Porter of Haywood, Sample, Seay, Staley, Thompson of Davidson, Thompson of Maury, Turner, Walters, Warner, Wright and President Brown—55.

Those voting in the negative are:

Messrs. Arledge, Bate, Brown of Henry, etc., Campbell, Carter, Cummings, Deavenport, Fentress, Gordon, Heiskell, Jones of Giles, Mabry, Shepard, Shelton, Stephens, Taylor and Williamson—17.

POINT OF ORDER.

Mr. JONES, of Giles, raised the following point of order:

A motion having been made to reconsider the vote adopting Section 1, Article IV, and that motion having been laid on the table, it could only be taken from the table by a vote of two-thirds of the Convention, and the motion of Mr. Kirkpatrick not having received a two-thirds vote failed—and that the vote subsequently taken to reconsider, and the reception and entertaining Mr. Fentress' amendment and the vote thereon were all out of order and void.

The Chair, Mr. TURNER presiding, decided the point of order well taken.

Mr. JONES, of Lincoln, appealed from the decision of the Chair and demanded the yeas and nays, which were ordered and the decision of the Chair sustained:

Yeas..43
Nays 27

Those voting in the affirmative are:

Messrs. Allen, Baxter, Brandon, Branson, Britton, Brown of Henry, etc., Burkett, Burton, Byrne, Carter, Chowning, Cummings, Deavenport, Doherty, Dromgoole, Fentress, Fielder, Finley, Gardner, Gaut, Gibson, Gordon, Heiskell, Hill of Gibson, House of Williamson, House of Montgomery, etc., Ivie, Jones of Giles, Kennedy, Key, Kirkpatrick, Mabry, Nicholson, Parker, Porter of Haywood, Shepard, Shelton, Staley, Stephens, Thompson of Davidson and Wright—43.

Those voting in the negative are:

Messrs. Arledge, Bate, Blizard, Brooks, Brown of Davidson, Cypert, Deaderick, Dibbrell, Gibbs, Henderson, Hill of Warren, Jones of Lincoln, Kyle, McDougal, McNabb, Martin, Meeks, Morris, Netherland, Sample, Seay, Taylor, Thompson of Maury, Walters, Warner, Williamson and President Brown—27.

On motion of Mr. SEAY the Convention adjourned until to-morrow morning at 9½ o'clock.

THURSDAY MORNING, FEBRUARY 17, 1870.

The Convention met pursuant to adjournment, Mr. President BROWN in the Chair.

Prayer by the Rev. Mr. INMAN.

The Journal of yesterday was read and approved.

THE BIBLE IN COMMON SCHOOLS.

Mr. SAMPLE offered the following resolution:

Resolved, That the Scriptures of the Old and New Testament shall never be prohibited or excluded from the Common Schools of this State.

ADJOURNMENT SINE DIE.

Mr. BLACKBURN submitted the following preamble and resolution:

WHEREAS, This Convention having now already been in session for thirty-four days, at an expense to the people of the State of twenty to thirty thousand dollars (the purpose whereof, the same was called, being to alter, amend or abolish the present State Constitution, neither of which has yet been done) therefore, be it

Resolved, That this Convention adjourn *sine die* on to-morrow, Friday, February, 18th, 1870, and that this Conventien be declared as adjourned on that day.

Which resolution lies over under the rule.

PLACE OF HOLDING COURT.

Mr. PORTER, of Haywood, offered the following resolution, which, on his motion, was referred to the Committee on the Judiciary:

"The General Assembly shall hereafter have no power to establish the Courts of Record, to be held elsewhere than at the county seat of the county for which such court is to be held."

WHEN LAWS TO TAKE EFFECT.

Mr. STEPHENS from the Committee on the Legislative Department made the following report:

To the PRESIDENT of the Convention:

I am instructed by a majority of the Committee on the Legislative Department to report the following amendment to Article II:

ARTICLE II.

Section 32. No law of a general nature shall go into effect until the fortieth day after its passage, unless such law, or its preamble, shall declare that the public welfare requires that it should take effect sooner.

Respectfully submitted,
W. H. STEPHENS,
Chairman, etc.

Mr. GARDNER moved that the Convention take up the report.

Mr. KEY moved to lay the amendment proposed by the Committee on the table.

Mr. GIBSON demanded the yeas and nays, which were ordered and the motion to lay on the table rejected:

Yeas..24
Nays..48

Those voting in the affirmative are:

Messrs. Allen, Arledge, Bate, Baxter, Blackburn, Blizard, Burkett, Carter, Dibbrell, Doherty, Hill of Warren, Ivie, Key, Kirkpatrick, Mabry, McDougal, Martin, Meeks, Morris, Sample, Staley, and Thompson of Maury—24.

Those voting in the negative are:

Messrs. Brandon, Branson, Britton, Brooks, Brown of Davidson, Brown of Henry, etc., Burton, Byrne, Campbell, Chowning, Coffin, Cummings, Cypert, Deaderick, Dromgoole, Fentress, Fielder, Finley, Gardner, Garner, Gaut, Gibbs, Gibson, Gordon, Heiskell, Henderson, Hill of Gibson, House of Williamson, House of Montgomery, Jones of Giles, Kennedy, Kyle, McNabb, Netherland, Nicholson, Parker, Porter of Haywood, Seay, Shepard, Shelton, Stephens, Taylor, Thompson of Davidson, Turner, Walters, Warner, Williamson and Wright—48.

Mr. BURKETT demanded the previous question, which was sustained, and the amendment reported by the Committee was adopted without a division.

MISCELLANEOUS.

On motion of Mr. KEY, the Convention proceeded to the consideration of the report of the Committee on Miscellenaeous Matters.

Mr. JONES, of Giles, offered the following amendment to the first amendment proposed by the Committee:

After the word "cast" insert, "which shall be a majority of all the votes in the last election for Governor preceding the vote," so that the section will read: "The Legislature shall have the right, at any time, by law, to submit to the people the question of calling a Convention to alter, reform, or abolish this Constitution, and when, upon such submission, a majority of all the votes cast, and which shall be a majority of all the votes cast in the last election for Governor preceding the vote, shall be in favor of said proposition, then delegates shall be chosen, and the Convention shall assemble in form, mode and manner as shall be prescribed."

Mr. BURKETT demanded the previous question, which was sustained.

Mr. JONES' amendment was rejected.

The amendment of the Committee to Section 3, Article XI, was adopted.

Yeas.. 37
Nays.. 32

Those voting in the affirmative are:

Messrs. Blackburn, Branson, Brooks, Brown of Davidson, Brown of Henry, etc., Byrne, Carter, Chowning, Dibbrell, Fielder, Finley, Gardner, Garner, Gaut, Gibbs, Gibson, Hill of Warren, House of Williamson, House of Montgomery, etc., Ivie, Jones of Giles, Key, Kirkpatrick, Mabry, McDougal, Martin, Meeks, Porter of Haywood, Porter of Henry, Sample, Seay, Staley, Taylor, Turner, Warner and Wright—37.

Those voting in the negative are:

Messrs. Allen, Arledge, Bate, Baxter, Blizard, Brandon, Britton, Burkett, Burton, Campbell, Coffin, Cummings, Cypert, Deaderick, Doherty, Dromgoole, Fentress, Gordon, Heiskell, Henderson, Hill of Gibson, Kennedy, Kyle, McNabb, Morris, Netherland, Nicholson, Parker, Shepard, Shelton, Stephens, Thompson of Davidson, Thompson of Maury, and Walters—32.

Mr. GIBSON offered the following in lieu of the section reported by the Committee, to follow Section 5:

"The Legislature shall have no power to pass special acts changing the names of persons, or for the adoption or legitimation of persons, or establishing fish traps or ferries, or remitting or releasing penalties due or accruing to the State, but shall by general laws confer this power on the courts."

Which was rejected by the Convention.

Mr. BLACKBURN demanded the yeas and nays on the adoption of the section as reported by the Committee, which were ordered, and the section adopted.

Yeas.. 43
Nays.. 26

Those voting in the affirmative are:

Messrs. Allen, Arledge, Bate, Baxter, Blizard, Branson, Britton, Brooks, Brown of Davidson, Burkett, Carter, Coffin, Cummings, Cypert, Deaderick, Dromgoole, Gibson, Gordon, Heiskell, Hill of Gibson, House of Williamson, House of Montgomery, etc., Ivie, Jones of Giles, Kennedy, Key, Kirkpatrick, Kyle, Mabry, McDougal, McNabb, Meeks, Morris, Netherland, Nicholson, Parker, Seay, Shepard, Shelton, Stephens, Taylor, Thompson of Maury, and Turner—43.

Those voting in the negative are:

Messrs. Blackburn, Brandon, Brown of Henry, etc., Burton, Byrne, Campbell, Chowning, Dibbrell, Doherty, Fentress, Fielder, Finley, Gardner, Garner, Gaut, Gibbs, Hill of Warren, Martin, Porter of Haywood, Porter of Henry, Sample, Staley, Thompson of Davidson, Walters, Warner and Wright—26.

Section —, to follow Section 11, as reported by the Committee, was adopted without a division.

Mr. KEY moved to reconsider the vote adopting the section, which was adopted.

Mr. JONES, of Giles, offered the following in lieu of the report of the Committee.

ARTICLE —.

AMENDMENT IN LIEU.

Any person holding office under the laws of this State who, except in payment of his legal salary, fees or perquisites, receives, or consents to receive directly or indirectly, anything of value or of personal advantage, or the promise thereof, for performing any official act, or with the express or implied understanding that his official actions, or omission to act, is to be in any degree influenced thereby, shall be deemed guilty of a felony, and on conviction shall be punished by imprisonment in a State prison for a term not exceeding five years, or by a fine not exceeding five thousand dollars, or both, in the discretion of the court. This section shall not affect the validity of any existing statutes in relation to the offence of bribery.

Mr. GIBSON offered the following in lieu of Mr. Jones' amendment:

"No State officer, or member of the Legislature, shall directly or indirectly act as counsel, agent, or attorney, in the prosecution of any claim against the State, or in advocating any measure in either House of the Legislature."

Which was rejected by the Convention.

Mr. HOUSE, of Williamson, offered the following amendment:

Insert after the word "receive," in second line, the words, "in consideration of being such member or officer;" and strike out all after the word "corporation" in third line.

Mr. ALLEN moved to lay the original proposition, and all pending amendments, on the table.

Mr. CYPERT demanded the yeas and nays, which were ordered, and the motion to lay on the table sustained.

Yeas..40
Nays..28

Those voting in the affirmative are:

Messrs. Allen, Arledge, Baxter, Blizard, Brandon, Britton, Brooks, Brown of Henry, etc., Burkett, Burton, Campbell, Carter, Chowning, Cummings, Cypert, Deaderick, Doherty, Dromgoole, Gibbs, Heiskell, Henderson, Hill of Gibson, Ivie, Kennedy, Key, Kirkpatrick, Kyle, Mabry, McDougal, McNabb, Meeks, Nicholson, Porter of Haywood, Seay, Shelton, Stephens, Thompson of Davidson, Thompson of Maury, Walters and Williamson—40.

Those voting in the negative are:

Messrs. Blackburn, Branson, Byrne, Coffin, Dibbrell, Fentress, Fielder, Finley, Gardner, Garner, Gaut, Gibson, Gordon, Hill of Warren, House of Williamson, Jones of Giles, Martin, Morris, Netherland, Parker, Porter of Henry, Sample, Shepard, Staley, Taylor, Turner, Warner and Wright—28.

Mr. PORTER, of Haywood, proposed to amend the section reported by the Committee in relation to a homestead, by striking out the words "one thousand" and inserting "five hundred."

On motion of Mr. GIBBS, the amendment was laid on the table.

Mr. GIBBS offered the following amendment:

Strike out "to the value of not less than one thousand dollars," and insert, "to the extent of fifty acres of land outside of corporated towns, or one town lot not exceeding one acre."

Mr. PORTER, of Haywod, moved to lay the amendment on the table, and demanded the yeas and nays, which were ordered, and the motion sustained.

Yeas..57
Nays.. 8

Those voting in the affirmative are:

Messrs. Allen, Arledge, Bate, Baxter, Blizard, Brandon, Branson, Britton, Brooks, Brown of Davidson, Brown of Henry, etc., Burton, Byrne, Campbell, Carter, Chowning, Coffin, Cummings, Cypert, Deaderick, Dibbrell, Dromgoole, Fentress, Fielder, Finley, Gardner, Garner, Gaut, Gibson, Gordon, Heiskell, Hill of Warren, House of Williamson, House of Davidson, etc., Ivie, Jones of Giles, Kennedy, Kirpatrick, Kyle, Mabry, McDougal, McNabb, Meeks, Morris, Netherland, Nicholson, Porter of Haywood, Sample, Seay, Shepard, Shelton, Staley, Turner, Walters, Warner, Williamson and Wright—57.

Those voting in the negative are:

Messrs. Doherty, Gibbs, Henderson, Hill of Gibson, Key, Martin, Porter of Henry, etc. and Thompson of Maury—8.

Mr. HILL, of Gibson, offered the following amendment:

Add to the end of the Section:

"The Legislature may increase the amount of this exemption."

Mr. ———— moved to lay the amendment on the table.

Mr. SHEPARD demanded the yeas and nays, which were ordered, and the motion to lay on the table sustained.

Yeas.. 44
Nays.. 24

Those voting in the affirmative are:

Messrs. Allen, Arledge, Bate, Baxter, Branson, Britton, Brooks, Brown of Davidson, Brown of Henry, etc., Burkett, Byrne, Campbell, Carter, Chowning, Coffin, Cummings, Cypert, Deaderick, Dibbrell, Doherty, Dromgoole, Fentress, Fielder, Gardner, Gaut, Gibson, House of Williamson, House of Montgomery, etc., Jones of Giles, Kennedy, McDougal, McNabb, Parker, Porter of Haywood, Porter of Henry, Sample, Shepard, Staley, Stephens, Thompson of Davidson, Turner, Walters, Williamson and Wright—44.

Those voting in the negative are:

Messrs. Brandon, Burton, Finley, Garner, Gibbs, Gordon, Heiskell, Henderson, Hill of Warren, Hill of Gibson, Ivie, Key, Kirkpatrick, Kyle, Mabry, Martin, Meeks, Morris, Netherland, Nicholson, Seay, Shelton, Thompson of Maury and Warner—24.

Mr. TURNER offered the following in lieu of the amendment reported by the Committee:

A homestead in the possession of each head of a family, and the improvements thereon, to the value in all of one thousand dollars shall be exempt from sale under legal process during the life of such head of a family, to inure to the benefit of the widow, and shall be exempt during the minority of their children occupying the same. Nor shall said property be alienated without the joint consent of husband and wife, when that relation exists. This exemption shall not affect debts contracted before the adoption of this Constitution, nor debts contracted for the purchase or improvement of said lot, nor public taxes.

Which was received by the Convention in lieu of the report of the Committee, and the section as thus amended adopted.

To the Section reported by the Committee to prevent marriage between whites and blacks, Mr. FENTRESS offered the following amendment:

Insert after the word prohibited, in the second line of 4th independent section of Committee on Miscellaneous Business, the following words:

No negro, mulatto, or mustee shall be allowed to sit on Juries or hold office in this State."

It will then read as follows:

"The intermarriage of white persons with negroes, mulattoes or persons of mixed blood, descended from a negro, to the third generation inclusive, is prohibited. And no negro, mulatto or mustee shall be allowed to sit on juries or hold office in this State."

Mr. BLIZARD moved to lay the amendment on the table.

Mr. GARNER demanded the yeas and nays, which were ordered and the motion to lay on the table rejected:

Yeas..13
Nays..57

Those voting in the affirmative are:

Messrs. Baxter, Blizard, Branson, Burkett, Coffin, Cypert, Deaderick, Gaut, Gibson, Heiskell, Hill of Warren, Key and Parker—13.

Those voting in the negative are:

Messrs. Allen, Bate, Blackburn, Brandon, Britton, Brooks, Brown of Davidson, Brown of Henry, etc., Burton, Byrne, Campbell, Carter, Chowning, Cummings, Dibbrell, Doherty, Dromgoole, Fentress, Fielder, Finley, Gardner, Garner, Gibbs, Gordon, Henderson, Hill of Gibson, House of Williamson, House of Davidson, etc., Ivie, Jones of Giles, Kennedy, Kirkpatrick, Kyle, Mabry, McDougal, McNabb, Martin, Meeks, Morris, Netherland, Nicholson, Porter of Haywood, Porter of Henry, Sample, Seay, Shepard, Shelton, Staley, Stephens, Taylor, Thompson of Davidson, Thompson of Maury, Turner, Walters, Warner, Williamson and Wright—57.

Mr. FENTRESS demanded the yeas and nays on the adoption of his amendment, which were ordered, and the amendment rejected.

Yeas.. 29
Nays.. 39

Those voting in the affirmative are:

Messrs. Allen, Arledge, Bate, Brooks, Brown of Henry, etc., Burton, Campbell, Carter, Chowning, Cummings, Dromgoole, Fentress, Fielder, Gardner, Heiskell, Hill of Gibson, House of Montgomery, etc., Ivie, Kennedy, Meeks, Porter of Henry, Seay, Shepard, Shelton, Stephens, Taylor, Turner, Wright and Williamson —29.

Those voting in the negative are:

Messrs. Baxter, Blizard, Brandon, Branson, Britton, Burkett, Byrne, Coffin, Cypert, Deaderick, Dibbrell, Doherty, Finley, Garner, Gaut, Gibbs, Gibson, Gordon, Henderson, Hill of Warren, House of Williamson, Key, Kirkpatrick, Kyle, Mabry, McDougal, McNabb, Martin, Morris, Netherland, Nicholson, Parker, Porter of Haywood, Sample, Staley, Thompson of Davidson, Thompson of Maury, Walters and Warner—39.

The Convention took a recess until 2½ o'clock P. M.

AFTERNOON SESSION.

Mr. DROMGOOLE offered the following amendment:

After the word "prohibited" insert "or the living together as man and wife in this State."

Which was adopted, and the Section as thus amended was adopted by the Convention.

The amendment, recommended by the Committee, to Article II, Section 25, having been incorporated in another part of the Constitution, was passed over informally.

Section 1, Article VII, reported by the Committee in lieu was taken up, when

Mr. TAYLOR offered the following amendment:

Insert after "Register" in second line, "and one Trustee" and insert after "Register" where it appears in second place in 2d line the words "and Trustee."

Mr. HOUSE, of Montgomery, etc., offered the following in lieu of Mr. Taylor's:

But the Legislature may authorise any of the counties to elect a County Trustee, to hold his office for two years.

Messrs. TAYLOR and HOUSE subsequently withdrew their amendments:

Mr. KIRKPATRICK submitted the following amendment:

Strike out in second line after the word "for" the word "*two*" and insert "*four*." Strike out at end of third line "*six*" and insert "*four*" in lieu thereof.

So that the Section will read:

Section 1. There shall be elected in each county, by the qualified voters therein, one Sheriff, one Register; the Sheriff for four years and the Register for four years; *Provided*, That no person shall be eligible to the office of Sheriff more than four years in any term of eight years.

Mr. KIRKPATRICK subsequently withdrew his amendment.

Mr. JONES, of Giles, moved to lay the amendment proposed by the Committee on the table, which was adopted; thereupon,

Mr. JONES, of Giles, proposed to re-adopt Section 1, of Article VII, of the Constitution, and it was accordingly adopted.

Mr. JONES, of Giles, offered the following amendment to Section 2, Article VII, of the Constitution of 1834:

"When any vacancy shall occur otherwise than by expiration of term in the office of Judge or Attorney General, except the Attorney General for the State, the same shall be filled for a full term at the next General election happening not less than thirty days after such vacancy occurs. And until the vacancy shall be so filled, the Governor, by and with the advice and consent of the Senate, if the

Senate shall be in session, or if not, the Governor alone may appoint to fill such vacancy. If the vacancy occurs in the Supreme Court, the powers and jurisdiction of the Court shall not be suspended for want of appointment or election when the number of Judges is sufficient to constitute a quorum."

Mr. BAXTER moved to lay the amendment on the table.

Mr. JONES of Giles, demanded the yeas and nays, which were ordered, and the motion to lay on the table was sustained.

Yeas.. 53
Nays.. 17

Those voting in the affirmative are:

Messrs. Allen, Arledge, Baxter, Blackburn, Blizard, Brandon, Branson, Britton, Brooks, Brown of Henry, etc., Burkett, Burton, Byrne, Carter, Chowning, Cummings, Deaderick, Dibbrell, Doherty, Dromgoole, Fielder, Finley, Gardner, Garner, Gaut, Gibbs, Gibson, Heiskell, Henderson, Hill of Warren, Hill of Gibson, House of Williamson, House of Montgomery. etc., Kirkpatrick, Kyle, McDougal, McNabb, Martin, Meeks, Morris, Nicholson, Parker, Porter of Henry, Sample, Seay, Shepard, Shelton, Taylor, Turner, Walters, Warner, Williamson and Wright—53.

Those voting in the negative are:

Messrs. Bate, Brown of Davidson, Campbell, Coffin, Cypert, Fentress, Gordon, Jones of Giles, Kennedy, Key, Mabry, Netherland, Porter of Haywood, Staley, Stephens, Thompson of Davidson, and Thompson of Maury—17.

Mr. FENTRESS proposed to amend by adding to the end of the section "occurring not less than forty days thereafter," which was rejected, and the section as it is in the present Constitution adopted.

Section 3, Article VII, was amended by inserting "and Comptroller" after the word "Treasurer," and by striking out the words "his or" in the third line, and as thus amended was adopted by the Convention.

Section 4, Article VII, was amended by striking out the words "that may happen by death, resignation or removal," and as thus amended was adopted by the Convention.

Section 5, Article VII, was amended by substituting the Report of the Committee on the Judiciary as follows:

Elections for Judicial and other civil officers shall be held on the first Thursday in August, 1870, and forever thereafter on the first Thursday in August next preceding the expiration of their respective terms of service.

The term of each officer so elected shall be computed from the first day of September next succeeding his election.

And as thus amended, was adopted by the Convention.

Paragraphs. The term of office of the Governor and other executive officers, shall be computed from the 15th of January next after the election of Governor, and

No appointment or election to fill a vacancy shall be made for a period extending beyond the unexpired term, and

Every officer shall hold his office until his successor is elected or appointed or qualified, were adopted by the Convention as reported by the Committee on the Judiciary.

Mr. McDougal moved to amend the paragraph in relation to filling vacancies in the office of Judge, etc., by striking out the words "time herein fixed for the general elections of civil officers" and inserting "time of the biennial elections of civil officers," which was adopted.

Mr. Fentress moved to amend by adding "occurring not less than forty days thereafter."

On motion of Mr. Porter, of Haywood, the amendment of Mr. Fentress was laid on the table.

The paragraph as amended by Mr. McDougal's amendment was then adopted by the Convention.

The Report of the Committee on Miscellaneous Provisions in relation to the preservation of game and fish was taken up, when Mr. Morris demanded the yeas and nays on the adoption of the section reported by the Committee, which were ordered and the section adopted.

Yeas..42
Nays..29

Those voting in the affirmative are:

Messrs. Allen, Arledge, Bate, Blizard, Brandon, Brown of Henry, etc., Burkett, Byrne, Campbell, Chowning, Coffin, Cypert, Deaderick, Dromgoole, Fentress, Garner, Gaut, Heiskell, Henderson, House of Williamson, Jones of Giles, Key, Kyle, Mabry, McDougal, Martin, Netherland, Nicholson, Parker, Porter of Haywood, Porter of Henry, Seay, Shepard, Shelton, Thompson of Davidson, Thompson of Maury, Turner, Walters, Warner, Williamson, Wright and President Brown—42.

Those voting in the negative are:

Messrs. Baxter, Blackburn, Branson, Britton, Brooks, Brown of

Davidson, Carter, Cummings, Dibbrell, Doherty, Fielder, Finley, Gardner, Gibbs, Gibson, Gordon, Hill of Warren, Hill of Gibson, House of Montgomery, etc., Ivie, Kennedy, Kirkpatrick, McNabb, Meeks, Morris, Sample, Staley, Stephens and Taylor—29.

Mr. BLIZARD moved to lay the section reported by the Committee, authorizing the receipt of the due coupons of the bonds of the State for taxes, on the table.

Mr. TURNER demanded the yeas and nays, which were ordered and the motion to lay on the table sustained.

Yeas..54
Nays..17

Those voting in the affirmative are:

Messrs. Allen, Arledge, Baxter, Blackburn, Blizard, Brandon, Branson, Britton, Brown of Henry, etc., Burkett, Burton, Campbell, Carter, Chowning, Coffin, Cummings, Deaderick, Dibbrell, Doherty, Dromgoole, Fielder, Gardner, Gaut, Gibbs, Gibson, Heiskell, Henderson, Hill of Warren, Hill of Gibson, House of Williamson, Ivie, Jones of Giles, Kirkpatrick, Kyle, Mabry, McDougal, McNabb, Martin, Meeks, Morris, Netherland, Nicholson, Parker, Porter of Henry, Sample, Seay, Shepard, Shelton, Staley, Stephens, Taylor, Thompson of Maury, Warner and Williamson—54.

Those voting in the negative are:

Messrs. Brooks, Brown of Davidson, Byrne, Cypert, Fentress, Finley, Garner, Gordon, House of Montgomery, etc., Kennedy, Key, Porter of Haywood, Thompson of Davidson, Turner, Walters, Wright and President Brown—17.

Mr. CYPERT submitted the following *proviso* to be attached to the amendment adopted to Section 3 of Article XI:

Provided, That nothing contained in this section shall be so construed as to deprive the people in their sovereign capacity from exercising the inherent right to alter, reform, change or abolish this Constitution, as declared in the Bill of Rights, independent of any legislative authority.

Which lies over until to-morrow.

Mr. THOMPSON, of Davidson, submitted the following independent section:

The due coupon bonds of the State legally issued prior to the year 1861, shall be received at par after January 1st, 1871, for all taxes or other dues to the State; *Provided*, That this section shall not apply during a rebellion or invasion of the State.

The consideration of which was postponed until to-morrow.

Mr. WARNER offered the following as an independent section:

Sec. —. That when any amendment or amendments to the Constitution of the United States shall be proposed to the several States thereof for ratification, no Legislature or Convention of this State shall ever ratify or reject such amendment or amendments, unless the Legislature or Convention shall have been elected by the people of this State after the period of time when the Congress or Convention of the United States shall have proposed such amendment or amendments to the several States for ratification.

The consideration of the proposed section was postponed until to-morrow.

Mr. TAYLOR moved that the Convention adjourn until 7 o'clock P. M., which was rejected.

On motion of Mr. STEPHENS, it was ordered that the hour of meeting hereafter be 9 o'clock A. M., take a recess at 1 P. M., meet again at 2, and sit as long in the afternoon as practicable.

Mr. THOMPSON, of Davidson, moved that the Convention adjourn until 9 o'clock to-morrow morning.

Mr. BAXTER demanded the yeas and nays, which were ordered, and the motion to adjourn adopted.

Yeas..40
Nays..27

Those voting in the affirmative are:

Messrs. Arledge, Blackburn, Branson, Brooks, Brown of Davidson, Brown of Henry, etc., Burton, Byrne, Campbell, Chowning, Coffin, Cummings, Cypert, Dibbrell, Doherty, Fentress, Gardner, Gibbs, Gordon, House of Montgomery, etc., Key, Kyle, Mabry, Martin, Morris, Netherland, Nicholson, Porter of Haywood, Porter of Henry, Sample, Seay, Shepard, Shelton, Stephens Taylor, Thompson of Davidson, Thompson of Maury, Turner, Walters and Wright—40.

Those voting in the negative are:

Messrs. Allen, Baxter, Blizard, Brandon, Britton, Burkett, Carter, Deaderick, Dromgoole, Fielder, Garner, Gaut, Gibson, Heiskell, Henderson, Hill of Warren, Hill of Gibson, House of Williamson, Ivie, Kennedy, Kirkpatrick, McDougal, McNabb, Meeks, Parker, Warner and President Brown—27.

FRIDAY MORNING, FEBRUARY 18, 1870.

The Convention met pursuant to adjournment, Mr. President BROWN in the Chair.

The Journal of yesterday was read and approved.

RESOLUTIONS, MEMORIALS AND PETITIONS.

Mr. ALLEN offered the following resolution:

Resolved, That this Convention proceed at once, without regard to the report of any committee or committees, to the consideration *seriatim,* of the various sections of the several articles of the Constitution adopted in 1834, that have not, as yet, been adopted, amended or rejected by this Convention.

Which lies over under the rule.

Mr. DROMGOOLE submitted the following resolution:

Resolved, That all the revenues of this State, after defraying the current expenses of government, and except the appropriations permitted by this Constitution to be applied to educational purposes, shall be applied to the payment of the just debts of the State, and no other application of its revenues shall be made until the debts of the State are paid.

Which lies over under the rule.

Mr. DOHERTY submitted the following resolution:

Resolved, That the Counties of Carroll, Gibson and Lauderdale, on the line of the Tennessee Central railroad, be excepted from the provisions in the Constitution requiring three-fourths of those voting in any county to authorize subscriptions to the stock of any railroad company.

Which lies over under the rule.

Mr. THOMPSON, of Davidson, presented a memorial from a number of Hebrew citizens, praying that they be allowed to observe their own Sabbath. Which was read and referred to the Committee on the Judiciary.

Mr. GIBSON offered the following as an independent section to Article XI:

All the revenue derived from the tax on polls, and such other revenues as the Legislature may from time to time designate, shall be set apart for the support of common schools, and shall never be applied to any other purpose.

Mr. SEAY offered the following as an independent section to Article II:

No county which has a representative at the date of the ratification of this Constitution, shall ever be deprived thereof, under any apportionment made hereafter under the provisions of this Constitution.

REPORT ON ORDINANCE.

Mr. NICHOLSON, from the Committee on Elections and Suffrage, made the following report:

The Committee have considered an ordinance presented to the Convention by Mr. Turner, of Sumner county, and have instructed me to recommend its adoption, with certain immaterial amendments. The ordinance, as amended and recommended for adoption, is as follows:

ORDINANCE.

1st. *Be it ordained by the Convention*, That it shall be the duty of the several officers of the State, authorized by law, to hold elections for members of the General Assembly and other officers, to open and hold an election, at the place of holding said elections in their respective counties, on the fourth Saturday in March, 1870, for the purpose of receiving the votes of such qualified voters as may desire to vote for the ratification or rejection of the Constitution recommended by this Convention. And the qualification of voters in said election shall be the same as that required in the election of delegates to this Convention.

2d. It shall be the duty of said returning officers, in each county in the State, to enroll the name of each voter on the poll-books prepared for said election, and shall deposit each ballot in the ballot boxes respectively. Each voter, who wishes to ratify the *new Constitution*, shall have written or printed on his ticket the words, "New Constitution," or words of like import; and each voter, who wishes to vote against the ratification of the new Constitution shall have written or printed on his ticket the words, "Old Constitution," or words of like import.

3d. The election shall be held, and the judges and clerks shall be appointed, as in the case of the election of the members of the General Assembly, and the returning officers, in the presence of the judges or inspectors, shall count the votes given for the new Constitution, and those given for the old Constitution, of which they shall keep a correct estimate in said poll-books. They shall deposit the original poll-books of said election with the Clerks of the County Courts, in the respective counties, and shall, within five days after the election, make out accurate statements of the number of votes polled in their respective counties for and against the new Constitution, and immediately forward, by mail, one copy of said certificates to the Governor, and one to the Secretary of State. So soon as the poll-books are deposited with the County Clerks, they shall certify to the Secretary of State an accurate statement of the number of votes cast for and against the new Constitution, as it appears on said poll-books. And if any of said returning officers shall fail to make the return herein provided for within the time required, the Secretary of State shall be authorized to send special messengers for the result of the vote in those counties whose officers have so failed to make returns.

4th. Upon the receipt of said returns, it shall be the duty of the Governor, Secretary of State, and the President of this Convention, or any two of them, to compare the votes cast in said election, and if it shall appear that a majority of all the votes was cast for "New Constitution," it shall be the duty of the Governor forthwith to make proclamation of the result, and thereupon the new Constitution shall be ordained and established as the Constitution of the State of Tennessee.

4th. The Governor of the State is requested to issue his proclamation as to the election on the 4th Saturday in March, 1870, herein provided for.

All of which is respectfully submitted.

A. O. P. NICHOLSON, Chairman.

VACANCIES IN JUDICIAL OFFICES.

On motion of Mr. Burton, the vote adopting Mr. McDougal's amendment to the paragraph providing for the filling of vacancies in judicial offices, etc., was reconsidered.

Thereupon Mr. Burton offered the following amendment:

Strike out "general" and insert "biennial," and add: "And such vacancy shall be filled at the next biennial election recurring more than thirty days after the vacancy occurs."

Which was adopted, and the paragraph, as thus amended, was again adopted by the Convention.

RATIFYING AMENDMENTS TO FEDERAL CONSTITUTION.

On motion of Mr. Mabry, the independent section, proposed by Mr. Warner on yesterday, prescribing the mode of ratifying amendments to the Constitution of the United States, was referred to the Committee on the Judiciary.

DUE COUPON BONDS.

The Convention proceeded to the consideration of the independent section, proposed by Mr. THOMPSON, of Davidson, in relation to receiving the due coupon bonds of the State for taxes, etc.

Mr. FIELDER demanded the question, which was sustained.

Mr. BAXTER demanded the yeas and nays, which were ordered, and the section rejected.

Yeas.. 7
Nays..62

Those voting in the affirmative are:

Messrs. Brown of Davidson, Chowning, Fentress, Finley, Gordon, Kirkpatrick and Thompson of Davidson—7.

Those voting in the negative are:

Messrs. Allen, Arledge, Bate, Baxter, Blackburn, Blizard, Brandon, Branson, Britton, Brooks, Brown of Henry, etc., Burkett, Burton, Bryne, Campbell, Carter, Coffin, Cummings, Cypert, Deaderick, Dibbrell, Doherty, Dromgoole, Fielder, Gardner, Garner, Gaut, Gibbs, Gibson, Heiskell, Henderson, Hill of Warren, Hill of Gibson, House of Williamson, Ivie, Jones of Giles, Kennedy, Key, Kyle, Mabry, McDougal, McNabb, Martin, Meeks, Morris, Netherland, Nicholson, Parker, Porter of Haywood, Porter of Henry, Seay, Shepard, Shelton, Staley, Stephens, Taylor, Thompson, Turner, Walters, Warner, Williamson and President Brown—62.

MISCELLANEOUS.

Mr. PORTER, of Haywood, entered a motion to reconsider the vote rejecting the amendment proposed by the Finance Committee in reference to the terms on which bonds shall be issued to railroad companies.

Mr. THOMPSON, of Maury, offered the following as an additional section to Article XI:

Sec. —. The tax on polls levied by the State under the provisions of the Constitution, shall be hereafter appropriated for the purposes prescribed in Section 10, Article XI, in such manner as the Legislature shall direct.

Mr. GIBSON offered the section proposed by him this morning in lieu of Mr. Thompson's.

Mr. BROWN, of Henry, etc., submitted the following in lieu of Mr. Thompson's proposition:

Sec. —. The State taxes derived from polls hereafter shall be appropriated to educational purposes, in such manner as the General Assembly shall from time to time direct by law.

Which was accepted by Mr. THOMPSON.

Mr. FIELDER moved to lay the pending propositions on the table.

Mr. GIBSON demanded the yeas and nays, which were ordered, and the motion to lay on the table rejected.

Yeas..18
Nays..52

Those voting in the affirmative are:

Messrs. Arledge, Bate, Blizard, Dromgoole, Fentress, Fielder, Garner, Gibbs, Heiskell, Hill of Warren, Hill of Gibson, House of Montgomery, etc., Jones of Giles, Kennedy, Porter of Haywood, Shelton, Stephens and Williamson—18.

Those voting in the negative are:

Messrs. Allen, Baxter, Blackburn, Brandon, Branson, Britton, Brooks, Brown of Davidson, Brown of Henry, etc., Burkett, Burton, Byrne, Campbell, Carter, Chowning, Coffin, Cummings, Deaderick, Dibbrell, Doherty, Finley, Gardner, Gaut, Gibson, Gordon, Henderson, House of Williamson, Ivie, Key, Kirkpatrick, Kyle, Mabry, McDougal, McNabb, Martin, Meeks, Morris, Netherland, Nicholson, Parker, Porter of Henry, Sample, Seay, Shepard, Staley, Taylor, Thompson of Davidson, Thompson of Maury, Turner, Walters, Warner and President Brown—52.

Mr. GIBSON'S amendment in lieu was rejected.

The section, as reported by Mr. BROWN, of Henry, was adopted by the Convention.

Mr. FENTRESS offered the following proviso to be added to Section 10, Article XI:

Provided also, That no school established or aided under this section, shall allow white and negro children to be received as scholars together in the same school.

Which was adopted by the Convention.

DIRECTORY TO THE CLERK.

Mr. SEAY introduced the following resolution:

Resolved, That the Secretary of the Convention be directed to remain after this Convention shall have finally adjourned, and complete the Journals by copying the reports of the different committees, and the Constitution, and other documents, and that the Journals be bound and deposited in the office of the Secretary of State, and that he also be directed to superintend the printing of the Journal of the Convention, and that the Committee on Expenditures report what compensation should be allowed him for such services.

Which lies over under the rule.

MISCELLANEOUS.

On motion of Mr. NETHERLAND leave of absence was granted Mr. Kirkpatrick.

Mr. STEPHENS moved to reconsider the vote adopting Section 13, Article VI.

Mr. HEISKELL offered the following resolution:

Resolved, That the Committee on Revision be authorized to strike out in Section 13, Article VI, after the words "Clerks of" the word "such" and after the words "inferior courts" the words "as may be hereafter established" which shall be "required to be" and after the word "counties" to insert "or Districts."

Which was ruled out of order by the Chair.

Mr. TURNER submitted the following resolution:

Resolved, That it is the sense of the House that the Committee on Revision and Enrollment have the right in preparing the draft of the Constitution to add or change such words as are necessary to produce harmony in the instrument, and to carry out its provisions, and to correct the verbiage and grammar of the same."

Which was adopted by the Convention.

Mr. JONES, of Giles, offered the following:

Clerks of Circuit and County Courts shall be elected by the qualified voters thereof for the term of four years; they shall be removed from office for malfeasance, incompetency or neglect of duty in such manner as may be prescribed by law.

Which was laid on the table.

Mr. KIRKPATRICK moved to take up the report of the Committee on New Counties and County Lines, which motion was rejected.

On motion of Mr. BAXTER the Convention proceeded to the consideration of Article VIII, of the Constitution of 1834, which was adopted without amendment.

On motion of Mr. BAXTER Article IX, of the Constitution of 1834, was taken up.

Mr. CYPERT demanded the yeas and nays on the adoption of the 1st Section, which were ordered and the Section adopted:

Yeas...41
Nays...27

Those voting in the affirmative are:

Messrs. Allen, Arledge, Bate, Baxter, Blizard, Brandon, Britton, Burkett, Byrne, Campbell, Carter, Chowning, Coffin, Cummings, Deaderick, Fentress, Fielder, Gardner, Garner, Gaut, Gibbs, Gordon, Heiskell, Henderson, Hill of Warren, Hill of Gibson, House of Williamson, House Montgomery, etc., Jones of Giles, Kennedy, Kirkpatrick, Kyle, Mabry, McNabb, Martin, Morris, Porter of Haywood, Shelton, Stephens, Thompson of Maury and Warner—41.

Those voting in the negative are:

Messrs. Branson, Brooks, Brown of Davidson, Brown of Henry, etc., Cypert, Dibbrell, Doherty, Dromgoole, Finley, Gibson, Ivie, Key, McDougal, Meeks, Netherland, Nicholson, Parker, Porter of Henry, Sample, Shepard, Staley, Taylor, Thompson of Davidson, Turner, Walters, Williamson and Wright—27.

Section 2, as it is in the Constitution of 1834, was adopted.

Mr. CAMPBELL moved to lay Section 3 on the table.

Mr. CYPERT demanded the yeas and nays, which were ordered, and the motion to lay on the table rejected.

Yeas...15
Nays...53

Those voting in the affirmative are:

Messrs. Allen, Baxter, Blizard, Brooks, Campbell, Gibson, Key, Mabry, Porter of Henry, Shelton, Thompson of Davidson, Thompson of Maury, Turner, Wright and Mr. President Brown—15.

Those voting in the negative are:

Messrs. Arledge, Bate, Brandon, Branson, Britton, Brown of Davidson, Brown of Henry, etc., Burkett, Byrne, Carter, Chowning, Coffin, Cummings, Cypert, Deaderick, Dibbrell, Doherty, Dromgoole, Fentress, Fielder, Gardner, Garner, Gaut, Gibbs, Gordon, Heiskell, Henderson, Hill of Warren, Hill of Gibson, House of Williamson, House of Montgomery, etc., Ivie, Jones of Giles, Kennedy, Kirkpatrick, Kyle, McDougal, McNabb, Martin, Meeks, Morris, Netherland, Nicholson, Porter of Haywood, Sample, Seay, Shepard, Staley, Stephens, Taylor, Walters, Warner and Williamson—53.

Mr. PORTER, of Henry, moved to amend by inserting the words "in this State" after the word "duel" in second line. And by inserting "in this State" after the word "duel" in the third line and by inserting after the word "duel" in the fourth line, the words "in this State."

Pending which the Convention took a recess.

AFTERNOON SESSION.

Mr. DROMGOOLE demanded the yeas and nays on the adoption of Mr. Porter's amendment, which were ordered, and the amendment rejected:

Yeas.. 16
Nays.. 49

Those voting in the affirmative are:

Messrs. Allen, Arledge, Baxter, Burton, Campbell, Dibbrell, Fentress, Gardner, Key, Mabry, Porter of Haywood, Porter of Henry, Shelton, Thompson of Davidson, Thompson of Maury and Wright—16.

Those voting in the negative are:

Messrs. Bate, Blizard, Brandon, Branson, Britton, Brooks, Brown of Davidson, Brown of Henry, etc., Burkett, Byrne, Carter, Coffin, Cummings, Cypert, Deaderick, Doherty, Dromgoole, Fielder, Finley, Garner, Gaut, Gibson, Heiskell, Henderson, Hill of Warren, Hill of Gibson, House of Williamson, House of Montgomery, etc., Ivie, Jones of Giles, Kennedy, Kyle, McDougal, McNabb, Martin, Morris, Netherland, Nicholson, Parker, Sample, Seay, Staley, Stephens, Taylor, Turner, Walters, Warner and Williamson—49.

Section 3, as it is in the Constitution of 1834, was adopted by the Convention.

The Convention proceeded to the consideration of Article X, of the Constitution of 1834.

Sections 1, 2 and 3 were adopted without amendment.

The 4th Section, relating to new counties, was postponed.

NEW COUNTIES AND COUNTY LINES.

The Convention took up the report of the Committee on New Counties and County Lines.

On motion of Mr. HOUSE, of Montgomery, the report was considered by sections or propositions.

Mr. HILL, of Gibson, moved to amend by striking out "two hundred and fifty" in the second line and inserting "three hundred."

Mr. MABRY moved to lay the amendment on the table.

Mr. KEY demanded the yeas and nays, which were ordered and the motion to lay on the table rejected:

Yeas.. 35
Nays.. 36

Those voting in the affirmative are:

Messrs. Allen, Blizard, Branson, Britton, Brooks, Burkett, Campbell, Carter, Cummings, Cypert, Dibbrell, Doherty, Fielder, Gardner, Gaut, Gibbs, Gibson, Henderson, Hill of Warren, House of Williamson, Key, Kirkpatrick, Kyle, Mabry, McNabb, Martin, Nicholson, Sample, Seay, Shepard, Taylor, Thompson of Maury, Turner, Warner and Wright—35.

Those voting in the negative are:

Messrs. Arledge, Baxter, Blackburn, Brandon, Brown of Davidson, Brown of Henry, etc., Burton, Byrne, Chowning, Coffin, Deaderick, Dromgoole, Fentress, Finley, Garner, Gordon, Heiskell, Hill of Gibson, House of Montgomery, etc., Jones of Giles, Kennedy, McDougal, Meeks, Morris, Netherland, Parker, Porter of Haywood, Porter of Henry, Shelton, Staley, Stephens, Thompson of Davidson, Walters, Williamson and President Brown—36.

Mr. WILLIAMSON moved to amend by striking out "two hundred and fifty" and inserting "three hundred and fifty," and demanded the question, which was sustained.

Mr. JONES, of Giles, demanded the yeas and nays on the adoption of Mr. Williamson's amendment, which were ordered, and the amendment rejected.

Yeas..22
Nays..47

Those voting in the affirmative are:

Messrs. Arledge, Baxter, Blackburn, Deaderick, Dromgoole, Fentress, Finley, Garner, Heiskell, House of Davidson, etc., Jones of

Giles, Kennedy, Kyle, McDougal, Morris, Netherland, Parker, Porter of Henry, Shelton, Staley, Stephens, Walters and Williamson—22.

Those voting in the negative are:

Messrs. Allen, Blizard, Brandon, Britton, Brooks, Brown of Davidson, Brown of Henry, etc., Burkett, Burton, Byrne, Campbell, Carter, Chowning, Coffin, Cummings, Cypert, Dibbrell, Doherty, Fielder, Gardner, Gaut, Gibbs, Gibson, Gordon, Henderson, Hill of Warren, Hill of Gibson, House of Williamson, Ivie, Key, Kirkpatrick, Mabry, McNabb, Martin, Meeks, Nicholson, Porter of Haywood, Sample, Seay, Shepard, Taylor, Thompson of Davidson, Thompson of Maury, Turner, Warner and Wright—47.

Mr. HILL, of Gibson, called "the question" and demanded the yeas and nays on the adoption of his amendment, which were ordered, and the amendment rejected.

Yeas.. 33
Nays.. 38

Those voting in the affirmative are:

Messrs. Arledge, Bate, Baxter, Blackburn, Brandon, Brown of Henry, etc., Burton, Byrne, Cummings, Deaderick, Dromgoole, Fentress, Finley, Garner, Gordon, Heiskell, Hill of Gibson, House of Montgomery, etc., Ivie, Jones of Giles, Kennedy, McDougal, Meeks, Morris, Netherland, Parker, Porter of Haywood, Porter of Henry, Shelton, Staley, Stephens, Walters and Williamson—33.

Those voting in the negative are:

Messrs. Allen, Blizard, Branson, Britton, Brooks, Brown of Davidson, Burkett, Campbell, Carter, Chowning, Coffin, Cypert, Dibbrell, Doherty, Fielder, Gardner, Gaut, Gibbs, Gibson, Henderson, Hill of Warren, House of Williamson, Key, Kirkpatrick, Kyle, Mabry, McNabb, Martin, Nicholson, Thompson of Davidson, Thompson of Maury, Turner, Warner and Wright—38.

Mr. MABRY moved to amend by striking out "fifty" in the second line and inserting "seventy-five," and demanded "*the question*" and the yeas and nays on his amendment, which were ordered and the amendment adopted.

Yeas..41
Nays..29

Those voting in the affirmative are:

Messrs. Allen, Arledge, Bate, Baxter, Blackburn, Brandon, Brown of Davidson, Brown of Henry, etc., Burton, Byrne, Campbell, Coffin, Cummings, Dromgoole, Fentress, Finley, Garner, Gordon, Heiskell, Hill of Gibson, House of Williamson, House of Montgomery, etc., Jones of Giles, Kennedy, Kyle, Mabry, McDougal, Meeks, Morris, Netherland, Nicholson, Parker, Porter of Haywood, Porter of Henry, Shelton, Staley, Stephens, Thompson of Davidson, Walters, Williamson and Wright—41.

Those voting in the negative are:

Messrs. Blizard, Branson, Britton, Brooks, Burkett, Carter, Chowning, Cypert, Deaderick, Dibbrell, Doherty, Fielder, Gardner, Gaut, Gibbs, Gibson, Henderson, Hill of Warren, Key, Kirkpatrick, McNabb, Martin, Sample, Seay, Shepard, Taylor, Thompson of Maury, Turner and Warner—29.

Mr. FENTRESS proposed to further amend the clause by striking out "four hundred and fifty" and inserting "seven hundred and fifty," which was rejected by the Convention.

Mr. HILL, of Gibson, moved to amend by striking out "four hundred and fifty and inserting "one thousand," which was rejected.

Mr. HILL moved to amend by striking out "four hundred and fifty" and inserting "seven hundred," which was adopted, and the clause as thus amended was adopted by the Convention.

Mr. MABRY moved to amend the second clause by striking out "twelve" and inserting "ten," and demanded the yeas and nays, which were ordered and the amendment rejected.

Yeas..30
Nays..41

Those voting in the affirmative are:

Messrs. Allen, Baxter, Blizard, Brandon, Branson, Britton, Brooks, Burkett, Chowning, Cummings, Cypert, Doherty, Fentress, Fielder, Gardner, Gaut, Gibbs, Gibson, Gordon, Henderson, Hill of Warren, Kirkpatrick, Mabry, Sample, Seay, Shepard, Thompson of Maury, Turner, Warner and Wright—30.

Those voting in the negative are:

Messrs. Arledge, Bate, Brown of Davidson, Brown of Henry, etc., Burton, Byrne, Campbell, Carter, Coffin, Deaderick, Dibbrell, Dromgoole, Finley, Garner, Heiskell, Hill of Gibson, House of Williamson, House of Montgomery, etc., Ivie, Jones of Giles, Kennedy, Key, Kyle, McDougal, McNabb, Martin, Meeks, Morris, Netherland, Nicholson, Parker, Porter of Haywood Porter of Henry, Shelton, Staley, Stephens, Taylor, Thompson of Davidson, Walters, Williamson and President Brown—41.

Mr. SEAY moved to amend by striking out "twelve" and inserting "nine," which was rejected.

Mr. MABRY moved to amend by striking out "twelve and inserting "eleven."

Mr. KEY demanded the yeas and nays, which were ordered and the amendment adopted.

Yeas..38
Nays..33

Those voting in the affirmative are:

Messrs. Allen, Baxter, Blizard, Brandon, Branson, Britton, Brooks, Burkett, Carter, Chowning, Cummings, Cypert, Doherty, Fentress, Fielder, Gardner, Gaut, Gibbs, Gibson, Gordon, Henderson, Hill of Warren, Hill of Gibson, Kennedy, Key, Kirkpatrick, Mabry, McDougal, Meeks, Nicholson, Sample, Seay, Shepard, Thompson of Davidson, Thompson of Maury, Turner, Walters and Warner—38.

Those voting in the negative are:

Messrs. Arledge, Bate, Blackburn, Brown of Davidson, Brown of Henry, etc., Burton, Byrne, Campbell, Coffin, Deaderick, Dibbrell, Dromgoole, Finley, Garner, Heiskell, House of Williamson, House of Montgomery, etc., Ivie, Jones of Giles, Kyle, McNabb, Martin, Morris, Netherland, Parker, Porter of Haywood, Porter of Henry, Shelton, Staley, tephens, Taylor, Williamson and President Brown—33.

The clause as thus amended was adopted by the Convention.

Mr. FENTRESS proposed to amend the third clause by adding after the words "taken off" at the end of the clause, "and a majority of the voters of the county from which such part is proposed to be taken," and demanded the yeas and nays, which were ordered and the amendment rejected.

Yeas.. 28
Nays.. 42

Those voting in the affirmative are:

Messrs. Arledge, Blackburn, Brown of Davidson, Campbell, Cummings, Deaderick, Dromgoole, Fentress, Finley, Garner, Heiskell, House of Williamson, House of Montgomery, etc., Ivie, Jones of Giles, Kennedy, McDougal, Morris, Netherland, Porter of Henry, Shepard, Shelton, Staley, Stephens, Turner, Walters, Williamson and Wright—28.

Those voting in the negative are:

Messrs. Allen, Baxter, Blizard, Brandon, Branson, Britton, Brooks, Brown of Henry, etc., Burkett, Burton, Byrne, Carter, Chowning, Coffin, Cypert, Dibbrell, Doherty, Fielder, Gardner, Gaut, Gibbs, Gibson, Gordon, Henderson, Hill of Warren, Hill of Gibson, Key,

Kirkpatrick, Kyle, Mabry, McNabb, Martin, Meeks, Nicholson, Parker, Porter of Haywood, Sample, Seay, Taylor, Thompson of Davidson, Thompson of Maury, and Warner—42.

Mr. GIBSON, moved to amend by striking out the words " a majority " in the sixth line, and inserting " two-thirds."

Mr. SEAY moved to lay the amendment on the table, which motion was rejected.

Mr. SEAY demanded the yeas and nays on the adoption of the amendment, which were ordered, and the amendment adopted.

Yeas..38
Nays..32

Those voting in the affirmative are:

Messrs. Arledge, Blackburn, Brandon, Branson, Brown of Davidson, Byrne, Campbell, Carter, Coffin, Deaderick, Dromgoole, Fentress, Finley, Gardner, Garner, Gibson, Gordon, Heiskell, Hill of Warren, Hill of Gibson, House of Williamson, House of Montgomery, etc., Ivie, Jones of Giles, Kennedy, McNabb, Morris, Nicholson, Parker, Porter of Haywood, Porter of Henry, Shepard, Shelton, Staley, Stephens, Williamson, Wright and President Brown—38.

Those voting in the negative are:

Messrs. Allen, Baxter, Blizard, Britton, Brooks, Brown of Henry, etc., Burton, Burkett, Chowning, Cummings, Cypert, Dibbrell, Doherty, Fielder, Gaut, Gibbs, Henderson, Key, Kyle, Mabry, McDougal, Martin, Meeks, Netherland, Sample, Seay, Taylor, Thompson of Davidson, Thompson of Maury, Turner, Walters and Warner—32.

The clause as thus amended was adopted by the Convention.

On motion of Mr. MABRY, the Convention adjourned until to-morrow morning at 9 o'clock.

SATURDAY MORNING, FEBRUARY 19, 1870.

The Convention met pursuant to adjournment, Mr. President BROWN in the Chair.

Prayer by the Rev. Mr. SAMPLE, a member of the Convention.

The Journal of yesterday was read and approved.

MEMORIALS AND PETITIONS.

Mr. STEPHENS presented a memorial from the Board of Trade of Memphis, praying a reconsideration of the action of the Convention on the subject of merchants' tax, which was read and laid on the table.

Mr. KENNEDY presented a protest from the Board of Trade of Clarksville against the passage of the section in relation to merchants' tax, and respectfully asking for a reconsideration of the same, which was read and laid on the table.

Mr. GIBBS presented a memorial from citizens of Obion County praying the formation of a new county out of territory west of Reel Foot Lake, which was read and laid on the table.

MISCELLANEOUS.

Mr. WARNER offered the following as an independent section to the Report of the Committee on Miscellaneous Provisions:

"That no white man shall be tried for life or liberty or property except by a jury of white men, and that the Legislature may regulate the trial by jury in accordance with this section and other sections embraced in this Constitution."

Mr. BRITTON offered the following resolution:

Resolved, That a Committee of five be appointed by the Chair, whose duty it shall be to prepare an address to the people of Tennessee, setting forth briefly the reasons for the action of the Convention on the changes made in the Constitution of 1834, the same to be printed and circulated contemporaneously with submitting the Constitution for the ratifying approval of the qualified voters of the State.

Mr. BRITTON moved to suspend the rules and take up the resolution.

On motion of Mr. BURTON, the motion to suspend the rules was laid on the table, and the resolution lies over one day under the rule.

Mr. DIBBRELL offered the following resolution:

Resolved, That it is the sense of this Convention that Clerks of the Supreme Court, and Clerks and Masters of the Chancery Court shall be elected by the people.

Mr. DIBBRELL moved to suspend the rules and take up the resolution.

Mr. CYPERT demanded the yeas and nays, which were ordered, and the motion to suspend the rules adopted.

Yeas..41
Nays..30

Those voting in the affirmative are:

Messrs. Arledge, Blackburn, Blizard, Brandon, Branson, Britton, Brooks, Burkett, Byrne, Chowning, Coffin, Cummings, Cypert, Deavenport, Dibbrell, Doherty, Dromgoole, Fentress, Fielder, Finley, Gibbs, Gibson, Heiskell, Henderson, Hill of Warren, Hill of Gibson, Ivie, Mabry, McDougal, McNabb, Martin, Morris, Parker, Sample, Seay, Shepard, Stephens, Taylor, Walters, Warner and Williamson—41.

Those voting in the negative are:

Messrs. Allen, Bate, Baxter, Brown of Henry, etc., Burton, Carter, Deaderick, Gardner, Garner, Gaut, Heiskell, House of Williamson, House of Montgomery, etc., Jones of Giles, Kennedy, Key, Kirkpatrick, Kyle, Meeks, Netherland, Nicholson, Porter of Haywood, Porter of Henry, Shelton, Staley, Thompson of Maury, Thompson of Davidson, Turner, Wright and President Brown—30.

Mr. President BROWN, Mr. NICHOLSON in the Chair, objected to the consideration of the resolution, as the subject matter had been disposed of by the Convention.

The Chair decided the objection well taken, and ruled the resolution out of order.

Mr. DIBBRELL appealed from the decision of the Chair, and demanded the yeas and nays, which were ordered, and the decision of the Chair sustained.

Yeas..45
Nays..24

Those voting in the affirmative are:

Messrs. Allen, Bate, Baxter, Blizard, Brandon, Branson, Britton, Brown of Davidson, Brown of Henry, etc., Burton, Carter, Coffin, Deaderick, Doherty, Fentress, Fielder, Gardner, Garner, Gaut, Gordon, Heiskell, Henderson, Hill of Gibson, House of Williamson, son, House of Montgomery, Jones of Giles, Kennedy, Key, Kirkpatrick, Kyle, McNabb, Meeks, Netherland, Nicholson, Porter of Haywood, Porter of Henry, Shepard, Shelton, Staley, Thompson of Davidson, Thompson of Maury, Turner, Williamson, Wright and President Brown—45.

Those voting in the negative are:

Messrs. Arledge, Brooks, Burkett, Byrne, Chowning, Cummings, Cypert, Deavenport, Dibbrell, Dromgoole, Finley, Gibbs, Gibson, Hill of Warren, Ivie, Mabry, McDougal, Martin, Parker, Sample, Stephens, Taylor, Walters and Warner—24.

Mr. TAYLOR offered the following resolution :

Resolved, That the rule requiring a motion to reconsider to be made within two days after the passage of a resolution, be suspended for the purpose of reconsidering the action of the Convention on the appointment of Clerks and Masters and Clerks of the Supreme Court.

Mr. TAYLOR moved to suspend the rules and take up the resolution.

Mr. BROWN, of Davidson, moved to lay the motion to suspend the rules on the table.

Mr. TAYLOR demanded the yeas and nays, which were ordered and the motion to lay on the table rejected :

Yeas..34
Nays..37

Those voting in the affirmative are:

Messrs. Allen, Bate, Baxter, Branson, Brown of Davidson, Brown of Henry, etc., Carter, Deaderick, Doherty, Gardner, Garner, Gaut, Gordon, Heiskell, Henderson, House of Williamson, House of Montgomery, etc., Jones of Giles, Kennedy, Key, Kirkpatrick, Kyle, Meeks, Netherland, Nicholson, Porter of Haywood, Porter of Henry, Shepard, Shelton, Thompson of Davidson, Turner, Williamson, Wright and President Brown—34.

Those voting in the negative are :

Messrs. Arledge, Blackburn, Blizard, Brandon, Britton, Brooks, Burkett, Burton, Byrne, Chowning, Coffin, Cummings, Cypert, Deavenport, Dibbrell, Dromgoole, Fentress, Fielder, Finley, Gibbs, Gibson, Hill of Warren, Hill of Gibson, Ivie, Mabry, McDougal, McNabb, Martin, Parker, Sample, Seay, Staley, Stephens, Taylor, Thompson of Maury, Walters and Warner—37.

Mr. HEISKELL demanded the yeas and days on the motion to suspend the rules, which were ordered, and the motion to suspend the rules adopted:

Yeas..39
Nays..31

Those voting in the affirmative are :

Messrs. Arledge, Blackburn, Blizard, Brandon, Branson, Britton,

Brooks, Burkett, Burton, Byrne, Chowning, Coffin, Cummings, Cypert, Deavenport, Dibbrell, Dromgoole, Fielder, Finley, Gibbs, Gibson, Hill of Warren, Hill of Gibson, Ivie, Mabry, McDougal, McNabb, Martin, Parker, Porter of Haywood, Sample, Seay, Stephens, Taylor, Walters Warner and Williamson—39.

Those voting in the negative are:

Messrs. Bate, Baxter, Brown of Davidson, Brown of Henry, etc., Carter, Deaderick, Doherty, Fentress, Garner, Gaut, Gordon, Heiskell, Henderson, House of Williamson, House of Montgomery, etc., Jones of Giles, Kennedy, Key, Kirkpatrick, Kyle, Meeks, Netherland, Nicholson, Porter of Henry, Shepard, Shelton, Thompson of Davidson, Thompson of Maury, Turner, Wright and President Brown—31.

Mr. WILLIANSON demanded a division of the question which was ordered, and a vote taken on that portion of the resolution in relation to Clerks and Masters.

Mr. CYPERT demanded the yeas and nays, which were ordered, and resulted as follows:

Yeas 38
Nays 34

Those voting in the affirmative are:

Messrs. Arledge, Blackburn, Blizard, Branson, Britton, Brooks, Burkett, Burton, Byrne, Chowning, Coffin, Cummings, Cypert, Deavenport, Dibbrell, Dromgoole, Fentress, Fielder, Finley, Gibbs, Gibson, Hill of Warren, Hill of Gibson, Ivie, Mabry, McDougal, McNabb, Martin, Morris, Parker, Sample, Seay, Staley, Stephens, Taylor, Walters, Warner, and Williamson—38.

Those voting in the negative are:

Messrs. Allen, Bate, Baxter, Brandon, Brown of Davidson, Brown of Henry, etc,, Gordon, Heiskell, Henderson, House of Williamson, House of Davidson, etc., Jones of Giles, Kennedy, Key, Kirkpatrick, Kyle, Meeks, Netherland, Nicholson, Porter of Haywood, Porter of Henry, Shepard, Shelton, Thompson of Davidson, Thompson of Maury, Turner, Wright and President Brown—34.

The proposition not having received a two-thirds vote was declared by the Chair rejected.

Mr. CYPERT appealed from the decision of the Chair, and demanded the yeas and nays, which were ordered and the decision of the Chair sustained:

Yeas 41
Nays 29

Those voting in the affirmative are:

Messrs. Allen, Bate, Baxter, Blizard, Brandon, Branson, Brown of Davidson, Brown of Henry, etc., Carter, Coffin, Deaderick, Doherty, Fentress, Fielder, Gardner, Garner, Gaut, Gordon, Heiskell, Henderson, House of Williamson, House of Montgomery, etc., Jones of Giles, Kennedy, Key, Kirkpatrick, Kyle, Meeks, Morris, Netherland, Nicholson, Porter of Haywood, Porter of Henry, Seay, Shepard, Shelton, Thompson of Davidson, Turner, Walters, Wright and President Brown—41.

Those voting in the negative are:

Messrs. Arledge, Blackburn, Britton, Brooks, Burkett, Burton, Byrne, Chowning, Cummings, Cypert, Deavenport, Dibbrell, Dromgoole, Finley, Gibbs, Gibson, Hill of Warren, Hill of Gibson, Ivie, Mabry, McDougal, McNabb, Martin, Parker, Sample, Staley, Thompson of Maury, Warner and Williamson—29.

ISSUANCE OF STATE BONDS.

On motion of Mr. BAXTER the motion of Mr. Porter, of Haywood, to reconsider the vote rejecting the amendment proposed by the Committee on Finance, in relation to the terms on which State bonds shall be issued was taken up.

Mr. DIBBRELL moved to lay the motion to reconsider on the table.

Mr. TAYLOR demanded the yeas and nays, which were ordered, and the motion to lay on the table rejected.

Yeas..27
Nays..44

Those voting in the affirmative are:

Messrs Allen, Britton, Byrne, Carter, Chowning, Cummings, Cypert, Deaderick, Dibbrell, Gardner, Gibbs, Gibson, Gordon, Heiskell, Key, Kirkpatrick, Kyle, Mabry, McNabb, Netherland, Nicholson, Parker, Seay, Shepard, Taylor and Williamson—27.

Those voting in the negative are:

Messrs. Arledge, Bate, Baxter, Blackburn, Blizard, Brandon, Branson, Brown of Davidson, Brown of Henry, etc., Burkett, Burton, Coffin, Deavenport, Doherty, Dromgoole, Fentress, Fielder, Finley, Garner, Gaut, Henderson, Hill of Warren, Hill of Gibson, House of Williamson, House of Montgomery, etc., Ivie, Jones of Giles, Kennedy, McDougal, Martin, Meeks, Morris, Porter of Haywood, Porter of Henry, Sample, Shelton, Staley, Stephens, Thompson of Davidson, Thompson of Maury, Turner, Walters, Warner, Wright and President Brown—44.

The motion to reconsider was then adopted.

Mr. GIBSON offered the following amendment:

Strike out all after the word "it" in the third line, so that the amendment will read: "No bonds of the State shall be issued to any railroad company which, at the time of its application for the same, shall be in default in paying the interest upon the State bonds previously loaned to it."

Which was rejected.

Mr. FENTRESS offered the following amendment:

Provided, That this clause shall not affect the obligation of any contract heretofore entered into by the State.

Mr. WILLIAMSON demanded the yeas and nays on the adoption tion of the amendment, which were ordered, and the amendment rejected.

Yeas.. 33
Nays.. 37

Those voting in the affirmative are:

Messrs. Allen, Branson, Brooks, Brown of Davidson, Byrne, Carter, Chowning, Coffin, Cypert, Dibbrell, Fentress, Finley, Gardner, Gibbs, Gibson, Gordon, Heiskell, Hill of Warren, Ivie, Key, Kyle, Mabry, Martin, Netherland, Nicholson, Parker, Seay, Shepard, Thompson of Davidson, Thompson of Maury, Warner, Williamson and Wright—33.

Those voting in the negative are:

Messrs. Arledge, Bate, Baxter, Blackburn, Blizard, Brandon, Britton, Brown of Henry, etc., Burkett, Burton, Cummings, Deaderick, Deavenport, Doherty, Dromgoole, Fielder, Garner, Gaut, Henderson, Hill of Gibson, House of Williamson, House of Montgomery, etc., Jones of Giles, Kennedy, Kirkpatrick, McDougal, McNabb, Meeks, Morris, Porter of Haywood, Porter of Henry, Sample, Shelton, Staley, Stephens, Turner and Walters—37.

Mr. DIBBRELL demanded the yeas and nays on the adoption of the amendment reported by the Committee on Finance, which were ordered, and the amendment adopted.

Yeas.. 52
Nays.. 20

Those voting in the affirmative are:

Messrs. Arledge, Bate, Baxter, Blackburn, Blizard, Brandon, Branson, Brown of Davidson, Brown of Henry, etc., Burkett, Burton, Carter, Chowning, Cummings, Deaderick, Deavenport, Doherty, Dromgoole, Fielder, Finley, Gardner, Garner, Gaut, Gordon, Heiskell, Henderson, Hill of Warren, Hill of Gibson, House of Williamson, House of Montgomery, etc., Ivie, Jones of Giles, Kennedy, McDougal, Martin, Meeks, Morris, Netherland, Parker, Porter of Haywood, Porter of Henry, Sample, Shelton, Staley, Stephens,

Thompson of Davidson, Thompson of Maury, Turner, Walters, Warner, Wright and President Brown—52.

Those voting in the negative are:

Messrs. Allen, Britton, Brooks, Byrne, Coffin, Cypert, Dibbrell, Fentress, Gibbs, Gibson, Key, Kirkpatrick, Kyle, Mabry, McNabb, Nicholson, Seay, Shepard, Taylor, and Williamson—20.

Ordered that the section be referred to the Committee on Revision.

PAYMENT OF THE STATE DEBT.

Mr. DROMGOOLE called up his resolution, offered on yesterday, in relation to the payment of the State debt.

Mr. PORTER, of Haywood, moved to lay the resolution on the table.

Mr. GARNER demanded the yeas and nays, which were ordered, and the motion to lay on the table sustained.

Yeas.. 41
Nays.. 27

Those voting in the affirmative are:

Messrs. Bate, Baxter, Blizard, Brandon, Branson, Britton, Burkett, Carter, Chowning, Cypert, Deaderick, Deavenport, Dibbrell, Finley, Gardner, Gaut, Gibbs, Gibson, Gordon, Heiskell, Henderson, Hill of Warren, Hill of Gibson, House of Williamson, Key, Kirkpatrick, Kyle, Mabry, McDougal, McNabb, Meeks, Morris, Nicholson, Parker, Porter of Haywood, Sample, Shepard, Stephens, Taylor, Thompson of Davidson, and Thompson of Maury—41.

Those voting in the negative are:

Messrs. Allen, Arledge, Brooks, Brown of Davidson, Burton, Byrne, Coffin, Cummings, Doherty, Dromgoole, Fentress, Fielder, Garner, Ivie, Jones of Giles, Kennedy, Martin, Netherland, Porter of Henry, Seay, Staley, Turner, Walters, Warner, Williamson, Wright and President Brown—27.

PUBLICATION OF NEW CONSTITUTION.

Mr. WILLIAMSON offered the following resolution:

Resolved, That for the information of the people an official copy of the amended Constitution, adopted by this Convention, be published in the two papers of largest circulation in the cities of Knoxville, Nashville and Memphis, and in one newspaper of largest circulation in each other county in which a newspaper is now published; and that 30,000 copies of the said amended Constitution be printed by the Public Printers for general distribution; and that the newspapers publishing an official copy of the amended Constitution be paid fifty dollars each.

Which lies over under the rule.

ADJOURNMENT SINE DIE.

Mr. JONES, of Giles, offered the following resolution:

Resolved, That the Convention will adjourn *sine die* on Tuesday next, at 12 o'clock at noon.

Which lies over under the rules.

REPORT OF THE JUDICIARY COMMITTEE.

Mr. HEISKELL, from the Committee on the Judiciary, reported the following in lieu of the amendment proposed by Mr. Warner:

"No Convention or General Assembly of this State shall act upon any amendment of the Constitution of the United States proposed by Congress to the several States, unless such Convention or General Assembly shall have been elected after such amendment is submitted.

Mr. GIBSON demanded the yeas and nays on the adoption of the amendment proposed by the Committee, which were ordered, and the amendment adopted.

Yeas..........62
Nays..........7

Those voting in the affirmative are:

Messrs. Allen, Arledge, Bate, Baxter, Blizard, Brandon, Britton, Brown of Davidson, Brown of Henry, etc., Burkett, Burton, Byrne, Carter, Chowning, Coffin, Cummings, Cypert, Deaderick, Deavenport, Dibbrell, Doherty, Dromgoole, Fentress, Fielder, Gardner, Garner, Gaut, Gibbs, Gordon, Heiskell, Henderson, Hill of Warren, Hill of Gibson, House of Williamson, House of Montgomery, etc., Ivie, Jones of Giles, Kennedy, Kirkpatrick, Kyle, Mabry, McDougal, McNabb, Martin, Meeks, Morris, Nicholson, Porter of Haywood, Porter of Henry, Sample, Seay, Shepard, Stephens, Taylor, Thompson of Davidson, Thompson of Maury, Turner, Walters, Warner, Williamson, Wright and President Brown—62.

Those voting in the negative are:

Messrs. Branson, Brooks, Finley, Gibson, Key, Parker, and Staley—7.

On motion of Mr. HEISKELL, the amendment was referred to the Committee on Revision.

REPRESENTATION.

Mr. SEAY called up the proposition submitted by him on yesterday, viz:

"No county, which has a representative at the date of the ratification of this Constitution, shall ever be deprived thereof under any apportionment made hereafter under the provisions of this Constitution;"

And demanded the yeas and nays on its adoption, which were ordered, and the amendment rejected.

Yeas..19
Nays..48

Those voting in the affirmative are:

Messrs. Branson, Brooks, Byrne, Cummings, Cypert, Deavenport, Dibbrell, Finley, Gibson, McDougal, McNabb, Meeks, Morris, Netherland, Parker, Sample, Seay, Staley and Taylor—19.

Those voting in the negative are:

Messrs. Allen, Arledge, Bate, Baxter, Blizard, Branson, Britton, Brown of Davidson, Brown of Henry, etc., Burkett, Burton, Carter, Chowning, Coffin, Deaderick, Doherty, Dromgoole, Fentress, Fielder, Gardner, Garner, Gaut, Gibbs, Gordon, Heiskell, Henderson, Hill of Warren, Hill of Gibson, House of Williamson, House of Montgomery, etc., Ivie, Jones of Giles, Kennedy, Key, Kirkpatrick, Mabry, Nicholson, Porter of Haywood, Porter of Henry, Turner, Walters, Warner, Williamson and Wright—48.

REVISION.

Mr. STEPHENS, from the Committee on Revision, made the following report:

I beg leave to report that in revising Section 13, of Article 6, I have caused it to read as follows:

"Sec. 13. Judges of the Supreme Court shall appoint their Clerks, who shall hold their offices for the term of six years. Clerks of inferior courts, holden in the counties or districts, shall be elected by the qualified voters thereof for the term of four years. Any clerk may be removed from office for malfeasance, incompetency, or neglect of duty, in such manner as may be prescribed by law.

Mr. Ivie raised the point of order, that the Committee had transcended their powers in making the alterations reported by them.

The Chair decided the point of order not well taken.

Mr. HEISKELL demanded the yeas and nays on receiving the report of the Committee, which were ordered, and the report received.

Yeas..46
Nays..16

Those voting in the affirmative are:

Messrs. Allen, Bate, Baxter, Blizard, Brandon, Branson, Brown of Davidson, Brown of Henry, etc., Burton, Byrne, Carter, Chowning, Coffin, Deaderick, Doherty, Fielder, Finley, Gardner, Garner, Gaut, Gibbs, Gordon, Heiskell, Henderson, Hill of Gibson, House of Williamson, House of Montgomery, etc., Jones of Giles, Kennedy, Key, Kirkpatrick, Kyle, Nicholson, Porter of Haywood, Porter of Henry, Seay, Shepard, Shelton, Staley, Stephens, Thompson of Davidson, Thompson of Maury, Turner, Williamson, Wright and President Brown—46.

Those voting in the negative are:

Messrs. Arledge, Britton, Brooks, Burkett, Dibbrell, Gibson, Hill of Warren, Ivie, Mabry, McNabb, Martin, Parker, Sample, Taylor, and Warner—16.

MERCHANTS' TAX.

Mr. STEPHENS introduced the following as an independent section:

"The portion of a merchant's capital used in the purchase of merchandise sold by him to merchants and sent beyond this State, shall not be taxed at a rate higher than the *ad valorem* tax on property."

On motion of Mr. STEPHENS, the rules were suspended and the section taken up.

Mr. GARNER demanded the yeas and nays on the adoption of the section, which were ordered, and the section adopted.

Yeas 42
Nays..24

Those voting in the affirmative are:

Messrs. Bate, Baxter, Blizard, Brown of Davidson, Brown of Henry, etc., Burton, Byrne, Carter, Coffin, Cypert, Deaderick, Deavenport, Dibbrell, Doherty, Dromgoole, Gardner, Gaut, Gibbs, Gordon, Heiskell, Henderson, Hill of Gibson, House of Williamson, House of Montgomery, etc., Jones of Giles, Kennedy, Key, Kirkpatrick, Mabry, McNabb, Nicholson, Porter of Haywood, Porter of Henry, Seay, Shepard, Shelton, Stephens, Taylor, Thompson of Davidson, Turner, Williamson and Wright—42.

Those voting in the negative are:

Messrs. Allen, Brandon, Branson, Britton, Brooks, Burkett,

Chowning, Fentress, Fielder, Finley, Garner, Gibson, Hill of Warren, Ivie, Kyle, Martin, Meeks, Morris, Netherland, Parker, Sample, Staley, Thompson of Maury and Warner—24.

Ordered, that the section be referred to the Committee on Revision.

Mr. House, of Williamson, offered the following as an additional section:

"Nor shall that portion of a merchant's capital used in the purchase of merchandise, sold by him to resident citizens of the State, be taxed at more than double the rate of the *ad valorem* tax on property.

Mr. House moved to suspend the rules and take up the section, which was rejected, and it lies over under the rule.

NEW COUNTIES AND COUNTY LINES.

The Convention proceeded to the consideration of the unfinished business of yesterday, the report of the Committee on New Counties and County Lines.

The first part of Clause 4, Section 1, was adopted without amendment.

Mr. Seay proposed to amend, by striking out in tenth line, the words "six hundred and twenty-five" and inserting "four hundred," which was rejected.

Mr. Arledge moved to amend by striking out "and twenty-five" in the tenth line.

On motion of Mr. Burkett, the amendment was laid on the table.

Yeas..46
Nays..24

Those voting in the affirmative are:

Messrs. Allen, Bate, Baxter, Blizard, Branson, Britton, Brooks, Brown of Henry, etc., Burkett, Carter, Chowning, Coffin, Cummings, Cypert, Deavenport, Dibbrell, Doherty, Fielder, Gardner, Gaut, Gibbs, Gibson, Gordon, Heiskell, Henderson, Hill of Warren, Hill of Gibson, House of Williamson, Ivie, Key, Kirkpatrick, Mabry, Martin, Meeks, Netherland, Parker, Porter of Henry, Sample, Seay, Shepard, Stephens, Thompson of Maury, Turner, Walters, Warner and Williamson—46.

Those voting in the negative are:

Messrs. Arledge, Brandon, Brown of Davidson, Burton, Byrne,

Deaderick, Dromgoole, Fentress, Finley, Garner, House of Montgomery, etc., Jones of Giles, Kennedy, Kyle, McDougal, McNabb, Morris, Nicholson, Porter of Haywood, Shelton, Staley, Taylor, Thompson of Davidson and Wright—24.

Mr. HILL, of Gibson, moved to strike out "six hundred and twenty-five," and insert "five hundred and fifty."

Mr. SEAY moved to lay the amendment on the table.

Mr. GARNER demanded the yeas and nays, which were ordered, and the motion to lay on the table sustained.

Yeas..35
Nays..33

Those voting in the affirmative are:

Messrs. Allen, Baxter, Blizard, Branson, Britton, Brooks, Brown of Davidson, Burkett, Burton, Carter, Chowning, Cummings, Deaderick, Deavenport, Dibbrell, Doherty, Fielder, Gardner, Gaut, Gibbs, Gibson, Gordon, Henderson, Hill of Warren, Ivie, Key, Kirkpatrick, Kyle, Mabry, Martin, Parker, Seay, Shepard, Thompson of Davidson and Warner—35.

Those voting in the negative are:

Messrs. Arledge, Bate, Brandon, Brown of Henry, Byrne, Coffin, Cypert, Dromgoole, Fentress, Finley, Garner, Hill of Gibson, House of Williamson, House of Montgomery, etc., Jones of Giles, Kennedy, McDougal, McNabb, Meeks, Morris, Netherland, Nicholson, Porter of Haywood, Porter of Henry, Sample, Shelton, Staley, Stephens, Taylor, Thompson of Maury, Turner, Walters, Williamson and Wright—33.

Mr. FIELDER proposed to amend by striking out "six hundred and twenty-five," and inserting "five hundred," which was adopted, and the clause, as thus amended, was adopted by the Convention.

Mr. HOUSE, of Montgomery, etc., offered the following as an independent section:

"Whenever any county may have taken stock in a railroad or other corporation, and a fraction of said county shall be taken to form a new county, or shall be added to another county by change of county lines, the inhabitants or property holders within said fractions shall continue liable to the payment of their relative proportions of all taxes necessary to pay the interest on any bonds that may have been issued in aid of any subscription of stock, and to pay said bonds until the same are fully paid."

Mr. GARDNER offered the following as an amendment to the section proposed by Mr. House:

"And the General Assembly shall have power, by appropriate legislation, to enforce the provisions of this section."

Which was accepted by Mr. HOUSE.

Mr. MABRY proposed to amend the section as follows:

"*Provided,* The railroad for which the liability was incurred passes through any part of the territory taken off to form a new county, or within three miles of the same."

Mr. HOUSE, of Montgomery, moved to lay the amendment of Mr. Mabry on the table.

Mr. MABRY demanded the yeas and nays, which were ordered, and the motion to lay on the table sustained.

Yeas.. 60
Nays.. 8

Those voting in the affirmative are:

Messrs. Allen, Arledge, Baxter, Blizard, Brandon, Branson, Britton, Brooks, Brown of Davidson, Brown of Henry, etc., Burton, Byrne, Carter, Chowning, Coffin, Cummings, Deaderick, Deavenport, Dibbrell, Doherty, Dromgoole, Fentress, Fielder, Finley, Gardner, Garner, Gaut, Gibson, Gordon, Heiskell, Henderson, Hill of Warren, Hill of Gibson, House of Williamson, House of Davidson, etc., Ivie, Jones of Giles, Kennedy, Key, Kirkpatrick, Kyle, McDougal, McNabb, Martin, Meeks, Morris, Netherland, Nicholson, Parker, Porter of Haywood, Sample, Shepard, Shelton, Staley, Stephens, Thompson of Davidson, Turner, Warner, Williamson and Wright—60.

Those voting in the negative are:

Messrs. Bate, Burkett, Gibbs, Mabry, Porter of Henry, Seay, Thompson of Maury and Walters—8.

Mr. HOUSE's amendment was then adopted.

Mr. FENTRESS offered the following amendment:

Provided, however, That no part of an old county shall be taken off without the consent of one-third of the qualified voters of such county.

Mr. SEAY demanded the yeas and nays on the adoption of the amendment, which were ordered, and the amendment rejected.

Yeas.. 22
Nays.. 47

Those voting in the affirmative are:

Messrs. Arledge, Blackburn, Brandon, Byrne, Coffin, Cummings, Deaderick, Dromgoole, Fentress, Finley, Garner, Heiskell, Jones of

Giles, Kennedy, Morris, Netherland, Porter of Haywood, Shelton, Staley, Stephens, Williamson and Wright—22.

Those voting in the negative are:

Messrs. Allen, Bate, Baxter, Blizard, Branson, Britton, Brooks, Brown of Davidson, Brown of Henry, etc., Burkett, Burton, Carter, Chowning, Deavenport, Dibbrell, Doherty, Fielder, Gardner, Gaut, Gibbs, Gibson, Gordon, Henderson, Hill of Warren, Hill of Gibson, House of Montgomery, etc., Ivie, Key, Kirkpatrick, Kyle, Mabry, McDougal, McNabb, Martin, Meeks, Nicholson, Parker, Porter of Henry, Sample, Seay, Shepard, Thompson of Davidson, Turner, Walters and Warner—47.

Mr. Gibbs moved to amend by striking out all after the word "voters" in the third line, to the word "provided" in the tenth line, and insert "no old county shall be reduced in forming a new county to a less territory than 450 square miles, and no section of an old county shall be taken off to form a new one, or be transferred to another, without a majority of the voters of said section voting therefor."

Mr. Baxter moved to lay the amendment on the table.

Mr. Hill, of Gibson, demanded the yeas and nays, and the motion to lay on the table sustained.

Yeas..44
Nays..16

Those voting in the affirmative are:

Messrs. Arledge, Bate, Baxter, Brandon, Britton, Brown of Davidson, Brown of Henry, etc., Burton, Byrne, Carter, Chowning, Coffin, Cummings, Cypert, Deaderick, Finley, Gardner, Garner, Gordon, Heiskell, Henderson, Hill of Gibson, House of Williamson, House of Montgomery etc., Ivie, Jones of Giles, Kennedy, Key, Kyle, McDougal, McNabb, Meeks, Morris, Nicholson, Parker, Porter of Haywood, Porter of Henry, Sample, Shelton, Staley, Stephens, Turner, Walters and Wright—44.

Those voting in the negative are:

Messrs. Blizard, Branson, Brooks, Burkett, Deavenport, Dibbrell, Doherty, Gaut, Gibbs, Gibson, Hill of Warren, Kirkpatrick, Mabry, Martin, Seay, Thompson of Maury, and Warner—16.

Mr. Kirkpatrick offered the following amendment:

"A new county may be formed out of territory made up of portions of Grainger, Jefferson and Greene Counties, but no line of such county shall approach the Court-house of Grainger County nearer than the Holston River at the point nearest said Court-house, nor shall any line thereof approach the Court-house of Jefferson County nearer than eleven miles, nor the Court-house of Greene County nearer than to begin at the town of Warrensburg, on the Nolichucky River, thence directly to Bull's Gap; *Provided,* That neither of said old counties shall be reduced below 500 square miles."

Which was adopted by the Convention.

Mr. GARDNER offered the following amendment:

Strike out lines one and two and insert "out of that portion of Obion County lying west of low water mark, on the east side of Reel Foot Lake."

Which was rejected, and the provision, as reported by the Committee, was adopted.

To the provision authorizing the formation of a new county out of portions of Smith, Macon and Sumner, Mr. ALLEN offered the following amendment:

Provided, That nothing herein contained shall exempt that portion of Smith County, thus detached, from the payment of its due proportion of the debts of said county, contracted previous to such separation.

Which was adopted, and the provision, as thus amended, was adopted.

Yeas..35
Nays..22

Those voting in the affirmative are:

Messrs. Allen, Blizard, Branson, Britton, Brooks, Brown of Davidson, Burkett, Byrne, Chowning, Coffin, Cummings, Deaderick, Deavenport, Dibbrell, Fielder, Gardner, Gibbs, Gibson, Gordon, Henderson, Hill of Warren, Hill of Gibson, Ivie, Kyle, Mabry, McNabb, Martin, Nicholson, Parker, Sample, Seay, Shepard, Taylor, Thompson of Maury, Walters and Warner—35.

Those voting in the negative are:

Messrs. Arledge, Bate, Baxter, Brown of Henry, etc., Burton, Doherty, Fentress, Finley, Garner, Gaut, House of Montgomery, etc., Jones of Giles, Kennedy, Key, Porter of Haywood, Porter of Henry, Shelton, Staley, Turner, Williamson and Wright—22.

Mr. MABRY entered a motion to reconsider the vote, the consideration of which, on motion of Mr. Thompson, of Maury, was postponed until Monday next.

To the proposition to form a new county out of portions of Jackson and Overton, Mr. BROOKS proposed to amend by adding:

"Said new county shall contain not less than 400 qualified voters, nor shall the area of either of said old counties be reduced below 450 square miles."

Which was adopted, and the section, as thus amended, adopted.

Mr. NICHOLSON offered the following amendment:

In line 1, paragraph 3, after the word "of" insert the word "Lewis," so that it will read: "The Counties of Lewis, Cheatham and Sequatchie," etc.

Which was adopted, and the paragraph as thus amended was adopted.

Mr. CARTER offered an amendment declaring that the county seat of Carter County shall not be removed without the concurrence of two-thirds of the Legislature.

Mr. BATE offered the following as an amendment to Mr. Carter's amendment:

Nor shall the seat of justice in the County of Tipton be removed without a majority of two-thirds of the qualified voters of said county vote therefor.

Mr. GARNER offered the following in lieu:

Nor shall the seat of justice of any county in this State be removed without the concurrence of two-thirds of the qualified voters in the respective counties.

Which was accepted by Messrs. CARTER and BATE, and adopted by the Convention.

Mr. FIELDER proposed the following amendment:

Out of territory made up of fractions of Haywood, Madison, Gibson and Dyer Counties, included in the bounds set forth in the second section of an act passed by the General Assembly of the State of Tennessee, on the 20th day of December, 1845, entitled "An act to establish the County of Crockett in honor of and to perpetuate the memory of David Crockett, one of Tennessee's distinguished sons."

Mr. GARDNER offered the following amendment to Mr. Fielder's proposition:

Add to the end of the proposition, "*Provided,* two-thirds of the qualified voters in each of the fractions taken to make said county shall vote for the same. *And provided further,* That neither of the counties from which such fractions are taken, shall be reduced below 500 square miles. *And provided also,* That said new county shall not contain less than 275 square miles."

Which was accepted by Mr. FIELDER.

Mr. PORTER, of Haywood, moved to lay the amendment on the table.

Mr. FIELDER demanded the yeas and nays, which were ordered and the motion to lay on the table rejected:

Yeas..24
Nays..35

Those voting in the affirmative are:

Messrs. Arledge, Bate, Baxter, Blizard, Britton, Brown of Henry, etc., Burkett, Burton, Coffin, Fentress, Gaut, Gibson, Henderson, Hill of Gibson, Jones of Giles, Kennedy, Key, Mabry, Porter of Haywood, Porter of Henry, etc., Sample, Shelton, Staley and Wright—24.

Those voting in the negative are:

Messrs. Allen, Brandon, Branson, Brooks, Brown of Davidson, Byrne, Carter, Chowning, Cummings, Deaderick, Deavenport, Dibbrell, Doherty, Fielder, Gardner, Garner, Gibbs, Gordon, Heiskell, Hill of Warren, House of Montgomery, etc., Ivie, Kyle, McNabb, Martin, Nicholson, Parker, Seay, Shepard, Taylor, Thompson of Maury, Turner, Walters, Warner and Williamson—35

On motion of Mr. BROWN, of Davidson, the further consideration of the proposition was postponed until Monday next.

Mr. MABRY entered a motion to reconsider the vote adopting Section 1, Article IX.

Mr. THOMPSON, of Maury, offered the following amendment:

"Out of territory made up of fractions of Maury, Williamson, Rutherford, Marshall and Bedford, a county may be established, but in no case shall the line of said new county approach the county sites of any of the counties from the territory of which said new county is made up nearer than eleven miles, except that the line of said new county may approach the Court-house of Marshall County as near as the northern bank of Duck River. But Marshall County shall not be reduced below 350 square miles.

The consideration of the amendment was postponed until Monday next.

Mr. PRESIDENT BROWN, Mr. Kennedy in the Chair, offered the following resolution:

Resolved, That the Counties of Tipton, Fayette, Henry, Lincoln, Haywood, Henderson, Rutherford, Giles, Bedford, Franklin, Robertson, Roane, Dickson, Blount, DeKalb, Sullivan, Hardeman, Madison, Carroll, Knox and Montgomery, shall not be reduced below the number of square miles now included in their present boundaries.

Mr. President BROWN called for the question on his resolution.

Mr. THOMPSON, of Maury, moved that the Convention adjourn until Monday morning at 9 o'clock.

Mr. GARNER demanded the yeas and nays, which were ordered, and the motion to adjourn adopted.

Yeas...33
Nays 27

Those voting in the affirmative are:

Messrs. Bate, Blizard, Brandon, Britton, Brown of Davidson, Burkett, Burton, Carter, Chowning, Coffin, Cummings, Deavenport, Dibbrell, Doherty, Fielder, Gardner, Gibbs, Gordon, Heiskell, Key, Kyle, Mabry, McNabb, Martin, Nicholson, Sample, Seay, Shepard, Taylor, Thompson of Maury, Warner, Williamson and Wright—33.

Those voting in the negative are:

Messrs. Allen, Arledge, Baxter, Branson, Brooks, Brown of Henry, Byrne, Deaderick, Fentress, Finley, Garner, Gaut, Gibson, Henderson, Hill of Warren, Hill of Gibson, House of Montgomery, etc., Ivie, Jones of Giles, Kennedy, Parker, Porter of Haywood, Shelton, Staley, Turner, Walters and President Brown—27.

MONDAY MORNING, FEBRUARY 21, 1870.

The Convention met pursuant to adjournment, Mr. President BROWN in the Chair.

The Journal of Saturday was read and approved.

REPORT ON MEMORIALS.

Mr. SEAY, from the Committee on New Counties and County Lines made the following report:

The Committee have directed me to report that they have had

under consideration the memorials from citizens of Coffee, Franklin, Lincoln and Bedford counties, and of citizens of Cannon, Smith, DeKalb, Wilson and Rutherford counties, and recommend them to the consideration of the Convention.

The memorial from the Justices of the Peace of Montgomery County asking for the restoration of fractions of Robertson County, is returned for the consideration of the Convention, and for such action as may be deemed proper; the Committee make no recommendation in regard thereto.

The memorial from citizens of Grundy asking that a portion of Grundy County be attached to Coffee County, is returned and recommended by the Committee to the respectful consideration of this body.

The memorials from citizens of Roane, Monroe and Blount asking for a new county to be formed out of territory made up of fractions of said counties, which were remanded to the Committee, are again returned, and the same recommended to the respectful consideration of the Convention, believing them to be entitled to such by this body.

The Committee ask to be discharged from the further consideration of the matters referred.

All of which is respectfully submitted.

GEORGE E. SEAY,
Chairman.

February 21, 1870.

PRINTING THE JOURNALS.

Mr. SEAY called up the resolution heretofore offered by him in relation to the printing of the Journal, etc., which was taken up, read, and on motion of ———————— was passed over informally.

JURY TRIALS.

Mr. SHEPARD offered the following as an independent section:

Article —, Section —. Every white person put upon trial, charged with any crime or misdemeanor, shall have empannelled for the trial of the same a jury of white men, and in all civil cases where the plaintiff or defendant is a white person the jury shall be composed of white men.

Which lies over under the rule.

NEW COUNTIES.

Mr. KEY offered the following amendment to the report of the Committee on New Counties:

Out of territory made up of fractions of the Counties of Monroe, Roane and Blount around the town of Loudon; but no line of such county shall ever approach the court-house of any of the old counties nearer than eleven miles, excepting that on the south side of the Tennessee River said lines may approach within ten miles of the county seat of Roane County, but on the north side of said river no line shall approach nearer than eleven miles.

Mr. STALEY offered the following amendment:

"*Provided*, That Roane County shall never be reduced below 625 square miles."

Mr. FINLEY offered the following amendment:

Provided, That such portions of said counties as may be taken off to form the new county shall still remain liable for their proportionable part of all debts contracted and owing prior to the formation of such new county.

Mr. KEY moved to lay the amendments on the table.

Mr. GIBSON demanded a division of the question, which was ordered, and a vote taken to lay the amendment of Mr. Finley on the table, and it was rejected.

Yeas..24
Nays..40

Those voting in the affirmative are:

Messrs. Blizard, Brown of Davidson, Burkett, Burton, Carter, Chowning, Deaderick, Dibbrell, Doherty, Fulkerson, Gaut, Gibbs, Gordon, Henderson, House of Williamson, House of Montgomery, etc., Kennedy, Key, Mabry, Nicholson, Thompson of Davidson, Walters, Warner and Wright—24.

Those voting in the negative are:

Messrs. Allen, Arledge, Bate, Baxter, Brandon, Branson, Britton, Brown of Henry, etc., Byrne, Campbell, Coffin, Cypert, Deavenport, Fentress, Fielder, Finley, Gardner, Garner, Gibson, Heiskell, Hill of Waren, Hill of Gibson, Ivie, Jones of Giles, Kyle, McDougal, McNabb, Martin, Meeks, Morris, Netherland, Parker, Porter of Haywood, Porter of Henry, Sample, Seay, Shelton, Staley, Stephens and Thompson of Maury—40.

A vote was taken on the motion to lay Mr. Staley's amendment on the table and it was adopted.

Yeas..49
Nays..16

Those voting in the affirmative are:

Messrs. Allen, Arledge, Baxter, Blizard, Brandon, Branson, Britton, Brown of Davidson, Brown of Henry, etc., Burkett, Burton, Byrne, Carter, Chowning, Cypert, Deaderick, Dibbrell, Doherty, Fielder, Fulkerson, Gardner, Garner, Gaut, Gibbs, Gibson, Gordon, Heiskell, Henderson, Hill of Warren, Hill of Gibson, House of Williamson, House of Montgomery, etc., Ivie, Kennedy, Key, Kyle, Mabry, McDougal, McNabb, Martin, Meeks, Nicholson, Porter of Haywood, Seay, Shepard, Thompson of Davidson, Thompson of Maury, Walters and Warner—49.

Those voting in the negative are:

Messrs. Brooks, Campbell, Coffin, Deavenport, Fentress, Finley, Jones of Giles, Morris, Parker, Porter of Henry, Sample, Shelton, Staley, Stephens, Turner and Wright—16.

Mr. FINLEY's amendment was then adopted.

Mr. STALEY demanded the yeas and nays upon the adoption of Mr. Key's amendment as amended, and it was adopted.

Yeas.. 45
Nays.. 14

Those voting in the affimative are:

Messrs. Allen, Arledge, Bate, Baxter, Blizard, Brandon, Branson, Britton, Brown of Henry, etc., Burkett, Burton, Byrne, Carter, Chowning, Cypert, Deaderick, Deavenport, Dibbrell, Doherty, Fielder, Fulkerson, Gardner, Gaut, Gibbs, Gibson, Gordon, Heiskell, Henderson, Hill of Warren, House of Williamson, Ivie, Kennedy, Key, Kyle, Mabry, McNabb, Martin, Netherland, Nicholson, Parker, Sample, Seay, Shepard, Thompson of Davidson, Thompson of Maury, Walters and Warner—45.

Those voting in the negative are:

Messrs. Brown of Davidson, Coffin, Fentress Finley, Garner, Hill of Gibson, Jones of Giles, Morris, Porter of Henry, Shelton, Staley, Stephens, Turner and Wright—14.

Mr. MARTIN offered the following amendment:

That portion of the territory of Marion County situated within the following boundary, viz: Beginning on the Grundy and Marion county line at the Nickajack trace, and running about six hundred yards west of Benjamin Posey's to where the Tennessee Coal Railroad crosses the line, and running thence south-east through the Pocket, near William Summers, crossing the Battle Creek Gulf at the corner of Thomas Wooten's field, thence running across the Little Gizzard Gulf at Raven Point, thence in a direct line to the bridge crossing the Big Fiery Gizzard, thence in a direct line to the mouth of Holy Water Creek, thence up said creek to Grundy County line, and thence running with said line to the beginning, shall be, and is hereby detached from Marion County and attached to the County of Grundy.

Mr. BYRNE demanded the yeas and nays on the adoption of the amendment, which were ordered, and the amendment adopted.

Yeas...... 44
Nays.. 18

Those voting in the affirmative are:

Messrs. Allen, Arledge, Baxter, Brandon, Branson, Britton, Brooks, Brown of Davidson, Brown of Henry, etc., Burton, Carter, Chowning, Cypert, Deaderick, Deavenport, Doherty, Fielder, Fulkerson, Gardner, Gibbs, Gibson, Gordon, Hill of Warren, Hill of Gibson, House of Montgomery, etc., Ivie, Kyle, Mabry, McNabb, Martin, Meeks, Morris, Netherland, Nicholson, Parker, Sample, Seay, Shepard, Staley, Stephens, Thompson of Davidson, Thompson of Maury, Warner and President Brown—44.

Those voting in the negative are:

Messrs. Bate, Byrne, Campbell, Coffin, Dibbrell, Fentress, Garner, Heiskell, Henderson, House of Williamson, Jones of Giles, Kennedy, Key, Porter of Haywood, Porter of Henry, Shelton, Turner and Wright—18.

On motion of Mr. TURNER, the motion of Mr. Mabry to reconsider the vote adopting the report of the Committee in relation to the formation of a new county out of portions of Smith, Macon and Sumner, was taken up, and the motion to reconsider adopted: Thereupon,

Mr. SEAY offered the following in lieu:

"Out of territory made up of fractions of Sumner, Smith and Macon counties, but no line of said county shall run nearer than ten miles to the Court-houses of Smith and Sumner counties—nor so as to include any territory of Macon county lying within nine and a half miles of the Court-house of Macon county—and not more than twenty square miles of Macon county shall be taken to form said county—nor shall any part of Sumner county be taken which lies west of the western boundary of Macon county.

No fraction shall be taken off unless two-thirds of the qualified voters of said fraction vote for it and the fraction so taken off shall pay its pro rata share of the debts of the old county contracted previous to such separation."

Which was adopted in lieu, and the clause as thus amended was adopted by the Convention.

Mr. SEAY moved to reconsider the vote adopting the amendment and further moved to lay the motion to reconsider on the table, which latter motion was adopted.

Mr. BROWN, of Henry, submitted the following resolution:

Resolved, That all further consideration of the subject of new counties and county lines, be indefinitely postponed, and that no proposition looking to the formation of a new county shall hereafter be considered except Section 5, Article X.

Mr. THOMPSON, of Maury, objected to the consideration of the resolution, and it was laid over under the rule.

Mr. PORTER, of Henry, moved the indefinite postponement of all pending propositions, and the report of the Committee on New Counties undisposed of.

Mr. GIBBS demanded the yeas and nays on the motion to postpone, which were ordered, and the motion adopted:

Yeas.. 34
Nays.. 21

Those voting in the affirmative are:

Messrs. Allen, Arledge, Baxter, Brandon, Britton, Brown of Davidson, Brown of Henry, etc., Burkett, Burton, Campbell, Chowning, Coffin, Doherty, Fielder, Gardner, Garner, Gordon, Heiskell, Henderson, Hill of Gibson, House of Williamson, Ivie, Kennedy, Meeks, Morris, Porter of Haywood, Porter of Henry, Sample, Shepard, Shelton, Stephens, Thompson of Davidson, Turner and Wright—34.

Those voting in the negative are:

Messrs. Branson, Brooks, Cypert, Deaderick, Dibbrell, Gibbs, Gibson, Hill of Warren, Jones of Giles, Key, Kyle, Mabry, McNabb, Martin, Netherland, Nicholson, Parker, Seay, Taylor, Thompson of Maury and Warner—21.

Mr. JONES, of Giles, offered the following *proviso:*

Provided, "That no territory shall be detached from any old county to form a new county, or to be attached to another county, without the consent of two fifths of the qualified voters of said old county—excepting such counties as have already been specially authorized by this Convention."

Mr. JONES demanded the yeas and nays on the adoption of the *proviso,* which were ordered, and it was rejected:

Yeas.. 24
Nays.. 35

Those voting in the affirmative are:

Messrs. Arledge, Bate, Brandon, Coffin, Deaderick, Doherty,

Fentress, Fulkerson, Heiskell, Hill of Gibson, House of Williamson, Jones of Giles, Kennedy, Key, Morris, Nicholson, Porter of Henry, Sample, Shelton, Stephens, Thompson of Davidson, Turner and Wright—24.

Those voting in the negative are:

Messrs. Allen, Baxter, Branson, Britton, Brooks, Brown of Davidson, Burkett, Burton, Campbell, Carter, Chowning, Cummings, Cypert, Fielder, Gardner, Garner, Gaut, Gibbs, Gibson, Gordon, Henderson, Hill of Warren, House of Montgomery, etc. Ivie, Kyle, Mabry, McNabb, Martin, Meeks, Netherland, Parker, Seay, Taylor, Thompson of Maury and Warner—35.

Mr. Gibbs submitted the following *proviso:*

Provided, That the foregoing provision requiring a two-thirds majority of the voters of a county to remove its county seat shall not apply to the counties of Obion and Cocke.

Which was adopted by the Convention.

REVISION.

Mr. Turner offered the following resolution:

Resolved, That it is the sense of this Convention that the Committee on Revision and Enrollment shall leave out of Article XI, Section 12, all after Common Schools in line 18.

Which was adopted.

NEW COUNTIES.

Mr. Deaderick offered the following as an independent section:

In all cases when a new county, or new counties, may be formed or created out of portions or fractional parts of other counties, that such portions or fractional parts as may be taken off of other counties in the formation of such new county or new counties shall be responsible and liable for such part of said old county or counties' indebtedness, in proportion to the amount of the taxable property in the several fractional parts so taken off, to the whole amount of taxables in the original county or counties from which said fractional part or parts may be taken.

Mr. Gibson offered the following in lieu:

"The fractions taken from old counties to form new counties, or taken from one county and added to another, shall continue liable for their pro rata of all debts contracted by their respective counties prior to the separation of such fractions.

Which was accepted by Mr. Deaderick.

Mr. Cypert demanded the yeas and nays on the adoption of the Section in lieu, which were ordered.

The hour of recess having arrived the Convention adjourned until 2 o'clock P. M.

AFTERNOON SESSION.

The Convention proceeded to vote on Mr. Gibson's proposition and it was adopted:

Yeas..37
Nays..16

Those voting in the affirmative are:

Messrs. Allen, Arledge, Bate, Brandon, Britton, Brooks, Brown of Henry, etc., Chowning, Coffin, Cummings, Cypert, Deaderick, Dibbrell, Fentress, Fulkerson, Gardner, Gibson, Heiskell, Hill of Gibson, House of Williamson, Ivie, Jones of Giles, Kennedy, Kyle, Mabry, McNabb, Netherland, Porter of Haywood, Porter of Henry, Shelton, Staley, Stephens, Thompson of Davidson, Turner, Walters, Williamson and President Brown—37.

Those voting in the negative are:

Messrs. Baxter, Brown of Davidson, Burkett, Carter, Fielder, Garner, Gibbs, Henderson, Hill of Warren, House of Montgomery, etc., Key, Martin, Nicholson, Seay, Thompson of Maury, and Warner—16.

On motion of Mr. House, of Williamson, leave of absence was granted to Mr. Burton.

The resolution of Mr. President Brown, declaring that certain counties shall not be reduced below their present limits was called up.

Mr. Fielder moved to lay the resolution on the table, and demanded the yeas and nays, which were ordered, and the motion to lay on the table sustained:

Yeas.. 41
Nays.. 22

Those voting in the affirmative are:

Messrs. Allen, Baxter, Blizard, Brandon, Branson, Britton, Brooks, Brown of Davidson, Burkett, Carter, Chowning, Cummings, Cypert, Dibbrell, Doherty, Fentress, Fielder, Gardner, Gaut, Gibbs, Gibson, Henderson, Hill of Warren, Hill of Gibson, House of Montgomery, etc., Key, Kyle, Mabry, McDougal, McNabb, Martin, Meeks, Netherland, Nicholson, Parker, Sample, Seay, Thompson of Davidson, Thompson of Maury,, Turner and Warner—41.

Those voting in the negative are:

Messrs. Arledge, Bate, Brown of Henry, etc., Coffin, Deaderick, Fulkerson, Garner, Heiskell, House of Williamson, Ivie, Jones of Giles, Kennedy, Morris, Porter of Haywood, Porter of Henry, etc., Shelton, Staley, Stephens, Taylor, Walters, Williamson and President Brown—22.

On motion of Mr. GARNER it was ordered that the action of this Convention on the subject of new counties and county lines, be adopted as Section 4, of Article X, of the new Constitution of Tennessee; and that the Committee on Revision have the same enrolled accordingly.

MISCELLANEOUS PROVISIONS.

On motion of Mr. TURNER the Convention proceeded to the consideration of Article XI.

Section 1, was amended by adopting the amendment recommended by the Judicial Department as follows:

"But ordinances contained in any former Constitution or schedule hereto, are hereby abrogated."

"The time which has elapsed from the 6th day of May, 1861, until the 1st day of January, 1867, shall not be computed in any case affected by the statutes of limitations, nor shall any writ of error be affected by such lapse of times."

Section 2 was adopted without amendment.

Section 3, having heretofore been amended, was adopted as amended.

Sections 4 and 5 were adopted without amendment.

Section 6, as amended, giving the Legislature power to pass a conventional rate of interest not to exceed ten per centum per annum was adopted.

Sections 7 and 8 were adopted without amendment.

Mr. House, of Williamson, demanded the yeas and nays on the adoption of Section 9, which were ordered and the amendment adopted.

Yeas..41
Nays..19

Those voting in the affirmative are:

Messrs. Allen, Baxter, Brandon, Branson, Britton, Brown of Davidson, Burkett, Carter, Chowning, Coffin, Cummings, Cypert, Deaderick, Dibbrell, Doherty, Fulkerson, Gardner, Gibson, Gordon, Henderson, Hill of Warren, Hill of Gibson, House of Montgomery, etc., Key, Kyle, Mabry, McDougal, McNabb, Martin, Meeks, Netherland, Nicholson, Parker, Porter of Henry, etc., Sample, Seay, Shepard, Taylor, Thompson of Maury, Warner and Wright —41.

Those voting in the negative are:

Messrs. Arledge, Bate, Brown of Henry, etc., Fentress, Fielder, Garner, Gibbs, Heiskell, House of Williamson, Ivie, Kennedy, Morris, Porter of Haywood, Shelton, Stephens, Thompson of Davidson, Turner, Walters and Williamson—19.

Section 10, having been previously acted on, was passed over informally.

Sections 11 and 12 were adopted without amendment.

On motion of Mr. Garner, it was ordered that the Article be referred to the Committee on Revision and Enrollment.

SCHEDULE.

On motion of Mr. Baxter, the Convention took up the Schedule reported by the Judiciary Committee, which is as follows:

Section 1. That no inconvenience may arise from a change of the Constitution, it is declared that the Governor of the State, the members of the General Assembly and all officers elected at or after the general election in March, 1870, shall hold their offices for the terms prescribed in this Constitution.

Mr. Heiskell proposed the following amendment, to be inserted at the end of the third line of said report:

Officers appointed by the Courts shall be filled by appointments, to be made and to take effect during the first term of the Court held by Judges elected under this Constitution.

Which was adopted by the Convention.

All other officers shall vacate their places thirty days after the day fixed for the election of their successors under this Constitution.

The Secretary of State, Comptroller and Treasurer shall hold their offices until the first session of the present General Assembly occurring after the ratification of this Constitution, and until their successors are elected and qualified.

The officers then elected shall hold their offices until the 15th day of January, 1873.

At the first election of Judges under this Constitution, there shall be elected six Judges of the Supreme Court, two from each grand division of the State, who shall hold their offices for the term herein prescribed.

In the event any vacancy shall occur in the office of either of said Judges at any time after the first day of January, 1873, it shall remain unfilled, and the Court shall, from that time, be constituted of five Judges.

While the Court shall consist of six Judges; they may sit in two sections and may hear and determine causes in each at the same time, but not in different grand divisions at the same time.

When so sitting the concurrence of two Judges shall be necessary to a decision.

The Attorney-General and Reporter for the State shall be appointed after the election and qualification of the Judges of the Supreme Court herein provided for.

Which was adopted by the Convention.

Mr. HEISKELL submitted the following as an additional section:

Every Judge and every officer of the Executive Department of this State, and every Sheriff holding over under this Constitution shall, within twenty days after the ratification of this Constitution is proclaimed, take an oath to support the same. And th [illegible] re of any officer to take such oath shall vacate his office.

Which was adopted.

On motion of Mr. GARNER, it was ordered that the Schedule be referred to the Committee on Revision.

ORDINANCE.

On motion of Mr. GARDNER, the Convention proceeded to the

consideration of the Ordinance reported by the Committeee on Elections and Suffrage.

Mr. NICHOLSON offered the following amendments:

On page 2, line 10, Section 3, strike out the words "Secretary of State," and insert the words "Speaker of the Senate," and in line 11 strike out the words "Secretary of State" and insert the words "President of the Convention," and in line 14, strike out the words "Secretary of State" and insert the word "Governor;" so that the clause will read as follows:

And immediately forward by mail one copy of said certificates to the Governor, and one to the Speaker of the Senate So soon as the poll books are deposited with the County Court Clerks, they shall certify to the President of the Convention an accurate statement of the number of votes cast for and against the "New Constitution," as appears in said poll books. And if any of said returning officers shall fail to make the returns herein provided for within the time required, the Governor shall be authorized to send special messengers for the result of the vote in those counties where officers have so failed to make returns.

Which was adopted by the Convention.

Mr. NICHOLSON offered the following amendments to Section 4:

In lines 1 and 2, of Section 4, strike out the words "Secretary of State," and insert the words "Speaker of the Senate." In line 4, after the words "duty of" insert the following words: "The Governor, Speaker of the Senate and the President of this Convention, or any two of them, to append to the Constitution a certificate of the result of the votes, from which time the Constitution shall be established as the Constitution of Tennessee.

In line 4, strike out the words "forthwith to" and insert the word "shall."

In lines 5 and 6, strike out the following words:

And thereupon the new Constitution shall be ordained and established as the Constitution of the State of Tennessee.

The section as amended will read as follows:

4. Upon the receipt of said returns it shall be the duty of the Governor, Speaker of the Senate and President of this Convention, or any two of them, to compare the votes cast in said election, and if it shall appear that a majority of all the votes cast for and against the "New Constitution" was cast for the "New Constitution," it shall be the duty of the Governor, Speaker of the Senate and President of this Convention, or any two of them, to append a certificate of the result to the Constitution, from which time the Constitution shall be ordained and established as the Constitution

of Tennessee, and the Governor shall forthwith make proclamation of the fact that the Constitution has been ordained and established.

Which several amendments were adopted, and the Ordinance, as thus amended, was adopted by the Convention.

Ordered that the Ordinance be referred to the Committee on Revision and Enrollment.

RELIGIOUS OBLIGATIONS.

Mr. HEISKELL, from the Committee on the Judiciary, made the following report:

The Committee on the Judicial Department, to whom has been referred the memorial of the Israelites, have considered the subject and beg leave to report, and recommend the passage of the following as a section of the Constitution:

No person shall, in time of peace, be required to perform any service to the public on any day set apart by his religion as a day of rest.

The Legislature may by law exempt any religious denomination or race of people from the operation of any law prohibiting the pursuit of secular callings on stated days.

On motion of Mr. HEISKELL, the report was taken up.

Mr. THOMPSON, of Davidson, offered the following amendment to the second clause:

Which shall not interfere with the observance of the Christian Sabbath by the community, nor authorize any violation of it as established by law.

Mr. CARTER demanded a division of the subject, which was ordered.

A vote was taken on Mr. THOMPSON's amendment, and it was rejected.

A vote was then taken on the first clause of the proposed amendment, and it was adopted.

The second clause was rejected.

Ordered that the amendment be referred to the Committee on Revision.

COUNTY SUBSCRIPTIONS TO RAILROADS.

Mr. DOHERTY called up his resolution to except certain counties from the requirement that a three-fourths vote shall be required to subscribe for stock in railroads, etc.

On motion of Mr. HILL, of Gibson, the resolution was laid on the table.

COMMITTEE DISCHARGED.

Mr. HEISKELL, from the Judiciary Committee, reported back the proposition of Mr. Porter of Haywood, limiting the power of the Legislature to establish Courts of Record, and asked to be discharged from its further consideration. The Committee was discharged accordingly.

DISQUALIFICATIONS.

Mr. MABRY called up his motion to reconsider the vote adopting Section 1, of Article IX, and the vote adopting said section was reconsidered.

Mr. CYPERT demanded the yeas and nays on the re-adoption of the section, which were ordered, and the section readopted.

Yeas.. 38
Nays.. 24

Those voting in the affirmative are:

Messrs. Allen, Arledge, Bate, Baxter, Brandon, Britton, Brooks, Carter, Coffin, Cummings, Deaderick, Fentress, Fielder, Fulkerson, Gardner, Garner, Gibbs, Gordon, Heiskell, Henderson, Hill of Warren, Hill of Gibson, House of Williamson, House of Montgomery, etc., Jones of Giles, Kennedy, Kyle, Mabry, McNabb, Morris, Netherland, Shepard, Shelton, Stephens, Thompson of Davidson, Thompson of Maury, Warner and Wright—38.

Those voting in the negative are:

Messrs. Branson, Brown of Davidson, Burkett, Chowning, Cypert, Dibbrell, Doherty, Gibson, Ivie, Key, McDougal, Martin, Meeks, Nicholson, Parker, Porter of Haywood, Porter of Henry, etc., Sample, Seay, Staley, Taylor, Walters and Williamson—24.

Ordered, that Article IX be referred to the Committee on Revision.

MERCHANTS' TAX.

Mr. HOUSE, of Williamson, offered the following in lieu of the proposition submitted by him on Saturday:

The capital employed by merchants, in the purchase of merchandise, shall not be taxed at a rate higher than the *ad valorem* tax on property.

Pending the consideration of said proposition, the Convention adjourned until to-morrow morning at 9 o'clock.

TUESDAY MORNING, FEBRUARY 22, 1870.

The Convention met pursuant to adjournment, Mr. President BROWN in the Chair.

Prayer by the Rev. Mr. CARTER, a member of the Convention.

The Journal of yesterday was read and approved.

REPORT ON PRINTING.

Mr. GARNER, from the Committee on Printing, made the following report:

The majority of the Committee on Printing, to whom was referred the resolutions of Messrs. Williamson, Turner and Seay, relative to copying and printing the Constitution adopted by the Convention, and the Journal of this Body, have instructed me to report the following resolution, and recommend its adoption:

Resolved, That the Secretary of this Body remain at Nashville after the final adjournment of the Convention, and procure the printing by the Public Printers, in pamphlet form, of thirty thousand copies of the Constitution adopted by this body, and deliver four hundred copies thereof to each one of the Delegates to this Convention for general distribution among the people with all practicable dispatch.

Also, that the Secretary have said Constitution printed, as early as possible, as an advertisement, in two newspapers of general circulation, printed at Nashville, two at Memphis, and two at Knoxville, and in one paper in every other county in the State wherein a newspaper is printed; and that the publishers of each of those papers be paid fifty dollars therefor.

Also, that the Secretary copy the Journal of the Proceedings of this Body in a well-bound book, written in a fair copy hand, and deposit said book at the Capitol among the archives of the State; and that he procure to be printed by the Public Printers, on good paper, and to be bound in sheep, 2500 copies of said Journal, first making out a full index thereto, and deposit 250 copies of said Journal with the State Librarian, and that he deliver 30 copies to each Delegate to this Body for distribution. For all which service the Secretary shall receive ——— dollars.

Respectfully submitted,

JOHN E. GARNER, Chairman.

On motion of Mr. GARNER, the report was taken up.

On motion of Mr. NICHOLSON, that part requiring the Secretary to cause the Constitution to be printed as an advertisement in different newspapers, was stricken out.

Mr. THOMPSON, of Davidson, moved that 100,000 copies of the Constitution be printed for general distribution, which was rejected.

Mr. BAXTER moved to print 75,000 copies of the Constitution, and demanded the yeas and nays, which were ordered, and the motion rejected.

Yeas...27
Nays...35

Those voting in the affirmative are:

Messrs. Allen, Baxter, Blizard, Brandon, Branson, Britton, Brooks, Brown of Davidson, Chowning, Garner, Gaut, Gibson, Henderson, House of Montgomery, etc., Ivie, Jones of Giles, McNabb, Martin, Netherland, Parker, Porter of Henry, Sample, Shepard, Shelton, Taylor, Thompson of Davidson and Wright—27.

Those voting in the negative are:

Messrs. Arledge, Brown of Henry, etc., Carter, Coffin, Cummings, Cypert, Deaderick, Dibbrell, Doherty, Dromgoole, Fentress, Fielder, Fulkerson, Gibbs, Gordon, Heiskell, Hill of Warren, Hill of Gibson, House of Williamson, Kennedy, Key, Kyle, Mabry, McDougal, Morris, Nicholson, Porter of Haywood, Seay, Staley, Stephens, Thompson of Maury, Turner, Walters and Warner—35.

Mr. GARNER moved to print 50,000 copies, and demanded the yeas and nays, which were ordered, and the motion was adopted.

Yeas...38
Nays...23

Those voting in the affirmative are:

Messrs. Allen, Baxter, Blizard, Brandon, Branson, Britton, Brown of Davidson, Chowning, Cypert, Deaderick, Doherty, Fulkerson, Garner, Gaut, Gibson, Gordon, Henderson, Hill of Warren, Hill of Gibson, House of Williamson, Ivie, Jones of Giles, Key, McNabb, Martin, Netherland, Nicholson, Parker, Sample, Seay, Shepard, Shelton, Taylor, Thompson of Davidson, Thompson of Maury, Walters, Warner and Wright—38.

Those voting in the negative are:

Messrs. Arledge, Brooks, Brown of Henry, etc., Carter, Coffin, Cummings, Dibbrell, Dromgoole, Fentress, Fielder, Finley, Gardner, Heiskell, Kennedy, Kyle, Mabry, McDougal, Morris, Porter of Haywood, Porter of Henry, Staley, Stephens, and Turner—23.

Mr. BROOKS moved to print 55,000 additional copies, which was rejected.

On motion of Mr. GARNER, the compensation to be allowed the Secretary for the services required in the resolution of the committee, was fixed at $400.

Mr. HOUSE, of Montgomery, etc., moved to reconsider the vote rejecting that part of the resolution which authorized the printing of the Constitution in the newspapers.

Mr. FIELDER demanded the yeas and nays, which were ordered, and the motion to reconsider rejected.

Yeas..30
Nays..34

Those voting in the affirmative are:

Messrs. Baxter, Blizard, Brandon, Brooks, Brown of Davidson, Burkett, Chowning, Cypert, Deaderick, Doherty, Dromgoole, Fulkerson, Garner, Hill of Warren, House of Williamson, House of Montgomery, etc., Ivie, Jones of Giles, Key, Martin, Porter of Henry, Sample, Seay, Shepard, Shelton, Thompson of Davidson, Thompson of Maury, Turner, Williamson and Wright—30.

Those voting in the negative are:

Messrs. Allen, Arledge, Branson, Britton, Brown of Henry, etc., Carter, Coffin, Cummings, Dibbrell, Fentress, Fielder, Finley, Gardner, Gaut, Gibbs, Gibson, Gordon, Heiskell, Henderson, Hill of Gibson, Kennedy, Kyle, Mabry, McDougal, McNabb, Morris, Netherland, Nicholson, Parker, Porter of Haywood, Staley, Stephens, Taylor, Walters and Warner—34.

On motion of Mr. WILLIAMSON, it was ordered that $25 additional be allowed the Secretary to purchase a book and stationery for the purpose of closing up the business of the Convention.

Mr. SHEPARD offered the following resolution:

Resolved, That the copies of the amended Constitution shall be distributed among the several counties in proportion to the voting population of the same.

On motion of Mr. GARNER, the resolution was laid on the table.

Mr. KENNEDY offered the following resolution:

Resolved, That the roll containing the draught of the amended Constitution adopted by this Convention, and by it submitted to the people for their ratification or rejection, be enclosed by the Secretary in a case suitable for its preservation, and deposited among the archives of the State.

Which was adopted by the Convention.

NEW COUNTY.

Mr. MARTIN offered the following resolution:

Resolved, That a new county may be formed out of fractions of the counties of Bedford, Lincoln and Franklin, so as to take a fraction off of the southeastern part of the County of Bedford, a fraction from the eastern part of the County of Lincoln, and a fraction from the northwestern part of the County of Franklin, so as the lines of said new county shall not approach the county seats of either of said Counties of Bedford, Lincoln and Franklin, nearer than eleven miles.

The resolution was ruled out of order by the Chair.

Mr. MARTIN appealed from the decision of the Chair and demanded the yeas and nays, which were ordered and the decision of the Chair sustained:

Yeas..54
Nays.. 5

Those voting in the affirmative are:

Messrs. Allen, Bate, Baxter, Brandon, Branson, Britton, Brooks, Brown of Davidson, Brown of Henry, etc., Burkett, Burton, Carter, Chowning, Coffin, Cummings, Cypert, Deaderick, Dibbrell, Doherty, Dromgoole, Fentress, Fielder, Fulkerson, Gardner, Garner, Gibbs, Gibson, Gordon, Hill of Warren, Hill of Gibson, House of Williamson, House of Montgomery, etc., Ivie, Jones of Giles, Kennedy, Key, Mabry, McDougal, McNabb, Meeks, Morris, Nicholson, Porter of Haywood, Porter of Henry, Sample, Seay, Shepard, Shelton, Stephens, Taylor, Thompson of Davidson, Walters and Wright—54.

Those voting in the negative are:

Messrs. Henderson, Kyle, Martin, Netherland and Warner—5.

THE AMENDED CONSTITUTION.

Mr. BAXTER moved that the Convention proceed to read the amended Constitution.

Mr. NETHERLAND demanded the yeas and nays, and the motion was adopted:

Yeas..31
Nays..29

Those voting in the affirmative are:

Messrs. Allen, Bate, Baxter, Brandon, Brown of Henry, etc.,

Burkett, Carter, Dibbrell, Doherty, Fentress, Fielder, Gardner, Garner, Gibbs, Gordon, Heiskell, Hill of Gibson, House of Williamson, House of Montgomery, etc., Kennedy, Mabry, McDougal, Porter of Haywood, Porter of Henry, Seay, Shepard, Shelton, Stephens, Thompson of Maury, Turner and Williamson—31.

Those voting in the negative are:

Messrs. Branson, Britton, Brooks, Chowning, Coffin, Cummings, Deaderick, Dromgoole, Fulkerson, Gibson, Henderson, Hill of Warren, Ivie, Jones of Giles, Key, Kyle, McNabb, Martin, Meeks, Morris, Netherland, Nicholson, Parker, Sample, Taylor, Thompson of Davidson, Walters, Warner and Wright—29.

In reading the Constitution it was discovered that the provision in relation to the State not being the owner or stockholder in any bank was omitted, and it was ordered to be interlined.

NEW COUNTY.

Mr. SEAY offered the following as an independent Section to Article II.

Resolved, That the new county provided to be established out of fractions of Sumner, Macon and Smith counties when established, shall be excepted out of the provisions of Section 29, of Article II, requiring the assent of two-thirds of the votes cast at an election for a county to become a stockholder with, or to give or loan its credit to or in aid of any person, company, association or corporation.

Which was adopted by the Convention.

TAXES AND EXEMPTIONS.

Mr. STEPHENS moved a modification of Section 28, line four, by adding after the word "producer" "and his immediate vendee."

Mr. GARDNER demanded the yeas and nays, which were ordered, and the amendment adopted.

Yeas..45
Nays..14

Those voting in the affirmative are:

Messrs. Allen, Blizard, Brooks, Brown of Davidson, Brown of Henry, etc., Burkett, Burton, Byrne, Carter, Chowning, Coffin, Dibbrell, Doherty, Dromgoole, Fentress, Fielder, Fulkerson, Gibbs,

Gordon, Heiskell, Henderson, Hill of Gibson, House of Williamson, Ivie, Jones of Giles, Kennedy, Key, Kyle, Mabry, McDougal, McNabb, Martin, Meeks, Nicholson, Porter of Haywood, Seay, Stephens, Taylor, Thompson of Davidson, Thompson of Maury, Turner, Walters, Warner and Williamson—45.

Those voting in the negative are:

Messrs. Baxter, Brandon, Branson, Britton, Gardner, Garner, Gaut, Gibson, Hill of Warren, House of Montgomery, etc., Morris, Netherland, Parker and Wright—14.

SUSPENSION OF RULES.

Mr. KYLE moved to suspend the rule, which requires a motion to reconsider to be made within two days after a vote has been taken.

Mr. THOMPSON, of Maury, offered the following resolution:

Resolved, That any rule of this Convention requiring a majority of two-thirds to take any motion to reconsider from the table be repealed, and it is declared to be the sense of this Convention that a majority can take from the table any motion to reconsider any vote of this Convention.

Mr. THOMPSON, of Maury, moved to suspend the rules to take up the resolution.

Mr. JONES, of Giles, demanded the yeas and nays to suspend the rule, which were ordered and the motion sustained:

Yeas..32
Nays..30

Those voting in the affirmative are:

Messrs. Arledge, Blizard, Britton, Brooks, Brown of Henry, etc., Chowning, Coffin, Cummings, Deaderick, Dibbrell, Doherty, Henderson, Hill of Warren, Hill of Gibson, Ivie, Key, Kyle, Mabry, McDougal, McNabb, Martin, Meeks, Morris, Netherland, Nicholson, Parker, Seay, Taylor, Thompson of Davidson, Thompson of Maury, Walters and Warner—32.

Those voting in the negative are:

Messrs. Brandon, Branson, Brown of Davidson, Burkett, Burton, Byrne, Carter, Dromgoole, Fentress, Fielder, Finley, Fulkerson, Gardner, Garner, Gaut, Gibbs, Gibson, Gordon, Heiskell, House of

Williamson, House of Montgomery, etc., Jones of Giles, Kennedy, Porter of Haywood, Shepard, Staley, Stephens, Turner, Williamson and Wright—30.

Mr. KENNEDY moved to lay the resolution on the table, which was adopted:

Yeas.. 35
Nays.. 30

Those voting in the affirmative are:

Messrs. Allen, Baxter, Blizard, Brandon, Brown of Davidson, Brown of Henry, etc., Burkett, Burton, Carter, Coffin, Cummings, Doherty, Dromgoole, Fentress, Fielder, Finley, Gardner, Garner, Gaut, Gibbs, Gibson, Gordon, Hill of Gibson, House of Williamson, House of Montgomery, etc., Jones of Giles, Kennedy, Key, Porter of Haywood, Shepard, Staley, Stephens, Turner, Williamson and Wright—35.

Those voting in the negative are:

Messrs. Arledge, Branson, Britton, Brooks, Byrne, Chowning, Cypert, Deaderick, Dibbrell, Fulkerson, Heiskell, Henderson, Hill of Warren, Ivie, Kyle, Mabry, McDougal, McNabb, Martin, Meeks, Morris, Netherland, Nicholson, Parker, Seay, Taylor, Thompson of Davidson, Thompson of Maury, Walters and Warner—30.

POLL TAX.

On motion of Mr. BRANDON Article IV, Section 1, was amended by adding after the word "poll tax"—"assessed against him"—and it was ordered that the alteration be made in the enrolled copy of the Constitution.

PROTESTS.

Mr. NETHERLAND presented the following protest:

The undersigned respectfully present to the Convention their protest against the action of this Honorable Body in requiring from every voter proof that he has paid his poll tax before he shall be allowed to vote in the elections in this State.

Their protest is made for the following reasons:

1. The elective franchise is a right, dear to every freeman, and necessary to protect him from unjust and unequal laws.

2. This provision may, and in some instances will prevent citizens from voting, as they may not have paid a poll tax because they have not been called on by the collector, or have been absent from home.

3. The provision discriminates in favor of the land holder, and against the citizen who owns no land, and who is only liable for a poll tax. Because the land holder is not bound to show by proof that he has paid the taxes due on his lands, and his age, in many instances, will be such as to exempt him from the payment of any poll tax. And the poor citizen can with justice say, "that you require me to pay the "*uttermost farthing*," *all* that I owe to the State, though I am poor, whilst my wealthy neighbor, who owns lands to the value of many thousand dollars, on which the taxes are due and unpaid, and when he is exempt by age from the payment of a poll tax, is allowed to vote, and therefore the provision of the Constitution is unjust and unequal, and discriminates in favor of the wealthy against the poor citizen.

4. The people of Tennessee have lately been relieved from the necessity of oaths and certificates before voting. This, to some extent, renews a system which the past has shown to be odious to the voters of the State. And although we will support the amended Constitution, as we believe it better than the old one, yet, we protest respectfully, but earnestly, against that feature which is contained in it, requiring proof of the payment of the poll tax before voting.

JOHN NETHERLAND,
A. A. KYLE,
THOS. C. MORRIS,
G. W WALTERS,
JAMES BRITTON,
T. B. IVIE,
MATT. MARTIN,
M. McNABB.

Mr. Fentress presented the following protest:

We protest against the adoption of the majority report of the Committee on Franchise and Elections, not only for the reasons assigned in the report of the minority of that Committee, but for the reason that it forces the people to endorse negro suffrage in that, if the people vote against the adoption of the Constitution as submitted, and thereby defeat it, they will be left as they are now, disfranchised, while the negro will remain an actual voter, (though we deny he would be legally so,) so that whether ratified or rejected the negro will be an actual voter. In one event the white man may lose his right to the elective franchise, under the present arbitrary laws, while the negro, in any event, is in the actual possession of a franchise that he has no capacity to exercise or appreciate.

We hold that this Convention has no right to force negro suffrage upon the people of Tennessee.

We hold further, that by adopting this principle of practical equality of races, it is a direct encouragement of a party whose object is, by usurpation, to destroy our republican system and to establish in its stead a consolidated despotism.

JAMES FENTRESS,
Of Hardeman.

WM. BLOUNT CARTER,
Of Carter.

WM. H. WILLIAMSON,
Of Wilson.

S. G. SHEPARD,
Of Wilson.

THANKS.

Mr. PORTER, of Henry, offered the following resolution:

Resolved, That the thanks of the Convention are hereby tendered to Messrs. JOS. A. MABRY & CO., for gratuitously furnishing the delegates copies of their able paper, the Daily Knoxville Whig, during the entire session.

The rules were suspended and the resolution unanimously adopted.

SIGNING THE CONSTITUTION.

Mr. JONES, of Giles, offered the following resolution:

Resolved, That this Convention will meet in this hall on to-morrow morning at half-past nine o'clock and resume the reading of the Constitution, and when the same shall be finished, the same will be signed by such delegates as may desire to do so, and no other business shall be in order or entertained by the Chair, until the Constitution shall be read and signed, when the President will adjourn this Convention without day.

Which, under a suspension of the rules, was adopted.

EXPENDITURES.

Mr. WILLIAMSON, from the Committee on Expenditures, made the following report:

STATE OF TENNESSEE

In account with

MEMBERS OF THE STATE CONSTITUTIONAL CONVENTION.

	Miles Travel'd	Mileage		Days Attend'e	Per diem	Total	
Allen, John	122	$ 19	52	45	$180	$ 199	52
Arledge, Jesse	168	25	88	45	180	205	88
Bate, Humphrey R.	438	70	08	45	180	250	08
Baxter, John	526	84	16	45	180	264	16
Blackburn, Joseph H	112	17	92	45	180	197	92
Blizard, Archibald	412	65	92	45	180	245	92
Brandon, Nathan	220	35	20	45	180	215	20
Branson, James W	574	91	84	45	180	276	85
Britton, James	674	107	84	45	180	287	84
Brooks, R. P	150	24	00	45	180	204	00
Brown, Neill S	....	....		45	180	180	00
Brown, James S	236	37	76	45	180	217	76
Burkett, T. M	450	72	00	45	180	252	00
Burton, John W	60	9	60	45	180	189	60
Byrne, William	270	43	20	45	180	223	20
Campbell, Alex. W	340	54	40	45	180	234	40
Carter, Wm. B.	762	121	92	45	180	301	92
Chowning, Z. R	500	80	00	45	180	260	00
Coffin, James A	454	72	64	45	180	252	64
Cummings Warren	112	17	92	45	180	197	92
Cypert, Robert P	192	30	72	45	180	210	72
Deaderick, W. V	776	124	16	45	180	304	16
Deavenport, T. D	150	24	00	45	180	204	00
Dibbrell, Geo. G	172	27	52	45	180	207	52
Doherty, W. F	182	29	12	45	180	209	12
Dromgoole, John E	66	10	56	45	180	190	56
Fentress, James	396	63	36	45	180	243	36
Fielder, A. T	380	60	80	45	180	240	80
Finley, W. H	572	91	52	45	180	271	52
Fulkerson, P. G	670	107	20	45	180	287	20
Gardner, John A	290	46	40	45	180	226	40
Garner, John E	50	8	00	45	180	188	00
Gaut, S. P	360	57	60	45	180	237	60
Gibbs, Chas. N	300	48	00	45	180	228	00

EXPENSE ACCOUNT, [*Continued.*]

	Miles Travel'd	Mileage	Days Attend'e	Per diem	Total
Gibson, H. R.	606	$ 96 96	45	$180	$ 276 96
Gordon, Bolling	122	19 52	45	180	199 52
Heiskell, J. B	472	75 52	45	180	255 52
Henderson, Richard	302	48 52	45	180	228 52
Hill, H. L. W	150	24 00	45	180	204 00
Hill, Sparrel	326	52 16	45	180	232 16
House, Samuel S	36	5 76	45	180	185 76
House, John T	120	19 20	45	180	199 20
Ivie, T. B	126	20 16	45	180	200 16
Jones, Geo. W	244	39 04	45	180	219 04
Jones, Thomas M	156	24 96	45	180	204 96
Kennedy, D. N	125	20 00	45	180	200 00
Key, D. M	302	48 52	45	180	228 32
Kirkpatrick, S. J	728	116 48	45	180	296 48
Kyle, A. A	678	108 48	45	180	288 48
Mabry, Jos. A	526	84 16	45	180	264 16
McDougal, A. G	341	54 41	45	180	234 41
McNabb, M	660	105 60	45	180	285 60
Martin, Matt	162	25 92	45	180	205 92
Meeks, John H	425	68 00	45	180	248 00
Morris, Thomas C	80	12 80	45	180	192 80
Netherland, John	678	108 48	45	180	288 48
Nicholson, A. O. P	88	14 08	45	180	194 08
Porter, James D. Jr	236	37 76	45	180	217 76
Porter, Geo. C	360	57 60	45	180	237 60
Parker, James C	650	104 00	45	180	284 00
Sample, William	622	99 52	45	180	279 52
Seay, Geo. E	84	13 44	45	180	193 44
Shepard, S. G	50	8 00	45	180	188 00
Shelton, E. H	574	91 84	45	180	271 84
Staley, W. B	472	75 52	45	180	255 52
Stephens, W. H	472	75 52	45	180	255 52
Taylor, John M	264	42 24	45	180	222 24
Thompson, John C	6	96	45	180	180 96
Thompson, W. Vance	88	14 08	45	180	194 08
Turner, James J	52	8 32	45	180	188 32
Walters, Geo. W	320	51 20	45	180	231 20
Warner, Richard, Jr	118	18 88	45	180	198 88
Williamson, W. H	60	9 60	45	180	189 60
Wright, W. M	214	34 24	45	180	214 24

EXPENSE ACCOUNT, [*Continued.*]

	Miles Travel'd	Mileage	Days Attend'e	Per diem	Total
Brown, Jno. C., President	156	$ 24 56	45	$270	$ 294 96
Russwurm, T. E. S., Secretary	.....	....	45	270	270 00
Jones, Thos. W. Ass't Sec'y	.....	....	45	270	270 00
Kyle, W. S., Sec. Ass't Secretary	.....	....	45	270	270 00
Stewart, L. G., Doorkeeper	.....	....	45	180	180 00
Bennett, John E., Ass't Doorkeeper	.....	....	45	180	180 00
Davis, H. N. C., Messenger	.....	....	45	180	180 00
Pearl, Henry, (colored) Porter	.....	....	45	180	180 00
Allowance to T. E. S. Russwurm Secretary, for copying the Journal, Reports of the Committees and other documents necessary to be copied and indexing the same and superintending the printing of the Journals and other documents	.....	....	...	......	400 00
Total amount of accounts of officers of the Convention	.....	....	...	......	1930 00

THE STATE OF TENNESSEE

In Account Current, as follows:

For sundry expenses incurred by the Convention, assembled at Nashville, on the tenth day of January, one thousand eight hundred and seventy (1870), for the purpose of revising, amending or forming anew the Constitution of said State.

Voucher No.	Account.	Amount.
Voucher No. 1	Aggregate due members as mileage	$ 3742 76
" "	Aggregate due delegates as per diem	13590 00
Voucher No. 2	Aggregate amount due officers of the Convention for services	1930 00
	To J. O. Griffith & Co., and Roberts & Purvis, $102 60 each	205 20
Voucher No. 3	Amount due Jones, Purvis & Co., (Pub. Printers)	943 38
Voucher No. 4	Amount of Buck, Barnes & Co	54 00

ACCOUNT CURRENT, [*Continued.*]

Voucher No.	Account.	Amount.
Voucher No. 5	Account of Paul, Tavel & Hanner, (Stationers	$ 124 90
Voucher No. 6	Account of Hicks, Houston & Co......	2 50
Voucher No. 7	Account of W. T. Berry & Co., (Booksellers)	341 46
Voucher No. 8	Account of A. A. Lemmon (receipted)..	2 00
Voucher No. 9	Balance of account of Buck, Barnes & Co	1 50
Voucher No. 10	Account of W. H. Woodcock & Co., (for Coal)..	50 00
Voucher No. 11	Account of W. H. Woodcock & Co., (for Coal)..	5 00
	Allowance to T. E. S. Russwurm, Sec'y, to purchase stationery........................	25 00
	Allowance to Dan Adams, for engraving Constitution..	225 00

All of which is respectfully submitted by the Committee,

W. H. WILLIAMSON,
Chairman.
GEO. C. PORTER,
T. W. BURKETT,
Committee.

The report was read, adopted and ordered to be certified to the Treasurer of the State.

The Convention then adjourned until to-morrow morning.

WEDNESDAY MORNING, FEBRUARY 23, 1870.

The Convention met pursuant to adjournment, Mr. President BROWN in the Chair.

The Rev. Mr. CARTER, a member of the Convention, offered the following prayer:

Almighty God! we adore Thee as the King of Kings and the Lord of Lords, and we desire to render unto Thee the homage which is justly due to Thy holy and reverend name! We acknowledge Thee as the author of all the blessings we have received, both as individuals and as a nation! Thou hast given to us this pleasant land, flowing with milk and honey, for our inheritance; and Thou hast also given to us the priviliges of free men. For these great and priceless mercies we thank Thee! And while we thank Thee for our mercies, we pray that none of our blessings may be taken from us, but that Thou wouldst continue to guide us, and to shield us from every danger, both from without and from within. May the wounds of the past be healed; may the wrongs we have done each other be forgiven and forgotten, and may the hearts of all our people be bound together with such cords of love as cannot be broken. We thank Thee for the peace and harmony which have prevailed in this body; and we also thank Thee that we, who but a little while ago, were enemies, and were engaged in deadly strife with each other, have learned how much more pleasant and profitable it is for brethren to dwell together in unity.

God of our fathers! spread Thy protecting wings over this great people, and let us learn war no more; but may we study those things which will best secure the peace and prosperity of our beloved country.

We know that we shall see each other's faces in the flesh no more; nevertheless, may the friendships we have here formed be lasting. We know that with many of us the work of life is well nigh finished; therefore we humbly pray, in the name of Thy Son, that when earth's fitful scenes are ended, and when heart and flesh shall fail us, Thou wouldst receive each and every one of us to Thyself in heaven, through Jesus Christ, our Lord, our King and our Redeemer! Amen.

EXPENDITURES.

On motion of Mr. WILLIAMSON, it was ordered that Daniel

Adams be allowed two hundred and twenty-five dollars for enrolling the amended Constitution on parchment.

On motion of Mr. KENNEDY, the Convention took a recess one hour.

FILLING OFFICES.

Upon reassembling, Mr. NICHOLSON offered the following as an independent section:

"No county office created by the Legislature shall be filled otherwise than by the people or the County Court."

On motion of Mr. NICHOLSON, the rules were suspended and the section unanimously adopted.

EXPENDITURES.

Mr. GARNER offered the following resolution:

Resolved, That Messrs. Roberts & Purvis, publishers of the Republican Banner, and Messrs. J. O. Griffith & Co., publishers of the Union and American, be paid the sum of $102 60 each for furnishing to the Convention eighty copies per day of said papers from January 10th, 1870, to February 23rd, 1870.

On motion of Mr. GARNER, the rules were suspended and the resolution adopted.

THANKS.

Mr. NICHOLSON offered the following resolution:

Resolved unanimously, That the thanks of this Convention are tendered to the Hon. John C. Brown for the courtesy, promptness, impartiality and ability with which he has discharged the duties of presiding officer.

Which was unanimously adopted.

The President made a suitable acknowledgment of the compliments contained in the resolution.

Mr. PORTER, of Henry, offered the following resolution:

Resolved, That the thanks of the Convention be hereby tendered to T. E. S. Russwurm, Secretary, Thos. W. Jones, Assistant Secretary, W. S. Kyle, Second Assistant Secretary, L. G. Stewart, Doorkeeper, John E. Bennett, Assistant Doorkeeper, H. N. C. Davis, Messenger, and Henry Pearl, Porter, for the faithful manner in which their duties have been performed.

Which was unanimously adopted.

DELIVERY OF CONSTITUTION TO THE GOVERNOR.

Mr. Brown, of Davidson, offered the following resolution:

Resolved, That when this Convention shall have adjourned *sine die* the members will proceed in a body to the Capitol, bearing with them the Constitution, enrolled on parchment, and deposit the same with the Governor of the State.

That they will embrace the opportunity thus afforded to call upon the Governor and the two Houses of the General Assembly with a view of tendering our respects and renewing the assurances of regard.

Which was adopted.

Thereupon the President appointed Messrs. House, of Williamson, Gardner and Kyle, to wait on the Governor and the General Assembly, and to notify them of the intended visit.

The Convention resumed the reading of the amended Constitution.

ORDINANCE.

1st. *Be it ordained by the Convention,* That it shall be the duty of the several officers of the State authorized by law to hold elections for members of the General Assembly and other officers, to open and hold an election at the places of holding elections in their respective counties, on the fourth Saturday in March, 1870, for the purpose of receiving the votes of such qualified voters as may desire to vote for the ratification or rejection of the Constitution recommended by this Convention. And the qualification of voters in said election shall be the same as that required in the election of delegates to this Convention.

2d. It shall be the duty of said returning officers, in each county in this State, to enroll the name of each voter on the poll-books prepared for said election, and shall deposit each ballot in the ballot-boxes respectively. Each voter, who wishes to ratify the new Constitution, shall have written or printed on his ticket the words "New Constitution," or words of like import, and each voter, who wishes to vote against the ratification of the new Constitution, shall have written or printed on his ticket the words "Old Constitution," or words of like import.

3d. The election shall be held, and the judges and clerks shall be appointed, as in case of the election of the members of the General Assembly; and the returning officers, in the presence of the judges or inspectors, shall count the votes given for the "New Constitution," and those given for the "Old Constitution," of which they shall keep a correct estimate in said poll-books. They shall deposit the original poll-books of said election with the Clerks of the County Courts in the respective counties, and shall, within five days after the election, make out accurate statements of the number of votes in their respective counties for and against the new Constitution, and immediately forward by mail a copy of said certificates to the Governor, and one to the Speaker of the Senate. So soon as the poll-books are deposited with the County Court Clerks, they shall certify to the President of the Convention an accurate statement of the number of votes for and against the "New Constitution," as appears in said poll-books. And if any of said returning officers shall fail to make the returns herein provided for within the time required, the Governor shall be authorized to send special messengers for the result of the votes in those counties where officers have so failed to make returns.

4th. Upon the receipt of said returns, it shall be the duty of the Governor, Speaker of the Senate, and President of this Convention, or any two of them, to compare the votes cast in said election, and if it shall appear that a majority of all the votes cast for and against the new Constitution, was for the "New Constitution," it shall be the duty of the Governor, Speaker of the Senate, and President of this Convention, or any two of them, to append a certificate of the result to the Constitution, from which time the Constitution shall be ordained and established as the Constitution of Tennessee, and the Governor shall forthwith make proclamation of the fact that the Constitution has been ordained and established.

5th. The Governor of the State is requested to issue his proclamation as to the election on the 4th Saturday in March, 1870, herein provided for.

EXPLANATION.

Mr. Fentress presented the following explanation, before affixing his name to the Constitution:

I sign my name to this Constitution merely to attest its genuineness, and to certify that it has been adopted by a majority of this Convention. As there have been words incorporated in it urging or recommending that the people of Tennessee adopt it, I feel it due to my people and myself so make this explanation.

For my position I refer to my record on the Journal. Time will disclose and posterity realize which of us is right. If the majority who have adopted this Constitution are right, and my fears unfounded, I will rejoice that their superior wisdom controlled our action. If the minority is right, and history shall declare that the action of the majority has tended to hasten our people into anarchy, or a consolidated despotism, a clear conscience shall be my reward.

Mr. CARTER, before signing the Constitution, gave the reasons in substance as above.

ABSENT MEMBERS TO SIGN AT PLEASURE.

Mr. HOUSE, of Williamson, offered the following resolution:

Resolved, That those members of the Convention who have not signed the Constitution, and who are absent from sickness or other cause, be permitted to sign the Constitution at their pleasure.

Which was adopted by the Convention.

The Convention then adjourned *sine die.*

JOHN C. BROWN, President.

Attest:
T. E. S. RUSSWURM, Secretary.

CONSTITUTION.

THE CONSTITUTION

OF THE

STATE OF TENNESSEE,

ADOPTED IN CONVENTION AT NASHVILLE, FEBRUARY 23d, 1870.

PREAMBLE AND DECLARATION OF RIGHTS.

WHEREAS, The people of the territory of the United States south of the River Ohio, having the right of admission into the General Government as a member State thereof, consistent with the Constitution of the United States, and the act of cession of the State of North Carolina, recognizing the ordinance for the government of the territory of the United States northwest of the Ohio River, by their Delegates and Representatives in Convention assembled, did, on the sixth day of February, in the year of our Lord one thousand seven hundred and ninety-six, ordain and establish a Constitution, or form of government, and mutually agreed with each other to form themselves into a free and independent State, by the name of the State of Tennessee; and,

WHEREAS, The General Assembly of the said State of Tennessee (pursuant to the third section of the tenth article of the Constitution,) by an act passed on the 27th day of November, in the year of our Lord one thousand eight hundred and thirty-three, entitled, "An Act to provide for the calling of a Convention, passed in obedience to the declared will of the voters of this State, as expressed at the general election of August, in the year of our Lord one thousand eight hundred and thirty-three, did authorize and provide for the election by the people of delegates and representatives, to meet at Nashville, in Davidson County, on the third Monday in May, in the year of our Lord one thousand eight hundred and thirty-four, for the purpose of revising and amending, or changing the Constitution; and said Convention did accordingly meet and form a Constitution, which was submitted to the people, and was ratified by them, on the first Friday in March, in the year of our Lord one thousand eight hundred and thirty-five; and,

WHEREAS, The General Assembly of said State of Tennessee, under and in virtue of the first section of the first article of the Declaration of Rights, contained in and forming a part of the existing Constitution of the State, by an act passed on the 15th day of November, in the year of our Lord, one thousand eight hundred and sixty-nine, did provide for the calling of a Convention by the people of the State, to meet at Nashville on the second Monday in January, in the year of our Lord, one thousand eight hundred and seventy, and for the election of delegates for the purpose of amending or revising the present Constitution, or forming and making a new Constitution; and,

WHEREAS, The people of the State, in the mode provided by said Act, have called said Convention, and elected delegates to represent them therein; Now, therefore,

We, the Delegates and Representatives of the people of the State of Tennessee, duly elected, and in Convention assembled, in pursuance of said Act of Assembly, have ordained and established the following Constitution and form of government for this State, which we recommend to the people of Tennessee for their ratification: That is to say—

ARTICLE I.

DECLARATION OF RIGHTS.

SECTION 1. That all power is inherent in the people, and all free governments are founded on their authority, and instituted for their peace, safety, and happiness; for the advancement of those ends they have, at all times, an unalienable and indefeasible right to alter, reform, or abolish the government in such manner as they may think proper.

SEC. 2. That government being instituted for the common benefit, the doctrine of non-resistance against arbitrary power and oppression is absurd, slavish, and destructive of the good and happiness of mankind.

SEC. 3. That all men have a natural and indefeasible right to worship Almighty God according to the dictates of their own conscience; that no man can, of right, be compelled to attend, erect, or support any place of worship, or to maintain any minister, against his consent; that no human authority can, in any case whatever, control or interfere with the rights of conscience; and that no preference shall ever be given, by law, to any religious establishment or mode of worship.

SEC. 4. That no political or religious test, other than an oath to support the Constitution of the United States and of this State, shall ever be required as a qualification to any office or public trust under this State.

SEC. 5. That elections shall be free and equal, and the right of suffrage, as hereinafter declared, shall never be denied to any person entitled thereto, except upon a conviction by a jury of some infamous crime, previously ascertained and declared by law, and judgment thereon by a court of competent jurisdiction.

SEC. 6. That the right of trial by jury shall remain inviolate, and no religious or political test shall ever be required as a qualification for jurors.

SEC. 7. That the people shall be secure in their persons, houses, papers and possessions, from unreasonable searches and seizures; and that general warrants, whereby an officer may be commanded to search suspected places, without evidence of the fact committed, or to seize any person or persons not named, whose offences are not particularly described and supported by evidence, are dangerous to liberty, and ought not to be granted.

SEC. 8. That no man shall be taken or imprisoned, or disseized of his freehold, liberties or privileges, or outlawed, or exiled, or in any manner destroyed, or deprived of his life, liberty, or property, but by the judgment of his peers or the law of the land.

SEC. 9. That in all criminal prosecutions, the accused hath the right to be heard by himself and his counsel; to demand the nature and cause of the accusation against him, and to have a copy thereof; to meet the witnesses face to face; to have compulsory process for obtaining witnesses in his favor; and in prosecutions by indictment or presentment, a speedy public trial by an impartial jury of the county in which the crime shall have been committed, and shall not be compelled to give evidence against himself.

Sec. 10. That no person shall, for the same offence, be twice put in jeopardy of life or limb.

Sec. 11. That laws made for the punishment of acts committed previous to the existence of such laws, and by them only declared criminal, are contrary to the principles of a free government; wherefore no *ex post facto* law shall be made.

Sec. 12. That no conviction shall work corruption of blood or forfeiture of estate. The estate of such persons as shall destroy their own lives shall descend or vest as in case of natural death. If any person be killed by casualty, there shall be no forfeiture in consequence thereof.

Sec. 13. That no person arrested and confined in jail shall be treated with unnecessary rigor.

Sec. 14. That no person shall be put to answer any criminal charge but by presentment, indictment or impeachment.

Sec. 15. That all prisoners shall be bailable by sufficient sureties, unless for capital offences, when the proof is evident or the presumption great. And the privileges of the writ of *habeas corpus* shall not be suspended, unless when, in case of rebellion or invasion, the General Assembly shall declare the public safety requires it.

Sec. 16. That excessive bail shall not be required, nor excessive fines imposed, nor cruel and unusual punishments inflicted.

Sec. 17. That all courts shall be open; and every man, for an injury done him in his lands, goods, person or reputation, shall have remedy by due course of law, and right and justice administered without sale, denial, or delay. Suits may be brought against the State in such manner and in such courts as the Legislature may by law direct.

Sec. 18. The Legislature shall pass no law authorizing imprisonment for debt in civil cases.

Sec. 19. That the printing presses shall be free to every person to examine the proceedings of the Legislature, or of any branch or officer of the Government; and no law shall ever be made to restrain the right thereof. The free communication of thoughts and opinions is one of the invaluable rights of man, and every citizen may freely speak, write and print on any subject, being responsible for the abuse of that liberty. But in prosecutions for the publication of papers investigating the official conduct of officers or men in public capacity, the truth thereof may be given in evidence; and in all indictments for libel the jury shall have a right to determine the law and the facts, under the direction of the court, as in other criminal cases.

Sec. 20. That no retrospective law, or law impairing the obligations of contracts, shall be made.

Sec. 21. That no man's particular services shall be demanded, or property taken or applied to public use, without the consent of his representatives, or without just compensation being made therefor.

Sec. 22. That perpetuities and monopolies are contrary to the genius of a free State, and shall not be allowed.

Sec. 23. That the citizens have a right in a peaceable manner to assemble together for their common good, to instruct their representatives, and to apply to those invested with the powers of government for redress of grievances, or other proper purposes, by address or remonstrance.

Sec. 24. That the sure and certain defense of a free people is a well-regulated militia; and, as standing armies in time of peace are dangerous to freedom, they ought to be avoided as far as the circumstances and safety of the community will admit; and that in all cases the military shall be kept in strict subordination to the civil authority.

Sec. 25. That no citizen of this State, except such as are employed in the army of the United States, or militia in actual service, shall be subjected to punishment under the martial or military law. That martial law, in the sense of the unrestricted power of military officers or others, to dispose of the persons, liberties or property of the citizen, is inconsistent with the principles of free government, and is not confided to any department of the government of this State.

Sec. 26. That the citizens of this State have a right to keep and to bear arms for their common defense. But the Legislature shall have power, by law, to regulate the wearing of arms with a view to prevent crime.

Sec. 27. That no soldier shall, in time of peace, be quartered in any house without the consent of the owner; nor in time of war but in a manner prescribed by law.

SEC. 28. That no citizen of this State shall be compelled to bear arms, provided he will pay an equivalent, to be ascertained by law.

SEC. 29. That an equal participation in the free navigation of the Mississippi is one of the inherent rights of the citizens of this State; it cannot, therefore, be conceded to any prince, potentate, power, person or persons, whatever.

SEC. 30. That no hereditary emoluments, priviliges or honors, shall be granted or conferred in this State.

SEC. 31. That the limits and boundaries of this State be ascertained, it is declared they are as hereafter mentioned, that is to say: Beginning on the extreme height of the Stone Mountain, at the place where the line of Virginia intersects it, in latitude thirty-six degrees and thirty minutes north; running thence along the extreme height of the said mountain to the place where the Watauga River breaks through it; thence a direct course to the top of the Yellow Mountain, where Bright's road crosses the same; thence along the ridge of said mountain, between the waters of Doe River and the waters of Rock Creek, to the place where the road crosses the Iron Mountain; from thence, along the extreme height of said mountain, to the place where Nolichucky River runs through the same; thence to the top of the Bald Mountain; thence along the extreme height of said mountain to the Painted Rock, on French Broad River; thence along the highest ridge of said mountain to the place where it is called the Great Iron or Smoky Mountain; thence along the extreme height of said mountain to the place where it is called Unicoi or Unaka Mountain, between the Indian towns of Cowee and Old Chota; thence along the main ridge of the said mountain to the southern boundary of this State, as described in the act of cession of North Carolina to the United States of America; and that all the territory, lands and waters, lying west of the said line, as before mentioned, and contained within the chartered limits of the State of North Carolina, are within the boundaries and limits of this State, over which the people have the right of exercising sovereignty, and the right of soil, so far as is consistent with the Constitution of the United States, recognizing the Articles of Confederation, the Bill of Rights, and Constitution of North Carolina, the cession act of the said State, and the ordinance of Congress for the government of the territory northwest of the Ohio; *Provided,* nothing herein contained shall extend to affect the claim or claims of individuals to any part of the soil which is recognized to them by the aforesaid cession act; *And, provided also,* That the limits and jurisdiction of this State shall extend to any other land and territory now acquired, or that may hereafter be acquired, by compact or agreement with other States or otherwise, although such land and territory are not included within the boundaries hereinbefore designated.

SEC. 32. That the erection of safe and comfortable prisons, and inspection of prisons, and the humane treatment of prisoners shall be provided for.

SEC. 33. That slavery and involuntary servitude, except as a punishment for crime, whereof the party shall have been duly convicted, are forever prohibited in this State.

SEC. 34. The General Assembly shall make no law recognizing the right of property in man.

ARTICLE II.

DISTRIBUTION OF POWERS.

SECTION 1. The powers of the Government shall be divided into three distinct Departments: The Legislative, Executive and Judicial.

SEC. 2. No person or persons belonging to one of these departments shall exercise any of the powers properly belonging to either of the others, except in the cases herein directed or permitted.

THE LEGISLATIVE DEPARTMENT.

SEC. 3. The Legislative authority of this State shall be vested in a General Assembly, which shall consist of a Senate and House of Representatives, both dependent on the people, who shall hold their offices for two years from the day of the general election.

SEC. 4. An enumeration of the qualified voters, and an apportionment of the Representatives in the General Assembly, shall be made in the year one thousand eight hundred and seventy-one, and within every subsequent term of ten years.

SEC. 5. The number of Representatives shall, at the several periods of making the enumeration, be apportioned among the several counties or districts, according to the number of qualified voters in each, and shall not exceed seventy-five, until the population of the State shall be one million and a half, and shall never exceed ninety-nine: *Provided,* That any county having two-thirds of the ratio shall be entitled to one member.

SEC. 6. The number of Senators shall, at the several periods of making the enumeration, be apportioned among the several counties or districts, according to the number of qualified electors in each, and shall not exceed one-third the number of Representatives. In apportioning the Senators among the different counties, the fraction that may be lost by any county or counties, in the apportionment of members to the House of Representatives, shall be made up to such county or counties in the Senate as near as may be practicable. When a district is composed of two or more counties, they shall be adjoining, and no county shall be divided in forming a district.

SEC. 7. The first election for Senators and Representatives shall be held on the second Tuesday in November, one thousand eight hundred and seventy; and forever thereafter, elections for members of the General Assembly shall be held once in two years, on the first Tuesday after the first Monday in November. Said elections shall terminate the same day.

SEC. 8. The first session of the General Assembly shall commence on the first Monday in October, 1871, at which time the term of service of the members shall commence, and expire on the first Tuesday of November, 1872, at which session the Governor elected on the second Tuesday in November, 1870, shall be inaugurated; and forever thereafter, the General Assembly shall meet on the first Monday in January next ensuing the election, at which session thereof the Governor shall be inaugurated.

SEC. 9. No person shall be a Representative unless he shall be a citizen of the United States, of the age of twenty-one years, and shall have been a citizen of this State for three years, and a resident in the county he represents one year immediately preceding the election.

SEC. 10. No person shall be a Senator unless he shall be a citizen of the United States, of the age of thirty years, and shall have resided three years in this State, and one year in the county or district immediately preceding the election. No Senator or Representative shall, during the time for which he was elected, be eligible to any office or place of trust, the appointment to which is vested in the Executive or General Assembly, except to the office of trustee of a literary institution.

SEC. 11. The Senate and House of Representatives, when assembled, shall each choose a Speaker and its other officers; be judges of the qualifications and elections of its members, and sit upon its own adjournments from day to day. Not less than two-thirds of all the members to which each house shall be entitled shall constitute a quorum to do business; but a smaller number may adjourn from day to day, and may be authorized by law to compel the attendance of absent members.

SEC. 12. Each House may determine the rules of its proceedings, punish its members for disorderly behavior, and, with the concurrence of two-thirds, expel a member, but not a second time for the same offence; and shall have all other powers necessary for a branch of the Legislature of a free State.

SEC. 13. Senators and Representatives shall, in all cases except treason, felony, or breach of the peace, be privileged from arrest during the session of the General Assembly, and in going to and returning from the same; and for any speech or debate in either House they shall not be questioned in any other place.

SEC. 14. Each House may punish by imprisonment, during its session, any person not a member, who shall be guilty of disrespect to the House, by any disorderly or any contemptuous behavior in its presence.

SEC. 15. When vacancies happen in either House, the Governor for the time being shall issue writs of election to fill such vacancies.

SEC. 16. Neither House shall, during its session, adjourn without the consent of the other, for more than three days, nor to any other place than that in which the two Houses shall be sitting.

SEC. 17. Bills may originate in either House; but may be amended, altered or rejected by the other. No bill shall become a law, which embraces more than one subject; that subject to be expressed in the title. All acts which repeal, revive or amend former laws, shall recite in their caption or otherwise, the title or substance of the law repealed, revived or amended.

SEC. 18. Every bill shall be read once on three different days, and be passed each time in the House where it originated, before transmission to the other. No bill shall become a law until it shall have been read and passed, on three different days in each House, and shall have received on its final passage, in each House, the assent of a majority of all the members to which that House shall be entitled under this Constitution; and shall have been signed by the respective Speakers in open session—the fact of such signing to be noted on the Journal; and shall have received the approval of the Governor, or shall have been otherwise passed under the provisions of this Constitution.

SEC. 19. After a bill has been rejected, no bill containing the same substance shall be passed into a law during the same session.

SEC. 20. The style of the laws of the State shall be, "*Be it enacted by the General Assembly of the State of Tennessee.*" No law of a general nature shall take effect until forty days after its passage, unless the same or the caption thereof shall state that the public welfare requires that it should take effect sooner.

SEC. 21. Each House shall keep a journal of its proceedings, and publish it, except such parts as the welfare of the State may require to be kept secret; the ayes and noes shall be taken in each House upon the final passage of every bill of a general character, and bills making appropriations of public moneys; and the ayes and noes of the members on any question, shall, at the request of any five of them, be entered on the journal.

SEC. 22. The doors of each House and of Committees of the Whole shall be kept open, unless when the business shall be such as ought to be kept secret.

SEC. 23. The sum of four dollars per day, and four dollars for every twenty-five miles traveling to and from the seat of government, shall be allowed to the members of each General Assembly elected after the ratification of this Constitution, as a compensation for their services. But no member shall be paid for more than seventy-five days of a regular session, or for more than twenty days of any extra or called session; or for any day when absent from his seat in the Legislature, unless physically unable to attend. The Senators when sitting as a court of impeachment shall each receive four dollars per day of actual attendance.

SEC. 24. No money shall be drawn from the treasury but in consequence of appropriations made by law; and an accurate statement of the receipts and expenditures of the public money shall be attached to and published with the laws at the rise of each stated session of the General Assembly.

SEC. 25. No person who heretofore hath been, or may hereafter be, a collector or holder of public moneys, shall have a seat in either House of the General Assembly, or hold any other office under the State Government, until such person shall have accounted for and paid into the treasury all sums for which he may be accountable or liable.

SEC. 26. No Judge of any court of law or equity, Secretary of State, Attorney-General, Register, Clerk of any Court of Record, or person holding any office under the authority of the United States, shall have a seat in the General Assembly, nor shall any person in this State hold more than one lucrative office at the same time: *Provided,* That no appointment in the militia, or to the office of Justice of the Peace, shall be considered a lucrative office, or operative as a disqualification to a seat in either House of the General Assembly.

SEC. 27. Any member of either House of the General Assembly shall have liberty to dissent from and protest against any act or resolve which he may think injurious to the Public or to any individual, and to have the reasons for his dissent entered on the journals.

SEC. 28. All property, real, personal or mixed, shall be taxed, but the Legislature may except such as may be held by the State, by counties, cities or towns, and used exclusively for public or corporation purposes, and such as may be held and used for purposes purely religious, charitable, scientific, literary or educational, and shall except one thousand dollars' worth of personal property in the hands of each tax-payer, and the direct product of the soil in the hands of the producer and his immediate vendee. All property shall be taxed according to its value, that value to be ascertained in such manner as the Legislature shall direct, so that taxes shall be equal and uniform throughout the State. No one species of property from which a tax may be collected shall be taxed higher than any other species of property of the same value. But the Legislature shall have power to tax Merchants, Peddlers, and privileges, in such manner as they may from time to time direct.

The portion of a Merchant's Capital used in the purchase of Merchandise sold by him to non-residents and sent beyond the State, shall not be taxed at a rate higher than the *ad valorem* tax on property. The Legislature shall have the power to levy a tax upon incomes derived from stocks and bonds that are not taxed *ad valorem.* All male citizens of this State over the age of twenty-one years, except such persons as may be exempted by law on account of age or other infirmity, shall be liable to a poll tax of not less than fifty cents nor more than one dollar per annum. Nor shall any county or corporation levy a poll tax exceeding the amount levied by the State.

SEC. 29. The General Assembly shall have power to authorize the several counties and incorporated towns in this State, to impose taxes for county and corporation purposes respectively, in such manner as shall be prescribed by law; and all property shall be taxed according to its value, upon the principles established in regard to State taxation. But the credit of no County, City or Town shall be given or loaned to or in aid of any person, company, association or corporation, except upon an election to be first held by the qualified voters of such County, City or Town, and the assent of three-fourths of the votes cast at said election. Nor shall any County, City or Town become a stockholder with others in any company, association or corporation, except upon a like election and the assent of a like majority. But the counties of Grainger, Hawkins, Hancock, Union, Campbell, Scott, Morgan, Grundy, Sumner, Smith, Fentress, Van Buren, and the new county herein authorized to be established out of fractions of Sumner, Macon and Smith counties, White, Putnam, Overton, Jackson, Cumberland, Anderson, Henderson, Wayne, Cocke, Coffee, Macon, Marshall and Roane shall be excepted out of the provisions of this section, so far that the assent of a majority of the qualified voters of either of said counties voting on the question shall be sufficient, when the credit of such county is given or loaned to any person, association or corporation: *Provided,* That the exception of the counties above named shall not be in force beyond the year one thousand eight hundred and eighty, and after that period they shall be subject to the three-fourths majority applicable to the other counties of the State.

SEC. 30. No article manufactured of the produce of this State shall be taxed otherwise than to pay inspection fees.

SEC. 31. The credit of this State shall not be hereafter loaned or given to or in aid of any person, association, company, corporation, or municipality; nor shall the State become the owner, in whole or in part, of any bank, or a stockholder with others in any association, company, corporation, or municipality.

SEC. 32. No Convention or General Assembly of this State shall act upon any amendment of the Constitution of the United States proposed by Congress to the several States, unless such Convention or General Assembly shall have been elected after such amendment is submitted.

SEC. 33. No bonds of the State shall be issued to any railroad company which, at the time of its application for the same, shall be in default in paying the interest upon the State bonds previously loaned to it, or that shall hereafter and before such application, sell or absolutely dispose of any State bonds loaned to it for less than par.

ARTICLE III.

EXECUTIVE DEPARTMENT.

SECTION 1. The Supreme Executive power of this State shall be vested in a Governor.

SEC. 2. The Governor shall be chosen by the electors of the members of the General Assembly, at the time and places where they shall respectively vote for the members thereof. The returns of every election for Governor shall be sealed up, and transmitted to the seat of government by the returning officers, directed to the Speaker of the Senate, who shall open and publish them in the presence of a majority of the members of each House of the General Assembly. The person having the highest number of votes shall be Governor; but if two or more shall be equal and highest in votes, one of them shall be chosen Governor by joint vote of both Houses of the General Assembly. Contested elections for Governor shall be determined by both Houses of the General Assembly, in such manner as shall be prescribed by law.

SEC. 3. He shall be at least thirty years of age, shall be a citizen of the United States, and shall have been a citizen of this State seven years next before his election.

Sec. 4. The Governor shall hold his office for two years, and until his successor shall be elected and qualified. He shall not be eligible more than six years in any term of eight.

Sec. 5. He shall be Commander-in-chief of the Army and Navy of the State, and of the Militia, except when they shall be called into the service of the United States; but the Militia shall not be called into service except in case of rebellion or invasion, and then only when the General Assembly shall declare by law that the public safety requires it.

Sec. 6. He shall have power to grant reprieves and pardons, after conviction, except in cases of impeachment.

Sec. 7. He shall, at stated times, receive a compensation for his services, which shall not be increased or diminished during the period for which he shall have been elected.

Sec. 8. He may require information, in writing, from the officers in the Executive Department, upon any subject relating to the duties of their respective offices.

Sec. 9. He may, on extraordinary occasions, convene the General Assembly by proclamation, in which he shall state specifically the purposes for which they are to convene; but they shall enter on no legislative business except that for which they were specifically called together.

Sec. 10. He shall take care that the laws be faithfully executed.

Sec. 11. He shall, from time to time, give to the General Assembly information of the state of the government, and recommend for their consideration such measures as he shall judge expedient.

Sec. 12. In case of the removal of the Governor from office, or of his death or resignation, the powers and duties of the office shall devolve on the Speaker of the Senate; and in case of the death, removal from office, or resignation of the Speaker of the Senate, the powers and duties of the office shall devolve on the Speaker of the House of Representatives.

Sec. 13. No member of Congress, or person holding any office under the United States, or this State, shall execute the office of Governor.

Sec. 14. When any officer, the right of whose appointment is by this Constitution vested in the General Assembly, shall, during the recess, die, or the office, by the expiration of the term, or by other means, become vacant, the Governor shall have the power to fill such vacancy by granting a temporary commission, which shall expire at the end of the next session of the Legislature.

Sec. 15. There shall be a Seal of this State, which shall be kept by the Governor and used by him officially, and shall be called the Great Seal of the State of Tennessee.

Sec. 16. All grants and commissions shall be in the name and by the authority of the State of Tennessee, be sealed with the State seal and signed by the Governor.

Sec. 17. A Secretary of State shall be appointed by joint vote of the General Assembly, and commissioned during the term of four years; he shall keep a fair register of all the official acts and proceedings of the Governor, and shall, when required, lay the same and all papers, minutes and vouchers relative thereto, before the General Assembly; and shall perform such other duties as shall be enjoined by law.

Sec. 18. Every Bill which may pass both Houses of the General Assembly, shall, before it becomes a law, be presented to the Governor for his signature. If he approve, he shall sign it, and the same shall become a law; but if he refuse to sign it, he shall return it, with his objections thereto, in writing, to the House in which it originated, and said House shall cause said objections to be entered at large upon its journal, and proceed to reconsider the Bill. If, after such reconsideration, a majority of all the members elected to that House shall agree to pass the Bill, notwithstanding the objections of the Executive, it shall be sent, with said objections, to the other House, by which it shall be likewise reconsidered. If approved by a majority of the whole number elected to that House, it shall become a law. The votes of both Houses shall be determined by yeas and nays, and the names of all the members voting for or against the Bill shall be entered upon the journals of their respective Houses. If the Governor shall fail to return any bill, with his objections, within five days (Sundays excepted) after it shall have been presented to him, the same shall become a law without his signature, unless the General Assembly, by its adjournment, prevents its return, in which case it shall not become a law. Every Joint Resolution or Order (except on questions of adjournment) shall likewise be presented to the Governor for his signature, and before it shall take effect shall receive his signature; and on being disapproved by him, shall, in like manner, be returned with his objections; and the same, before it shall take effect, shall be re-passed by a majority of all the members elected to both Houses, in the manner and according to the rules prescribed in case of a Bill.

ARTICLE IV.

ELECTIONS.

SECTION 1. Every male person of the age of twenty-one years, being a citizen of the United States, and a resident of this State for twelve months, and of the county wherein he may offer his vote for six months next preceding the day of election, shall be entitled to vote for members of the General Assembly, and other civil officers for the county or district in which he resides; and there shall be no qualification attached to the right of suffrage, except that each voter shall give to the judges of election, where he offers to vote, satisfactory evidence that he has paid the poll taxes assessed against him for such preceding period as the Legislature shall prescribe, and at such time as may be prescribed by law, without which his vote cannot be received. And all male citizens of the State shall be subject to the payment of poll taxes and the performance of military duty within such ages as may be prescribed by law. The General Assembly shall have power to enact laws requiring voters to vote in the election precincts in which they may reside, and laws to secure the freedom of elections and the purity of the ballot-box.

SEC. 2. Laws may be passed excluding from the right of suffrage persons who may be convicted of infamous crimes.

SEC. 3. Electors shall, in all cases, except treason, felony, or breach of the peace, be privileged from arrest or summons, during their attendance at elections, and in going to and returning from them.

SEC. 4. In all elections to be made by the General Assembly, the members thereof shall vote *viva voce,* and their votes shall be entered on the journal. All other elections shall be by ballot.

ARTICLE V.

IMPEACHMENT.

SECTION 1. The House of Representatives shall have the sole power of impeachment.

SEC. 2. All impeachments shall be tried by the Senate. When sitting for that purpose, the Senators shall be upon oath or affirmation, and the Chief Justice of the Supreme Court, or if he be on trial, the Senior Associate Judge, shall preside over them. No person shall be convicted without the concurrence of two-thirds of the Senators sworn to try the officer impeached.

SEC. 3. The House of Representatives shall elect, from their own body, three members, whose duty it shall be to prosecute impeachments. No impeachment shall be tried until the Legislature shall have adjourned *sine die*, when the Senate shall proceed to try such impeachment.

SEC. 4. The Governor, Judges of the Supreme Court, Judges of the Inferior Courts, Chancellors, Attorneys for the State, Treasurer, Comptroller, and Secretary of State, shall be liable to impeachment whenever they may, in the opinion of the House of Representatives, commit any crime in their official capacity which may require disqualification; but judgment shall only extend to removal from office, and disqualification to fill any office thereafter. The party shall, nevertheless, be liable to indictment, trial, judgment and punishment according to law. The Legislature now has, and shall continue to have, power to relieve from the penalties imposed, any person disqualified from holding office by the judgment of a Court of Impeachment.

SEC. 5. Justices of the Peace, and other civil officers, not hereinbefore mentioned, for crimes or misdemeanors in office, shall be liable to indictment in such courts as the Legislature may direct; and upon conviction, shall be removed from office by said court, as if found guilty on impeachment; and shall be subject to such other punishment as may be prescribed by law.

ARTICLE VI.

JUDICIAL DEPARTMENT.

SECTION 1. The judicial power of this State shall be vested in one Supreme Court, and in such Circuit, Chancery and other inferior courts as the Legislature shall, from time to time, ordain and establish, in the Judges thereof, and in Justices of the Peace. The Legislature may also vest such jurisdiction in Corporation Courts as may be deemed necessary. Courts to be holden by Justices of the Peace may also be established.

SEC. 2. The Supreme Court shall consist of five Judges, of whom not more than two shall reside in any one of the grand divisions of the State. The Judges shall designate one of their own number who shall preside as Chief Justice. The concurrence of three of the Judges shall, in every case, be necessary to a decision. The jurisdiction of this Court shall be appellate only, under such restrictions and regulations as may, from time to time, be prescribed by law; but it may possess such other jurisdiction as is now conferred by law on the present Supreme Court; said Court shall be held at Knoxville, Nashville and Jackson.

SEC. 3. The Judges of the Supreme Court shall be elected by the qualified voters of the State. The Legislature shall have power to prescribe such rules as may be necessary to carry out the provisions of Section 2, of this Article. Every Judge of the Supreme Court shall be thirty-five years of age, and shall, before his election, have been a resident of the State for five years. His term of service shall be eight years.

SEC. 4. The Judges of the Circuit and Chancery Courts, and of other inferior courts, shall be elected by the qualified voters of the district or circuit to which they are to be assigned. Every Judge of such courts shall be thirty years of age, and shall, before his election, have been a resident of the State five years, and of the circuit or district one year. His term of service shall be eight years.

SEC. 5. An Attorney-General and Reporter for the State, shall be appointed by the Judges of the Supreme Court, and shall hold his office for a term of eight years. An Attorney for the State for any circuit or district for which a Judge having criminal jurisdiction shall be provided by law, shall be elected by the qualified voters of such circuit or district, and shall hold his office for a term of eight years, and shall have been a resident of the State five years, and of the circuit or district, one year. In all cases where the Attorney for any district fails or refuses to attend and prosecute according to law, the Court shall have power to appoint an Attorney *pro tempore.*

SEC. 6. Judges and Attorneys for the State may be removed from office by a concurrent vote of both Houses of the General Assembly, each House voting separately; but two-thirds of the members to which each House may be entitled, must concur in such vote. The vote shall be determined by ayes and noes, and the names of the members voting for or against the Judge or Attorney for the State, together with the cause or causes of removal, shall be entered on the Journal of each House respectively. The Judge or Attorney for the State, against whom the Legislature may be about to proceed, shall receive notice thereof, accompanied with a copy of the causes alleged for his removal, at least ten days before the day on which either House of the General Assembly shall act thereupon.

SEC. 7. The Judges of the Supreme or Inferior Courts shall, at stated times, receive a compensation for their services, to be ascertained by law, which shall not be increased or diminished during the time for which they are elected. They shall not be allowed any fees or perquisites of office, nor hold any office of trust or profit under this State or the United States.

SEC. 8. The jurisdiction of the Circuit, Chancery, and other inferior courts, shall be as now established by law, until changed by the Legislature.

SEC. 9. Judges shall not charge juries with respect to matters of fact, but may state the testimony and declare the law.

SEC. 10. Judges or Justices of the inferior courts of Law and Equity, shall have power in all civil cases, to issue writs of *certiorari*, to remove any cause or the transcript of the record thereof, from any inferior jurisdiction into such court of law, on sufficient cause, supported by oath or affirmation.

SEC. 11. No Judge of the Supreme or inferior courts shall preside on the trial of any cause in the event of which he may be interested, or where either of the parties shall be connected with him by affinity or consanguinity, within such degrees as may be prescribed by law, or in which he may have been of counsel, or in which he may have presided in any inferior court, except by consent of all the parties. In case all or any of the Judges of the Supreme Court, shall thus be disqualified from presiding on the trial of any cause or causes, the Court or the Judges thereof, shall certify the same to the Governor of the State, and he shall forthwith specially commission the requisite number of men of law knowledge, for the trial and determination thereof. The Legislature may, by general laws, make provision that special Judges may be appointed to hold any Court, the Judge of which shall be unable or fail to attend or sit; or to hear any cause in which the Judge may be incompetent.

SEC. 12. All writs and other process shall run in the name of the State of Tennessee; and bear test and be signed by the respective clerks. Indictments shall conclude, "*against the peace and dignity of the State.*"

SEC. 13. Judges of the Supreme Court shall appoint their Clerks, who shall hold their offices for six years. Chancellors shall appoint their Clerks and Masters, who shall hold their offices for six years. Clerks of the inferior courts, holden in the respective counties or districts, shall be elected by the qualified voters thereof, for the term of four years. Any Clerk may be removed from office for malfeasance, incompetency, or neglect of duty, in such manner as may be prescribed by law.

SEC. 14. No fine shall be laid on any citizen of this State, that shall exceed fifty dollars, unless it shall be assessed by a jury of his peers, who shall assess the fine at the time they find the fact, if they think the fine should be more than fifty dollars.

SEC. 15. The different counties of this State shall be laid off as the General Assembly may direct, into districts of convenient size, so that the whole number in each county shall not be more than twenty-five, or four for every one hundred square miles. There shall be two Justices of the Peace and one Constable elected in each district, by the qualified voters therein, except districts including county towns, which shall elect three Justices and two Constables. The jurisdiction of said officers shall be co-extensive with the county. Justices of the Peace shall be elected for the term of six, and Constables for the term of two years. Upon the removal of either of said officers from the district in which he was elected, his office shall become vacant from the time of such removal. Justices of the Peace shall be commissioned by the Governor. The Legislature shall have power to provide for the appointment of an additional number of Justices of the Peace in incorporated towns.

ARTICLE VII.

STATE AND COUNTY OFFICERS.

SECTION 1. There shall be elected in each county, by the qualified voters therein, one Sheriff, one Trustee, one Register; the

Sheriff and Trustee for two years, and the Register for four years; but no person shall be eligible to the office of Sheriff more than six years in any term of eight years. There shall be elected for each county, by the Justices of the Peace, one Coroner, and one Ranger, who shall hold their offices for two years. Said officers shall be removed for malfeasance, or neglect of duty, in such manner as may be prescribed by law.

SEC. 2. Should a vacancy occur, subsequent to an election, in the office of Sheriff, Trustee or Register, it shall be filled by the Justices; if in that of the Clerk, to be elected by the people, it shall be filled by the courts; and the person so appointed shall continue in office until his successor shall be elected and qualified; and such office shall be filled by the qualified voters at the first election for any of the county officers.

SEC. 3. There shall be a Treasurer or Treasurers, and a Comptroller of the Treasury, appointed for the State by the joint vote of both Houses of the General Assembly, who shall hold their offices for two years.

SEC. 4. The election of all officers and the filling of all vacancies not otherwise directed or provided by this Constitution, shall be made in such manner as the Legislature shall direct.

SEC. 5. Elections for judicial and other civil officers, shall be held on the first Thursday in August, one thousand eight hundred and seventy, and forever thereafter on the first Thursday in August next preceding the expiration of their respective terms of service.

The term of each officer so elected shall be computed from the first day of September next succeeding his election. The term of office of the Governor and other executive officers, shall be computed from the 15th of January next after the election of the Governor. No appointment or election to fill a vacancy shall be made for a period extending beyond the unexpired term. Every officer shall hold his office until his successor is elected or appointed and qualified. No special election shall be held to fill a vacancy in the office of Judge or District Attorney, but at the time herein fixed for the biennial election of civil officers. And such vacancy shall be filled at the next biennial election recurring more than thirty days after the vacancy occurs.

ARTICLE VIII.

MILITIA.

SECTION 1. All militia officers shall be elected by persons subject to military duty, within the bounds of their several companies, battalions, regiments, brigades and divisions, under such rules and regulations as the Legislature may, from time to time, direct and establish.

SEC. 2. The Governor shall appoint the Adjutant-general, and his other staff officers; the Major-generals, Brigadier-generals, and commanding officers of regiments, shall respectively appoint their staff officers.

SEC. 3. The Legislature shall pass laws, exempting citizens belonging to any sect or denomination of religion, the tenets of which are known to be opposed to the bearing of arms, from attending private and general musters.

ARTICLE IX.

DISQUALIFICATIONS.

SECTION 1. WHEREAS, Ministers of the Gospel are, by their profession, dedicated to God and the care of souls, and ought not to be diverted from the great duties of their functions; therefore, no Minister of the Gospel, or Priest of any denomination whatever, shall be eligible to a seat in either House of the Legislature.

SEC. 2. No person who denies the being of God, or a future state of rewards and punishments, shall hold any office in the civil department of this State.

SEC. 3. Any person who shall, after the adoption of this Constitution, fight a duel, or knowingly be the bearer of a challenge to fight a duel, or send, or accept a challenge for that purpose, or be an aider or abettor in fighting a duel, shall be deprived of the right to hold any office of honor or profit in this State, and shall be punished otherwise, in such manner as the Legislature may prescribe.

ARTICLE X.

OATHS, BRIBERY OF ELECTORS, NEW COUNTIES.

SECTION 1. Every person who shall be chosen or appointed to any office of trust or profit under this Constitution, or any law made in pursuance thereof, shall, before entering upon the duties thereof, take an oath to support the Constitution of this State, and of the United States, and an oath of office.

SEC. 2. Each member of the Senate and House of Representatives, shall, before they proceed to busines, take an oath or affirmation to support the Constitution of this State, and of the United States, and also the following oath: "I, ——— ———, do solemnly swear (or affirm) that, as a member of this General Assembly, I will, in all appointments, vote without favor, affection, partiality, or prejudice; and that I will not propose or assent to any bill, vote or resolution, which shall appear to me injurious to the people, or consent to any act or thing whatever, that shall have a tendency to lessen or abridge their rights and privileges, as declared by the Constitution of this State."

SEC. 3. Any elector who shall receive any gift or reward for his vote, in meat, drink, money or otherwise, shall suffer such punishment as the laws shall direct. And any person who shall directly or indirectly, give, promise or bestow any such reward to be elected, shall thereby be rendered incapable, for six years, to serve in the office for which he was elected, and be subject to such further punishment as the Legislature shall direct.

SEC. 4. New counties may be established by the Legislature, to consist of not less than two hundred and seventy-five square miles, and which shall contain a population of seven hundred qualified voters. No line of such county shall approach the court-house of any old county, from which it may be taken, nearer than eleven miles, nor shall such old county be reduced to less than five hundred square miles. But the following exceptions are made to the foregoing provisions, viz: New counties may be established by the present or any succeeding Legislature, out of the following territory, to-wit: Out of that portion of Obion county which lies west of low water mark of Reel Foot Lake; Out of fractions of Sumner, Macon and Smith counties; but no line of such new county shall approach the court-house of Sumner or Smith counties nearer than ten miles, nor include any part of Macon county lying within nine and a half miles of the court-house of said county; nor shall more than twenty square miles of Macon county, nor any part of Sumner county lying due west of the western boundary of Macon county, be taken in the formation of said new county; Out of fractions of Grainger and Jefferson counties, but no line of such new county shall include any part of Grainger county north of the Holston River; nor shall any line thereof approach the court-house of Jefferson county nearer than eleven miles. Such new county may include any other territory which is not excluded by any general provision of this Constitution; Out of fractions of Jackson and Overton counties, but no line of such new county shall approach the court-house of Jackson or Overton counties nearer than ten miles; nor shall such county contain less than four hundred qualified voters, nor shall the area of either of the old counties be reduced below four hundred and fifty square miles; Out of fractions of Roane, Monroe and Blount counties, around the town of Loudon, but no line of such new county shall ever approach the towns of Maryville, Kingston or Madisonville nearer than eleven miles, except that on the south side of the Tennessee River, said lines may approach as near as ten miles to the court-house of Roane county. The counties of Lewis, Cheatham and Sequatchie, as now established by legislative enactments, are hereby declared to be constitutional counties. No part of Bledsoe county shall be taken to form a new county, or a part thereof, or be attached to any adjoining county. That portion of Marion county, included within the following boundaries: Beginning on the Grundy and Marion county line, at the Nick-a-jack Trace, and running about six hundred yards west of Ben Posey's, to where the Tennessee Coal Railroad crosses the line, running thence south-east, through the Pocket, near William Summers', crossing the Battle Creek Gulf, at the corner of Thomas Wooten's field; thence running across the Little Gizzard Gulf at Raven Point; thence in a direct line to the bridge crossing the Big Fiery Gizzard; thence in a direct line to the mouth of Holy Water Creek; thence up said creek to the Grundy county line, and thence with said line to the beginning, is hereby detached from Marion county, and attached to the county of Grundy. No part of a county shall be taken off to form a new county, or a part thereof, without the consent of two-thirds of the qualified voters in such part taken off; and, where an old county is reduced for the purpose of forming a new one, the seat of justice in said old county shall not be removed, without the concurrence of two-thirds of both branches of the Legislature, nor shall the seat of justice of any county be removed without the concurrence of two-thirds of the qualified voters of the county. But the foregoing provision, requiring a two-thirds majority of the voters of a county to remove its county seat, shall not apply to the counties of Obion and Cocke. The fractions taken from old counties to form new counties, or taken from one county and added to another, shall continue liable for their *pro rata* of all debts contracted by their respective counties prior to the separation, and be entitled to their proportion of any stocks or credits belonging to such old counties.

SEC. 5. The citizens who may be included in any new county shall vote with the county or counties, from which they may have been stricken off, for members of Congress, for Governor, and for members of the General Assembly, until the next apportionment of members of the General Assembly after the establishment of such new county.

ARTICLE XI.

MISCELLANEOUS PROVISIONS.

SECTION 1. All laws and ordinances now in force and use in this State, not inconsistent with this Constitution, shall continue in force and use until they shall expire, or be altered or repealed by the Legislature. But ordinances contained in any former Constitution or schedule thereto, are hereby abrogated.

SEC. 2. Nothing contained in this Constitution shall impair the validity of any debts or contracts, or affect any rights of property, or any suits, actions, rights of action, or other proceedings in courts of justice.

SEC. 3. Any amendment or amendments to this Constitution may be proposed in the Senate or House of Representatives; and, if the same shall be agreed to by a majority of all the members elected to each of the two Houses, such proposed amendment or amendments shall be entered on their journals, with the yeas and nays thereon, and referred to the General Assembly then next to be chosen; and shall be published six months previous to the time of making such choice; and if, in the General Assembly then next chosen as aforesaid, such proposed amendment or amendments shall be agreed to by two-thirds of all the members elected to each House, then it shall be the duty of the General Assembly to submit such proposed amendment or amendments to the people, in such manner, and at such times as the General Assembly shall prescribe. And if the people shall approve and ratify such amendment or amendments, by a majority of all the citizens of the State, voting for Representatives, voting in their favor, such amendment or amendments shall become a part of this Constitution. When any amendment or amendments to the Constitution shall be proposed, in pursuance of the foregoing provisions, the same shall, at each of the said sessions, be read three times on three several days in each House. The Legislature shall not propose amendments to the Constitution oftener than once in six years. The Legislature shall have the right, at any time, by law, to submit to the people the question of calling a Convention to alter, reform or abolish this Constitution, and when, upon such submission, a majority of all the votes cast shall be in favor of said proposition, then delegates shall be chosen, and the Convention shall assemble in such mode and manner as shall be prescribed.

SEC. 4. The Legislature shall have no power to grant divorces, but may authorize the courts of justice to grant them for such causes as may be specified by law; but such laws shall be general and uniform in their operation throughout the State.

SEC. 5. The Legislature shall have no power to authorize lotteries for any purpose, and shall pass laws to prohibit the sale of lottery tickets in this State.

SEC. 6. The Legislature shall have no power to change the names of persons, or to pass acts adopting or legitimatizing persons, but shall, by general laws, confer this power on the Courts.

SEC. 7. The Legislature shall fix the rate of interest, and the rate so established shall be equal and uniform throughout the State; but the Legislature may provide for a conventional rate of interest, not to exceed ten per cent. per annum.

SEC. 8. The Legislature shall have no power to suspend any general law for the benefit of any particular individual, nor to pass any law for the benefit of individuals, inconsistent with the general laws of the land; nor to pass any law granting to any individual or individuals, rights, priviliges, immunities, or exemptions, other than such as may be, by the same law, extended to any member of the community who may be able to bring himself within the provisions of such law. No corporation shall be created, or its powers increased or diminished by special laws, but the General Assembly shall provide by general laws, for the organization of all corporations hereafter created, which laws may, at any time, be altered or repealed; and no such alteration or repeal shall interfere with, or divest, rights which have become vested.

SEC. 9. The Legislature shall have the right to vest such powers in the courts of justice, with regard to private and local affairs, as may be expedient.

SEC. 10. A well-regulated system of internal improvement is calculated to develop the resources of the State, and promote the happiness and prosperity of her citizens; therefore, it ought to be encouraged by the General Assembly.

SEC. 11. A homestead, in the possession of each head of a family, and the improvements thereon, to the value, in all of one thousand dollars, shall be exempt from sale under legal process during the life of such head of a family, to inure to the benefit of the widow, and shall be exempt during the minority of their children occupying the same. Nor shall said property be alienated without the joint consent of the husband and wife when that relation exists. This exemption shall not operate against public taxes, nor debts contracted for the purchase money of such homestead, or improvements thereon.

SEC. 12. Knowledge, learning and virtue, being essential to the preservation of republican institutions, and the diffusion of the opportunities and advantages of education throughout the different portions of the State being highly conducive to the promotion of this end, it shall be the duty of the General Assembly, in all future periods of this Government, to cherish literature and science. And the fund called the *common school fund,* and all the lands and proceeds thereof, dividends, stocks and other property of every description whatever, heretofore by law appropriated by the General Assembly of this State for the use of common schools, and all such as shall hereafter be appropriated, shall remain a *perpetual fund,* the principal of which shall never be diminished by Legislative appropriation; and the interest thereof shall be inviolably appropriated to the support and encouragement of common schools throughout the State, and for the equal benefit of all the people thereof; and no law shall be made authorizing said fund, or any part thereof, to be diverted to any other use than the support and encouragement of common schools. The State taxes derived hereafter from polls shall be appropriated to educational purposes, in such manner as the General Assembly shall, from time to time, direct by law. No school established or aided under this section shall allow white and negro children to be received as scholars together in the same school. The above provision shall not prevent the Legislature from carrying into effect any laws that have been passed in favor of the Colleges, Universities or Academies, or from authorizing heirs or distributees to receive and enjoy escheated property under such laws as may be passed from time to time.

SEC. 13. The General Assembly shall have power to enact laws for the protection and preservation of game and fish within the State, and such laws may be enacted for and applied and enforced in particular counties or geographical districts designated by the General Assembly.

SEC. 14. The intermarriage of white persons with negroes, mulattoes, or persons of mixed blood, descended from a negro to the third generation, inclusive, or their living together as man and wife, in this State, is prohibited. The Legislature shall enforce this section by appropriate legislation.

SEC. 15. No person shall, in time of peace, be required to perform any service to the public on any day set apart by his religion as a day of rest.

SEC. 16. The declaration of rights, hereto prefixed, is declared to be a part of the Constitution of this State, and shall never be violated on any pretense whatever. And to guard against transgression of the high powers we have delegated, we declare that every thing in the Bill of Rights contained is excepted out of the general powers of the government, and shall forever remain inviolate.

SEC. 17. No county office created by the Legislature shall be filled otherwise than by the people or the County Court.

SCHEDULE.

SECTION 1. That no inconvenience may arise from a change of the Constitution, it is declared that the Governor of the State, the members of the General Assembly, and all officers elected at or after the general election of March, 1870, shall hold their offices for the terms prescribed in this Constitution.

Officers appointed by the courts shall be filled by appointment, to be made and to take effect during the first term of the court held by Judges elected under this Constitution.

All other officers shall vacate their places thirty days after the day fixed for the election of their successors under this Constitution.

The Secretary of State, Comptroller, and Treasurer, shall hold their offices until the first session of the present General Assembly occurring after the ratification of this Constitution, and until their successors are elected and qualified.

The officers then elected shall hold their offices until the 15th day of January, 1873.

SEC. 2. At the first election of Judges under this Constitution, there shall be elected six Judges of the Supreme Court, two from each grand division of the State, who shall hold their offices for the term herein prescribed.

In the event any vacancy shall occur in the offices of either of said Judges at any time after the first day of January, 1873, it shall remain unfilled, and the Court shall from that time be constituted of five Judges.

While the Court shall consist of six Judges they may sit in two sections, and may hear and determine causes in each at the same time, but not in different grand divisions at the same time.

When so sitting the concurrence of two Judges shall be necessary to a decision.

The Attorney-General and Reporter for the State shall be appointed after the election and qualification of the Judges of the Supreme Court herein provided for.

SEC. 3. Every Judge and every officer of the Executive Department of this State, and every Sheriff holding over under this Constitution, shall, within twenty days after the ratification of this Constitution is proclaimed, take an oath to support the same, and the failure of any officer to take such oath shall vacate his office.

SEC. 4. The time which has elapsed from the 6th day of May, 1861, until the 1st day of January, 1867, shall not be computed in any cases affected by the statutes of limitation, nor shall any writ of error be affected by such lapse of time.

Done in Convention, at Nashville, the 23d day of February, in the year of our Lord one thousand eight hundred and seventy, and of the independence of the United States the ninety-fourth. In testimony whereof we have hereunto set our names.

JOHN C. BROWN, President.

John Allen,
Jesse Arledge,
Humphrey R. Bate,
John Baxter,
A. Blizard,
Nathan Brandon,
R. P. Brooks,
James Britton,
Neill S. Brown,
James S. Brown,
T. M. Burkett,
Jno. W. Burton,
Wm. Byrne,
Alex. W. Campbell,
Wm. Blount Carter,
Z. R. Chowning,
James A. Coffin,
Warren Cummings,
Robt. P. Cypert,
W. V. Deaderick,
Thos. D. Deavenport,
G. G. Dibrell,
W. F. Doherty,
J. E. Dromgoole,
James Fentress,
A. T. Fielder,
P. G. Fulkerson,
Jno. A. Gardner,
John E. Garner,
S. P. Gaut,
Chas. N. Gibbs,
B. Gordon,
J. B. Heiskell,
R. Henderson,
H. L. W. Hill,
Spl. Hill,
Sam. S. House,
John F. House,
T. B. Ivie,
Thomas M. Jones,
David M. Kennedy,
D. M. Key,
Sam. J. Kirkpatrick,
A. A. Kyle,
Jos. A. Mabry,
A. G. McDougal,
Malcom McNabb,
Matt. Martin,
John H. Meeks,
Thos. C. Morris,
J. Netherland,
A. O. P. Nicholson,
Geo. C. Porter,
Jas. D. Porter, Jr.,
George E. Seay,
Samuel G. Shepard,
E. H. Shelton,
Wm. H. Stephens,
Jno. M. Taylor,
J. C. Thompson,
W. Vance Thompson,
James J. Turner,
Geo. W. Walters,
Richard Warner, Jr.
Wm. H. Williamson,
W. M. Wright.

Attest:

T. E. S. RUSSWURM,
Secretary.

Thos. W. Jones,
Assistant Secretary.

W. S. Kyle,
2d Ass't Secretary.

ORDINANCE.

---

1. *Be it ordained by the Convention,* That it shall be the duty of the several officers of the State, authorized by law to hold elections for members of the General Assembly and other officers, to open and hold an election at the place of holding said elections in their respective counties, on the fourth Saturday in March, 1870, for the purpose of receiving the votes of such qualified voters as may desire to vote for the ratification or rejection of the Constitution recommended by this Convention. And the qualification of voters in said election be the same as that required in the election of delegates to this Convention.

2. It shall be the duty of said returning officers, in each county in this State, to enroll the name of each voter on the poll-books prepared for said election, and shall deposit each ballot in the ballot-boxes respectively. Each voter who wishes to ratify the new Constitution shall have written or printed on his ticket the words, "New Constitution," or words of like import; and each voter who wishes to vote against the ratification of the new Constitution shall have written or printed on his ticket the words, "Old Constitution," or words of like import.

Sec. 3. The election shall be held, and the judges and clerks shall be appointed, as in the case of the election of the members of the General Assembly, and the returning officers, in presence of the judges or inspectors, shall count the votes given for the "New Constitution," and of those given for the "Old Constitution," of which they shall keep a correct estimate in said poll books. They shall deposit the original poll books of said election with the Clerks of the County Courts in the respective counties, and shall, within five days after the election, make out accurate statements of the number of votes in their respective counties, for and against the "New Constitution," and immediately forward by mail, one copy of said certificates to the Governor, and one to the Speaker of the Senate. So soon as the poll books are deposited with the County Court Clerks, they shall certify to the President of the Convention, an accurate statement of the number of votes cast, for and against the "New Constitution," as appears on said poll books. And, if any of said returning officers shall fail to make the returns herein provided for, within the time required, the Governor shall be authorized to send special messengers for the result of the vote in those counties whose officers have so failed to make returns.

4. Upon the receipt of said returns, it shall be the duty of the Governor, Speaker of the Senate, and the President of this Convention, or any two of them, to compare the votes cast in said election; and if it shall appear that a majority of all the votes cast for and against the New Constitution were for "New Constitution," it shall be the duty of the Governor, Speaker of the Senate, and President of this Convention, or any two of them, to append to this Constitution a certificate of the result of the votes, from which time the Constitution shall be established as the Constitution of Tennessee, and the Governor shall make proclamation of the result.

5. The Governor of the State is requested to issue his proclamation as to the election on the fourth Saturday in March, 1870, herein provided for.

JOHN C. BROWN, *President.*

Attest:

T. E. RUSSWURM, *Secretary.*

CERTIFICATE OF RATIFICATION.

STATE OF TENNESSEE:

In pursuance of the fourth Ordinance of the late Constitutional Convention of the State of Tennessee, adopted on the twenty-third of February, one thousand eight hundred and seventy, in the City of Nashville, we, D. W. C. SENTER, Governor of said State, and JOHN C. BROWN, President of said Convention, and D. B. THOMAS, Speaker of the Senate, do hereby certify that we have carefully compared the votes for and against the New Constitution, in the election on the fourth Saturday of March, one thousand eight hundred and seventy, and we certify that the vote cast in the entire State, leaving out the Counties of Knox, Grainger, Reane and Overton (from which there are no official returns), was one hundred and thirty-two thousand. Of these, ninety-eight thousand one hundred and twenty-eight votes were for the New Constitution, and thirty-three thousand eight hundred and seventy-two votes were for the old Constitution, and that the majority for the New Constitution was sixty-four thousand two hundred and fifty-six, and we certify, accordingly, the ratification of the New Constitution.

Done at the Executive Department, in the City of Nashville, this fifth day of May, A. D. one thousand eight hundred and seventy, and of the American Independence the ninety-fourth.

D. W. C. SENTER,
Governor.

JOHN C. BROWN,
President, etc.

D. B. THOMAS,
Speaker of the Senate.

THE GOVERNOR'S PROCLAMATION

DECLARING THE

RATIFICATION OF THE NEW CONSTITUTION.

STATE OF TENNESSEE, EXECUTIVE DEPARTMENT,
NASHVILLE, May 5, 1870.

In pursuance of the fourth Ordinance of the late Constitutional Convention, I have carefully examined the official returns of the election held on the 26th day of March last, for the ratification or rejection of the proposed New Constitution for the State of Tennessee, (except the Counties of Knox, Grainger, Roane and Overton, which returns have not been received,) and find the number of votes cast for "New Constitution" to be (98,128) ninety-eight thousand one hundred and twenty-eight, and for the "Old Constitution" (33,872) thirty-three thousand eight hundred and seventy-two, being a majority of (64,256) sixty-four thousand two hundred and fifty-six for the New Constitution.

Now, therefore, I, D. W. C. SENTER, Governor of the State of Tennessee, by virtue of the power and authority in me vested, do hereby declare and proclaim that the "New Constitution," as submitted to the people, was ratified by them at the ballot-box, on the 26th day of March last, by said majority of (64,256) sixty-four thousand two hundred and fifty-six votes.

In testimony whereof, I have hereunto subscribed my official signature, and ordered the Great Seal of the State [SEAL.] to be affixed. Done at the Department in the City of Nashville, this fifth day of May, A. D., 1870, and of the American Independence the ninety-fourth.

By the Governor: D. W. C. SENTER.

A. J. FLETCHER,
Secretary of State.

ACT AUTHORIZING THE CONVENTION.

THE ACT

OF THE

GENERAL ASSEMBLY

AUTHORIZING THE CONVENTION.

[Laws of 1869-70, Chapter CV.]

AN ACT *to authorize the people to call a Convention, and for other purposes.*

WHEREAS, According to Section 1, Article I, of the Declaration of Rights, all power is inherent in the people, and all free governments are founded on their authority and instituted for their peace, safety and happiness ; and,

WHEREAS, It is declared that, for the advancement of these ends, the people have, at all times, an inalienable and indefeasible right to alter, reform or abolish the Government in such manner as they may think proper ; and,

WHEREAS, In the opinion of this General Assembly, the public exigencies do now demand the exercise of these inherent and reserved powers on the part of the people of the State: Therefore,

SECTION 1. *Be it enacted by the General Assembly of the State of Tennessee,* That every male person not convicted and rendered infamous for crime, of the age of 21 years, being a citizen of the United States and a citizen of the county where he may offer his vote, six months next preceding the day of election, is hereby authorised to assemble an the third Saturday of December, 1869, at the several places of holding elections in the several counties, and vote for or against calling a Convention to amend, revise, or form and make a new Constitution for the State; and no certificate or other qualification than the foregoing shall be required by the Judges holding said election.

SEC. 2. *Be it further enacted,* That in submitting the question of a Convention to the people, they shall have written or printed on their ballots the words "Convention," or "No Convention," and if the number of votes cast for a Convention be greater than the votes cast against a Convention, then there shall be a Convention.

SEC. 3. *Be it further enacted,* That an election for delegates to a Convention of the people of the State shall be held in the several counties thereof at the same time and places, and that said election shall be held at all the precincts and voting places established by law, and shall be managed and conducted by the Commissioners of Registration and other proper officers of the counties respectively, in the same manner and under the same rules and regulations that members of the General Assembly are now elected. And it is hereby declared to be the duty of the Governor to issue his proclamation to the several Commissioners of Registration of the State immediately after the passage of this act, requiring them to hold and conduct the same as herein provided. The said Commissioners of Registration shall advertise the time and places of said election as in cases of members of the General Assembly.

SEC. 4. *Be it further enacted,* That the whole number of delegates elected to said Convention shall be seventy-five.

SEC. 5. *Be it further enacted,* That each one of the Representative Districts, as established by the apportionment act of 19th of February, 1852, shall constitute a district, and elect and send to said Convention exactly the same number of delegates that they have Representatives in the General Assembly by said act of apportionment.

SEC. 6. *Be it further enacted,* That each one of the Floaterial Districts, as established by said act of apportionment, shall constitute a district, and elect and send to said Convention one delegate.

SEC. 7. *Be it further enacted,* That the votes in the several

Representative and Floaterial Districts shall be compared at the several places where the votes for members of the General Assembly were compared in the last August election.

Sec. 8. *Be it further enacted,* That no person shall be eligible to a seat in said Convention who is not twenty-one years of age, and who has not been a citizen of the State for twelve months, and of the county and district from which he is elected six months immediately preceding the election.

Sec. 9. *Be it further enacted,* That all laws requiring test-oaths to enable persons to become candidates for office, or requiring Judges and Clerks of elections to take such oaths, shall not apply to the election under this act.

Sec. 10. *Be it further enacted,* That in case of the death, refusal to serve, resignation or removal from this State of any delegate, the vacancy occasioned thereby shall be filled in the same manner prescribed by law for the filling of vacancies in the representation to the General Assembly.

Sec. 11. *Be it further enacted,* That it shall be the duty of the Commissioner of Registration of each county in the State, immediately after said election, to make a complete return to the Secretary of State of the votes cast "for Convention" or "no Convention," and for delegates in his county. The certificate of election of the returning officer or officers of the county or districts, shall be *prima facie* evidence of the right of any delegate to a seat in said Convention, subject, if contested, to be decided in the manner the Convention may prescribe.

Sec. 12. *Be it further enacted,* That it shall be the duty of the Governor and Secretary of State to compare the returns made by the Commissioners of Registration, and if a majority of those voting be in favor of a Convention, it shall be the duty of the Governor immediately to issue his proclamation announcing the result, and said Convention shall convene in the city of Nashville, on the second Monday in January, 1870; and when so assembled, said delegates shall organize themselves into a Constitutional Convention, by the election of a President and such other officers as they may deem necessary.

SEC. 13. *Be it further enacted,* That said Convention shall adopt such rules and regulations for its government, and the transaction of business as it shall think proper, and that the members and officers of said Convention shall receive the same compensation as is now allowed by law to the members and officers of the General Assembly of the State, and to be paid in the same manner by the Treasurer.

SEC. 14. *Be it further enacted,* That the Constitution or form of government which said Convention may adopt, shall not be of any binding force or efficacy until the same has been submitted to and ratified by the people of the State, in such manner and at such time as the Convention shall provide.

SEC. 15. *Be it further enacted,* That should any county have no Commissioner of Registration at the time of said election, or should the Commissioner of Registration fail or refuse to hold said election, then in that event, it shall be the duty of the Sheriff of each county to open and hold such an election, subject to the same rules and regulations as imposed upon Commissioners of Registration by this act.

SEC. 16. *Be it further enacted,* That in all cases when the Commissioner or Sheriff fails or refuses, or from any other cause, fails to hold said election, it shall be lawful for any freeholder to hold said election, by summoning as many bystanders as may be necessary to hold said election, all of whom shall be freeholders.

SEC. 17. *Be it further enacted,* That this act shall take effect from and after its passage.

W. O'N. PERKINS,
Speaker of the House of Representatives.

D. B. THOMAS,
Speaker of the Senate.

Passed Nov. 15, 1869.

INDEX.

INDEX.

A

B

C

D

F

G

H

I

J

K

M

N

O

P

R

S

T

W

www.ingramcontent.com/pod-product-compliance
Lightning Source LLC
LaVergne TN
LVHW020933110826
845150LV00004B/855

* 9 7 8 1 4 2 5 5 5 1 8 8 9 *